It's All About Business: Lifetime Lessons For Success

It's All About Business: Lifetime Lessons For Success

A Business Memoir

Allen H. Lipis

Contents

Preface 11

Acknowledgments 13

Chapter 1: Introduction 17
Chapter 2: Childhood Traits 20
Chapter 3: High School 41
Chapter 4: My Family 73
Chapter 5: College 96
Chapter 6: Iowa State University 130
Chapter 7: Finding a Career and a Wife 151
Chapter 8: Learning About Business 181
Chapter 9: Consulting and Citibank 193
Chapter 10: Atlanta Payments Project 207
Chapter 11: Payment Systems Inc. 230
Chapter 12: Electronic Banking, Inc. 256
Chapter 13: Bank Earnings International 275
Chapter 14: Global Concepts: Partners.................................295
Chapter 15: Global Concepts: On My Own 321
Chapter 16: Selling Global Concepts, Inc.............................377
Chapter 17: McKinsey and Retirement 408

In memory of my parents, Sophie and Leo Lipis, who started me out in life with love, with family and with unconditional support for the paths I took in life, and to everyone else that helped to create me along the way.

He who learns from his fellowman a single chapter, a single verse, a single statement, or even a single letter must treat him with honor and call him his teacher, his guide, his intimate.

—Pirkei Avos 6.3

Preface

How do I begin to tell you about the things that have molded my life? How can I describe the events that have shaped me as a person and mean the most to me? How do I pass on the things that made a difference in my life? How do I know if anything I will say will really matter to anyone else? These are the thoughts that drove me to put on paper the things that mattered to me most in my life. I felt compelled to write them in the hopes that they will matter to you.

Unconsciously, the paths that I took in life, the people I met, and the experiences I had did change me. Some things are planned, but most things just happen, and we deal with them, both good and bad. We make decisions without knowing the ramifications because our vision is short, our experience is limited, and our world is much more complicated than we can ever understand.

I wrote this book because I wanted to pass on the lessons that I learned over a lifetime of experience, especially my business experiences. I consider my life a success in many ways: I have a successful marriage, children and grandchildren that admire me and me them, and I was very successful in business.

I didn't know whether anyone would be interested in my life, except perhaps my children and grandchildren, so I wrote for me. I was content to understand what happened throughout my life that made me the man that I am—the good, the bad, and the ugly. I wanted to look at the experiences I had, explain what impact those experiences had on me, and provide the lessons that I learned from them. I thought it might be useful for my children to know why I turned out the way that I did; this is a kind of self-introspection about the changes that affected me the most.

This book is filled with the events in my life that had the most impact on me. Many of these events changed me from who I was to who I am. They also became part of the reason why I succeeded in business. Everyone is changed by the experiences they have, so what I have to say should be relevant to others. In each chapter, I highlighted the lessons I learned to pass on what my experiences taught me. No one had my experiences, but many other people might have grown up shy, or saw others smarter than they were, or failed in business, or worked for tough bosses. If any of those are you, then perhaps this book will help you.

I didn't think that my own story in and by itself would interest many people. Memoirs are usually about famous people or people who did something special. I never won a race, held public office, or was in the movies. I just did my thing, minded my own business, and pressed on day after day, year after year. And as I write this at age seventy-four, I think I have made something useful out of my life, but more important than that, I think the experiences I had that changed me might make you understand yourself a little more and perhaps even provide some guidance for your life. Only you can decide.

Since I did succeed in business, I focused on that aspect of my life more than any other. I thought that would be the most useful aspect of my life for most people who want to succeed in business. But the experiences in business are the experiences in life, and business is just another extension of who I am. For the most part, business provides a broad set of experiences that I would not have gotten any other way.

Perhaps, you will see the need to assess just who you are by reviewing your life's experiences. I assure you, it is an awesome journey, and I encourage you to take the plunge. It will do you a world of good.

Allen Lipis
June 2012

Acknowledgments

In a book about my life, it is not possible to acknowledge everyone that had an impact on me. As my quotation from above states, if you learn even a single thing from a person, then that person is your teacher. I learned from so many people, too numerous to mention.

The greatest acknowledgement must go to my parents, who started me off in life, taught me through example, and introduced me to their families, making me an integral part of them. I have much to be thankful for having grown up surrounded by family who taught me how to speak and how to act. In so many ways they demonstrated how to treat people properly, how to raise a family, and how to enjoy life.

The encouragement for this book comes from my wife and my children. They wanted to know about my family, where I went to school, how I met my wife, where they were born, and how I succeeded in business. My wife believed that my story would be of great value to my family and gave me the time and support I needed to work on this book for several years. It was only when the full extent of the effort materialized that we both began to recognize that my story would be of interest to a wider audience. I owe her a great deal for being a part of my life for almost fifty years and providing advice in my business whenever I asked. Indeed, she was an active participant in the most successful business I created.

All of my teachers had a material impact on changing me, some much more than others. I attended the fiftieth reunion of Erasmus Hall High School in Brooklyn not because I wanted to see a few friends I knew but to honor the teachers I had. The greatest impact on my growing into an adult was at the Baruch School of Business, a part of City College of New York. I learned much, not just from my teachers, but also from my college friends. They opened my eyes about the rich variety of people that exist in the world and made me understand the vast choices I had that would allow me to create myself the way I wanted to be. Finally, graduate school taught me how to become a professional, how to define a problem, how to analyze it, and how to solve it with a vast set of analytical tools. I am especially indebted to Professor H. T. David at Iowa State University for showing me how to produce original research. I never used all the tools I was taught, but the process of approaching a problem professionally became a part of my life.

Looking back on the companies that hired me, I consider myself fortunate to have worked for Battelle Memorial Institute, a first-class scientific research company, and M&M Candies, one of the most successful private companies in the world. At M&M Candies, I worked for Dr. Larry Friedman, who showed me how to analyze data in many meaningful ways. He was a master at it, and a little of what he knew spilled over into me. At Citibank, one of the greatest banks in the world, I had an opportunity to work under John Reed and to appreciate what strategy was all about. In Atlanta, I worked for the top five banks in the early 1970s: Citizens & Southern National Bank, First National Bank of Atlanta, Trust Company Bank, Fulton National Bank, and National Bank of Georgia. I was never actually employed by the Federal Reserve Bank of Atlanta, but they treated me as though I were an employee.

I am especially indebted to Brown Rawlings at the Atlanta Fed for having confidence in me when he hardly knew me. He was instrumental in making me the project director of the Atlanta Payments Project, which catapulted me forward into the world of electronic banking. Many of my colleagues on that project taught me how to conduct a major research effort, taught me how to lead, to write, and to work as a team. Forty years later, a few of us still meet out of friendship.

At American Express, I had the privilege of seeing top management up close and I took what I could from James Robinson III, Louis Gerstner, and George Waters. I learned how to sell consulting from Dale Reistad, Bob Cady, and Steve White. I had great backup staff with Bill Moore and Mary Floyd during my early years in business. And finally, I had the privilege to work with a very talented group of people at Global Concepts, especially Steve Ledford, Jenny Johnson, Dave

Stewart, Jay Mehaffey, Michael Fisher, John Mateker, Anne Sullivan, and many others.

Roger Orloff and the staff at Powell Goldstein were extremely professional in helping me sell my company, and this book would not have been written had the sale of my company not have occurred so successfully.

Lisa Stroll served me well as my editor. She not only improved my writing but also forced me to stay on the mission of this book, which was to provide the lessons I learned in life and in business. Working collaboratively, she urged me to eliminate extraneous comments and rewrite sections that were not clear. The book is much the better because of her, though I take full responsibility for what remains.

Finally, I thank a good part of my family, my wife, my son, Leo, my daughter, Pamela Glinsky, and my son-in-law, Ron Beilinson, for having been a part of my business. They saw things I could never see and taught me the value of asking advice from family.

Chapter 1

Introduction

Retirement. It was December 1, 2005, and my retirement party was to occur that evening at the Atlanta Historical Society, a beautiful building in the heart of the wealthy part of Atlanta. My three children and my wife would be there, along with my extended family. My staff would be there, as well as colleagues that I had worked with across a forty-year professional career, and even a few customers were coming, some from as far away as Omaha.

I had sold my company, Global Concepts, to McKinsey & Company fourteen months earlier and continued on as the advisor to my old company. It was time to retire, and it was both sad and happy at the same time. I was sad because I was leaving the payment system world, a world I had come to love, and a field I had become an expert in. I would be walking away when there were so many issues still to be addressed. But I was happy to have the money from the sale of my business and to be able to retire in comfort. I was also thrilled that I could travel, see my grandchildren, and become involved in activities I had put off because of business.

As the days passed after my retirement party, I could not get the thought out of my mind that I had a story to tell about how I achieved the success that I had, the failures that I had to overcome, and the support that I received from so many unusual places. The more I thought about it, the more challenging the book would be because I didn't just want to tell my story of success. The lessons I learned over my professional career might be more valuable to other people who might think they were a nobody, thought they could not reach their dreams, and didn't think they had the courage to take on their challenge. I wanted to inspire them through my own story. I thought this book might help them. Still, I had my doubts about writing this book. How will I know if anything I will say will really matter to anyone else? That's what I asked myself. I thought that I had at least two answers.

People in the banking industry have not only asked me for advice, criticism, and new ideas for years and years but also paid me well for them. They wanted me to give speeches on my banking innovations, to forecast trends, and to analyze why their customers loved them or hated them. My first answer was that some people made a lot of money because of what I told them, so I knew that what I had to say mattered to them.

That was a narrow group of people. My wife and children would cringe if I stopped with that—and so would I. There is another dimension to the question. Will what I say matter to anyone besides those people, and if so, why?

Circumstances of birth placed me in a family with two kinds of wealth, and neither had anything to do with money. Because I came from a family with emotional and spiritual wealth, I had to rely on good judgment, morality, hard work, and a couple of brain cells to give me the stuff I needed to go from struggling to successful. Very successful.

My success was not an accident. Yours will not likely be either. It's safe to say the chairman of the board for Big Deal Corporation will not "discover" you on the street and invite you to assume the role of president. If you want to be the boss of something, whether it's a bank or a coffee house or a sole proprietorship, you will need to do a lot of the same things I did. Regardless of what year it is when you read this or what technologies are molding business operations around the world, you will accelerate your advancement with the help of a mentor—and I propose that this book be a start in that direction. I will give you lessons that are not dependent on having my background or looking anywhere else.

Many of the events that happened in my life were not of my doing. I was not in control, and I believed that luck played a major role in how my life unfolded. The key was to recognize an opportunity when it presented itself and then decide whether to take advantage of that opportunity or not.

I wanted to write this book not because the public cared to know about me, although my grandchildren might want to know about their grandfather. I was not a celebrity, I was not known by the public, and I had no dramatic story about corruption or drugs or sex. I was an ordinary kid growing up in a low-to-middle-income neighborhood in Brooklyn, New York. I was naïve to believe that what I had most everyone else had—loving parents, a large family with grandparents, uncle and aunts, plenty of cousins, and lots of friends. I went to Brooklyn public schools and gradually recognized that I had to change if I wanted to succeed in life and in business.

I overcame some of my weaknesses early in my life, married well, raised three great kids, and succeeded beyond my wildest expectations in business. I wanted to tell my story not to boast about my successes but to pass on what I learned over a professional career that spanned more than forty years and was part of the dramatic development of electronic banking. I had played a significant role in its development along with so many others, and I had learned many lessons along the way. I thought the lessons I learned might be useful to others wishing to be their own boss.

Given my business experience, I want you to feel as though I'm a mentor for you. This book is filled with the events in my life that had the most impact on me. Many of these events changed me from who I was to who I am. They also became part of the reason why I succeeded in business. No one else has had my exact experiences, but many other people have grown up shy, seen others who are smarter than they were, failed in business, or worked for tough bosses. If any of those are you, then perhaps this book will help you.

If nothing else, perhaps I will help you see the need to assess just who you are by reviewing your life's experiences—to codify your own lessons. I assure you, it is an awesome journey, and I encourage you to take the plunge. You will learn to be your own mentor.

Chapter 2

Childhood Traits

Call me Zeyda. When I started having grandchildren, I didn't want to be called grandfather, but Zeyda, the Yiddish name I called my grandfather. He was a mentor to me along with my parents and many of my other relatives. Zeyda is the name all of my grandkids now call me, and even my children and their spouses have gotten used to calling me by that name. For me it is sign of respect and of love, and I while I respond to that name, I never take it for granted. I know that so many other people did not have my background, and they did not have the mentoring I had. Zeyda reminds me that as the patriarch of my family, I should continue to provide mentoring to family, friends, and business associates when they request it.

My cousin once told me that she grew up taking twists and turns while I grew up straight and tall as an oak tree. I never wavered from the tradition of being surrounded by family. I was focused on getting a good education and wanted to do something important. In many ways, she was right. I went to an outstanding high school, a great college, excellent graduate schools, and worked for some of the most prestigious companies in the world. I had the luxury of great teachers and remarkable bosses who have become legends by virtue of their amazing success in business. From one job to another, I did work for the cream of American business and banking. In addition, I worked for a company when it was beginning its amazing growth as one of the fastest-growing companies in the United States. I received mentoring on many different levels: how to grow a business, how to handle people, and how to make a profit.

When I finally started my own firm, I had a tremendous background to be able to do what I had I seen others successfully do, and it made it much easier to find my way in business and eventually create my own success. Selling my company to McKinsey & Company, one of the most prestigious consulting firms in the world, is indicative that I did indeed build a successful business.

This book is not so much about the successes I had, but rather about the characteristics that I had to acquire to become that success. Some of these traits were copied from the people that I admired. I saw how they operated and decided that I wanted to be like them, so I copied their style as much as I could, knowing that I could never be them exactly. For others, I saw their weaknesses and decided that I did not want to act the way they acted, so I tried to avoid their traits. I want to identify for you what I learned over the past seven decades. I have tried to make my observations simple, but not too simple because success is dependent on many factors. It isn't easy to simplify the process, nor is it easy to indicate the path necessary for success. The simplest approach I know is to tell you my story, focusing on the characteristics that it took me to succeed. In the end, the burden still fell on me to find my own way, to find my own style, taking whatever I could from the many people who entered my life. Nothing, of course, guarantees success.

My journey begins by telling you that *the most important thing a parent can give their child is unconditional love*. This is especially true when things go wrong. It's easy to kiss and hug your child when things go right, but the real test is when things go wrong. I found this out at an early age.

I was born in Brooklyn in 1938 near Brighton Beach. When I was three years old, my parents moved to New Britain, Connecticut, because my father was fearful that he would be drafted into the army for World War II even though he had two children. My father found a job in New Britain at Fafner Ball Bearing working for the war effort. That kept him deferred throughout the war.

During our stay in New Britain, my family lived in a government project that had attached homes. We had a living room and kitchen downstairs and two bedrooms and a bath upstairs. When I was five years old, I got hold of some matches and started playing with them. I was alone with my two-year old sister, upstairs in my parents' bedroom. My parents were downstairs in the kitchen. All of a sudden, the lit match came in touch with the curtains and they caught on fire. As the fire began to spread up the curtains, I yelled for my father who came running upstairs. By then the curtains where all aflame, and the fire was moving up toward the ceiling. My father quickly pulled the curtains down and stamped out the fire, partly burning his hands. While he was doing that, he yelled down to my mother, "Sophie, bring up some water!" My mother, hearing the urgency in my father's voice, but not really understanding why the water was needed, showed up with a small glass of water. It was hardly enough to put out the fire, but it was a story my father loved to tell.

I was really frightened about the fire and scared at what my father might do to me. I thought I would be spanked or severely criticized for letting the curtains catch fire. My parents knew that being only five years old, I could be excused for my ignorance, and it was a real life lesson about what happens when you play with fire. That incident made me cautious about playing with fire, but more importantly, it subconsciously told me that my father loved me—he did not punish me for making a stupid mistake. For the first time, I knew how forgiving my father was; *my father loved me even when I made a big mistake.* He saw how scared I was about the fire, and I would remember what I did. Punishment was not necessary. I am thankful that my curiosity was not snuffed out by a harsh punishment.

I don't know where my curiosity came from, but it has been with me all my life. *Curiosity can get you in trouble, but it is how you learn.* Uncontrolled curiosity is not just dangerous. It can kill you. Controlled, curiosity is how inventions occur, how scientists operate, and how breakthroughs happen. At five years old, my curiosity was uncontrolled, and I was lucky my father was in the house and knew exactly what to do.

When I was about ten years old, my father came home with an air rifle he picked up somewhere. The rifle was enticing because it was unusual for our family to have a gun or a rifle in our house. The rifle was put away in the closet, but I knew where it was located. One day when my parents were not home, I thought I would shoot it out the back window of our apartment. Since I didn't know anything about rifles—and I certainly didn't want to use bullets and didn't think we had any in the house—the idea occurred to me that I could use a long wooden match, the match my mother used to light the stove. The rifle used air pressure to shoot what was in the barrel, so I tried the matches and they worked. When I shot matches at a brick wall across the backyard about seventy-five feet away, the idea worked perfectly. The match would hit the brick wall and light up, hurting no one. I was proud of the fact that I was shooting the rifle. Of course, I knew that my parents, especially my father, would be totally opposed to my using the rifle at all, let alone shooting matches against someone else's brick wall, so I was definitely not going to say anything about this to anyone. However, the matches were obvious to the neighbors who heard the sound of the rifle and saw the matches strike the brick wall. One of them told my father what I was doing, and that was the end of the rifle in our house and the end of my little game of fun.

My father was a relatively easygoing father and rarely hit me, but once in a while, I just went too far and then I got spanked. The spanking hurt, and I am sure it was justified in my father's eyes, but for me, I always thought the spanking was not deserved. One time I got so mad about being punished that I decided to get even. But what could I do to get even? I finally thought that I could hide my father's favorite leather slippers, slippers he used to keep beside his bed and use only in the apartment. It wasn't a big loss to my father, but it would be a little bit of revenge for hurting me and making me cry. I decided that the best place to hide the slippers was under my parents' bed on top of the wooden slat that held up the box springs. I shoved the slippers up between a wooden slat and the mattress in the middle of the bed so it would be difficult to see even when you looked under the bed. I was determined to keep my mouth shut and not say a word to anyone and see if I could punish my father because he had punished me.

My parents looked for those slippers for weeks and couldn't find them, and every time I heard them talk about not knowing where the slippers were, I smiled inwardly. I was getting my sweet revenge. Finally, after several months had gone by, I decided to tell my parents what I had done. While they watched, I climbed under their bed and produced the lost slippers. All they could do was laugh, be happy that the slippers were returned, and that was the end of the mystery of the lost slippers.

Even when I hid the slippers for months, my father didn't get angry about it. He could have been angry with me, but rather he saw the cleverness in what I did. I was smart enough to hide them for months.

Because I was not punished, it made me feel good that even though I was just the little boy in the family, I could get sweet revenge by being clever about it, so clever that my parents could laugh instead of punishing me. My parents overlooked this prank and saw it for what it was—a young boy needing to get some satisfaction. By laughing instead of punishing, they reinforced once again their unconditional love of me.

To prove how much the family loved me, my family was often at my grandparents' apartment. They only had one bathroom, a rather ordinary room with a toilet and bathtub. The toilet seat was made of wood, and one day when I was sitting on the toilet and had nothing to do, I started to carve my first name in the front of the toilet seat between my thighs with the small pocket knife I owned. I finished the first three letters of *Allen*, so that it was obvious that I was the culprit. I was then ten years old.

Of course, it didn't take long for people to discover the carved toilet seat. When they asked me if I did the carving, I lied and pleaded innocent. When they said my name was the only one beginning with the letters *A-L-L*, I said nothing; I couldn't bring myself to openly admit I was the one. I was innocent and naïve, it was a stupid thing to do, and most of all everyone knew I was the guilty culprit. It became a big joke around the family that I carved my name on the toilet seat. That toilet seat was never changed, and the story was repeated for years. Indeed, every time anyone went to the bathroom, there were my initials. Up until my grandmother moved out of that house, the wooden toilet seat with the start of my first name carved in it stayed there. For my family, everyone saw it as a cute thing and nothing more. I was never punished for it, and I never did it again. *People will minimize your mistakes if they love and respect you.*

When I shot wooden matches from my father's rifle out the back of my apartment, I thought no one would know and that I could hide this little secret from my parents. I wasn't smart enough to know how to cover my tracks when I did something wrong. I thought that I could get away with it, but I got caught. That taught me an important lesson: *Crime doesn't pay. In the end you do get caught.* Someone will find out that you are doing something wrong, and you won't get away with it.

When I carved part of my name on the toilet seat in my grandparents' bathroom, everyone knew it was me that did it. It was an innocent but stupid thing to do, and I heard that story repeated again and again. It was cute, but it was also embarrassing. These were good lessons to learn early in life when no one got hurt and nothing was damaged. It helped me stay away from trouble most of my life.

Next to loving me, *my parents constantly tried to give me confidence.* While they tried, confidence is an internal feeling, and I had to find it in my own way, as you will see. It took me a long time to get there.

When I was six years old, I used to go sledding in the winter down a huge hill about a half mile away from my house. It was several hundred feet high and the ride down the hill lasted for a quarter mile or more, so it was a really good ride on snow. One day, my father came along, and we both went down the hill on my sled, me on top of my father. The sled was not very big, and my father's legs hung off the back. The ride was faster than ever with all the weight on the sled; we flew down the hill. When we got to the end of the ride, my father told me in the most serious face he could muster that he was scared to go down the hill again, but I could go back up the hill because he knew I wasn't scared. As he was leaving to go home, I told him that I wasn't scared at all and went back up the hill for another ride. I went down that hill many times that day and many days after that, but my father never went sledding down that hill again. At that tender age, every time I went down that hill, it built my confidence. I could do something my father was scared to do.

This story is the case where *a parent gave me confidence for an accomplishment that I hardly deserved.* I took my father's words at face value, and thought I was more confident about riding my sled down the hill than he was. I had more courage than my father and that was a real confidence builder for a six-year-old.

Early training builds confidence. It can last a lifetime. In New Britain, our government housing was surrounded by a number of farms. Besides the farm that had the sled-riding hill, there was a farm in back of our house that had a small pond that froze up in the winter. I learned to ice-skate on that pond at a very early age. I would go ice-skating there every winter with a bunch of other kids. One time a kid fell through the ice in one section where it was just too thin. He wasn't hurt, just wet as someone pulled him out quickly. Since I could ice-skate every winter, ice-skating became a part of my life and it built my confidence because I did it well. I never forgot how. Even when I was not on the ice for many years, ice-skating came back to me naturally.

Traveling alone also built my confidence. During that same era, because my father did not own a car, I had to travel somewhere in New Britain by bus. I took the bus some time after school. I was six years old, yet my mother allowed me to ride alone on the bus, knowing that I knew where to go, I could get off the bus at the right stop, and then take another bus back home. New Britain was a safe town, and my parents never worried about my being kidnapped or molested. They knew I knew my way. That level of trust by my parents gave me a level of confidence at an early age; I could be trusted to find my way by myself. That level of trust didn't matter for anyone else, but it had an important impact on me.

Trust builds confidence in a young child. When you are young, you have no fear when your parents trust you. You know they will not want you to be hurt, even if you are not sure about something. If they think you can do it, you give it a try. The more they trust you, the more risk you are willing to take and the more you will learn. Even if you are scared, you gain the courage to do more, and eventually, it is second nature.

After the war, my family moved back to Brooklyn to the area that is called Brownsville. When I lived there in the late 1940s, Prospect Avenue between Hopkins Avenue and Saratoga Avenue was a beehive of activity; it was the main market for the neighborhood. There were pushcarts along the entire length of the street selling fruit, bread, clothes, and household items. The street was jammed with people buying and selling, and I always enjoyed walking along it watching people doing business.

The kosher butcher we used had a small store on that street. Once inside the store past the butcher block and glass showcases that displayed the meat, there was a back area where live chickens were kept, killed, and plucked. My mother asked the butcher if they needed a delivery boy to deliver telephone orders to customers. By coming with her one day, I got my first job delivering those orders because I had my own bicycle and a basket to carry the food. The butcher didn't pay me at all. I was willing to work for tips from the customers. After all, I was only twelve.

I would make the deliveries late in the day for several hours, rain or shine, perhaps delivering to two to three customers. The ladies that accepted the deliveries usually gave me a dime or a quarter, which amounted to a couple of dollars a week, but that was enough for me since I didn't need much money. This was a win for the butcher who didn't have to make the deliveries and for the customer who didn't or couldn't come to the store. I was mostly busy on Thursday and Friday as customers were getting ready for the Sabbath.

On a couple of occasions when the road was slick from rain, my bike skidded off the road, and I scraped a knee or my hands. I just got up, got back on the bike, and delivered the order. I intended to be a reliable delivery boy, and I was. As my very first job, I was determined to make good. I felt a part of that butcher shop, a part-time employee even though they didn't pay me.

I learned for the first time what it was like to make money on my own. *Making money when you're young teaches you the value of money and the responsibility to do a job well: be on time to your employer and to the customer.* The butcher and the customer depended on me, and I did not fail them. I felt important. I was doing something useful for people and getting paid for it.

I also felt that my mother had enough trust in me to let me ride a bicycle all over the neighborhood alone, knowing that I would be out in traffic and crossing trolley tracks. I delivered rain or shine and accepted the tips without complaining. I gained a small amount of confidence in my ability to make deliveries, to go to houses that I had never been to before, and to protect the meat from being stolen. My mother knew the neighborhood was totally safe, and the butcher trusted me with his meat. The job didn't last long, for we moved away to another neighborhood, but I had my first taste making money, and I liked it. Succeeding in my first job set the tone for succeeding in all my subsequent jobs.

A father can mentor a son by doing anything the son cannot do. During the winters in New Britain, there was a fair amount of snow. One winter, my father made a huge snowman by rolling a small snowball around on the ground until the ball was about three feet in diameter. He didn't do it alone; other fathers joined in the fun, but for me, it was my father doing it. The fathers made three huge snowballs and put one on top of the other, creating a snowman that was bigger than my father. We decorated the snowman with pieces of coal for the eyes and nose, put a scarf around his neck and a wooden handle for a mop at his side. Seeing a snowman much bigger than I was made me feel small, and it also left me in awe of my father who could create something so big and lifelike—almost human—from snow. I was impressed with my father's ability, and it taught me that it was possible to create something from almost nothing. Seeing him create a snowman when I was six years old had an impact on how I saw my father. That incident convinced me that I might be able to create when I got older too.

The worst thing that happened to me intellectually was flunking out of Yeshiva Chaim Berlin. When we returned to Brooklyn from Connecticut, my grandparents, who were very religious Orthodox Jews, insisted that my parents send me to an Orthodox yeshiva. That turned out to be Chaim Berlin on Eastern Parkway, a short distance from my apartment. I probably started there in the second grade, a year after the other students, since I was seven when we came back to Brooklyn. Chaim Berlin was a very Orthodox Jewish school designed around the Jewish yeshivas that existed in Eastern Europe before World War II. It was an all-boys school. We prayed every morning and afternoon, and we ate strictly kosher food. The school was organized for religious studies in the morning and secular studies in the afternoon. The Jewish studies were conducted in Yiddish, not English, and this was a major problem for me. While I was an excellent student in secular studies, getting straight As there, I did not speak Yiddish even though my parents spoke it at home to one another. I picked up a word or two, phrases that were used often, but never enough to really speak the language. That hurt me at school where other students spoke fluent Yiddish and understood what the teacher was saying. I could not do well in my Judaic classes because I did not understand the language my teacher was speaking.

Coming into the school in the second grade from a public school in Connecticut, I was behind the others in the class, and the school did not believe in remedial help. I needed to learn Yiddish before I could move forward with my Hebrew studies. The entire morning was a complete disaster because I could never understand what was being said in class. One Hebrew teacher believed in putting the children in seats in priority order of their knowledge. Seating every child in class according to how smart they were was just his way of organizing his class. The best students were in the front row, the next best group in the second row, and so on. I was in the back of the class in the last row with two other students. I felt totally inferior, and everyone in the class knew it. Sitting in that class day after day told me I was stupid, and it created an inferiority complex in me that lasted for many, many years.

I had no other means of comparison except to feel inferior. This feeling of inferiority went on for three years until I left the school. Only much later in life did I realize that the teacher's seating rule was a stupid idea because it made every student in the class, except the first few, believe that they were not as good as other students. Even though I was smart in secular studies, the impact of sitting in the back of the classroom day after day, year after year had a huge negative impact on me as a person, making me shy and reserved, and for a long time thereafter, I could not get over thinking that I was inferior.

I don't want to make light of my three years at Chaim Berlin. It had a major impact on my overall confidence, not just in school but overall. This wasn't a single event but a recurring feeling day after day for years. Three years is a long time to continuously fail in school. *For a child, one serious failure negates a hundred successes.* This extended failure altered my personality for a decade, contributing to my shyness and my feelings of inferiority. This is not like falling off a bicycle or striking out at bat or even failing to win a game. This is about a major failure, one that makes a child feel inferior to all the other children. Because of my experience there, I came to think of myself as intellectually below other kids my age, incapable of learning the work when others were doing quite well.

My mother often repeated afterwards that she met with the headmaster of the school, and the rabbi did not want to directly tell her what to do, so he said to her, "Give yourself an idea." My mother told that story often because she hated to admit that I was not right for that school. Finally, my father took matters into his own hands even though he knew my grandparents pushed hard for me to get a good Jewish education. My father saw that I was failing at Chaim Berlin, pulled me out, and sent me to public school for my fifth grade, which was only a half a block away from my apartment. Those three years at Chaim Berlin made me into a shy person for a long time. It gave me the feeling that I could not succeed in school and perhaps in life. It made me believe that I could not master languages. That experience haunted me until I got to college.

You can receive a lot of praise again and again, but a little criticism hurts much more and is remembered for years, especially for a youngster growing up. *Be careful with the failures you allow young people to have; it will influence them for a lifetime.* We learn from failures even more than successes. Let the failures be small failures, not one that will impact a child's personality.

The most memorable story about my father was the day we traveled by train to Central Park in Manhattan for a Sunday afternoon outing. We were all dressed up nicely. My father was wearing a suit and tie, he had his shoes shined, and he was sporting a Benrus watch. My father, my mother, my sister, and I were all together enjoying a lovely spring afternoon walk in the park. As we passed by the lake in Central Park, a little five-year-old boy slipped on the edge of the lake and fell into it close to us. He couldn't swim. He was floundering and drowning about six to eight feet from the edge of the water. His mother was beside herself, screaming, "Save my boy! Save my boy! He's drowning!" Why she didn't jump in to save her son is still a mystery, but there was no one else around but my family.

My father looked around, hoping someone else would be the hero, but there was no one. Once he knew it was up to him, without hesitation, he jumped into the lake up to his chest and pulled the boy to safety. My father was a good swimmer, but he didn't have to swim a stroke. Still, he was soaking wet, his pants and coat were muddy, his shoes and socks were disgusting, and his watch was full of water. The lady was extremely grateful and offered to pay to clean my father's suit. My father took nothing from her except her grateful thanks. He traveled home on the train in that wet suit, wet socks and shoes, and a ruined watch. Between cleaning the suit and fixing the watch, it was an expensive day as well as a wet and uncomfortable one. As the days went by, all I could remember was that my father, without hesitation, jumped into the lake to save someone he didn't know, knowing he had to do the right thing. He gave no thought to the consequences to himself, his suit, or his watch. He showed me what it means to help others in serious need of help. From then on, I wanted to help others. He became my hero. He was my only hero!

I often wondered why the mother did nothing except to scream. Why didn't she jump in to save her child instead of my father? I didn't know the woman, and I had no idea if she could swim, whether she was fearful of getting wet or whatever. I didn't walk in her shoes. *If you don't know why someone does what they do, then don't judge their actions—you aren't walking in their shoes.*

One thing happened that shows you the mentor my father was for me, and the lack of confidence I still had occurred at my bar mitzvah. The evening party was at my grandparents' synagogue many miles away and included all the relatives and friends. It was a nice turnout, perhaps 150-200 people. I was supposed to give a speech to this audience, a speech that my Hebrew teacher had written for me. I was incapable of writing the speech myself even though I had graduated from the local Hebrew school. I had the knowledge but lacked the courage.

Although I only had to read it, I was still shy and completely unfamiliar with public speaking. I had never given a speech before. I was nervous, scared, and uncomfortable reading someone else's words, so I panicked and I told my father that I could not give the speech. I could always tell my father my deepest feelings because I could always count on him to understand. I told him I was too scared to speak. He did understand because he was not a public speaker either. He talked to me gently, never insisting, always trying to reason with me. Somehow he convinced me that it wouldn't be that bad, that the speech was all written out, that it would be an embarrassment for him and my mother if I didn't speak, and that everyone would understand if I slipped up reading a word or two. With a little confidence boost from my father, I gave that speech. I don't remember a word I said, but I remember my father was always on my side.

I really never had anyone I would call my hero except my father. Although I rooted for the Yankees, I just wasn't that interested in sports to have a real hero. My uncle Sammy once brought me an autograph of Joe DiMaggio, whom he met traveling on a plane somewhere. I kept the autograph for a short time and promptly lost it. I loved the Yankees; they were my baseball team. I liked going to a baseball game, but that was it. I never had a baseball hero. I didn't have a rabbi outside of my uncle to admire, and I had no interest in admiring movie stars, politicians, or TV personalities. The reason was clear to me. They did not know me, could not help me to grow, and whatever I knew about them was superficial.

Everyone seemed to have flaws or problems. I was so focused on studying, on learning, and on growing up that I didn't have time to admire people way beyond my league. For me, they were not real. They were outside my world of reality. I was self-centered, trying to grow up.

I had no time for heroes, for then I would not be focusing on growing my own abilities but only admiring theirs.

But when my father spoke about his automobile mechanic as though he was a genius at auto repair, I was impressed. We often would go to the Shell station on Atlantic Avenue with our old Studebaker, my father's first car, for it always seemed to need work. The mechanic there would find the problem and promptly fix the car. Since my father was mechanically inclined, he knew a good mechanic when he saw one. If my father was impressed, then so was I. This mechanic was as close to being my hero because my father thought he was a genius. I never really talked to the man, knew him only from the reputation my father had of him, but he was the best there was because my father said so.

The old apartment building we moved to from Connecticut was a third-floor walk-up in the Brownsville section of Brooklyn. It was a lower middle-income area with old coal-heated buildings built in the early 1900s. By any definition, it was a low-income area for families that could not afford much more, but I never noticed that it was low income. Since everyone that lived on that street was in the same category, I knew nothing else. When you are eight years old, you don't focus on what life could be like. I took life as it came to me. I did not have any other choice. For me, it was my home, so I made friends on the block, went to school like all the other kids, and made do with what life brought me. In many respects, it was a great time in my life, for I had no worries and did what little kids do—play and study.

My parents made it clear to my sister and me that *children have a single job—get a good education.* My parents took care of all the other issues. I didn't have to worry about my health or about money, the two things older people worry about most. I worried about doing well in school, about studying for tests, about turning in my homework, and about staying out of trouble. That was my real job. The rest of the time I could play and have fun.

In my first year of junior high school, I took a shop class, and the teacher required each student to build something out of wood. The wood was provided by the school for little projects, like a set of bookends or making a wooden cat or some other easy to make item. My parents had just bought a twenty-gallon fish tank, and we had purchased guppies, mollies, and swordfish for the tank, all tropical fish that are easy to take care of and have live-bearing fish. I suggested to my shop teacher that I wanted to build a wooden stand for the fish tank to hold my twenty-gallon fish tank. The stand would sit three feet off the floor and would have a shelf under the fish tank to hold supplies and the pump to clean the tank. The teacher agreed to let me build the fish tank stand provided I brought enough wood from home to replace the wood I would use in school because the fish tank stand would require much more wood than what the other students would be using.

When I told my father about the project, he said he could bring enough wood from work to satisfy the teacher, and he did. One morning, my father and I brought several ten-foot sections of wood up the stairs at school to the shop. I worked hard on that fish tank stand, measuring all the dimensions and building the stand with a shelf. In the end, the stand was very basic, made out of two-by-fours and plywood, but it was very strong. It held the fish tank quite well, and my parents proudly displayed it in the living room for all to see.

I appreciated the fact that my parents were willing to have my elementary carpentry skills displayed in their living room and that they were willing to show off my handiwork for relatives and friends to see. The lesson I learned from this experience is *you can break the rules if you are creative*. I could exchange my wood for the shop's wood. I also recognized that my carpentry was weak; my fish stand was not well made as far as furniture goes. And finally, even at twelve years old, I recognized that the only reason that fish tank stand was accepted in my mother's living room was because I made it. When we moved a short time later, the fish stand disappeared and was never seen again, but it didn't matter to me anymore.

In our new apartment, my parents gave me the twenty-gallon fish tank for my bedroom. At first, I continued with live-bearing mollies, guppies, and swordfish. As they died, I decided that I would move up a level and breed egg-laying fish, which was much more difficult. I chose small zebra fish that have black stripes on a white background and are generally easy to breed. I put several layers of marbles on the bottom of the fish tank so the fertilized eggs would fall down between the marbles away from the adult fish who would eat the eggs if they could. After several months, the zebra female was loaded with eggs, and I watched daily for the time when she would drop her eggs. Once she did, the book said that the male would lay sperm down to fertilize them. One night, I actually saw it happen just as the book said it would happen.

The female dropped her eggs, the male swam over them, sending a spray of his sperm, and the eggs gradually settled to the bottom of the tank in between the marbles. Several days later, I could see hundreds and hundreds of tiny fish attached to the glass near the bottom of the tank. A few of them gradually found their way to the plants to hide in the leaves away from their carnivorous parents. Over time, most of the zebra fish died out; they were either eaten by the mature zebra fish or died for some other reason. A few of them actually made it to become adult fish, but not very many, and I was sad to see them die out so quickly.

The most interesting part of my tropical fish experience occurred when I moved on to breed fighting fish. The male fighting fish is beautiful in color and fascinating to watch. Two males in the same tank will fight each other until one is dead, so it is never a good idea to put them together. The female is not as pretty. Breeding them is very interesting as the male first blows a huge number of bubbles, one on top of the other to make a nest. When he is done, one huge corner of the fish tank at the surface is covered with empty bubbles. Once the female is ready to lay her eggs, the male wraps his body around the female and squeezes out the eggs. Then the male swims down to the bottom, picks up an egg in his mouth, and places the egg inside one of the bubbles to protect the egg, allowing it to hatch. I actually saw it happen, and I was so astonished to see it that I could only watch and be impressed.

Tropical fish are a specialty like most things in life. It is easy to get a fish tank and put tropical fish in it. Most anyone can do that. It takes, however, a level up to breed them, especially egg-laying fish. In doing that as a teenager, I knew more and was doing more than most people having tropical fish. I thought that I was becoming an expert, but it was obvious that *it takes lots of knowledge to become an expert.* I didn't continue much beyond that point, but the acquisition of knowledge beyond what others knew in tropical fish made me feel that I could become an expert at something down the road. Tropical fish was a start for me, but any subject wherein you know more than the public is a way for a young person to believe they can become someone important.

I don't know why I started to save coins. I just did. I began by saving pennies and quickly realized that I needed a coin book to store the various pennies I found in circulation. The coin book left space for every year and every mint, and gradually I moved from saving pennies to nickels, to dimes, to quarters, and to half dollars. In 1947, many of the valuable US coins were still in circulation. My mother would give me $5 to buy coins, and I would go to the bank and get $5 in pennies. I would then read the mintmark on the pennies to add to my coin collection. After picking out a few pennies I needed for my collection, I would fill the wrapper with the remaining pennies, add replacement pennies, and return the coins to the bank to get another $5 of coins to begin again.

I looked for coins for my coin collection for many years over and over again, filling in my collection. I made a list of the coins that were missing and carried that list with me in my wallet. Every coin was a possibility for me. Everywhere I went, I would look at the change I got, and I would look at the change my parents got, always looking for mintmarks to add to my collection. I never bought a coin in all my years of collecting. I look back today and admire my determination and commitment to continue looking for a few good pennies, nickels, dimes, quarters, and half dollars during that decade.

I saved coins because it was fun and because I had a commitment to build a coin collection from scratch. It was only much later that I discovered that my coins were worth a great deal more than their face value. I still have the collection today, and it gives me great satisfaction to look at them and realize that every single one of them was handpicked by me from the thousands and thousands of coins I reviewed in my youth. That type of diligence and commitment has stayed with me for most of my life. It gave me the feeling that I understood more about US coins than the average person using them to buy something.

On one occasion, I filled two coin wrappers with fifty pennies each and took them to a small grocery store in the neighborhood to get a dollar. The grocer didn't trust me and counted the coins to be sure there were fifty pennies in each wrapper. One of the wrappers had forty-nine coins in it, and I was totally embarrassed. I had no desire to stiff the grocer and had made an honest mistake, but the grocer was certain that I was trying to get an extra penny out of him.

When I shortchanged the grocer, that mistake affected my integrity, even if it was an honest mistake. That embarrassment taught me a penny lesson—when others trust you, especially when it concerns money, you must be accurate. Fifty pennies cannot be forty-nine pennies, and the one time it was checked, it was wrong. My integrity was at issue. *My good name was worth more than diamonds and rubies.* The thought that a single penny could insult my integrity has stayed with me, and it became a part of my desire to never be embarrassed again for trying to cheat someone.

My uncle Maxie was an avid stamp collector, and he encouraged me to become a stamp collector too in addition to my coin collecting. While I started collecting US stamps, I quickly gravitated to collecting stamps from all over the world. It was interesting looking at these stamps, and I got an early education about where countries around the world were located. Since my uncle had a much larger collection than I, he graciously gave me hundreds of stamps from his collection, most of them doubles for him, but it gave me a quick start in stamp collecting.

My uncle suggested that I send a postcard to the American embassy at countries all over the world asking them to send me their cancelled stamps off of the mail they regularly received, which cost them nothing. On my postcard, I mentioned that I was ten years old, a stamp collector, and I would be very appreciative if they could help out a very young stamp collector. The cost of a postcard was small, yet the results were amazing. Most of the embassies replied with some stamps, and a few of them sent dozens of them. These stamps were torn off envelopes so I had to soak the stamps in water to remove the glue on the back of the stamp. I looked forward to getting mail from all over the world and then adding the stamps to my ever-growing collection.

What I learned was *if you don't ask, you'll never know what others will do for you.* It is better to ask and be refused than not to ask at all. I was getting stamps for free, feeling great about it, and thankful that my uncle had put me onto stamp collecting. Whenever I look at my stamp collection, I am reminded about how much can be accomplished for free—if you're willing to ask.

My passion began with coin collecting and then went on to stamp collecting. Those passions continued for many years, and they taught me the value of persistence. It also taught me the joy and happiness that comes from having a passion in life. *Give a child one passion, and that passion leads to other passions.* I learned a lot more about a subject than most people know, and that made me feel like an expert. It was exciting learning something in great detail, and that spurred my interest in other matters. It led to my career as a consultant.

One day my parents gave me a small chemistry set with about fifty different containers of various chemical items, including several test tubes. One night my parents went out and left me alone with my sister who was then eight. I was about eleven. I decided that I would find out how the chemicals reacted by placing them in the test tube. I had no idea what these chemicals were, how they would react with one another, and did not bother to read anything about them.

At first, nothing much happened. I tried various chemicals one at a time then mixed several at a time and shook the test tube vigorously. Nothing happened. I had no idea what I was doing, I had no idea about chemistry, and I certainly didn't know the differences among all the chemicals that were in the kit. My curiosity, however, got the better of me, and I was determined to get some kind of chemical reaction. In my ignorance, I decided to heat the test tube over the gas burner on the stove. Nothing happened with one chemical. I added several together and nothing happened. In frustration, I put a cork in the test tube and continued heating it. The mixture in the test tube was jet-black and quite liquid. With the cork in the test tube, pressure built up until an enormous explosion occurred.

The explosion sprayed black liquid everywhere: on the walls, on the ceiling, on the light fixture, on the floor, and all over my sister and me. It was a disaster. I was petrified about what would happen to me when my parents came home, which they did shortly thereafter. Once again, they merely scolded me about not playing with things I did not understand. Again, this reinforced subconsciously that my parents loved me even when I screwed up badly. Curiosity will get you in deep trouble if you don't know what you're doing. Those were lessons that have remained with me for most of my life. Fortunately, the black stuff all over the kitchen could be easily cleaned up, which my parents did that night, so there was no lasting damage. This was, of course, the end of my chemistry experiments.

St. Marks Avenue was a declining neighborhood even when I lived there. There were mostly old tenements attached to each other that were coal heated with a walk-up as high as four floors. Several of the tenements were in such bad shape that they were condemned by the city as uninhabitable. These buildings had broken windows, no lights inside, and I was scared to go in them at all. One time, a guy in the neighborhood went into the abandoned building, climbed out on the third floor, and hung out of the building, holding on to the ledge by his hands. As he dangled there, his feet in mid-air, he was trying to show off how macho he was. I watched him trying to impress all of us standing in the street. I thought to myself, "What a stupid thing to do—to put your life in danger to impress your friends." I could not understand why a person would put his life in danger just for fun. I thought it was stupid, but he didn't. I became convinced that *there is no sense in taking dangerous risks with little reward.*

One night during the summer when I was about eleven years old, a bunch of my friends were playing kick the can on the sidewalk and the street. Someone is picked to be "it," and that person has to find the other kids. Someone not "it" kicks a can on the sidewalk out into the street as far as he can, and then the rest of us run and hide while the person that's "it" has to find us before we touch the safe pole, like the street lamp. One of the guys named Red tried to reach the street lamp and ran across the street without looking. He didn't see the car coming and was hit and sent sliding along the ground for twenty-five feet and ended up under a parked car. Fortunately, Red wasn't killed, but he broke one of his legs in several places. The car stopped, an ambulance was called, and several days later, Red returned home in a cast. After that, Red always walked with a limp. I have thought about that incident many times because I could easily have been Red. It was only by the grace of God that it wasn't me. *In the excitement and emotion of having a lot of fun, you still need to be careful about what you do.*

I had a friend named Melvin who was about my age. We used to play ball in the street since that was often the only place for us to play. I don't remember the incident, but one afternoon, I pushed Melvin a little too hard, and he went crashing headlong into a car and broke half of his front tooth. It was an accident pure and simple, two eleven-year-olds playing a little rough with each other. Melvin's mother did not take too kindly to that fact and gave me the worst looks for months every time she saw me. She had to take Melvin to the dentist and fix a permanent front tooth, which not only was expensive but also altered Melvin's smile for life. His mother never let me forget it because playing *rough can cause a lifetime of grief.* Still, I prefer that than to not experiencing any risk and the opportunity to see what you are made of. In the end, Melvin was still my friend.

One of the accomplishments of my sixth grade class resulted in a class picture. That picture was made of the entire class after each student in the class deposited money once a week into a savings account at a local savings bank for eight weeks in a row. Each student did not want to be the one that undermined the picture, and with the encouragement of Mrs. Moskowitz, our teacher, we all succeeded in depositing money each week to get a picture of our class. When the picture was made, I put that photograph into a frame and hung it on my wall to remind me that *commitment to an objective can be achieved if we all work together.*

The most positive thing I accomplished in my early education was winning the American history award, a competition with all sixth grade students. Some time in the middle of the year, the teachers organized an American history competition. Any student could apply, and like a spelling competition, the students were asked questions about American history, one student at a time in the main auditorium with the entire school in attendance. All questions were to be taken from the sixth grade American history textbook that we were studying.

I studied that book every day for a couple of months, memorizing as much of the material as I could because I wanted to win the contest. During the competition, one by one the students dropped out. The missed question was then asked of the next student until the correct answer was given. Because there were so many contestants, at first the questions were easy, and I only had to answer a few questions to remain in the competition. With twenty-five to thirty students participating, it took some time before the competition narrowed down to just a few. Finally, we were down to two students, and the other boy missed a question related to Lake Champlain. I knew the answer. I was the winner, and the teachers gave me a certificate with my name on it, proclaiming that I had won the American history contest for the sixth grade. I was so proud of that award. It was the first time I had won anything competitively. I framed that certificate and hung that award on the wall of my house to see day after day. That award boosted my confidence, and I thought that I was a winner.

When real accomplishment happens, like winning the American history contest, that win stays with you for a lifetime. I was the winner, a win I won because I studied hard. I was determined to do my very best, and I was better prepared than my competitors. Every time I looked at that award, it made me feel great.

In the seventh grade, my homeroom teacher was the typing teacher for all the classes at the junior high school. She knew that typing would be a very useful skill, and she took every available time in our homeroom to teach us to type. I thought at the time that I would never find this skill useful, first, because I wasn't going to be a secretary, second, because I did not have a typewriter at home, and third, because I was used to writing in a book. I could not understand how typing would be useful for me. That was 1951, long before computers. I didn't need to type for many years until the computer age came into existence, and then those typing skills became extremely useful. *Some things you think are worthless turn out to be very useful later in life.* Learning to type in the seventh grade was one of them.

There is a small picture of my father, my sister, and me in front of my apartment building on St. Marks Avenue. I must be about eleven years old, and my sister is about eight. My father is standing between us, hugging us both. My father is wearing a hand-knit sweater vest my mother made, and I am wearing the exact same designed sweater vest as my father's. Behind us is a small set of steps leading up to the entrance of our apartment building, with the two small front doors that swung open and had no locks. Besides the same sweaters that my father and I wore, I am wearing a long coat that is too big, my hair makes me look like a wimp, and I am clinging to my father as though he were my safety insurance. My sister is looking just as helpless, also close to my father and looking very innocent as she was. The front of my apartment building looks very old and worn and very typical of the turn-of-the-century brownstones that covered the block I lived on. Together, the picture is one of a small family living in a low middle-income neighborhood without a concern for fashion yet clinging together because family is what counts the most.

This picture sits on my dresser at home today, and I look at it often, for it sums up my past as much as anything else. The picture talks to me. Keep life in perspective. Family still counts the most. Children need to feel safe. Money is not everything. Fashion is not that important. Handmade clothing is more valuable than anything purchased. *One picture can keep your life in perspective.* I am one lucky guy.

Chapter 3

High School

My father started his own business with a partner, Sol Faberman, repairing sewing machines late in the 1940s. Faberman was responsible for bringing in sewing machines for repair, and my father would repair them. The business did not work out for them, and they closed their business after a year or so, not because the business failed, but because my father could not take the pressure of being in business for himself. He did not know how much income he would make from week to week, and his partner was not a very aggressive salesman.

When that business closed down, Faberman went into a totally different business selling various household items that he bought wholesale from Japanese importers. He offered them for sale over the weekend at outdoor markets in New Jersey. He lived in Brooklyn as my family did, so he would travel to New Jersey on a Friday and come home late Sunday evening. He needed an extra pair of hands to unload the hand-painted plates, vases, lamps, ashtrays, glasses, and other household items, and my father consented to let me help him.

Faberman picked me up late Friday afternoon after school, and we traveled to New Jersey and stayed overnight in a motel. I was his helper as he sold his merchandise at a different market on Sunday than Saturday. He rented one of the booths at these markets stalls with a roof overhead that could be locked up for the week. These markets attracted a lot of people each weekend for food, clothing, and other items. I helped by packing and unpacking the goods and wrapping up packages sold to customers. I had no idea how successful the business was, but we sold quite a few items each weekend.

I didn't make much money, and I was outside most of the day. I did this for quite a few months in the fall, winter, and into the spring. I watched how Faberman would sell, but I had no idea how to negotiate the sale or whether the profit was decent or not. I was just too young to understand business. I did what I was asked to do, and I didn't learn much about business other than to conclude that lots of people bought junk that I wouldn't keep in my house.

Even though Faberman was kind to me and paid for my food and the motel, I didn't really enjoy the experience. I stopped because I didn't like being away from my family every weekend, I wasn't making much money, I wasn't learning about business, and it was cold being outside for six to eight hours. The combination kept me in the job a short time, and that was a good thing. I learned that not every job is fun.

That job convinced me that *a good job should be fun and be a learning experience.*

I tried to follow that advice most of my life. I know that many people do a job for the money, not because they like doing it. Many people feel trapped in their job, don't enjoy the job they are in, and don't think they can change. I feel sad for them, for a job consumes at least a third of their life. To devote that much time to a task that is not fun and does not provide much experience is sad. Try hard to enjoy every job you have and learn as much as you can from each of them. When you are learning on the job, you will find that the job is more fun. Learning and fun should go hand in hand. *When your job is no longer fun, leave it; the sooner the better.* Even though I sometimes didn't follow my own advice, it was always a mistake to stay. I should have acted sooner.

In March 1952, my family moved from Brownsville to Flatbush; we were moving up. The neighborhood was much better, and my mother managed to get me into an elementary school a few blocks from our apartment. I was put in the eighth grade, and there were only three months left until graduation. It was unlike the junior high school I left that went from the seventh grade to the ninth grade; my new school only went up to the eighth grade.

Somehow I discovered that it was possible to take a special exam to get into the highly regarded engineering high school—Brooklyn Tech. Brooklyn Tech was well known for its engineering training. It was available to all kids in Brooklyn, but you had to pass a tough exam to get in. I was pretty good in math and convinced my parents to let me take the exam since the cost of going to that high school was free.

I was actually a little surprised when I found that I had passed the exam and was accepted. On reflection, I decided that I didn't want to be an engineer. I had my heart set on becoming an accountant. Everyone in my family thought that a good math student should become an accountant, and accounting was business—engineering wasn't. When I turned Brooklyn Tech down, the principal of the school insisted that I was making a very dumb mistake because Brooklyn Tech was a great school. She forced my parents to come to her office and told them that my going to Brooklyn Tech would be an honor for her school and for me. In advance of that meeting, I told my parents that I just didn't want to go to Brooklyn Tech. They supported my decision even though the principal insisted that I go there. My parents trusted my judgment over an authority figure. It was my life, not the principal's.

What I did learn from the experience was that my parents supported my decision, not the principal's, and they trusted my judgment. There seems to be great reluctance to trust the judgment of children, for the argument is made that they are not mature and are easily swayed. While true, children still know what they like and don't like. Children want to learn, they know when they are learning, and parents also know when their children are learning. When your child tells you that he/she does not have a good teacher, accept the premise that *your child has good judgment. Trust them.* Children know when they are excited about learning, when they are bored and not learning, and when they have a teacher who can teach. I was clear that I did not want to go to Brooklyn Tech.

As I got older, the decisions became more difficult, but I had to decide. Don't put off decisions by living in the past. Live in the present and decide for the future. *When the decision is all yours to make, be sure about what you really want to do.*

Only God knows what might have happened to me had I taken the other road. It reminds me of the famous Robert Frost poem "The Road Not Taken." I made many decisions in my life that could have taken me down an entirely different path, and I will never know how it would have turned out. I have fantasized about the roads not taken on many occasions, but it was just for fun, never seriously. Regret about what you do in your life is for others. *Do not regret the decisions you make. You cannot go back.* Never look back with longing for having missed or regretted some other path. I made the best decision that I could with the information then available to me, and I am satisfied with those decisions. When you know that you made the best decision that you could have made, you should have no regrets.

I don't remember much about my three months at my elementary school except that much of the material was different from what I had been learning in junior high school. However, the math teacher was impressed with me because of one small incident. One day, he gave the class a math problem that he thought no one would solve quickly. While everyone was hard at work trying to solve the problem, I solved it in a few minutes before anyone else, and he was very impressed. I was so proud of myself. I can still remember the problem.[1]

On the strength of my quick and correct solution, I was asked to take the math test for the best math student in the graduating class, but I was behind in my math knowledge and did not win. Still, I was impressed with myself for solving that one problem, and this triumph has stayed with me for more than sixty years.

At any age, winning is a valuable experience that improves your self-confidence, especially that of a child. It doesn't matter what you win so long as the winning is legitimate. Getting that math problem right faster than anyone else may not have mattered to anyone else in the class, but it mattered a great deal to me.

---

[1] There are exactly 100 coins. Some are gold coins worth $5 each; some are silver coins worth $3 each; some are bronze coins worth $.50 each. Using exactly 100 coins, how many gold, silver, and bronze coins are there?

There are two solutions to this problem. The problem is tricky because there are three unknowns—gold, silver, and bronze—and only two possible equations, so setting up algebraic equations, which is what the class was learning, did not work by themselves, and that's what most of the students were doing. The answer lies in the restriction that the coins must be a whole number, not 6.5 gold coins, but either 6 gold or 7 gold, etc. Once you understand that only whole numbers work for gold, silver, and bronze coins, and you realize that most of the coins must be bronze because they are worth less than a dollar and must compensate for the expensive gold and silver coins, you should be able to try various combinations to reach the answers.

Competition can be hurtful for anyone that does not win, especially for those who do poorly. Still, winning is the American way, and competition is what capitalism is all about. There are hundreds of ways for children to win: in sports, in class, on exams, for fun and games, at home and away, anywhere and anytime. Winning is important for self-esteem, and there are so many ways to be a winner.

Not everyone needs to know that you are a winner. Only you need to know. You can win when others don't even know it, like winning at a computer game or finishing a Sudoku puzzle or a crossword puzzle. Winning is an attitude; you can carry that attitude with you always and not feel bad when you lose. *Once a winner, always a winner.* Vince Lombardi, the legendary coach of the Green Bay Packers, is quoted as saying that, "Winning isn't everything, but the will to win is everything." Winning is a habit and so is losing.

Partly because of my shyness and partly because of my upbringing, I didn't have a strong desire or the courage to take an aggressive interest in girls until I was about eighteen. I never dated until I went to college even though I wanted to go out with certain girls. In my teenage days, a boy had to make the first move to ask a girl for a date, and I just couldn't bring myself to do that in person or over the telephone. I just thought about it a lot and never did it. I never thought I was the best looking or the most talkative; I just wasn't very comfortable around girls my age. I admired good-looking guys, like Steve, who was outgoing, handsome, and an excellent roller skater. He was always going to the roller rink on Eastern Parkway, and there were always girls around him. Several years later, I was astonished to hear that another friend named Joel, a guy two years older than me, was going to marry one of the most attractive girls in our neighborhood. I could never have had the courage to ask her out, yet I knew I was smarter than Joel. I couldn't understand what she could see in Joel, for there were many other guys more attractive and more intelligent than he was. She was so beautiful; she could do better. Joel was an outspoken guy, not that smart and had a bad temper. I could not understand what any girl could see in him. And yet, he had convinced a really gorgeous girl to marry him. My ego was bruised, and to this day, I just don't get what some women see in some men.

As a senior in high school, a beautiful girl who sat next to me in our history class, a girl that I found very attractive, was engaged. She was getting married, and I had not even taken a girl out on a date. I was very naive about girls. It was all part of being shy and reserved; I didn't have the courage to be outgoing with women. Getting over my shyness took a long time, and it prevented me from meeting women. Being analytical didn't help either; I was always analyzing a situation and never living in the present.

While guys my age were dating and even getting married, I was only dreaming about women, nothing more. With no organized sport to consume my time, I had nothing else to do except study. *Being shy and naïve does have its advantages—you compensate by getting good grades.*

When I started at Erasmus Hall High School, I found that the teachers were exceptionally strong, that I was learning a lot, and I needed to do a lot of homework at night to stay up with all my classes. I was living in a three-bedroom apartment. My bedroom was in the middle of the apartment, close to the living room where my parents watched TV every night. In 1952, my father had just spent four hundred dollars on a sixteen-inch RCA TV, and he and my mother enjoyed watching it nightly. With the walls in the apartment very thin, I could hear the TV clearly, and the noise was totally distracting from the homework I had to focus on. How could I drown out the talking on the TV? I couldn't ask my parents to stop watching TV when they had just bought it. I decided that I needed music in my own bedroom to drown out the TV, but I had no idea what kind of music I was going to use to accomplish this.

After much study, I bought a Columbia 360K stereo for eighty dollars in one of the local stores and hooked it up. There were no separate speakers; the phonograph had two speakers built into the wooden box that allowed for stereophonic sound. I had no records, but I thought I might be able to find something to listen to while I studied.

Downstairs in the same apartment building, Arthur Solomon, one of my friends, introduced me to his father. He just happened to love classical music because he had more than a hundred classical music albums. When he heard that I was looking for some kind of music to listen to while studying, he proposed to sell me six to ten of his albums that he was looking to get rid of because he was looking to upgrade his collection. He proposed selling his used albums to me for a dollar per album. Quickly, I took him up on that offer. That was the start of my classical music collection and my love for classical music.

I still have most of these 33 1/3 long-playing albums. I have never adequately thanked him for putting me on to classical music, but even more important, he is the man that helped me get good grades in high school. Without that music, I doubt that I would have been able to focus as strongly on my homework, and I doubt that I would have gotten the good grades I got in high school. The music drowned out the TV, and most importantly, I discovered the music that works best for studying is slow classical music.

My most favorite of all these records is Sibelius's Symphony No. 1. Over the years, I have played that record more than a few hundred times, sometimes several times in a single night. Over the four years of high school, my record collection increased, and I gradually enlarged my appreciation for all kinds of music, including jazz, Broadway shows, and popular music. But in the end, I returned to classical music because it soothed me, it drowned out the TV, and it focused me so I could direct 100 percent of my mind on studying. Later I learned that *slow classical music is a proven technique to concentrate more effectively, thereby improving your study habits.*

In the book *Super Learning*, the author describes scientific studies in Europe that have concluded that slow Baroque classical music is the best music to study with as it focuses the mind, eliminating all distractions without the listener being distracted by the music. The largo or slow section of classical music is best because it is slow, quiet, and trancelike, making it perfect to listen to while studying. The book lists a number of classical music albums that are best for studying although I listened to slightly more energetic music from what was recommended. Still, I was pretty close in my choice to what the book recommends as ideal. This confirmed something I had found on my own, and it reinforced my belief that classical music was the savior for me in high school.

In addition to Mr. Solomon, my humble thanks to Sibelius, for he alone was with me almost every evening for four years. Even after I had graduated to better music equipment, I kept my Columbia 360K stereo in my basement because it was an old friend, a friend that had made a big impact on my life. It gave me the opportunity to acquire an excellent education.

For any student, *studying is best done in the same place with the right atmosphere to focus 100 percent on the material to be learned.*

What worked for me is classical music, a big desk, and good lighting. Today, I don't need the music because I don't have distracting sounds, but my high school years taught me to focus my mind on the material in front of me. That training stayed with me over the years. Whatever can concentrate the mind to focus on learning the material without being distracted is the answer. A standard place to study and slow quiet music worked for me.

Partly because I was smart, partly because I finally had good teachers, and partly because I had organized an atmosphere conducive to studying, I found that studying was the most exciting thing in my teenage life. Studying took me to places I had never seen or heard of, opened my horizons, challenged my mind, and excited me as nothing had done before. I would spend hours at my desk doing my homework. I liked doing it because I enjoyed the learning process. Because I was studying areas that I had a strong interest in, I continued to be fascinated throughout high school with the body of knowledge that was so new to me. It set me on a course for the rest of my life.

It's not odd that I should remember some of my teachers more than fifty years later. Some teachers leave an impression on you, both good and bad, that you never forget. Mr. Sanderson was one of them. He was quite old, probably close to sixty when I took his freshman math class, but that was not the problem. Sanderson gave only one test for each of the three grading periods of the semester, and the entire grade was based on that one test. Worse, there were only a few math problems on these tests, and you either got the problem totally right or totally wrong. He never gave partial credit as other teachers did. His first exam had four problems, each one worth twenty-five points. I got three problems right, and thought I had gotten a 75 on the exam. I expected a 75 on my first report card, but I was surprised when my first report card showed me failing the course with a 50. I knew I was a good math student, and yet I had a failing grade that I did not deserve. I had to show the report card to my parents and then explain that my idiot teacher had made a mistake. What a way to begin my math studies in high school. Fortunately, I had the test in my possession, showed it to him, indicated that he had made a mistake, and sure enough on the next report card, he changed the grade to 75. The 50 was still there on the report card, crossed out and replaced by a 75, and I had to look at it until I finished the class. I remembered that teacher because it was the only time I had a failing grade in math even though it was the wrong grade. In math, I knew a bad teacher when I spent a semester with him; Mr. Sanderson fit the profile. He proved to me that teachers controlled my destiny even when they were wrong.

Mrs. Altchler, my next math teacher, was a great math teacher. The first day I came to class, she took complete control of the class and scared me. She was a big woman with a booming voice, and she made it quite clear that she insisted on perfect discipline, or else she would throw you out of the class. Within half an hour, I knew she was not to be fooled with; she insisted on absolute obedience. Her manner was intimidating, but that didn't matter to me. I wanted to learn geometry, and she knew how to teach it. I listened intently all semester long; there was no other way to be in her class. It was a huge change from Mr. Sanderson. Teaching required not just knowledge of the subject but also an interesting personality to make the subject come alive. She had both. I think it was because of that class that I love geometry. That love has stayed with me all my life.

Teachers can be boring or inspiring. One inspiring teacher is all you need to offset all the others. I had many great teachers in my life and a good number of boring ones as well. I forgot the boring ones and remembered the inspiring ones. The inspiring teachers had a major impact on my life, and I thank them all for what they did for me. I wish that all teachers were inspiring, but they aren't. You just need to put up with them as best as you can and move on. Seek out inspirational teachers. You may only need one. *It's not the school that matters; it's the teachers that are in it.*

I always wanted to play the trombone. I had taken piano lessons when I was ten years old, and those lessons taught me how to read music, but I could not imagine playing any other instrument than the trombone. I just knew I would like it. I had heard Tommy Dorsey play the trombone as the leader of his orchestra, and I liked the sound of the trombone, the way the instrument looked, and that was it. When I started at Erasmus High School, they had a band and I joined. The school gave me one of their trombones at first, but eventually, I bought my own trombone. I was not a great trombone player, but I was good enough to play in the high school band.

There were only a few trombone players in the band, perhaps three to four of them, and I was determined to improve to become as good as I could be. Since Erasmus had a football team, the band would go to the football games and play throughout the game, but we never went onto the field during halftime to give a performance. The band was not that good, and we didn't practice marching into various formations as they do today.

Mr. Bowdoin, our band teacher, would work with us on our music a couple of times a week in the afternoon, and gradually I started to improve. I was impressed by three things while playing in the band. The first was that I started out at an equal level with Stanley Kaplan who was in my class and played trombone. We were both beginners, but I took lessons throughout high school while Stanley didn't. I took a lesson each week, and the teacher forced me to focus on basic technique—reading music, playing in tune, and training my lips to make clear notes. I was diligent though I can't say I was a good player. In my senior year, it was quite obvious that I could play much better than Stanley could play because I was practicing and had a teacher outside of class while Stanley didn't practice at all. I was proud of the fact that I ended up first trombone while Stanley played second trombone. *Practice makes a difference.*

The second thing I learned was how little I knew about trombone playing. One day, Mr. Bowdoin invited a professional trombone player to visit our band practice. I thought my trombone was the problem, not my playing, but the professional trombone player took my trombone and played it significantly better than I had ever played it. He proved in one minute that I was the problem, not my trombone. The third thing I learned was that the trombone player in the orchestra, who was the same age as I was, was a much better player than I could ever be. I was playing simple marches while he was playing serious classical music. He could improvise, and I didn't have a clue about improvisation. He could play jazz, he could play without sheet music, and I could do none of the above. I knew then that while I loved the trombone, while I loved to play in the band, I would never amount to much as a trombone player. That was an important experience. I tried to succeed at one of the great desires of my youth, to play the trombone, and I succeeded. I had worked at it for four years, not hard but hard enough. *I loved the trombone, but the trombone didn't love me.*

I had a love affair with my trombone, but after four years of playing, the trombone did not love me back. I was an okay player. I could read music and I could play the easy music for a high school band. I just wasn't that good, and I knew it. I gave it a decent try, I practiced, and I did become the best player in my high school band. But in the end, I was not that good. I enjoyed playing music and no other instrument pleased me more, but I had to admit that my talents lay elsewhere. It was a sad day when I put my trombone away, but *I could not see myself committed to a pursuit that I was never going to be any better than mediocre.* I wish it were otherwise, but at eighteen years old, I had to face the facts. There were many things that I knew I could do well, but the trombone was not one of them. I loved the trombone from the earliest time I could remember. I wanted to continue to play it, but I knew I would not be much good at it, and I gave it up for things I knew I could be good at. My high school trombone still lies on a shelf in my basement, and I look at it lovingly from time to time, but it is now only a memory.

When I was fifteen, I thought I could play football. I borrowed a standard one-speed bike and rode to a football field about two miles away. It was the huge parade ground near Prospect Park where teenage kids played football. I thought if I showed up, I would be able to get into a game. I had no football outfit, and neither did the other guys playing. I thought I could protect myself by merely wearing a heavy sweater and long pants. No one wore a helmet or shoulder pads or any kind of protection, for this was a friendly game, so I thought. Since I never played football, I had no idea how risky it was without protection of any kind. I could catch the ball, but I had never played organized football. It was totally stupid to think this way, but teenagers tend to think first about having fun and not about the risks of getting hurt.

I stood around for a while until there was room for another player, and then I was asked to join the team. I didn't know anyone playing, and I didn't think I needed to know anyone since this was just a fun game. I played one of the ends, and I quickly discovered that there was more to football than just being fast or strong. I remember two things during the fifteen minutes I played. The first was that the opposing team had real football players, guys that played on high school football teams and knew how to block and tackle. The second thing was that our team had none of that. We were a disorganized bunch of guys just having fun.

Our team didn't have any training at all. When the opposing team scored a touchdown and were kicking for the extra point, they could spread their feet after the ball was in play so that no one could get through the line. I was impressed that they knew how to play football because I had no training whatsoever. I would not have remembered such a game except for one incident. After playing for about fifteen minutes as an end, I went out for a pass. The quarterback threw the football to me, and I caught it nicely and headed for the end zone. I was determined to make a touchdown no matter what even though two men were closing in on me. I kept running hard for the end zone. Near the goal line, I was hit by two guys simultaneously, one on either side of my body. I went down hard, tackled at the knee and the waist at the same time. I fell into a heap a few yards before the end zone. I knew I had a problem as soon as I hit the ground. They hurt my knee so bad that I could not continue in the game.

At first, I thought I broke something, for I was in severe pain. I was out of the game and could hardly stand up, let alone walk. I limped around for the next half an hour with no improvement in sight. No bones were broken, but my knee was hurting really bad; it was beginning to swell up and walking was very painful. Gradually, I limped along, but I couldn't walk well. How was I to get home? I didn't want to leave the bike at the park. I had borrowed a bike from the basement of my apartment, and I had to get that bike home. Eventually, I got the courage to get on the bike and ride it home. Every rotation gave me severe pain. Fortunately, the road home was flat and did not require the tough exertion that a hill would require. I thought I would never get there, but I made it.

Having managed to make it home, I hobbled down into the basement, put away the bike, hobbled back upstairs to the third floor of my apartment, and slowly undressed. Without saying a word, I got undressed and headed for the hottest bathtub I could stand. My mother asked me what I was doing, and I told her I hurt my knee and was soaking it. I was never happier to take a bath. The knee healed up a few days later, but that was the end of my football career. I had played football, I had almost scored a touchdown, but winning wasn't worth it.

I gave little thought to the risks and focused on having fun. It was a youthful way of thinking. In business, in investing, and even in a normal situation, trying something new, and in doing something you don't know much about, *when you don't know the risks, don't take them.*

In the early '50s in Brooklyn, my friends and I didn't have access to a baseball field or a schoolyard or even a dirt lot, but we loved to play baseball. Since we had to play on our own block, we devised a baseball game we could play with cars parked and cars traveling on the street. The game was called punch ball. We used a pink ball that was soft enough to punch with your fist without needing a bat. We called the soft pink ball a Spaldeen because it was made by Spalding.

We would designate a sewer in the middle of the street as home base, a second sewer a hundred feet away also in the middle of the street as second base, pick a car fifty feet away from the first sewer on the right as first base, and a car fifty feet away from the first sewer on the left as third base. Depending on the number of kids available, we would put men in the street and on the sidewalks as fielders, allowing the batter to punch the ball on the street or on the sidewalk. The game was played just like baseball, three outs for an inning, the ball had to be thrown to first base before the batter got there and catching the ball on the fly was an out. The batter threw the pink ball up in the air and punched it with his fist just like hitting a baseball with a bat.

One day I was playing punch ball in the street. We had a good game going with about six boys on each team. I was pretty good at this game because I could punch the ball hard and long. We were behind in runs, it was the last inning, and I was the batter with a man on base. I stood between winning and losing. I threw the pink ball up and hit it hard with my fist, and it went clear over the heads of the outfielders. I couldn't believe that I had hit the ball so far and so well. I ran as hard as I could and touched all the bases while the outfielders retrieved the ball way down the street. I beat the throw to home plate and won the game with a home run. I had hit an inside-the-block home run and won the game! I was a hero. I got lots of congratulations, and I walked on air for days thinking about it. I knew I could play a very mean punch ball.

I have thought about that punch ball homer many times over the years because it was the only time I really thought of myself as a hero, as the guy who made all the difference between winning and losing. I only needed to do this feat once to believe I could do it again, and it gave me the confidence to believe in myself, not just for punch ball or even for sports, but in everything I did in life. No one else will remember that I hit a home run in a punch ball game in Brooklyn in the early '50s, but I do and that has helped to shape my life. *Once a winner always a winner; once a hero makes you a hero forever.*

There is one fishing story I will never forget. I was sixteen years old and had gone fishing in the summer for years. In the middle of the winter, Bernie, my friend next door, persuaded me that winter fishing would be neat since we could catch whiting, cod, and other cold-water fish. I went to my father and pleaded for him to let me go. He was familiar with winter fishing in New York, and he said something like this, "Fishing in winter is a very stupid idea. It's cold and miserable and you will get seasick. The fishing is not easy, and the chances are high that you will not catch a thing. The type of people who fish in winter are tough, not like the easygoing people you will see in the summer. These fishermen like to smoke, drink, and play cards, so if you get sick and are stuck in the cabin below deck, the air will stink and you won't be able to sleep or breathe. I know because I did it."

Still, I persisted. I had never gone fishing in the winter, I had a friend to go with, and it wasn't expensive. After a long, tough argument, my father finally relented. He said he was doing it so I would learn from my experience and understand that not everything had to be understood firsthand to know it was a stupid idea. He had gone winter fishing, and he knew what he was talking about.

I went winter fishing, and everything my father predicted happened. I got seasick. I hardly fished at all. The waves and the sea were very rough. I ended up below deck in a foul, smelly bed listening to men playing cards and drinking whiskey. It was one of the most miserable days of my life. But it was also one of the great lessons I learned early in life. *Trust good advice. You don't have to experience something to know it is bad for you.* Your parents are looking out for your best interests, and they often know what they are talking about. Don't be attracted to something stupid just because your friends want to do it. That experience at sixteen may have kept me out of drugs, gambling, drinking, and a whole host of other stupid experiences you think you must experience. Thank God my father let me have the experience of going winter fishing. It taught me a lesson for a lifetime.

I already described my dislike for Joel. I found him crude, not interested in studying, and a pushy guy. He was two years older than me and six inches taller. I could never beat him in a physical fight. Still, I hung around him because he was one of the guys on the block.

He lived in an apartment two buildings away. One day, I was in his apartment with a couple of other friends, and we discussed masturbation while no one else was at home. Joel claimed that he could masturbate whenever he wanted, and I thought that was not possible, so I bet him a dime that he couldn't masturbate right then and there in his parents' living room while we watched. Well, he took me up on the bet and proceeded to masturbate just as he promised. We were all astonished at this performance, and we argued that he really didn't do it. There was some question about whether he actually had completed the job or not, and I argued that he didn't do it and refused to pay him the dime.

A week or so later, he was in my apartment with a couple of other guys, and he was still insisting that I owed him a dime. He knew I was a coin collector, saw my coin collection lying around on my desk, and proceeded to take a dime out of that collection. He didn't know anything about coin collecting, but he could read the total production for each of the years the dimes were minted. To hurt me, he selected the coin with the lowest production because it was one of the most valuable coins in the collection. He was right. Since he was bigger than me and I didn't want to fight about it, I let him have it. I couldn't have stopped him anyway. He selected the 1921 mercury dime, certainly one of the rare coins I had found. I never got the coin back, and I don't know what Joel ever did with the coin; he probably just spent it.

For months, I was angry with him for taking one of my most valuable coins, and we were never close after that. I tried to find a 1921 mercury dime after that, hoping that I could find a replacement, but it never happened. Today, I have almost all the mercury dimes except the very rare ones, and the 1921 mercury dime is still missing in my coin book. I suffered a hundred times more anguish over losing that dime than just paying Joel off, but I was stubborn and refused to admit that he had actually masturbated. Today, I would say that I lost that bet, and I should have paid the dime. I was stubborn at the time, I refused to admit that I lost the bet, and I paid a heavy price for it.

Every time I was stubborn and insisted I was right when it was possible I was wrong, I suffered. It happened when I refused to pay the dime bet, it happened when I didn't listen to my father and went fishing in the wintertime, and it happened when I held my ground against other boys and ended up fighting with them. There are times when you need to hold your position, but most of the time the situations are trivial.

Being stubborn indicates an unwillingness to negotiate—it's my way or else. *There is no cure for stubbornness.* It is tough to live with those kinds of people. Reduce the number of things you are stubborn about. The fewer they are, the better.

One of my friends was Billy. He was one of the really smart guys on our block. He got into Brooklyn Tech, the school I turned down. Billy kept to himself, and one day I discovered that he had bought a bike and was riding it all over Brooklyn to stay fit. Most of the guys I hung around were not physically fit. We just hung around going to the local candy store, playing cards, or got involved in some nonphysical game. I was physically out of shape, overweight, and not interested in sports. Billy was riding his bike all over Brooklyn and setting an example. I thought he was weird and a loner. It was twenty years later before I entered the aerobics revolution, and by then, it took me four years of running to work up to run the Peachtree Road Race, a 10K race in Atlanta. *Physical fitness is essential for growing up and for life.* When I was physically fit, I could concentrate for most of the day and not feel tired. When you are physically fit, you are mentally strong and able to do most anything. You can be on the field playing, being in the action, instead of watching on the sidelines.

I admired Billy for not only being physically fit, smart, and good looking, but also for doing his own thing when the rest of us were just wasting time. He became a medical doctor. I knew he was going to become someone important.

I never joined the Boy Scouts; it wasn't the thing a good Jewish boy in Brooklyn did. None of my friends were Boy Scouts, and only later did I learn the value of scouting, too late to do me any good. One day, my friend Michael suggested that we camp out overnight during the summer in a Boy Scout camp in Staten Island. I didn't know a thing about camping and neither did Michael, but we were willing to try. How bad could it be? I thought it was a good idea and convinced my parents that we would not get in trouble. Michael and I had no idea about camping. We just threw a few things together to keep ourselves warm, enough food for one night, and decided to take the ferry to Staten Island. My mother was concerned that we did not have anything to put on the ground for us to sleep on, so she gave me an old quilt that was in our closet that no one used anymore. We gave no thought whatsoever about needing a tent, a shovel, an axe, or any of the other items a good

Boy Scout troop might bring with them when camping overnight. We didn't think we needed a tent or any other type of gear. All we had was a backpack. With basic clothes and food and a couple of flashlights, we set off.

At the Boy Scout camp, we noticed that there were many Boy Scouts camping there. They had erected quite a few tents for the night, and clearly we were not as prepared as they were. The Boy Scout tents looked very inviting, and I thought to myself how unprepared we were. We found a good location on a little slope because we did not have a pillow and thought we would be fine for the night. We would sleep outdoors; we would be braver than the Boy Scouts. We cooked a nice meal over a fire we made and enjoyed the warm summer evening.

Some time late in the evening, it started to rain. At first, the rain was light and did not seem to be a problem, so we covered ourselves as best we could with the blankets we had and hoped for the best. We pulled the covers over our heads and prayed for it to stop. When the rain didn't let up, we knew we were in trouble. It was then the middle of the night, there were no lights, there were plenty of trees, slopes and hills, and the rain became increasingly heavy. Finally, it started to rain hard. Michael and I covered up as best we could, but the rain was getting into everything. We were getting wet, the quilt on the ground was soaked, everything was soaked, it was pitch black outside, and we had no idea where to go. Finally, we could stand it no longer; we were drenched from head to toe, and the blanket my mother had given me was soaked through and through and ruined. We could no longer stay where we were with everything soaked; we had to head for shelter. With the quilt completely soaked and too heavy to carry, we had to leave it behind. We picked up the rest of our gear and headed for any shelter we could find. The rain was now coming down in sheets. As we trudged through the rain, we could see the Boy Scouts comfortably sleeping in their tents. I envied them and their preparation.

After about fifteen minutes in the rain, with everything soaked through and through, we found an outhouse with an overhang that could at least keep us out of the rain. The outhouse was nothing more than a wooden cover surrounded by wood on three sides with two toilet seats inside. One side was completely open, and there was just enough room for us to stand there out of the rain. The place stunk of urine and feces, had flies and other insects all over the place, but it was the only dry spot around. The worst thing was the smell of shit all around us. We didn't like the spot. In fact, we hated the spot, but it was out of the rain, and we were soaked. How could we dry off? For some unexplainable reason, we had brought along a huge container of talcum powder. I thought that the talcum powder could absorb some of the water on our bodies since nothing else was dry, so we started to undress and began to cover ourselves with talcum powder. The rain lasted another half an hour or so and then stopped, but we were still soaked. We took off our wet clothes, one piece at a time, and covered ourselves with talc to dry off.

Since it was the middle of the night and very humid, it took several hours before our shirts felt a little dry. Next, we took off our pants and underwear and covered ourselves with talcum powder, again hanging our pants up to dry. We did the same thing with our socks and shoes. Imagine, standing in that outhouse in our shorts, waiting for our clothes to dry, covered all over with talcum powder, smelling the urine and feces, and putting up with the flies. We stood that way for several hours, not knowing what else to do. We couldn't leave since everything was wet. We couldn't get home in the middle of the night since the buses and ferry were not in service, so we put up with the mess we were in all night long. We stayed standing in that outhouse until the sun rose. As day broke, we put on our still-wet clothing, threw away anything no longer worth carrying, and went back to our quilt. It was soaked, torn, and totally unusable for anything, so we left it there. We were miserable going home in wet clothing, without my mother's blanket, without any sleep, and smelling from pee and shit. Little by little, our clothes dried on our bodies.

After we came home, I thought how foolish we were to go camping unprepared, without thinking about the uncertainties of the weather. The Boy Scouts knew what they were doing. They trained for it. They brought what they needed to stay dry, and we had to pay the price standing in an outhouse the entire night because we had no idea what we were getting into. Being prepared is not just a slogan; lack of it has consequences.

The Boy Scout motto of being prepared is an important element in life. When a pilot gets ready to fly, he checks off his list to be sure the plane is ready. Lawyers spend most of their time preparing their case for court. *Being prepared is planning for the worst while working for the best.* Preparation is the essential element for winning in everything. Throwing something together at the last minute may work for some people, but preparation is always to be preferred. It is the secret to success.

I did stupid things as a teenager, like tossing balloons filled with water off the roof of my apartment building. It seemed like fun at the time, but it was a stupid thing to do, and I stopped doing it once we hit a taxicab with one of our balloons. I knew it was wrong, and it might've seriously hurt someone. Playing football without protection was a stupid thing to do. When the tackles hurt my knee, I suffered for days. When I went fishing in the wintertime against my father's advice, it was stupid thing to do, and I suffered during the entire trip. I learned from my stupidity. I hope you learn from yours. *When you do something stupid, don't do it again.*

When you grow up in a low-income neighborhood where everyone doesn't have much extra money, you accept that type of life, for that's the only type of life you know. I didn't understand how wealthy people lived, and I didn't care. I was enjoying my childhood, I kept busy, and I had the essentials. I didn't miss what I didn't know much about. From time to time, I would go to one of my friend's private homes. Some of my more-distant relatives had private homes too. But it never registered on me that my family had less money than these wealthier families had. I never thought about it; it wasn't that important. If you are happy with your lot, and I was—perhaps because I wasn't exposed to any other environment—you are a rich man. I don't think I ever felt jealousy that some other family had more. This was because all the other people in my life, family and friends, never had more than we had. The simple fact was that we *lived within our means.*

I never discussed money when I was young or talked about lacking money. My parents never complained openly in my presence about what they needed or couldn't buy, so I never felt I was missing something. We were low-middle income, but I didn't know the difference. I accepted my family's financial status easily simply because it did not affect me until it was time to go to college.

I got my first real job from a close friend of my father's, Myron Finklebrand. Mr. Finklebrand owned a shoulder pad factory in a loft in Manhattan. It was right in the heart of Soho. I got the required working papers and worked there during the summer at age sixteen. I started in the shipping department and later went on to cutting a circle of fabric in half to make two shoulder pads. The shipping and receiving department received cotton in huge bales. The cotton went into shoulder pads that were usually for military uniforms. After the shoulder pads were ready to be shipped, I would package them up for another company in Manhattan that would put them into the uniform.

Near the end of the summer, I was asked to be a cutter. I would cut the round sewn material with cotton inside into two equal pieces. It was a boring job, but I became efficient at it and kept up with everyone else doing that job. I didn't make much money that summer. What I learned was that I could work with others, that I could learn on the job, that I was a hard worker, that I could get promoted from assistant in shipping to a cutter, and that I could be as good as anyone else.

My second job came from a neighbor downstairs who worked in a fake fur clothing company. I was standing outside my apartment one afternoon late in the spring when one of the men that lived in the apartments near mine asked a group of us teenagers if we wanted a summer job just when school was ending. The man was a cutter for a coat company in Manhattan that made fake fur into coats called Fur No. 9. The company wanted someone to package up the cut material for another location so the coat could be sewn together.

He first asked Bernie because he knew him. Bernie just wasn't sure whether he wanted the job or not. I immediately stepped forward and said I wanted the job, and the man picked me. I got that job because I didn't hesitate and forcefully said I wanted the work. I didn't care what I did; I wanted to work. I was seventeen, and I wanted a job and took it unhesitatingly. I didn't ask why or even care; I just wanted a job. I went with my gut and took the first job that came my way. There were probably four to five kids standing around, and I was the first to step forward and take the offer. I didn't know anything about this neighbor, and I didn't know anything about working in a real company, but I was game. Because I spoke up first, I got the job.

At the company, the materials for the coats were laid out on long tables. Once the material was cut, I had to bundle it all up into a huge paper package and tie it up with twine nice and tight so it could be delivered to the sewing machine operators in another location. I had a huge roll of heavy wrapping paper and a huge roll of twine that I would cut with a knife. The packages were made about three feet high, two feet wide, and three feet long and weighed about thirty to forty pounds.

On the first day on the job, the older men that did the cutting thought they would have some fun with me and asked me to bring them a pail of steam. The men made it sound like a very serious request. Of course, it was a joke, but I took the request seriously, for it was my first day on what I thought was a real paying job, and I wanted to make a good impression. Being naïve, I took the request seriously. I didn't have a pail, and I had no idea where I could find steam in the place. Being intelligent, naïve, and serious to not know a practical joke when it was played on me, I thought it might be possible to put the lid on the pail fast enough to keep the steam in the pail. However, the men did not give me a cover and didn't tell me where to go for steam. When I went looking for the steam and the cover in a most serious way, they all had one good laugh. I still think it is possible, but I was too naive then to understand that my leg was being pulled.

It was a good idea to be the brunt of a joke the first day on the job, for it established a good relationship with the rest of the staff. With all the men laughing at me, it was probably the best thing I could have done to get on with them. It didn't take long before they told me it was a joke, and I laughed at how stupid I was. After that, I was treated like a junior member of the company probably because they all had a good laugh on me on my first day on the job. Sometimes it pays to make a fool of yourself. Stupidity does have its benefits. I never had any trouble with the rest of the staff for the rest of the summer.

Once during the summer, I had an accident with the knife that I used to cut the twine, and I cut my left index finger. Then another time, I cut my right ring finger with the paper. In both cases, I had to go to a doctor close by since I was covered under workmen's compensation. I never paid for the doctor visits. These were bad cuts though the doctor decided that I didn't need stitches for either cut. I suspect that I could have used a stitch or two to minimize the scar.

If there were no packages to wrap, which could occur for several hours during the workday, I would sit down and read a book. No one seemed to care that I was reading, for as soon as there was something that I had to do, I would put the book down and get back to work.

Fake Fur No. 9 was a good job for me. It paid me real wages, and it was the first job I got entirely on my own. I learned a little about business, and I found that older men, men old enough to be my father, would accept me on the job. I learned that *if you do what the boss or supervisor expects, people will leave you alone to do your job.* There was an acceptance that I could read a book or just take it easy if there was no work to be done, but I had to be ready to jump back into work as soon as there was work.

When you're hired to do a job, do the job you are asked to do and do it well. In all my early jobs, I focused on doing them well. As a delivery boy, I made sure that the deliveries were made as promised. For my first real job, I showed up on time and worked hard all day. For my second job, I learned to make packages that did not come apart and got the work out as quickly as possible. As a junior person, I did not question what management wanted done, nor did I try to tell other people what to do or think about whether the process could be improved. I had a job as part of a system, and the only thing I was asked to do was to do my job. Until I knew more, and that was much later, I did what I was told. That is the best way to work when you are just starting out in business.

I have, for the longest time, believed that if I had to select one event that changed my life for the better, it would my special English class as a junior in high school. As a junior, the English department offered a special class on speech that was available to thirty-six students. I applied for it and was accepted. I think the selection process was based partly on grades because I quickly discovered that some of the best students at Erasmus Hall High School were in this class. The number one kid in the entire school was in the class, as were a dozen other kids with high academic grades. While I was in the top 20 percent of the class, I was nowhere near as bright, polished, or capable as the rest of the class, but *I was willing to risk the pain of failure for the chance of improving myself.*

The class was divided into six groups of six students each. Each group was to make four presentations throughout the semester as follows: the first presentation was an analysis of a TV show, the second and third presentations were on some other topics that the students had to select, and the final presentation was a debate by breaking the group of six into two teams of three, each side having two speakers supporting their position and the last speaker being the rebuttal speaker. Having been a quiet, reserved boy, almost unable to read his bar mitzvah speech a few years earlier, and never having given a formal presentation to anyone, the prospect of having to get up in front of the class four times during the semester was worse than a life-threatening disease. I was petrified at the thought of having to get up in front of the class and present. I knew I would be a failure; I couldn't sleep at night thinking about it. I had panic attacks that I would lose my train of thought, that whatever I said would not be good enough, that other students would run rings around me and make me look stupid, that I would not carry my fair share of the load with the other students in my group, and a thousand other negative thoughts. Every day I was in pain thinking about failing the class, thinking about being tongue-tied, thinking that I would have nothing to say or worse. I was convinced that I would open my mouth to speak, and the other students would laugh at me. These thoughts went on day after day, week after week. It is hard to convey the fear I felt about having to speak in front of an audience. The school year began in September and finished some time in January, so the sense of fear remained with me for nearly five months. I couldn't stop thinking about it. I dreaded it, I didn't know how to confront it, and I didn't think I was prepared to give a speech in front of anyone.

Finally, it was my turn to give my first presentation, and it went as badly as I thought. I was flustered. I was totally unsure of myself, but I got up in front of the class and did my presentation. The teacher sat in the back of the room, took good notes on each presentation, and went over the results with each of us individually. I was amazed that I didn't get a failing grade for the first presentation; I think it might have been given a very generous B-, but I thought that I was awful, and the teacher was merely being kind to me. This process continued this way for the entire semester. As my turn to speak approached, I panicked—I was going to fail. I would speak and make a stupid fool of myself. The other students were so much better than I was and on and on and on. But each time I got up in front of the class and gave it my best, recognizing that my best was not very good. Finally, it was time for the debate. I had two other students to argue our side of the debate, and the only thing I remember was going over to one of my teammates' home to prepare for the debate. She had a much nicer home than my apartment, and this too gave me a sense of inferiority. I was petrified to get up and debate; here was a situation where other students were encouraged to attack me, to make my arguments look stupid and make me look stupid. A debate was not something I had bargained for. I knew I was going to be outclassed by superior students, by superior poise, and by superior arguments. It was bad enough having to present my analysis of a situation on some topic, but a debate was the last straw. I was going to look stupid. Definitely.

I don't remember how well I did or even what we debated. What I remember is that getting up and making four presentations in front of my peers forced me to overcome my shyness. It forced me to deal with the fear of failure and do my best; it caused me to assess myself as not being as stupid as I thought I was. No one laughed at my presentations even though I knew those presentations were not as good as the best students in the class. I had a long way to go to improve myself, but I knew I was capable of improving. I was not as polished, as poised, as intelligent, or as mature as the best students in my high school, but I was determined to stay up with them. That class changed my life in many ways. It forced me to confront myself, to assess my desire to lead, to build confidence in me, to argue rationally, to defend myself intellectually, to speak before a group, to think on my feet, and to be more confident about my own verbal ability. Nothing changed me so quickly—so painfully—as that one class did. I think I would not be the kind of person I am today without the benefit of that one class. I owe a great deal to the teacher who led it, and I don't even remember his name.

I knew I was shy, and I knew that I wanted to get over it. I had no idea that a speech class in high school would be tremendously helpful in getting me over being so shy. The months and months of agony day after day worrying about having to speak before my classmates helped me come to grips with my shyness. I didn't realize it then, for I was suffering. It was only after the course was over that I realized that I had changed. I had created myself by facing a flaw in my personality. I wanted to change myself, and the class forced me to change. It wasn't a case of wanting to succeed, but a case of not wanting to fail. I did not want to fail the class, and I did not want to remain a recluse, unwilling to start a conversation and unable to give a speech. My shyness defined me, and I didn't want to be defined that way. *The bigger the flaw, the more it defines you as a person.* My high school speech class convinced me that I could change who I was. It was the first step in making that change.

At Erasmus, there was something called Senior Day near the end of my senior year. Many of my friends talked about it, but most of them seemed too afraid to really take it seriously. On Senior Day, seniors were to come to school in some crazy outfit, dressed like a cowboy, an Indian, a convict, or some other outlandish costume. The administration of the school did not support Senior Day, and seniors could expect to be thrown out of school or get suspended for wearing such outfits. None of us seniors knew the ramifications. As the day approached, a few of us swore to come in costume, but I wasn't sure whether anyone else would have the guts to do it. Finally, I decided that I would dress in costume to look like a pirate. I took one of my sister's gold shirts, too short and too small for me but just right to tie the bottom of the shirt into a knot near my stomach. I took a pair of black pants, cut them off about ten inches at the bottom, and ripped the pants to above the knee about ten times so they would give the shredded look of a pirate. I found some sort of scarf that I could wear on my head and tied it tight, so it too gave me the pirate look I had seen in the movies. I even found a hunting knife that I fit into some scabbard that attached to my pants. My mother took a picture of me the night before in this getup with the knife in my mouth. I thought this was healthy fun, and perhaps I could get through most of the day without getting caught because the school was so big.

That morning, I got on the BMT train at Newkirk Avenue for the one stop to Church Street to go to school. The train was crowded, and naturally, everyone took a look at me in my pirate outfit. I told myself, "You have the courage to get on the train and let everyone look at you, so you must have the courage to go to school in that outfit." When I walked into Erasmus, many of my friends wished me well, for they did not have a costume on, and they admired my guts for doing it. I lasted about half an hour in school; I don't think I made it to my first class before the assistant principal, a big burly man who could handle anyone physically and was tough as nails on anyone having a discipline problem, caught me in the hall and hauled me into the administration area. He told me that what I was wearing was unacceptable and sent me home to change. Stupidly, I had not brought any change of clothes with me, thinking I could get away with this pirate getup all day. I thought the administration would look the other way. I had no backup. I took the train home, changed clothes, and returned to school.

One of my friends wore a cowboy outfit, and he suffered the same consequences that I did. The price for taking a risk in this situation was small. We knew that in previous years other seniors had done this. It taught me to break the rules when it didn't hurt anyone. Even today, the memory of taking that small risk to have fun lingers on.

Facing the fear I had about speaking in front of my English class as a junior gave me the courage to be a pirate for a day as a senior. Without that speech class, I would never have had the courage to dress up as a pirate. The pirate outfit was my way of saying that I wasn't completely shy anymore, and it was worth it to be able to tell myself that I had the courage to stand out from the crowd. It took several more years in college to make the transition permanent.

After graduating from high school, my uncle Philip Lipis and my aunt Shoshanah were kind enough to ask me to spend the summer in Chicago in their home. My uncle was the rabbi of Beth El Synagogue in Highland Park, one of the rich suburbs of Chicago. He raised the money to build that synagogue, and it became a dynamic Jewish enterprise. My uncle was also a member of a golf club nearby, and he got me a job as a caddy for the club along with dozens of other boys my age. There wasn't a salary associated with being a caddy, so it didn't take much convincing at the club.

In the morning, my aunt would drive me over to the club with a book in my arm. I would put my caddy number in a hat with all the other caddies, and the caddy manager would draw out the numbers at random to see the order in which the caddies would work that day. Since there were many kids interested in being caddies and the club was only busy on the weekends, there was the possibility that I would not get to be a caddy for the entire day if my number was drawn near the bottom. If my number was drawn among the first few numbers, then I might be able to carry for two rounds of golf—one in the morning and one in the afternoon.

There were only a few members that would carry their own clubs, and there were no golf carts used on the course, so the caddies would carry the clubs for two members in a foursome, one set of clubs on each shoulder. With no salary, a caddy depended entirely on tips. The standard tip was four dollars per person, so I could make eight dollars a day, and if I was lucky enough to have my caddy number drawn early and the course was busy that day, then I could made two trips to earn the huge sum of sixteen dollars that day, but this was a rare event.

I was not making much money, but I enjoyed sitting under a tree outside the first hole reading a book for several hours every day. I read a dozen books or more that summer. And I learned to play golf, as I had never been on a golf course before. Once in a while when the course was empty, I would borrow a club and hit a few golf balls. Gradually, I understood how to hit the ball with accuracy though I was totally untrained and never did learn to play golf properly . . . and didn't much care.

One time I got into an argument with another caddy about whose number was drawn first. I thought my number was ahead of his, and he thought his was drawn ahead of mine. I was sure I was right, and the caddy manager would not decide the matter. I thought he favored the other caddy because he knew him, and I was just there for the summer. In any event, the other caddy got so mad that he punched me right in the mouth and split my lip inside my mouth. That started a fight because I wasn't going to stand there to take it, but the people close by broke it up quickly. I don't remember who won the fight or who went out to caddy first; I was bleeding from the punch. When my aunt picked me up, she was astonished to find that I had had a fight with another boy, and that I was bleeding though not badly. She insisted that I see a doctor, and he put a couple of stitches in my mouth. Eventually, my mouth healed fine, and I had no lasting effects physically, but it would be the last time that I would fight physically over some stupid issue, such as who was first as a caddy. Thereafter, I had no trouble with the caddy manager or any other caddy, for they knew I would be willing to stand up for my rights. Because I was unwilling to be a patsy, I had no trouble after that getting the proper rotation as a caddy. In some small way, I think I won.

The first time I fought was over some ballgame I was playing with another boy my age, and we stood toe to toe arguing about who was right. The other boy got mad enough that he took a punch at my face and hit me on the jaw. I then jumped on him, and we wrestled for a bit before we stopped with neither of us getting the better of the other. The second time, I was pushed to fight over a brief scuttle in the hallway. He then challenged me to a wrestling match in our gym class to settle the score, which I wisely refused.

What I learned for the third time as a golf caddy was that standing up for my rights against another boy my age over some small issue usually leads to getting hurt, and fighting never proves anything. The only thing it leads to is getting hurt. *In a typical fight, there are no winners, only losers.* I was confident that I wouldn't have a physical fight again, and I never did.

My aunt tried hard to hook me up with other boys my age, but there were only a few occasions when I spent time with them. After all, I was just there for the summer, and there was no real opportunity to make long-lasting friendships. However, one incident did teach me about underage drinking. One night, two boys my age picked me up for an evening out. I had no idea where we were going but was happy to be with them. We had little in common, for they were relatively wealthy, owned their own cars, and lived in a fancy neighborhood in Chicago. I was from a very modest apartment in Brooklyn.

The three of us drove out to some deserted area with me in the backseat. They parked the car and turned off the lights, and then the boys took out some wine they had either taken from their home or bought and started drinking from the bottle. For them, this was forbidden territory. They were not permitted to drink alcohol at home, so they were drinking this forbidden fruit against their parents' wishes. I had a sip or two and thought how different their family was from mine. I grew up drinking wine all the time at our Friday night dinner to usher in the Sabbath and on Jewish holidays like Passover, where one was obligated to drink four cups of wine, and on other occasions. Drinking wine was no big deal for me. It was a normal activity in my life. I was drinking wine on religious occasions for perhaps a decade or more. It seemed odd to me to have to steal away to some secret location to drink wine against the wishes of your parents when I drank wine in front of my parents on a regular basis.

Drinking wine did not offer me some special satisfaction or a way to feel high or even a way to disobey my parents' wishes, but for my friends it was exciting. I naturally kept my mouth shut about it to the other boys, had a couple of sips, and enjoyed knowing that in this regard I was more mature than they were. It just pointed out to me how different I was from them and how thankful I was to have parents and family that thought that drinking wine was okay in moderation and certainly okay on religious occasions.

This incident taught me that allowing children to enjoy a small amount of wine or liquor on occasions when adults were drinking in moderation would teach a child how to handle their liquor when they grew up. As a result, I never had a drinking problem; I do drink wine and liquor on occasion but only moderately. This one incident helped to keep my alcoholic drinking in perspective. I never had to drink secretly or consider drinking to be a way to fight for my freedom of expression or a way to have fun. Drinking liquor was just a normal part of my life growing up.

When you are young, new experiences provide a golden opportunity to see entirely new perspectives on life. The summer in Chicago living with my aunt and uncle did that for me. I saw how wealthy people lived in fancy homes. I worked on a golf course and attended dinners at the country club. I attended a very upscale synagogue and met wealthy people. I had a chance to meet boys my age who drove cars, had lots of money in their pockets, and see that they led completely different lives than the one I was used to in an apartment in a low-income area in Brooklyn. It was an eye opener for me.

I certainly don't mean to suggest that my Chicago experience proved that I was living an inferior existence. I was quite comfortable with my life. I had many friends and relatives, my parents loved me, I had a good education, and I was going to college. What I did find, however, was a different world—a world I had never experienced before—and there were some experiences I did want to emulate, even if it was unconscious. Memories stay with you a long time, some for a lifetime. My summer in Chicago showed me that if other ordinary people could become rich, then I could too, that there was more than one brand of Judaism, and if my uncle could speak beautifully, then maybe I could too. Those were long-term goals, and it would be decades before I could believe they were possible to achieve. But those goals did not exist at all until the end of my summer in Chicago.

During that summer I went to the synagogue regularly with my uncle for a morning or an evening religious service. Although he was the conservative rabbi in a conservative synagogue, he was Orthodox in his training as was I, so the service was easy for me. I was comfortable at a synagogue, having gone to my grandfather's Orthodox synagogue on most of the major holidays. On each occasion, there was my uncle as the leader of the service. It was an example I could not hope to emulate at my age, but it was leadership by my family that I saw daily.

Since I lived in my uncle's home, I had the opportunity to become much more deeply involved in Jewish events that he participated in, as well as see the enormous Jewish library that he had in his study. By osmosis, I got back in touch with my own Judaism in a nonthreatening way without being pushed. Compared to the European-oriented Judaism of my Orthodox grandparents and the lack of synagogue participation that my own father had, that summer with my uncle rejuvenated my interest in becoming a more modern Jew, whatever that meant.

On several occasions, I had the wonderful opportunity to hear my uncle speak on a Jewish topic or two, as he was a wonderful speaker. He was one of the best storytellers I have ever met, and he could influence people to do what he wanted, though not necessarily what they wanted. He had a big, deep, sonorous voice and a huge command of English. He was always well prepared on whatever he spoke about, especially Jewish history. This was my chance to see and hear a first-class speaker up close and personal. It convinced me how important public speaking was. I was still a rather shy kid, so being able to speak like my uncle was not even a possibility then, but the memory of hearing those speeches provided an unconscious goal to become a public speaker later in my life.

In the fall of my senior year in high school, my uncle called to say that he was in New York for a few days staying with the Permuts. Mr. and Mrs. Permut lived on Long Island in a private home, and they were close friends of my uncle. Naturally, my father wanted to see his brother, so we drove out to see him.

During the evening, the conversation turned toward my future since I had to decide where I was going to go to college. Since I was set on becoming an accountant, the obvious conclusion was that I would go to the Baruch School of Business at the City College of New York (CCNY). It was the best business school in New York, and it was free for students that were accepted. At the time, CCNY provided free tuition for their students, a benefit that had been in place for decades to give New Yorkers the opportunity of a college degree. Acceptance was based on either having an 86 average or better in high school or by passing an entrance exam similar to the SAT today. I had an average better than 86, and I knew I would be accepted to Baruch although I did take the entrance exam anyway.

My uncle suggested that if became a certified public accountant (CPA), then the best combination was to also obtain a law degree. The combination would prove extremely valuable in business. I just listened. Mr. Permut then said that he was an alumnus of the Wharton School of Business at the University of Pennsylvania, and he thought the Wharton School would be the outstanding school for me to go to for accounting. We all knew that Wharton was a topflight business school, much more prestigious than Baruch, but going to an Ivy League school like Wharton seemed way out of reach. My uncle encouraged me to apply for admission to Wharton, and Mr. Permut announced that he was a major contributor to the school and would be a reference for me if I applied. My uncle was adamant that I apply to Wharton, and it was always difficult to go against my uncle who was a great salesman. Mr. Permut said that it might be possible that I could get a scholarship of some kind. It was difficult for my parents to say no even though they had no idea how they would pay for me to go to Wharton if I got in. Nevertheless, I did apply to Wharton, and with my decent grades and the reference from Mr. Permut, I was accepted to the Wharton School. The annual tuition was about two thousand dollars.

At Baruch, the tuition was ten dollars per semester. The comparison between one of the most expensive Ivy League schools and free tuition at CCNY made the decision easy. I was going to Baruch; my parents never thought about taking out a student loan. For them, Baruch was a more than an acceptable school, and going into debt didn't make sense.

In all the years of growing up, it was the only time that the lack of money ever mattered to me. I wanted to go to Wharton because it was an Ivy League school and had a great reputation, but I knew my family's finances, and I knew that Wharton was a reach way beyond what they could afford. I didn't dwell on the loss. That's the way life is; you take what life throws at you, and you do the best you can do with what is available. Once I entered Baruch, I forgot completely about Wharton. It was another road not taken, and there was no way to know how it would have turned out.

To sum up my early years in terms of who I was and how I changed, I had wonderful parents who always supported me and worked hard to give me confidence in myself. They had limited experience intellectually, and they were not used to dealing with lots of money or complicated business issues. Neither of my parents was confident in dealing with strong-willed people or institutions. They gave me confidence in myself, but I had to deal with the outside world.

At Chaim Berlin, I felt inferior because I didn't speak Yiddish. Getting bruised intellectually for several years in my early school years contributed to my shyness and lack of confidence. That one negative experience overwhelmed all the positive experiences I had with friends and family. I did not feel positive about myself until my junior year in high school. Then one English speech class required me to speak in front of my classmates and forced me to confront my shyness and my lack of confidence. This began the process of change inside of me. One English class was not enough, but it forced me to confront the issue head on.

Chapter 4

My Family

In providing the lessons I learned to transform myself from an ordinary kid to an extraordinary entrepreneur, I would be remiss if I did not discuss the major impact that my parents had on me, as well as my extended family. There is, of course, much more that I could say about my family, but my focus here is on the lessons I was taught by osmosis that ultimately shaped my entrepreneurial culture. The best approach for me is to discuss my mother first, then her parents, my grandparents, and finally my father. Each had a significant impact on how I grew up.

My mother was Sophie Lipis. She was born in Szamos Ujvar (pronounced Shamashava), Hungary. She was the only daughter of Frieda and Jacob Klein. She was the only sister of seven brothers: Harry, Saul, Abe, Sammy, Maxey, Nathan, and Reuben. She married my father on December 7, 1935, and they stayed married for over thirty-two years until my father's death in 1968. She never married again. No one could replace my father, and my mother was a strong and independent woman quite capable of taking care of herself.

My mother made you feel important when you talked with her. She listened to you, really listened, and you always felt she understood. And she always made light of your problems. "Don't worry," she would say, "it's okay. It will be all right."

My mother was way ahead of this country in not seeing why she should hate anyone. Hatred was not in her vocabulary. She was too busy loving, too busy caring, too busy helping to hate. She had love in her heart for everyone that she met even though she could point out how they could improve. When I came to live in Atlanta, the motto was that the city was too busy to hate; there was a desire to move beyond discrimination. My mother passed that on to me: *be too busy to hate.*

My mother was the bedrock of optimism. No matter what the problem, she was in your corner supporting you, giving you comforting advice, making you feel just a little bit better. You always knew where to turn when you needed a friendly ear. And you were never disappointed. When I got in small trouble at school, she would come to the principal's office with me, listen attentively to the principal's complaint, nod quietly, and never argue with authority. Once the lecture was over, she would return to loving me again as though nothing at all happened. She was always in my corner.

Everyone in the family loved my mother, and she loved them in return. But mostly because she cared so much about her family, she stayed in touch with all of them mainly by phone and often by insisting that we visit with them in their homes. As a result, I found myself at the home of my grandparents, my aunts and uncles, my cousins, my great-aunt, and friends of the family. My mother always had a kind word for each of them although her sharp eye could be critical in a nice way as well.

On the occasion of her seventy-fifth birthday, I told her that I loved her dearly. I said, "You have been an inspiration to me all my life, believing in me, supporting me, nurturing me, and making me see the goodness in life. You have always been ready with a helping hand, a kind word, a sweet hug, and a friendly smile. It is a comfort for me to have you in my corner, always and without doubt. You have a basic faith in the goodness of people; you have an optimistic spirit that the world is meant for good, that everything is for the best. You live a highly ethical life; you're not interested in cheating others, and you're always committed to doing what is right; you are at peace with yourself because you always do your very best, not just for yourself, but also for others."

My mother did not see gray. She did not even see black or white. She only saw right; it was the right thing to do. Period—end of discussion. And she told you. She took a position, and it was always the high ground. It was always the proper thing to do.

You did not say no to Sophie because she never said no to you. My mother never demanded, she never insisted, she never requested. She told you what needed to be done when it needed to be done, made you feel that you would be doing a mitzvah, a good deed, and you ended up doing it and liking it.

When all that I heard from my mother was the right thing to do, it taught me ethics when I did not know what ethics meant. I heard over and over again that this was the proper thing to do and I had to do it. End of story! I had to write a thank-you note. I had to go to my grandparents' house because they wanted to see me. I had to put on a suit and tie and look nice. I had to visit so and so. I had to call this one and say this to them, and many, many more. My mother knew what had to be done and told me what I needed to do on many different occasions, even after I was married. She would take me aside and tell me the right thing to do.

When you have had that kind of training, the first thought is, "What would my mother do?" The more times you ask that question, the easier it is to do the right thing simply because it shows up in your head automatically. So when it came time for me to run my own business, I often said to myself, *"Do not see black or white or even gray. See right."*

My mother loved to laugh. Her laugh was infectious. When she laughed, you laughed. She loved to dance. At every wedding, at every celebration, there she was up there in the thick of it dancing and enjoying herself. She went to her last celebration because she insisted on attending all celebrations. "Who knows," she said, "how many more I will be able to attend?" Little did we know!

Henry James once said that there are three most important qualities of a person: "The first is to be kind; the second is to be kind; the third is to be kind." My mother stood for much of what is good with humanity: for responsibility, for kindness, for honesty, for modesty, for helping others. She sunk her roots deep, and when I think of her, I hear her echo: family, kindness, tradition.

When I don't want to do something I must do, my mother guides me. When I am scared, her memory inspires me. When I am worried, her smile and the twinkle in her eye are a comfort to me. Her sense of doing right is my conscience.

The story of Sophie Lipis is more than anything else the story of my remarkable Klein family. When I was growing up, I thought our family was normal. I thought all families got together often, called each other daily, celebrated together on holidays and on joyous occasions, and pulled together in times of trouble. I did not know about broken homes, divorce, or family fights that never ended. In our Klein family, we follow the slogan of the Three Musketeers, "All for one, and one for all." We still do. My mother was always out there leading the way.

That culture has stayed with me in life and in business. I see people with rose-colored glasses. I got that from my parents. While that can be hurtful in seeing only the positive side of people, it turned out to be positive even though my staff or my family had a different perspective. Eventually, I listened to them, but my optimistic attitude did cause conflict. For a small company, it was especially important to be optimistic, but this applies to every company. The bigger the company, the more internal strife there seems to be, and it is partly why small companies that work as a team can be more efficient and provide better service than their much bigger competitors.

Having spoken about the values I got from my mother, I now turn to her family, the Klein family, especially her father and her brothers, my uncles. I spent my childhood at my grandparent's house on Passover and on many other occasions in Brooklyn, New York. They had a subconscious impact on my values because I grew up surrounded by my mother's family.

As a young man, my grandfather, my Zeyda, came to live in the Hungarian territory though he was from Romania. When he married my grandmother, my Bubbe, they moved into a very big farmhouse with barns and stables in the back and a big backyard. The house had a kitchen, dining room, and three or four bedrooms. There were cows and horses and sheep and geese and chickens running around in the back.

Before World War I, Zeyda worked for the government, and gradually the government was putting in cobblestone streets. He would take a team of men and horses to lakes four to five miles away, pick up cobblestones and gravel from the side of the lake, and deliver them to other teams that were paving roads being built by the government.

In 1914, World War I broke out, and Hungary sided with Germany. As the war progressed, Hungary started drafting soldiers for its army. Zeyda didn't want to fight in the Hungarian army. He had four children, and in 1916 when he thought he might be drafted, he was twenty-seven years old and physically fit. He had no political views about the war; he just wanted to avoid military service and risk the possibility of being killed. Had he stayed in his hamlet, he would have been drafted. Because the United States was not in the war at that time, he learned that Hungary still permitted him to leave the country to go to the United States. Other men were migrating to the United States to avoid the draft too. He filled out the required application for the United States just before the Hungarian government closed the borders on emigration because there were just too many people migrating out of the country. Within twenty-four hours of being approved, he packed up his belongings, said good-bye to his wife and four children, and left for the United States.

Zeyda was the first of my family to come to America, so there was no special attraction to stay in New York City or anywhere else. He knew a few people in Youngstown, Ohio, a few Romanian people from Europe that had gone there. The company in town was looking for people to work in the steel mill. As soon as he heard about the company, he went to Youngstown and got a job at Youngstown Sheet & Tubing and started to earn good money. He started at the company as a laborer, learned quickly, and was promoted to foreman. He was strong, reliable, and capable of managing people from his work in Europe. By working overtime with foreman wages, he accumulated a good deal of money.

I am amazed at how much money he saved in the few years he first stayed in America. He had few expenses and worked all the time, so when he returned to Europe after the War, he had twelve thousand dollars. That was a huge amount of money. Keep in mind that there was very low income tax at that time. The income tax was established in 1913 with the Sixteenth Amendment to the Constitution. While it made the income tax a permanent fixture in the US tax system, the tax was initially quite small, especially for the salary Zeyda was making. Virtually all the money he made could be saved, except for a small amount of living expenses. In 1916, the first three thousand dollars was exempt from taxes, and there was a 2 percent tax after that up to twenty thousand dollars, so Zeyda's tax at four thousand dollars per year, his approximate salary, would have been twenty dollars. In 1917, his tax would have been about sixty dollars.

In 1919, he decided that it was safe to return to Hungary. He hadn't seen his family for three years. He was certain that he was leaving the United States to go back to Hungary. He took his money with him because he was going to live in Europe. Coming back to his home with twelve thousand dollars in cash was a small fortune.

As a safety measure before he returned to Europe, Zeyda went to a shoemaker in the United States, had the shoemaker open up the bottom of the shoe, and put two thousand dollars there in case, he said, "if anything ever happens, I am coming back to the United States." He wore those shoes all the time.

With his accumulated money, his relatives wanted him to go into business. He was not a great businessman, and his relatives were only students. They were students who stayed home studying, hoping business would come to them. They first opened a soap factory. The soap business didn't do well, and it eventually closed down. The second business was a piece goods factory, and there was a third business, a factory. All these businesses failed because there was a major depression in Hungary after losing World War I, and Zeyda's relatives were not good businessmen. In two years, these business losses ate up ten thousand dollars. When business continued to be very bad, he naturally thought about coming back to America. Still, Bubbe did not want to go; she didn't want to leave her family. With only two thousand dollars left, Zeyda was scared that he would run out of money. To be sure about returning to America, he got passports for all of the family and stayed in touch with the US consulate in Hungary.

In 1921, the United States was about to cut the quota of Hungarians allowed into America. A few weeks before immigration to America was stopped, the consulate got in touch with Zeyda and told him, "You've got to make up your mind—you either have to go to America now, or you will have to stay in Hungary because the United States is cutting the quota." Once they cut the quota, Zeyda knew that he wouldn't be able to bring his family to America, or that it would be much more difficult.

After two years of business failures in Europe, losing most of his money, Zeyda decided to return to the United States with his family. The reasons were obvious: he lost most of his money, and he knew there was opportunity in the United States. He could get a job back in Youngstown. Bubbe didn't want to leave her home because she didn't want to leave her mother and the rest of the family. It was not easy for her. She would be leaving all her relatives back in Hungary. She thought she might never see them again, and she was right. She knew her husband had tried to earn a living in now Romania (their area in Hungary was given to Romania after the war), and it wasn't working.

Finally, she agreed that they had to come to America. There was no big fight over it. She said to her husband, "All right, we'll go. If you want to go, we'll go." My family came to America in 1921, when my mother was nine years old.

And that is why I can say that the odds favored that I should not have been born. My Zeyda did not want to fight in World War I and was smart enough to come to America on his own to avoid going into the Hungarian army. If he had joined the army, he might have been killed, and Bubbe would not have come to America with four small children. Even if Zeyda survived the war, he would not have known about America and might have stayed in Romania only to die in the Holocaust twenty years later. It was World War I that brought him to America, and so my sister and I and the rest of my cousins must be thankful for my Zeyda's persistence and vision.

This was just one of the probabilities against my being born. The other one was that Zeyda was a poor businessman, and several businesses that he started failed. Had these businesses succeeded, he almost certainly would have remained in Europe, and he, my mother, and the rest of the family would have died in the Holocaust. While I wish my Bubbe and Zeyda had a less difficult time financially throughout their lives, I am thankful that the result of business failures in Europe created the opportunity for me to be born. A world war affecting millions of people in Europe, business failures by my relatives after the war, and the knowledge my Zeyda gained firsthand that real opportunities existed in the United States all came together to make it possible for me to exist.

In 1921, Hungary wouldn't let emigrants take money out of the country when they left. With the two thousand dollars in the sole of his shoe, whenever he needed more pocket money, Zeyda would go to a shoemaker to take out some money. One time he found that the outside of the shoe was wet from perspiration or water, and the water had eaten away part of the money. When he went to the bank to change the money, the bank wouldn't give him the full value of the money because they said part of the US currency was eaten away. That was a ridiculous statement, but he couldn't argue with the bank.

Because Zeyda kept enough money to get back to the United States with his family, he had a safety net. It was a story worth remembering and trying to emulate. It isn't easy to create a safety net, and while I wanted to do it and knew I needed to do it, I never did it. For many years, my wife would ask me whether we had enough money to buy a house. Then later, we didn't have money to pay for the education of our children. And still much later, we didn't know where the money would come from when we retired. I never had a serious plan for each of these situations. The answer is that I bet on myself. I put all my effort into becoming successful financially, and it worked out. That's the only answer: *if you want a safety net, bet on yourself.*

When my family left their home, they walked away and left everything they couldn't carry. The family gave away their furniture and their clothing. They only took what they could carry. No one bought their house; they just abandoned it. The family was moving to a new country that spoke a new language without knowing anyone. They walked away from the world they knew and the relatives that were part of their life to a new world that they didn't know and didn't understand. That was the decision my Bubbe had to make, and she had to trust her husband's judgment. It wasn't easy for either of them, but they did it.

All four children carried knapsacks. Abe, then five years old and the youngest, had a little knapsack. As they were traveling from one destination to another, moving from one train to go to another, someone asked Abe, "Abe, is the knapsack heavy?" Abe said, "It isn't heavy, but I can't carry it!" They all laughed and repeated that for many, many years. Someone would say, "No, no, it isn't heavy, but I can't carry it!"

At every border, Zeyda bought off the guards by giving them a few American dollars. When they got to the boat, Zeyda paid off some more people to get tickets for the boat they were booked on. They missed the first boat because they weren't insect clean. One of them had lice.

On the second boat, someone fainted. Evidently they didn't feel good, so someone called out, "Water, water, get some water! Someone fainted!" Everyone thought the boat was sinking, that water was coming into the boat. The passengers were not familiar with being on the high seas and were obviously scared about being on the boat.

There were about four hundred passengers on the boat: first class, second class, and steering. The passengers were offered awful food, but my family was prepared with lots of nuts. With the bread they took, they would spread a handful of nuts on a slice of bread for a peanut sandwich and finish the snack with a lot of fruit. They also took salami with them to eat kosher even on the boat. They were traveling in March, in wintertime, and the boat was cold. The trip took ten days, and everyone was seasick for days except little Abe. When they saw land, Abe came down running, "We're there! We're there!" He was elated. My family came to America on March 21, 1921, landing on Ellis Island in New York City.

When later in my life I thought of the risks of becoming an entrepreneur and the possibility that I might fail, I have often thought about the much greater risks that my Zeyda took. He left home to escape from being drafted into the Hungarian army. He didn't see his family for three years. He came to a country he did not know and had to learn a new language on his own. And then he moved his entire family to America not knowing whether they would be happy. I never had to take risks that great. I have the luxury of living in America, safe and secure. I have kept that in my mind often, and even though I was scared to do some of the things I did, I moved forward with the recognition that my risks were small compared to my Zeyda. It made risk taking much easier.

Life is risk. You may worry—move forward anyway. You may be told no—keep asking. You may fail—try anyway. Be bold, take chances, be courageous, and think about the rewards as well as the risks. People like my grandfather took much greater risks than you will take, so march on and make your life exciting. *Compare your risk to others you know or read about, and you will find risk taking much easier.* It is better to have risked and lost than never to have risked at all. Make your life an adventure.

When my family arrived in New York, an uncle came to greet them with a food basket and a big bunch of bananas for the kids. They gave Harry, my mother's oldest brother, a banana, and he didn't know enough to peel it. He had never seen a banana before, so he ate the banana with the peel, and his mouth puckered out. Who knew from bananas?

At Ellis Island, the family had to indicate a destination. The only reasonable destination was Youngstown. From New York, they took a train to Youngstown, a twelve-hour trip. On the way, the bedspreads Bubbe brought from Europe were stolen from her luggage. She had put so much effort into taking them and then lost them just before her journey ended.

In Youngstown, Zeyda thought he would return to work at Youngstown Sheet & Tubing, but Bubbe had a problem with that. During the war, he worked on Saturday because he needed the money, and the company insisted that it was part of their workweek. The company wanted to hire him, but he had to work on Saturday as he did before. However, Bubbe was an observant Jew and didn't want him to work on their Sabbath. Zeyda conceded to his wife's wishes and decided to find other work.

Religious people pay a price for their commitment to their religion. People used to relocate to a new city when their company demanded the change. Today, many people pick the place they want to live and then find a job in that location. People will accept less pay for less traveling. It all depends on your values. Once you decide on your values, the decision will make itself clear. For many people, *there are more important things than a higher-paying job.*

Zeyda bought a horse and wagon and started peddling fruits and vegetables. He bought his fruits and vegetables at the wholesale market and went out during the week selling from his wagon. As a fruit peddler, he could live anywhere and continue that business. At the same time, he was now an American citizen, so he could sponsor relatives from Europe to move to the United States, and he did. By the mid-1920s, Bubbe's immediate family, her two sisters, her brother and their spouses, along with a couple of cousins were living in New York, so the family decided to move to New York City. All the other relatives that stayed in Europe were killed in the Holocaust.

In New York, Zeyda tried to become a kosher butcher. He worked for a butcher for a short while, but since he was learning a new trade butchers wouldn't pay enough until he had experience. In the fruit business, he made at least fifty dollars per week, so he gave up the butcher business and went back to what he knew. There would always be plenty of potatoes, string beans, and vegetables in their house. He began with a horse and wagon as he did in Youngstown but soon rented a store with an apartment in the back. Between the fruit store in the front and peddling with a horse and wagon, the family managed. Eventually, the children convinced Zeyda to buy a truck.

All the children learned English in school, but they spoke Yiddish at home. The only time my grandparents spoke Romanian or Hungarian was when they didn't want the children to know what they were saying. The children spoke English to their mother because she wanted to learn English. She learned to speak English with her children as they went through the first and second grade. When the children did their homework, she did the same homework. After that, she learned how to read on her own and studied the questions in the booklet to become a citizen. When she went before the judge for her citizen papers, he was very surprised that she had learned to read and write without going to school. The judge said, "I must take my hat off to you." Both Bubbe and Zeyda never went to school to learn English. They learned it on their own, a remarkable accomplishment.

If you want to succeed in business, then you need to *learn the language in the business you are in.* You've got to know the territory. Just like speaking a foreign language, every business world has its own language and it can often be complex. The more you know about that language, the easier it will be to succeed. It will open up opportunities that otherwise would not be available for you.

Although Harry followed in his father's footsteps and worked in the fruit business most of his life, he never worked with his father because they never did enough business for the two of them to work together. He didn't finish high school because he, as the oldest, felt an obligation to go to work to help support the family. The pressure during the Depression was so bad that all of the children old enough to work went to work. He got his first job for twelve dollars a week working in a grocery store even though he was very good in printing. In school, he learned to set type and feed the printing machine. His printing teacher asked him why he quit school, and he said, "Everyone has a blue serge suit when they graduate and look what I came to graduate with—a pair of old pants and a torn shirt." He said, "My parents need money, and I am dedicated to my parents." The teacher said that he could get him a job in printing for eight dollars per week. Harry thought he might have to work on Saturdays to be in the printing business, and he didn't want to go against his parents who observed the Sabbath.

When Harry decided to work in a grocery store, he told his printing shop teacher, and the teacher said, "Harry, don't go into the grocery business. Go into the printing business. It will pay better dividends in the long run." Harry didn't even know what dividends meant, so he said, "I don't need eight dollars a week. I need twelve dollars per week. The grocery business pays four dollars per week more." But the teacher continued to say it would pay better dividends in the long run. Harry said, "No. I need twelve dollars."

He worked for the grocer for one year, and then the grocer gave Harry the key to the store and told him to open and close it. He then worked from six in the morning until nine at night and eventually worked himself up to twenty-five dollars a week, becoming a manager at the age of eighteen. Harry was still going to continuation school, so he went to his printing teacher and said, "You see, I'm making twenty-five dollars per week in one year's time." His teacher still said the printing business would pay better dividends in the long run. Harry told me, "About three to five years later to show you what a shmuck I was, I met a printer that was living next door to me. I was then making thirty-five to forty dollars per week. I asked him what he did for a living. Finally, I found out that he was a printer and that he was making $150 per week. I wasn't smart enough to throw away the fruit business and become an apprentice as a printer."

In the end, Harry couldn't succeed in his own business. He wound up working in Brooklyn for fruit men all his life. He tried to go into business a couple of times, but it was the Depression years and nothing worked. He tried three businesses on his own, but he was never successful. He could make other people's businesses successful, but not for himself.

Finally, Zeyda opened a store with his son Saul on Pitkin Avenue and Autumn Street, a major shopping street where Brooklyn meets Queens. It was an Italian and German neighborhood, so they figured that they would do pretty well. They called the store Saul's Fruit Market. Saul worked for his father for a while, and after he married, he left the fruit business and tried to start his own business. But it was Depression years, and he had no luck.

My mother and my father started seeing each other in 1931, and it continued for about four years. During that time, he worked for a bank that went bankrupt, and he was out of a job. Finally, they decided to get married as long as he was working. For a while, he wasn't working, so they waited. Finally, my father found a job with the US Bronze Sign Company. Even then, he was afraid to get married because he was only making twenty-five dollars per week. My mother told him, "Let's try being married and see what happens." There was no such thing as an engagement. There was just a verbal agreement between them. That was the engagement. Unfortunately, my father's mother, Leah, died soon after my parents became engaged, so they delayed their wedding for ten months. They married on December 7, 1935.

They didn't go on a honeymoon because they couldn't afford it. They rented a room and a half apartment in Brooklyn, and my mother went looking for a permanent job. My father's sister was working for a publishing company, and she was instrumental in finding a job for my mother at one of the magazines owned by the company. She worked in the mailroom for sixteen dollars a week. When my sister and I were small, my mother wanted to be home for us, so she stopped working. She returned to work part-time to support our family only after we were older and in high school.

My parents and the rest of my extended family all lived in a low middle-income environment. My grandparents never had their own home; they lived in a small two-bedroom apartment with one bathroom. None of my family had much money, and vacations were rare. Yet through it all, they lived within their means. No one had serious debt; no one got in serious financial trouble. There was little money for luxuries.

Living within your means was a lesson I learned by osmosis. I lived it, and it taught me that I could do the same thing for my family and later for my business. *You must live within your means, especially in business.* I avoided borrowing money. I hired staff only when I knew I had the revenue to support them, and when I didn't follow that rule, I ran into trouble. If you live within your means in your personal life and in business, your worries over finances will be much easier.

With America likely to be drawn into World War II and the draft in place, my father wanted to stay out of the military because he had two children. He knew that working in the defense industry would get him deferred. He tried to get into defense companies on Long Island, but he couldn't find a job. A friend of his got a job at the Fafner Ball Bearing Company in New Britain, Connecticut; they were doing work for the defense industry. When my father found that they were hiring, he went there and got a job. For the next four to five months, he came home to Brooklyn on weekends. He took the train home on Friday night and went back to New Britain on Sunday night. This lasted until he was selected to move into a prefabricated government apartment built for defense workers.

My Zeyda turned to the people he knew to live and find work. My father had a friend that told him about a company that was hiring, and that got him a job. The same was true for my mother and my uncles. Friends will get you leads for a job.

However skilled or experienced you are, introductions are a critical element in finding a job. People do business with the people they know and trust. Friends can vouch for your capability more than you can and can introduce you to more people than you know. *The best that can be said about you is what others say about you.* Count on them as your first source to find a job. In the end, of course, you have to sell yourself.

In Connecticut, my parents stayed in touch with the rest of the family, but they didn't have a phone because they couldn't afford one. My mother asked her neighbor, "Is it all right if my mother calls me or if my brother calls me?" The neighbors were nice about it and had no problem having my mother come into their apartment for a phone call.

Zeyda had the ability to pick up languages on his own. He eventually spoke six languages: Yiddish, English, Romanian, Hungarian, Italian, and German. When he had his fruit store, he used to talk to customers in their own language—how much this weighed, how much that weighed, all in Italian or in German.

Nadie, my mother's second youngest brother, was retarded. He was born normally, but infantile paralysis affected his brain and his walking, and the doctors didn't have the medicine they have today. Bubbe took him to all types of doctors, and the only thing they wanted to do was operate on his brain. She didn't do it because it was potentially fatal. Until he was fourteen years old, Nadie lived at home. Finally, the family decided to put him in Letchworth Village, a place for retarded people run by the State of New York. He was there for over forty years. In spite of that, the family stayed committed to visiting him regularly throughout his life. Nadie spoke almost normally. My mother was always grateful to be able to see him and saw him regularly as did other members of the family.

The Kleins individually and separately made a living, but they never made serious money. There were hundreds of little stores like their fruit store, yet they managed to make a living for their families. Zeyda took two of his younger boys, Maxie and Sammy, into the business, and after Zeyda died, they ran it together. In time, they gave up the store. Maxie continued to remain in the fruit business working for a chain store while Sammy took jobs working for a friend or a relative.

The amazing part of the story is that Zeyda came to America to avoid fighting in a war, returned to Europe, and failed in business. Because he wasn't a good businessman, he saved his family and many of his relatives from the Holocaust. The family stayed together in the United States even after they married, and they organized a "Cousin's Club" so they could continue to meet and for their children to stay in touch with each other. Without a great deal of money, they all had solid marriages, raised great kids, and marveled at the education that their children and grandchildren mastered, many of them becoming professionals as doctors, lawyers, stock brokers, teachers, consultants, entrepreneurs, and businessmen. I am but one of those professionals.

I grew up where family was the center of my world. I was with loving parents, aunts and uncles, plenty of cousins, and two grandparents that served as role models for me. As I grew up, I heard the stories that began in Europe about how my Zeyda left home to protect himself and his family, sent home money regularly, and returned from America to be with them as soon as World War I was over. I heard the story that my grandparents moved back to New York so their immediate family and their extended family could be together again. I would visit my uncles and aunts regularly, and I often went to "Cousin's Club" meetings. I even attended weddings of my uncles and aunts when I was a small child, and I certainly attended other celebrations of the family when I was young and impressionable. All this had an impact on me. Family was not just important; it was the center of my life. As a result, *family became my paramount responsibility*.

When you grow up with family, it puts responsibility into your life. You will be a part of a community that worries about you, that helps you and that cares about you. Family will help you move away from being self-centered and focus your life on helping others. Family will give you a sense of stability, a world that you belong to, a group of people you can trust, and a feeling that others in your family will help you grow and succeed in whatever you do. Family will produce a responsibility to be a part of their lives and to help them in any way that you can. Done well, that responsibility to family will stay with you all of your life; you will pass it on to your children and grandchildren.

I took that family responsibility into my business world. As the owner of the business, I had a paternal responsibility. I had given jobs to people, and I felt a responsibility to not just make a profit but also to treat my employees well, to find work for them, and to have them share in the rewards of a company they had a significant role in making a success.

In addition to feeling responsible for others, I knew I had to be responsible for myself. While never expressed, I sensed that there was regret among my parents and my relatives that they did not get the education they wanted. They had to stop their education too early. The Depression forced them to go to work to support their families. They didn't have the time or money to continue their formal education.

Without a good education, the jobs available will be low-paying jobs. A strong formal education is the single most important strategy for the survival of the child. The education you receive will make all the difference in your life. You will conclude that you could not have accomplished what you did accomplish without it.

Although I discussed the major influence that my father, Leo Lipis, had on my upbringing, there are a few stories about my father's life that had an impact on me. My father was born in 1909 in Tiraspol, Russia, and came to America in 1913 when he was three years old. His personality later in life was a product of his childhood, and it prevented him from being the businessman he longed to be. His father constantly told him that he was a do-nothing kid. He was compared to his older brother who was a more disciplined student.

When it came time to go to college, my father didn't have his mother in sound health to support him, and his father was nowhere to be found. He convinced his uncle to support his first year of law school since back then, he could go to law school right out of high school. After his first year, his uncle didn't have the resources to support him any longer. It was 1929—the Depression stopped him from going on as it did for many others. He had to drop out of school.

My father once told me a remarkable story that convinced him that he was a lucky guy. He used to walk to Hebrew school on Sunday mornings. One Sunday, he found a dime in the street while walking to school, then the next week he found another dime in almost the exact same spot, and the next week, he again found a third dime in almost the same spot. He never forgot that he found three dimes three weeks in a row in nearly the same spot because the probabilities were so low. Sometimes, a small event like that can change your outlook on life. For my father, that story helped give him the optimistic attitude he always had about life. He always thought he was a lucky guy.

My father told me a story about a high school friend of his that never went to college but became a big success because of the way he dressed. His friend always wore a suit and put a fresh flower in his lapel every day. Eventually, this friend became head of the personnel department of his company because of his dress and style. My father was impressed with the fact that there were other ways to succeed besides pure intellect. His friend succeeded because his attire was impressive. That story impressed me because no one I knew in our family dressed stylishly. *Clothes make the man.*

My father was an avid reader. We couldn't afford to buy our own books, so he always took me to the public library where we both took out books. He liked to suggest books for my reading pleasure, books he enjoyed reading. At first, I took his advice and tried his suggestions, but gradually I found my own way and my own taste. Still, we went to the library often.

My father's nightstand was always full of books, and gradually, my mother had her nightstand full of books too. My father went to bed reading, and I thank him for instilling the joy of reading in me. Today, my nightstand is full of books, and it reminds me from where I got that habit. My mother always said, *"Read and you will never be lonely."* She's right.

In the late forties, my father took the one great entrepreneurial plunge of his life. He quit his job at US Bronze Sign Company and started his own sewing machine repair business with a lifelong friend, Sol Faberman. Sol was responsible for bringing in the business, and my father was responsible for repairing the sewing machines. It was a decent business because the war was over for several years, sewing machines were a big item, people were making their own clothes, and there were many clothing manufacturers in New York.

Unfortunately, my father had two major problems. First, his partner was not a strong salesman. He was not aggressive enough in finding new customers and not concerned about it. Second, my father did not have the confidence to withstand the pressure of not knowing next week's work and the possibility that he would not be able to take home enough money to feed his family. The business lasted one year.

My mother was very encouraging; she urged him to stick it out, to get rid of his partner, to let the business mature, but my father could not stand the uncertainty of the business. The business was making money, and it could have continued on, but my father was unable to stand the rigor of a mediocre partner and an uncertain future. *Being an entrepreneur requires confidence*, and my father didn't have it. He packed it in and went back to US Bronze Sign Company.

My Zeyda went into business for himself. My father tried his own business too, and so did my uncles. None of them were wildly successful. The point is that *people have a basic desire to own their own businesses*. Whether it is being fearful of religious intolerance, a desire to make a lot of money, or a need for control, most people think about starting their own business. That is why there are so many start-ups in this country and why the bulk of American businesses are small companies. The most important factor is not to focus on making a profit but on developing a good idea. If you think about what you know and can do well, you will find a good idea. Have the courage to find your own way. If you need encouragement, my story will help.

Failing in his own business hurt my father badly, both emotionally and professionally. He was still dealing with his childhood experiences of being criticized by his father and losing his mother at an early age. He lacked the confidence in business, the confidence to deal with uncertainty, and the willingness to be at risk. He did go for psychiatric help by meeting with Dr. Robbins, a cousin of his, but he never made great progress to try another business venture again. He had too much family responsibility and too little money to risk it. He stayed at US Bronze Sign in various capacities.

Of all the jobs my father had at US Bronze Sign Company, he loved being a sign hanger the most. When I was about ten to twelve years old, my father asked me to be his helper. We changed the name of the bank by putting up individual bronze letters above the entrance of the bank branch. My father's job was to climb up a ladder about ten to twenty feet high, remove the old letters, design the layout for the new letters, drill the holes in the brick facade of the building, and mount the letters one by one. It was a demanding job, requiring an ability to center the name, space the letters properly, keep each letter straight, drill the three to four holes for each letter, ensure they all fit just right on the building, and do all of that neatly without marring the rest of the building.

My father loved that job because he was his own boss, the quality of the work was entirely his own, he traveled all over New York City, he set his own hours, and few others did the job as well or as fast as he could do it. I loved to go with him on assignments even though I only went a handful of times. He told stories about lifting a 150-pound bronze sign in a synagogue with a couple of other people who worked there. He would lift the heavy sign and have it fit perfectly the first time. As we drove around New York, he would point out where he had put that plaque up or that sign or those letters. He loved being a sign hanger, and he taught me to *love the job you do*.

My father loved to say, "When I hang 'em, they don't come down." He had chisels, hand bits, electronic drills, and a tool chest full of pliers, screwdrivers, and bolts. He knew his sign hanging business, and I was impressed with his mechanical ability. He believed he was the expert in his work because he was. What he did, he did well, and he took great pride in his work.

My father's sign hanging career came to an abrupt end when he fell off a ladder in 1954, breaking his pelvis and shattering the bones in his left wrist. He was alone trying to hang a sign without a helper, and he overextended himself. He ended up in Meadowbrook Hospital on Long Island near where he fell.

In the hospital, it was the middle of the summer, and the temperature every day was in the '90s. My father was in a body cast from the middle of his chest down to just above his knees to let his pelvis heal properly. His left hand was in a cast. He was a mess in a bed in the middle of a ward with fifteen to twenty other beds. He had no privacy. My mother went to see him as often as possible, but she did not drive. We depended on my uncles to pick us up and take us to the hospital, and they were there whenever we needed them.

Within a week, my father's hand began to close. The fall had severed a nerve in his wrist, which prevented his fingers from working. My mother quickly got another medical opinion, and we hastily moved my father to Brooklyn to a doctor more experienced with this issue. That doctor operated on the wrist, attached the nerve back together, and saved my father's left hand from becoming a closed fist.

Through it all, my father never complained. He was a man about having made a mistake, and he accepted the consequences calmly without anger or shame. He screwed up, fell off the ladder, hurt himself, and he had to live with the result.

Eventually, the body cast was removed, and he gained strength back in his hand. Never once in all the years that followed his recovery did I ever hear him complain about that accident. More than anything, it taught me to *accept responsibility for your stupidity*. His pelvis recovered back to normal, and his left hand was nearly normal although he could not totally bend his hand back. He was proud of his recovery and the little disability resulting from such a nasty accident.

Like many Jews, he believed that some good comes from bad situations. That was the case here as my father received a monthly payment from Workman's Compensation for becoming partially disabled from his accident on the job. It wasn't much, about ten to twenty dollars per week to reflect the loss of salary from having to work at a desk job instead of being a sign hanger, which paid better. The monthly payment went on for several years until my father decided to accept a six thousand dollars lump sum payment in place of his monthly disability payments for life. The six thousand dollars was a significant windfall of money. It enabled my parents to put together the down payment to buy their first and only home.

Because my father worked for a company with a foundry that poured molten bronze into molds, he felt capable of doing smaller but similar things at home. One day we melted lead over a gas flame in the basement and poured the molten lead into fishing molds to make sinkers. He had all the right equipment: a long metal spoon, large amounts of lead, a metal mold to make sinkers of various sizes, and a burner that would melt the lead in the metal spoon. I was impressed to see him melt lead at a high temperature. Slowly, he poured it into the molds and let it cool. I was a teenager making my own sinkers: four, six, eight, and ten ounces. It was fun to do, and I was excited that we could do that on our own. It taught me that *know-how is a valuable skill to have*. We used those sinkers whenever we went fishing from Sheepshead Bay.

As I grew up, I obtained the know-how that I acquired through hard work and experience. I learned how to play all kinds of games, how to fish, how to collect stamps and coins, how to breed tropical fish, how to do well in school, how to ice skate, how to be a busboy, how to swim, and how to use tools. Later in my life, I learned how to speak, how to write, how to teach, how to make money, how to negotiate and how to invest, and much more. In each case, it took time, experience, and mistakes to figure out how to do many of these things well.

We should measure ourselves according to our know-how. Can you cook or live outdoors or fly a plane or fix a car or speak a language or make money in the stock market? The more know-how you have, the more capable you become in a variety of situations. In this world with so much variety and so many trades, it isn't possible to do it all, so you have to pick the areas in which you want to be an expert. I have always thought that having a large variety of skills gave me the flexibility to change my career and to be able to change my life. The earlier you acquire know-how, the more likely it is that your know-how will remain with you all your life. It will make you a much more interesting person.

My father was a very big smoker. He smoked from his teenage years and was a two-pack-a-day smoker for many years. He knew it was a disgusting habit, but he was addicted to it. When he broke his pelvis and was in great pain, he refused to take a shot of morphine or some other painkiller after the first few days because he did not want to become addicted to drugs. He knew what cigarettes had done to him.

Sometime in the late '50s, he stopped smoking cold turkey. He attributed it to his brother-in-law, Harry, who had stopped smoking. He didn't think Harry was any better than he was, and if Harry could stop smoking, so could he. He quit cold and stopped smoking for years. He never lost the taste for a good cigarette, however, and eventually returned to smoking, but at a much slower pace.

At the time he stopped smoking, it was not that fashionable to stop. The Surgeon General's report was not yet out that proved that smoking caused cancer. Smoking was a normal activity, and my father and my uncle were way ahead of their time. I admired my father for stopping cold turkey, for disciplining himself to live without cigarettes for years, even when he knew he missed it and enjoyed it. *When you have the discipline to give up something you like doing, like smoking, you know you have the discipline to accomplish other goals too.*

Inspiration can come from many sources. When you know you can do better, seek out someone to inspire you; it is likely that you will find that someone. My parents inspired me in many ways: how they acted toward each other, how they accepted their responsibilities, how they raised their children, how they dealt with lack of education, how they handled other people, and how they dealt with each other's differences regarding religion.

I was inspired by music, by winning in competition, by well-educated people, by some of my teachers, by a few of my relatives, by the jobs I had, by the bosses I had, by my wife, my children and my grandchildren. If you look for inspiration, you will find it. My father stopped smoking because a brother-in-law did it. I started running after I read a book called *Aerobics* by Ken Cooper. My uncle inspired me to start stamp collecting, and Tommy Dorsey inspired me to play the trombone. The world is full of people who can inspire you by how they live, how they train, what they accomplish, what they say and do. *There is nothing more exciting than a person who motivates you to be the best you can be.* If you look for them, you will find them—on TV, on the radio, in books, in the movies, in sports, in school, in churches and synagogues, in politics, and in your own family. Seek and you will find, and that inspiration will change your life. It changed mine.

I never had any heroes growing up except for my family members. My father was my hero because he could fix almost anything, he read avidly, and he was my mentor whenever I needed advice. My father was fond of saying, "This too will pass." He was optimistic about life, devoted to his wife and family, and never complained about what life tossed at him. I rarely saw him angry with people, only with himself. He was first, last, and always for his family, not just his immediate family but also the wider family we were intimately a part of for so many years. He was quick to drive to pick up and take family and friends somewhere. I rarely saw my parents argue; I think they were careful to keep their arguments for only when they were alone.

As an adult after leaving home to go to graduate school, I kissed my father on the lips when I returned home. It was our way of saying that we loved each other, that we were special for each other, and that we meant it. I kissed my mother's uncles on the lips too, and now I do the same with my son. It is a special feeling I reserve for the men I love dearly.

My father was only fifty-nine years old when he died. I missed him back then, and I miss him now, more than forty years later. In many ways, the distance in time seems like yesterday. I can recall the conversations we had, the places we went, and the personality that was his as though he had died only a few days ago. I shall always miss his smile, his advice, his guidance on living, and his commitment to the family. He was a role model I tried to emulate.

With both of my parents being optimistic people, with most of my relatives always talking about the future and telling stories of the past that had happy endings, it was easy for me to become an optimistic person. I had little to worry about as a child, and my failures were smoothed over by all of them. My father's expression, "This too will pass," was his clear indication that better times were ahead. I had a roof over my head, clothes to wear and food always on my table, no worries about my health or money, and I was living in the United States, not having to worry about war or chaos. With all of that, I had nothing serious to worry about, and optimism was a natural outcome for me as it should be for most children in America today. My family always saw the glass as being half full. It is a Jewish trait in spite of the many difficulties we have had in our history. We are an optimistic people; it is partly the result of our religion and partly the result of our outlook on life. *For business and for life, it is better to be optimistic than pessimistic.*

Chapter 5

College

What continued to contribute to my self-confidence's growth wasn't the classes I took or the professors; it was the extracurricular activities I took part in. Because Baruch College was a business school, many of the students went off to work in the afternoons; they were more interested in making money than becoming involved in student life. Since Baruch was a small school and few students were really active, it gave me many opportunities to grow as a leader, providing the self-confidence I so desperately wanted. I hadn't planned on becoming active in college, but it was what I needed. As it turned out, Baruch was the best thing that ever happened to me in all of my education. It made me grow in so many ways and changed me into a totally different person. It was just a lucky break that Baruch had so many opportunities for me to grow in the ways I needed to grow.

As I entered Baruch, I was convinced that I was not active enough in high school to get the most out my school. I was determined to become involved in college life, so I showed up at the college a week before school got underway to see what was going on and to try to find ways to become involved. What I found was the early planning for class registration that was then entirely manual. Professor Andrew Lavender was responsible for the entire process, and he was looking for students to help. I immediately offered my services and found myself being a runner from the registration process to the gym to let students know when a class was closed out and no longer available.

The process for registering for a class was simple in theory but complicated for students. All the classes for the entire school were listed on a huge wall in the gym, and each student would select the classes they wished to take on their registration card. Students registered by class, seniors first and freshmen last. Once you selected your classes in the gym, you took your card to the registration line where your class selections were read to Professor Lavender, who marked his master list to track the number of students in each class. He knew the maximum class size for every class, so when that number was reached, he would close the class. I would then go to the gym and indicate on the huge board that a class had closed out. At that point, anyone contemplating that class would have to revise their schedule.

Since I was working for the registration process, I knew exactly when the freshman class was allowed to register. As a result, I was among the very first freshman to register for my classes, and I never failed to get the classes I wanted. I did the registration process for the two semesters of my freshman year and then stopped because I became involved in other activities.

There were a few incidents at Baruch that have stayed with me most of my life. The first one occurred on the first day of school. Bernard Baruch was still alive in 1956, and he made an appearance in the auditorium where all the freshmen were sitting. He had a hearing aid on and spoke eloquently about City College, having graduated there himself. At the end of his talk, the dean got up and said that we should turn to our left and then to our right and introduce ourselves to the two people next to us. He then went on to say that one of the three of us would never graduate, for that was apparently the dropout rate. I was scared upon hearing that remark, for I thought that might mean me, and that remark stayed with me throughout the first semester. *Being scared guarantees that you will be motivated.*

When you start something new, it can be scary. That is often a good thing, especially if you want to do well. That's what I felt entering college. Being a little scared was good for me. It kept me focused on succeeding, and it was exciting because the future was unknown. When you are scared, there is a tendency to avoid jumping in because failure looks much more likely than success. Beginnings always look scarier than they are. That's because at first you know so little. Ask yourself one question: "Have many others have done this before?" If yes, then you know that others have succeeded. Once you know it is the right thing for you to do, then go for it. That's why I got involved in college life, and it changed me in the direction I wanted to go. I was scared at the beginning, and I used that fear to work hard at succeeding. Failure was not an option.

The greatest benefit about becoming involved in the registration process was that I met a lot of other people at Baruch early, and some of them were looking for freshmen to join their fraternity. Within a short period of time, I decided that I would pledge Alpha Phi Omega (APO), the service fraternity. It was the best decision in my college career for a variety of reasons. First, the fraternity was unlike any other fraternity on campus, driven to serve the school and not just a place for fun, sports, or other activities. APO was deeply involved in the school's activities and had a group of men devoted to helping the school raise money as well as serve the student body.

The best activity that APO ran was the used-book exchange. At the start of the semester, students had the ability to put their books up for sale at the used-book exchange. Each book was accepted on consignment and evaluated at a quarter, a half, or three-quarters of the list price of the book, depending on the book's condition. APO charged ten cents to the seller and ten cents to the buyer of the book. If the book did not sell, the seller would get the book back but would still pay the ten cents. Books were sold on a first-come, first-sold basis with buyers selecting what price they wanted to pay, a quarter, a half, or three-quarters. Books that were no longer required for a class were not accepted though most of the books were used for several years.

With over a thousand students taking four to six classes and many classes requiring more than one book for the class, the used-book exchange would handle five thousand books, and APO would clear a thousand dollars for their work. The used-book exchange took a tremendous amount of time, requiring a room to keep the books, accepting books on consignment, logging the student's name for that book, evaluating the book, putting the book on the shelves in its proper place, staying open most of the school day for students to buy their books, managing the money, paying the students whose books were sold, and returning the books to the students whose books did not sell. The used-book exchange required several fraternity brothers to organize the effort, put together a time schedule for most of the other fraternity brothers to staff the exchange, and deal with student issues as they arose, such as losing a book or taking a book in for sale that was not required for any class, etc. Only a fraternity dedicated to service could pull this effort off, and APO did a magnificent job through all the years that I attended the school.

Another service APO provided was a silk screening process for anyone that wanted an eight and a half by eleven inches poster in color. If an organization wanted to advertise a play, a dance, a movie, or lecture, they would come to APO with their design, select the colors they wanted, and we would silk screen the design, producing a single copy at a time. Usually, the organization wanted twenty-five to a hundred copies, and the charge was about a dollar per copy. APO also orchestrated the semi-annual blood drive for the school working with the Red Cross.

As a pledge, I had a pledge book that required me to get three signatures a week from every member of the fraternity. With the school in only one building on the corner of Twenty-Third Street and Lexington Avenue in Manhattan, and the campus on the ninth floor of the building, it wasn't difficult finding members of the fraternity—everyone was in the same building. I got signatures running up and down staircases or riding elevators between classes or during lunch and even at the fraternity house. The signatures were a great way for pledges to meet fraternity brothers and to feel a part of the fraternity quickly. It made me feel a part of the school and the fraternity almost immediately. It also gave me a sense of purpose, something I did not have in high school.

But most importantly, *if you want to get involved, then show up early and make your presence known.* I wanted to overcome my shyness, and I needed to reinforce my desire to be a leader. To grow as a person, I had to become involved in college, not just to get good grades, but also to change myself. I wanted to be a different person—a leader—full of passion and excitement. The only way to do this was to get involved at Baruch as much as possible. What I learned was that once you commit to becoming involved, the doors open wide and the opportunities show up. You may not know where the doors are when you begin, but they do show up.

APO had a sister organization named Boosters, which was composed of women who also had a commitment to give service for the school. As a result, Booster women were always visiting the APO fraternity house, which was located on the second floor of an apartment building a few blocks from the school. The fraternity house was a nice place to hang out, a place to discuss fraternity business, but there was no place to sleep. I lived at home and took the train home every night no matter how late fraternity business took.

Fraternity meetings were held at the fraternity house, and I was introduced to XXX-rated French films there, too. One of the brothers would bring in the movie, and we would set up the projector in the large room of the fraternity house that served as our meeting room—our all-around gathering place. The movies would usually be shown at night after school, and naturally, they were well attended. It was a real eye opener, for I was still a very naïve kid. These movies were pure sex, and it was the first time I saw explicit sexual activity. As the movie played out, the brothers would make funny comments about the lewd details going on in the movie, and that is how I got my first introduction to sex. They were fun to watch, especially with a fun group of guys my age.

An incident occurred when one of the fraternity brothers borrowed money from the fraternity checking account and was found out. There was a big discussion about whether to report him to the police or have him pay back the money. Our advisor, Professor Levy from the English department, whom all of us respected and admired, made an impassioned plea to let the brother pay back the money and let it be a lesson for him and for us. We followed his wishes. It taught me to *make amends as quickly as possible if you screw up, so the punishment is as small as possible*.

On another occasion, Professor Levy asked a select group of students to go with him to visit Eleanor Roosevelt at her home in Hyde Park, New York. I was one of the privileged to do so, and this was the first time that I was ever close to a world-class personality, especially a woman as admired as Mrs. Roosevelt. She had just returned from Russia and spoke in detail about her trip. The twenty students who went sat at her feet, taking in every word, thankful that we had a chance to meet such a well-known political personality.

On a third occasion, Professor Levy invited a small group of students to his home for an evening of discussion and dinner. After dinner, being the English professor that he was, he asked us all to read a play out loud. We were awful at it. We weren't used to reading out loud, let alone with passion, and it was enlightening to see how poorly college students were at reading material with emotion. We were not used to acting, and it showed how ill-prepared we all were to act outside of our own daily lives.

At the end of my sophomore year, I was deeply involved in changing my majors, in thinking about leaving Baruch to major in mathematics at the uptown CCNY campus and in finding other outlets beyond APO. APO had been my life outside of class for two years, it had a tremendous influence on my growth, and I was extremely thankful that APO played such an influential role in my life. I wanted to take on more responsibility, so I put myself in the running to become the treasurer of APO. It was an important job at the fraternity, but I was not the only one running for the job. Naturally, there was politics involved. All the brothers had a vote, and they voted for their friends and for other reasons. I lost. I thought my intelligence and existing friendships would carry the day, but they didn't. I was hurt at losing and that turned me off to APO for the remaining two years at Baruch. I was still a brother. I would go to a meeting once in a while, but I turned my attention to other activities at Baruch.

I learned three very important things from my two active years at APO. The most important thing I learned was how to emulate upperclassmen who I admired at the fraternity. These guys were bright, articulate, confident, and politically savvy. They could lead, they could manage, they could persuade, and they could produce results. I had none of that and tried to be like them by working closely with them. It was clear that *to become a leader, emulate the people who are leaders*. It was an experience that changed me for the better. The second thing the fraternity did was to give me a sense of purpose for college life. I was not going to go through college as I did in high school, merely taking classes and not enjoying the extracurricular activities. APO got me involved in many activities in the school that made me feel important, made me feel that college was a part of my life, and gave me the chance to gain leadership skills—skills that changed me for the rest of my life. The third thing the fraternity taught me was how to dance. I had never danced until coming to college but wanted to learn. When the Booster girls showed up, we would often play foxtrot, cha-cha, or rock-and-roll music. The girls taught me to dance. I learned slowly, but eventually, I could hold my own on the dance floor. Even to this day, I am thankful for being able to ballroom dance.

As a freshman, I became the business manager of the *Ticker*, the student newspaper. It wasn't a demanding job—I paid a few bills each month—but I felt a part of the school. Over my four years at Baruch, I became very active in the school. I ran a blood bank drive, served on the student council, was president of the junior class, was chairman of a Flower Sale Day, and served as chancellor of Sigma Alpha, the honor service society.

One of the accomplishments I am most proud of is receiving the award of high honors from the student council at the end of my senior year at Baruch. It was recognition from my peers that I was among the very few who gave a great deal of their time to their school and deserved to be honored for their selfless service.

Had I gone to the Wharton School at the University of Pennsylvania, I might not have had the same opportunities I had at Baruch. In many ways, Baruch was a better choice for me, but I didn't realize it at first. As I became deeply involved in extracurricular activities, I began to realize that those activities were having a deeper impact on me than the classes I was taking. I was changing as a person, I was learning to lead, I was meeting a lot of smart people, I was serving the school and improving myself in the process, and I was excited to go to college each and every day. Being involved in *extracurricular activities can change you far more than classes can.*

There were, no doubt, great classes that I loved, and they taught me a great deal about the world, but it was the extracurricular activities that changed me more. Almost certainly, I would not have had as many opportunities to grow at Penn where the competition would have been stronger and everyone lived on campus. Because students at Baruch lived at home and many of them left in the afternoon for a job, the few of us that were involved at Baruch outside of class had opportunities for personal growth—opportunities that I desperately needed. *Sometimes what you think is second best turns out to be the best choice after all.*

At the end of my freshman year, I was taking my first economics class, and there was a lot of material to review for the final exam. I had a fraternity brother named Nat who was in my class, and we decided to study for the exam together. He came over to my apartment, and we stayed up all night reviewing the material. We took a couple of No-Doz pills to keep us alert. We both took the exam without an hour's worth of sleep, and we both did extremely well. Nat was a good student, and we complemented each other, but it was the first and last time I was going to give up an entire night's sleep for an exam.

I found that under pressure, I learn a great deal more than I usually learn without pressure. I learned to not only live with pressure but also to appreciate what it did for me. As we approached the end of a class with the final exam looming just ahead, the pressure was on to learn the material and be prepared for whatever the teacher asked. Some friends in college goofed off during the entire semester and then had the ability to learn most of the material in a few days to pass the final exam. Other friends worked hard all semester long and didn't feel any pressure at all as the final exam approached. They were always ready. I was in the middle. I did my work all semester long, but the pressure of the final exam pushed me hard. I was amazed at how much I could learn in a short period of time under pressure. I learned to summarize a course in five pages of notes using short phrases and keywords. I then could shorten those notes down to a single page to summarize the essence of the material. I could only do that at the end of a semester because it took me that long to let the material sink in. Time and review made the material more understandable, and pressure to know forced me to summarize it all on a single page. This technique helped me in business and in life as I developed a skill to summarize a complex problem down to its essential issues.

I took one class from Professor Lavender. He was an English teacher and suggested at first that we focus on reading *Tom Jones* by Henry Fielding. The novel is a classic, and I suppose that Professor Lavender had not read it but thought it would be just right for our class. After several weeks into the semester, he showed up for class and told us that he was removing *Tom Jones* from our reading list and replacing it with *Crime and Punishment* by Dostoyevsky. I had no idea why he did this until much later in my life when I saw the movie *Tom Jones*, an explicitly sexual tale of a young man growing up in England. I suppose Professor Lavender didn't need to deal with the sexually explicit parts of the book even though it was a classic. It was a good decision.

The most remarkable statement I heard in college came from the lips of Professor Lavender. One day, in the hallway in the afternoon after my classes were over, I was talking with him about school, about extracurricular activities, and about getting a good college education. He then said, *"Don't go through college. Let college go through you."*

It was a beautiful statement, short, clear, and powerful. Somehow that remark summed up what I was looking for in college. I had been a shy and quiet guy throughout elementary school and high school, and I didn't like being that way. I wanted to get the most out of college that was possible. It convinced me that staying around campus after class, getting involved in serving the school, and getting to meet the faculty after class on an informal basis was extremely important for my growth. I was just beginning to rid myself of my shyness, and I needed training on how to become a leader, on how to speak in public, and on how to become a mature adult. I now know how important those words are, so I can say unequivocally, *"Don't go through life. Let life go through you."* Be in the moment, experience your life, give your life the best experience you can afford and desire, and don't be a writer sitting in the stands reporting on what happened. Be on the field of action, involved in life, making decisions, and moving forward.

I wasn't entirely serious as a student though I did study hard. I had trained myself in high school to sit and study for hours, and I was determined to succeed. One time, a number of guys went to a bar a few blocks from the college for a beer chug-a-lug contest. The winner was the one that could down a pitcher of beer in the shortest amount of time. I entered the contest, didn't win, but had fun drinking large amounts of beer. There were plenty of times when a group of us would go for pizza and beer—and pizza in New York is the best pizza anywhere in the world. There was another time when a large group of us went to a sing-along bar on Third Avenue for hamburgers and beer. The bar had a piano player who would play a variety of sing-along songs, and the entire bar would sing with him. The place was always crowded, and I have often thought that a bar like this would be a big hit and very profitable located near a college campus.

I probably would have joined the Baruch band if they had one, but alas, there was no band, and there was no football team. As a result, I stopped playing the trombone even though I loved it. I found a bugle somewhere and took it to a number of basketball games. Given my trombone experience, it wasn't difficult to play. I would play "charge" on the bugle, and it helped me take an interest in CCNY basketball. It was a fun thing to do, no one else brought along a bugle, and I felt important playing it. The team was not that good, only played in a minor league, but it did once get an invitation to play in the NIT tournament.

I took my bugle with me as a bunch of fraternity brothers drove down to Maryland to see the game. We got there during the first half, the team lost, but I played the bugle a couple of times. It was fun to be a part of real college basketball and to cheer my team on even though I did not know any of them.

The summer after my freshman year was an eye opener for me. It was the first time I actually lived away from home. I heard about a job at a camp from a friend, and I managed to meet the owner. When I told him that I had just completed a Red Cross swimming badge and passed the exam, he hired me as an assistant swimming coach on the lakefront where the children went swimming. A small part of the lake was roped off for that purpose.

The owner offered me $125 for the entire summer, plus tips as a counselor in one of the bunks for twelve-year-old boys. I thought the tips might add a couple of hundred dollars more. I accepted the offer, for I had never really been to a camp. I thought that being in camp for the summer would be fun, and I would make a little money though the money was miserly.

I shared the bunk with another counselor that was a rising junior at Dartmouth College. I was impressed with him because I thought he went to a better school than I, was more sophisticated than I, took charge of the kids in our bunk all day, and probably deserved more of the tips than I. I felt inferior to him all summer long.

Nevertheless, my co-counselor and I split the tips from the parents of the kids in our bunk. Since the guy from Dartmouth met the parents while I worked on the waterfront, I never really knew whether I got 50 percent of the money or not. I was too scared to press the issue, although I sensed that other counselors were making more than I was. I didn't want to confront my co-counselor. I felt intimidated by his intellect the first day I met him. Not only did he go to an Ivy League college, but he was also reading some book on political life in Russia when I had no understanding of foreign affairs at all. I felt that he had a deeper understanding of the world because I knew nothing about either Russia or politics. I was just a naïve kid.

While all the other counselors were playing baseball or hiking or boating or rafting or doing some other things during the summer, I spent virtually all of my time in or near the waterfront, teaching seven—to thirteen-year-old kids how to swim. That was all I did the entire summer.

I had little interaction with the other counselors, especially the female counselors in the camp. I didn't date; I didn't really have time to meet anyone except the counselor in my own bunk. As a result, I felt isolated from the counselors my age for most of the summer. It was a lonely summer.

In midsummer, two of the counselors were caught sleeping together, and both were summarily fired. Since I was just beginning to date, I was astonished to learn that two counselors were having sex and scared to see that counselors could be fired on the spot. I couldn't believe that counselors would get involved that way, for I could see no justification even though I was eighteen years old. The owner of the camp made it clear that anyone else not doing their job or involved sexually with another counselor would be fired. There was a time when the director yelled at me for doing something wrong, and I thought I would be fired. That set me straight quickly, for I had no other place to go except back home, and I didn't want my parents to think that I was not good enough or got fired on my first job away from home. I worked hard at the lake, but I still felt that my job was in jeopardy all summer long. I was scared that I would be fired. Of course it did not happen. I minded my business and stayed out of trouble for the rest of the summer.

There was something else about Tunis Lake Camp that really was intimidating. At the end of summer, the camp put on Color War. Color War in this camp was beyond anything I could imagine or create because the camp was designed for artistic kids and many of the counselors were creative too. During Color War, the camp split into three sides, and each side made designs, created songs, built structures, costumes, organized large groups of kids into a chorus, and put together a performance for the judges that lasted an hour or more. I had no idea that this would happen, having spent all my time on the waterfront, so I was totally amazed and impressed when the counselors created new librettos to music, taught the campers dance routines, and made up scenes to be acted out on stage. In addition, costumes were made and sets were built. This all took place for several weeks prior to the event, so the competition was very impressive. I was blown away by the decorations, the designs, the organization, the songs, the singing, everything. I was a nerdy math guy that had never dealt in the creative arts. I could never do what they did. To see other counselors my age organizing these creative arts and crafts really made me feel inferior. It was not just beyond my ability. It was way beyond it. I did not have that kind of creativity or leadership. I came home feeling that I was vastly inferior to the other counselors and in need of gaining much more confidence in my own abilities.

I did not enjoy camp that summer. I was scared of being fired, I wasn't making much money, and I was on the waterfront all summer long. But it was my job. *Once I accepted the job, I stuck it out.* I wish I had the perspective back then that I have today.

At camp, the counselors were given one day off each week to do with as they pleased. Many of us preferred to get out of camp and go to some town to see a movie or just leave to see the surrounding area. With the camp so far north of most of the activities going on in the Catskills, it was necessary to travel south at least ten to twenty miles to get to a major town. Since my parents only had one car, I had to hitchhike to get anywhere at all. In the mid-1950s, hitchhiking was not difficult because many people would pick you up. I hitched rides every time I had a day off, often traveling as much as fifty miles away from camp before turning back. Hitching a ride from camp was an amazing experience in survival. I traveled with one of the other counselors to have company and to share the experience.

Three incidents are worth mentioning. The first occurred when a man picked us up in a late model Oldsmobile. As I sat in the backseat, I looked down to see a rifle lying between the front and back seats. I had never held a rifle except for the few times I shot matches out of my apartment when I was ten years old, so the gun scared me. In upstate New York, having a rifle in the car was not a big deal, but for a Brooklyn boy, the gun was scary. Why would he have a rifle in his car? It just didn't sit well with me because I was not used to guns being so readily available. Heck, I had access to the rifle before the driver did, so he sure was a trusting soul.

That was not as scary as the speed I found myself traveling with a man I did not know. The new Olds was moving at over a hundred miles an hour, and the speedometer read 108. I had never gone that fast before in my life. I was used to speeds of fifty, sixty, seventy miles per hour, but 108 was another matter. I was too scared to even talk, and I just sat there hoping that nothing would happen. I was sure that if we crashed, I would be dead—dead from a man I did not know in a car I probably shouldn't have been in. This guy was driving completely differently from the way my family drove a car, and he lived differently than the way my family lived. Of course, nothing happened, and I managed to get out of the car safe and sound. I even thanked the man for the ride. The experience convinced me beyond anything else I had experienced before that *it was time to grow up and recognize that a lot of people did not resemble any of my family. Not even close!*

The second incident occurred early one day when we hitched a ride to Oneonta to see a movie. In 1957, Charlton Heston was playing Moses in *The Ten Commandments*. The movie was great, but it was long and ended late in the afternoon. When we decided to hitch back to the camp, it was very late in day. We tried to hitch a ride, but no one seemed interested in picking us up. As the sun starting to sink toward the horizon, I had to get more and more aggressive in wanting to find a ride. Finally, a family of four stopped for gas. The father was driving with his teenage son next to him. In the back of the car sat the mother and her young daughter. As they were filling up their car, my friend and I told our sob story about being far from our camp, that it was late in the day, and that we were worried about getting back to the camp. Finally, the family agreed to give us a ride, and we agreed to pay them three dollars. Back then you could fill a gas tank for three dollars.

Since it was dinnertime, the wife had some food with her and fed the family on small paper plates while we drove to their home. I watched the father take a drink of soda from a bottle while he was driving, and that really scared me. I had just learned to drive, and I thought that it was really dangerous to drink soda and drive because it would take your eyes of the road. I have no problem doing the same thing now, but at nineteen, I thought it was a dangerous thing to do. The father dropped his wife and daughter off first, and then he and his son drove us to our camp. I was sure the father brought his son along for protection in case we decided to give him some trouble, which, of course, was never an issue. We just wanted to get back to camp and were thankful that it was happening. We were glad to pay him the money and equally glad to get out of the car. They were very kind to us, but I was really scared. I was thrilled to have gotten back by sundown and pleased that it only cost us a few dollars to get there.

The last hitch was the scariest event of all. I don't recall exactly where my friend and I hitched to, but it was quite a long way, maybe thirty or forty miles from the camp, and I wasn't sure exactly how to get back to the camp. Eventually we found a hitch, but as I looked on the map, it was clear that we were traveling in the wrong direction.

As the car sped north, it was going farther and farther away from where camp was located. If we didn't get out of the car, it would be almost impossible to get back to camp that night. Finally, we asked to get out at a crossroad that we thought would be a better direction to get home. The crossroad was not a main road, but we thought it was better to take our chances on that road than to go farther away from our destination.

Unfortunately, it was the wrong place to get a hitch because it was a back road, and we never saw a single car going down that road for fifteen to twenty minutes. As the afternoon waned, we decided that the only thing to do was to keep walking down the deserted road until we reached some sort of help.

It was a very lonely walk, and the day was fast drawing to a close. We were nowhere, and I was worried that we wouldn't make it back to the camp, let alone find a place to stay for the night. As we walked, we constantly watched the sun head down toward the horizon. After half an hour without seeing a single car, I was becoming really nervous. The chance of a hitch was becoming remote. Finally, we reached a small intersection that was a tiny hamlet of twenty or so houses. We looked up and down the street for any cars that were moving. Nothing was moving! We were tired from our walk and ready to give up about finding our way back to camp that night. We had no idea what we would do or where we would stay. We were scared and frustrated that there was literally no one around. I thought that we might have to sleep outdoors for the night, and I wasn't happy about it. There wasn't a single gas station or a restaurant there, only private homes. I was nervous about knocking on a strange door to tell our miserable story.

All of the sudden out of nowhere, a car came into sight and passed us. There were two young guys in it, not much older than we were. They saw us, and out of curiosity, they turned around and stopped to ask what we were doing there. I told them that we took the wrong car for a hitch, and we were trying to get back to the main highway about four to five miles away, which would put us on the highway toward camp. I could see that they were not that interested in helping us, but I was certain that we wouldn't be able to get back to camp without their help. I proposed to them that if they could take us to the main highway, my buddy and I would give them two dollars for gas. They were still reluctant to do it since it was way out of their way. I think we finally offered to fill their tank completely, and that did the job. I didn't want to spend the money, but I also didn't want to sleep by the side of the road either. Paying for their gas was a much better alternative. While the two guys in the car were talking to each other about whether to drive us or not, I took the aggressive step of opening the back door of their car and got in. My buddy followed me, and the two guys in the front seat had their minds made up for them. I think they reluctantly agreed to do it and drove us to a diner that had a gas station attached.

On the way, the driver told us that this was his eighteenth car; they just got old, broken cars, fixed them, and drove them until they no longer would run. Then they took the parts off the broken car and used them to fix up another car. They were self-taught mechanics, and I was impressed that they were creative enough to fix cars that easily. When we got to the main road, it was just about dark, so we literally threw three dollars at the boys while they were filling up their gas tank. We ran into the diner at the gas station, not to get away from the boys, but to find another hitch to the camp.

My friend and I walked to every table where people were eating dinner, and we directly asked them if they were heading in the direction of the camp and, if they were, could they give us a lift. Luckily, we found a truck driver who took us. By then, it was totally dark. I sat up in this big eighteen-wheeler and enjoyed the last bit of the trip without fear, for I had been thoroughly scared from the time we started walking on the deserted road to the time we found the boys that drove us to the main road to finding someone to take us to the camp. It was a trip I would not want to do again, and it unnerved me about hitch hiking anymore. Once again, I was not prepared. We did not have a detailed map of the area; we only had a rough idea about which way to go, and thankfully it worked out. *That was one scary day, but it taught me negotiation skills when in a bad situation.*

The art of persuasion is an essential skill for leadership. I learned it out of necessity when hitching. I had to return to camp, the day was dwindling down, and I needed a ride. You may not want to ask for a ride, but necessity pushes you hard. You begin by explaining your situation, then you negotiate, then you try to persuade, and finally you focus on convincing. *The art of persuasion is essential for achieving your goal.* It's all about selling, selling yourself, and getting others to agree on your point of view.

There are a few things you can succeed at without persuasion, but they are usually done alone, like writing a book or creating a painting. Most things require other people to work with you, and persuasion is essential to achieving your goal. The only way to learn to persuade is to do it again and again, reviewing your failures and successes. There is a famous saying at Symphony Hall in Atlanta by Robert Woodruff, the great CEO of the Coca-Cola Company. His famous quote is, "There is no limit to what a man can do or how far he can go if he doesn't mind who gets the credit." That is persuasion at its best: giving the credit to others for what you want done.

In my sophomore year, I was still interested in accounting as a career, but I needed some extra money for school since my parents were struggling to make a living themselves. The summer job at Tunis Lake Camp did not pay well. Even though I was reluctant to find a job and wanted to enjoy the benefits of a full-time education at CCNY, many of the students were in a similar situation and had a part-time job in the afternoon. The Baruch School was geared to teach most classes in the morning, so that faculty and students could leave in the afternoon for jobs outside of school. It wasn't what I wanted to do, but I decided that I had to do it to put a little extra money in my pocket.

I found a part-time job at a small two-man CPA firm called Fass & Buchalter, located on Nassau Street in Manhattan, a short subway ride from school. I worked there for the better part of a year doing two things: adding up the sales in small companies in Manhattan and filling out the basic data for federal income tax returns. I worked two to three days a week for about ten to twelve hours in total.

I would go to small firms that used the accounting firm, talk to the bookkeeper, and she (it was usually a she) would give me the sales figures line by line written by hand in her revenue book. There were thirty to forty lines on a page with each sale in the hundreds or thousands of dollars. My job was to verify the total sales that the bookkeeper had calculated at the bottom of the page. I had to add columns of numbers for ten to twelve hours a week. After a short time, I became very fast at it. The fastest, easiest, and most accurate way to add a column of numbers was to add in terms of nine, ten, or eleven. In this way, I would count by tens. I could add ten and subtract one if the number was nine, add ten if the number was ten, or add ten and one if the number was eleven. The key was finding nines, tens, and elevens. For example, if the numbers down a column were 6, 4, 5, 8, 2, 5, 1, 7, 3, 4, then I would combine 6+4=10 in my head, 5+5=10, 8+2 =10 to get 30, then 1+7+3=11 to get 41 and 4 to make 45. I could do that in two seconds. I continued that way down a column of thirty to forty numbers in ten seconds or less and reached a total to compare against the total in the book. I would then do the next column and so on, rarely making a mistake and having the bookkeeper's total to compare to. If I found a difference from the total in the book, I would double-check the calculation to be sure. The bookkeepers generally used a calculator, so they were rarely wrong. After several months, I could go faster than a calculator, and I was rarely wrong either because I was practicing every week for ten to twelve hours. That technique has stayed with me all my life, and people are amazed at how quickly I can add a column of numbers.

After the New Year when the CPA firm started on taxes, I spent much of my time filling in the basic information for clients' federal income tax returns. I took last year's tax return and copied the name, address, business number, and a variety of other boilerplate items to save the two partners time. The work was boring, and it had to be done in the office down on Nassau Street. I worked a few weekends, in addition to verifying sales records, and that combination took away a lot of my free time.

Adding a column of previous sales and worrying about last year's information for tax purposes convinced me that I really didn't want to be an accountant. As an accountant, I thought I would always be focused on the past, on reviewing the books and paying taxes for a business based on what had already occurred. I wanted to focus on the future. I found accounting work very repetitive. I was problem oriented. I liked the intellectual challenge of a new problem rather than doing the same thing over and over again. It was fine for others to do, but not for me. *Working in my field taught me that I didn't want to work in that field.*

After I changed majors from accounting to statistics in my junior year, I stopped working for Fass & Buchalter. I had lost my passion for accounting, and I didn't want to continue in it as a career. I also had made enough money during my sophomore year to not worry about needing extra cash during the coming school year.

I considered transferring to the uptown campus to become a math major, but by then, I was halfway through college, I was deeply involved in Baruch, I had joined a wonderful fraternity, and I knew a lot of people on campus. I just didn't want to start anew and give up all that I had accomplished in my first two years in college. I turned to Professor Lavender for advice. He knew me quite well. He told me to change majors to statistics, which I knew I wanted to do, and I could do that at Baruch. He also recommended that it would be smart to finish my major in accounting since I only had a few more courses to go. As a result, I became a double major, majoring in accounting and statistics. I didn't want to take another accounting course, but I took his advice. *It is responsible to finish what you start, and it is also right to quit when the result is not useful.*

I finished Hebrew school to satisfy my parents, but it was a waste of time. I majored in accounting in high school to follow the recommendation of my uncle when I should have taken chemistry and physics. My two years of accounting was covered in one semester in college. The two years of high school accounting was a waste of time. I finished my last two accounting classes in college to follow the advice of a teacher I respected; it too was a waste of time.

Early in the jobs I had, I never quit and finished them even when I did not like what I was doing. I always finished a book that I started reading, and I never dropped a class in college once I signed up for it. I always ate what was on my plate, and I always stayed to the end of the movie even when I did not like the movie.

It took me much later in life to walk away from an activity in the middle of it because it was a waste of time. I didn't want to be a quitter, but I also didn't want to waste my time. Eventually, I learned to be more discriminating and avoid things that were a waste of time and to have the courage to quit in the middle when the result had no value for me. *The sooner you quit what you don't need or don't want, the more effective you will be in your life.*

Nassau Street had a lot of coin and stamp stores in the 1950s, and I was still interested in growing my coin collection. However, I had been collecting coins since I was ten years old, and I no longer had the same interest I had when I was younger. There was one interesting item that caught my attention in one of the coin stores. It was a 1909 S VDB

Lincoln penny for sale for twenty dollars. The penny was the first year the Lincoln penny was made. The "S" indicated it was minted at the San Francisco mint, and the "VDB" on the reverse side of the penny in small print stood for the designer of the penny, Victor D. Brenner. This penny had the smallest volume of pennies minted for the Lincoln cent, it was a very valuable coin, and it was impossible to find in circulation. I wanted to buy the coin, but twenty dollars was a lot of money for a penny. Even more important, the one principle that I never violated was that I would only find coins from circulation; I would not pay any more for them than their face value. Nevertheless, I looked at that coin every time I passed that coin store, wishing I had the courage to pay twenty dollars for a penny that I knew would be much more valuable someday. Twenty years ago, that penny was selling for four hundred dollars. I recently looked up the price in a coin book; it is selling at retail for $750 to $1,200, depending on the fineness of the penny. In fifty years, the coin went up about fifty times in value, not a bad investment. If only I had as much courage to make a good investment as I did to change my major.

The most influential intellectual event in my college career occurred during the second semester of my sophomore year. I was frustrated at the end of my freshman year with all the accounting and business courses that I had to take, not just because I didn't enjoy them, but also because I was missing out on a more liberal education—an education that would deal with history, literature, and social sciences. I didn't want just a business education. I wanted a more complete education, and I was determined to get it. In the second half of my sophomore year, I registered for a class on European history by Professor Gadol and an English class by Professor Levy. Those two classes helped to reinforce my determination to switch majors from accounting to a more mathematical orientation.

Mrs. Gadol was a beautiful woman, and I loved looking at her as well as listening to her talk about the history of Europe. The class was extremely well attended with a lot of bright people, and the discussions about history were both interesting and inspiring. I looked forward to that class eagerly even though I knew so little about the subject. Near the end of the semester, we were required to write a paper on some aspect of the history we were studying, but I was so frustrated about my life and my lack of commitment to becoming an accountant that I decided that

I would write about myself, about my innermost thoughts as a young man. I was going to write about my life, my frustrations, my inhibitions, my ethics, and any other subject that dealt with my maturation process in college. I knew this would not fit with what Professor Gadol had in mind and that I might get a failing grade in this class because it was not the subject matter of the class. I didn't care! I was going through a crucial time in my life—at least I thought I was—and I needed a way to come to grips with my future. That term paper was going to get me to focus on what to do with my professional life, and I was willing to risk a low grade to deal with the most pressing issue I had.

I wrote that paper; it was called "The Changing Values of a Young Man." I handed the paper in and hoped that Mrs. Gadol would be kind to me, and she was. She wrote on the cover page that it was the wrong topic, that I should have written on some history topics, and that I should read *The Autobiography of Henry Adams*, which talked about the same issues I dealt with. She marked the rest of the paper extensively for the grammatical mistakes that I made, and there were many of them, but in the end, she gave me a B- for the paper. I was thrilled that she was so kind to me.

To give you a sense of what I wrote back then, here are a few excerpts from the paper, "The Changing Values of a Young Man" written in May 1958:

> I am still absolutely lost as to what I am looking for, what meaning or purpose all this may have for me, and how long I will remain actively interested. I feel myself on the borderline, slowly being built up by my education to an awareness of what intellectualism can be. Yet, I cannot discover what path to take to satisfy my interests. What I am seeking is some sense of direction, which will give me enough stimuli to keep me striving for the values I know I want, and for those that I see in my teachers.

> Education, or liberal education, gives an unending choice of values. I have tried out new ways and ideas, letting myself drift along from one island to another, not having any pattern or goal except this: to learn and understand.

I reject the view that everything is predetermined, that I will never make a decision, that I am following my fate written in the "big book." Life would be worthless if this were true. Every decision I make is creative in that I am searching within myself to find the best answer.

The class lecture often produces information without any purpose. It is no exaggeration to say that students are often treated as long-playing records on which is impressed a set of words to be reproduced when necessary. The skill of the student is rated on how well he or she can reproduce the sounds that he or she has heard.

A bored instructor creates boredom. Textbooks are a means to learning and not the end. When they are the central tools of learning, they dull thoughts. The chief reliance is the give and take of ideas from a teacher and the members of the class. The only way we can be human is to keep extending our interest beyond ourselves and to understand the world in which we live.

The second class that sophomore year was with Professor Levy, a man I knew well. I was a great admirer of the man. During the semester, I had to read a famous book called *Liberal Education* by Mark Van Doren and write a report about it. That book reinforced the feeling I had sitting in Mrs. Gadol's class. I was being excited by two great classes that had nothing whatsoever to do with accounting or business. Together they forced me to reevaluate what I wanted to do with my life. It was both thrilling and frustrating to go through the process, but it reshaped the rest of my life. I am thankful that I had such good teachers to open my eyes to a world I knew I wanted but did not know how to get. Here are some excerpts from the book *Liberal Education* by Mark Van Doren and my comments about them:

"No one," says T. S. Eliot, "can become really educated without having pursued some study in which he took no interest—for it is a part of education to learn to interest ourselves in subjects for which we have no aptitude."

By training our minds to understand difficult subjects, we are better able to understand new problems, judge them, and overcome them. If a man wants to study only subjects that are interesting to him, he must first study all subjects. How else can he find the subjects he likes? The artist must study all subjects, for life is the basis of art. The more one knows, the more interesting one becomes and, in turn, life becomes more interesting.

> Age and experience are necessary; young men have not lived long enough to know why temperance and wisdom are good. Principles can be memorized, but their meaning waits upon their application—itself perhaps the most difficult of human tasks, since in a given situation it is so easy either to apply the wrong principle or to rest in a statement of the right one, as if by magic it would apply itself . . . It is only as we grow older that we learn why we have learned.

Experience is the best teacher. To know life, you must live it. You cannot feel certain emotions until you live them. Knowledge can be gained through study, but the wisdom to apply this knowledge comes from experience. We learn from our mistakes, and experience teaches us not to repeat them. This is education.

The most painful single thing about contemporary American education is the system of "vocational choice," which extends down as far as the high schools. In college this would be an evil, and in fact it is; but even the high school student is nagged until he declares what he wants to do when he grows up. The boy who knows that much about himself is one out of a thousand. The rest pretend they know; and from that moment on are channeled toward a life that they may not discover to be the wrong one until they are middle-aged. All men are specialists at last, but there is a time for choice and it is not the time of youth.

The time of youth is the best time of life. It is the time when a boy wants to do everything and be everything. While doing these things, the youth has to pick one field that he thinks he would enjoy doing for the rest of his life. This time of choice is a bad one because a boy choosing his career doesn't have enough information about himself to adequately choose his profession. But if some specialty is not chosen early enough, the future of a nation may be at stake; its future is dependent upon its youth. Each man must realize that he must have a talent that he can rely on to live even if he should find that some other field "calls him." Until we find out what we want, we should support ourselves. It is this means to an end that enables us to have the life we want. Yes, "youth is wasted on the young," but that is the reality of our society.

> The teacher is kind, but to someone he is training to forget him. "My son is coming to do without me," wrote Emerson in his journal. "And I am coming to do without Plato." The good teacher disappears out of the student's life as Virgil and Beatrice disappear out of *The Divine Comedy*. They are remembered as persons, and so is every good teacher remembered; but when the student has found his own way in the world he cannot recall how much of his wisdom he owes to another. It is his now, and that is what his teacher had intended.

Teaching is an art that all of us possess. Some have more talent than others, yet we are all capable of communicating our knowledge to others. In this way we influence all those to whom we speak. The good teacher can influence you to take the right path when you are in the dark. The teacher does not tell you which path it is but gives you enough information to help you make the right decision. The goal is to have the student see the light, recall the advice, but know that the wisdom gained was discovered alone.

I was a strong math student, but I wanted a liberal education in a business school. I wanted to know what the great minds had to say about civilization, about science, about life. I learned that it was possible to get a liberal education if you looked for it, and if you knew what you wanted, you could find it in college or outside of it.

Education allows you to become the person you want to be. I wanted to change to someone else. I didn't know who that someone else was, but I knew that education would lead me in the right direction and it did. It wasn't just liberal education classes alone. It wasn't just the many extracurricular activities I participated in or the jobs I had. It was all of them working together, letting me explore new ways of thinking, new ways of speaking, and new ways of behaving. I worked at changing myself because I wanted to change; education led me all along the way.

At Baruch, statistics classes taught how to use statistical techniques rather than the mathematical theory behind them. I knew statistics was closer to what I wanted to do than accounting. I took the only class in basic calculus, and it had only five students because business students at Baruch were not interested in calculus. I loved the class, enjoyed the small size, and I did well enough to believe I could go to graduate school to major in mathematical statistics. I took the only other math class on probability and would have taken more math classes, but they were not available. Nevertheless, the math and statistics classes were satisfying enough for my mathematical urge and gave me a taste of what statistics could be as a profession.

One story that my friend Jake told was that he took Eco 15 with me, the only statistics class required of all students. Eco 15 was a basic statistics class. For most students, it was one of the hardest classes in the school because it required a decent background in mathematics. For me, it was easy; at the end of the course, I knew the material well. Jake knew he didn't. At the final exam, there were a hundred or so students taking the exam in a huge room, and we were allowed to take any seat we wanted. Naturally, Jake sat right next to me and encouraged our friends to do the same. As he tells it, I got an A on the final and an A in the class. Jake and others surrounding me also got As on the final or close to it. The next circle around them got Bs, and the circle around them got Cs as though I was the source of all knowledge for the class. I never knew if he was right or not or whether others cheated off my exam or not, but it was a great story, and it certainly improved my confidence.

At the end of my sophomore year, I got the best summer job I ever had in college for two reasons: I made a substantial amount of money, and I had a girlfriend for the entire summer. My sister had a friend who was close friends with the owners of Keim's Hill Top Lodge, a small German Jewish hotel in Mountainside, New York, in the heart of the Catskill Mountains. The hotel held 120 guests, and they needed one busboy for half the tables because there were only two waiters and two busboys for the entire dining room. I interviewed for the job and got it.

I took care of six tables, ten people to a table. While that wasn't difficult, it was a demanding job from six in the morning until after dinner at eight. Between those hours, I had some free time: one hour off after breakfast and a few hours off in the afternoon. I had to set the tables for breakfast, lunch, and dinner and clean them after each meal. I was in charge of beverages during the meal. Compared to making almost no money in camp the previous summer, as a busboy I made substantial tips from guests and finished the summer with six hundred dollars in cash, the most amount of money I had ever made. This was enough money to last for much of my next college year.

In addition to earning good money, I found a girlfriend just down the road from the hotel. She had a girlfriend, and the two girls would come over to our hotel almost every day to hang out. My girlfriend was seventeen, a couple of years younger than me, so within a few weeks, we were a couple for the six to eight remaining weeks of the summer. With a girlfriend, the evenings with her made the summer fly by.

We used to make out in the top bed in my bunk, lie down on a blanket near the pool, or take a walk in the woods alone. I wasn't lonely, and I was having a decent love life for the first time in my life. It was a thrilling summer to be able to have a girlfriend who enjoyed being with me and me with her. I was in good health, I was making money, I was learning about the opposite sex, and I was on my own. It was a carefree time in my life.

Unfortunately, my girlfriend lived in the Bronx, and I lived in Brooklyn. After the summer was over, not having a car meant I had to take the train to the Bronx to take her out on a date. I found that the time from my apartment to her apartment took one and a half hours to get there, so I had a three-hour commute to see her. I liked her, and I thought she was great for a summer romance, but I didn't think she was worth the time it took to get to her apartment and back. One time I took her on a hayride in Staten Island. We double-dated as she set up a friend of mine with a date. It took three to four hours for us to pick up our dates, take the train downtown to the ferry to Staten Island, and then take a bus to get to the hayride. Taking our dates home began at midnight when the trains and buses weren't running as often. By the time I got home, the sun was coming up at five o'clock. That was the end of my summer romance. She was still in high school, and I was a rising junior, and I wasn't ready for a serious relationship. I was focused on getting a good education, and dating was not a high priority for me. I knew it could also be expensive, and I wanted to conserve the few hundred dollars I made that summer for the entire school year.

I didn't start dating until I went to college. I wanted to date, but I was scared to ask a girl for a date because I didn't know how to begin. I was a nerd and would have nothing to say on the date, and I didn't have much money to impress a girl. I lacked confidence in myself partly because I wasn't dating, and I thought that girls would not want to date me. I talked about it with a few friends and had many thoughts about dating, but it took a long time to find a girlfriend.

My first girlfriend was a lucky break. She built confidence in me as a man even though she was still in high school. It didn't matter. That summer, I gained confidence that at least one girl liked me, and I wasn't such a loser. She liked me well enough to spend a lot of time with me. I needed her confidence, and she gave it willingly by spending time with me. *The right woman can build confidence in a man like nobody else can.*

Once I knew that a woman was not put off by me, I acquired the courage to ask other women for a date. It was a long time in coming, given that I was twenty years old, but at last I was confident enough to think that I could begin dating seriously. Only a woman could give me that kind of confidence.

In my junior year, I joined Sigma Alpha, the undergraduate honor service society that reduced my interest in my fraternity. I was happy to be a part of another service-oriented organization full of bright students who were elected not just because they were smart but also because they wanted to serve their school. In the fall of my senior year, I ran for the chancellor of Sigma Alpha, the president of the organization. I lost to Rita, but I liked her a great deal and dated her several times. She was a beautiful person inside and out, and I have often thought about where she ended up. She wanted to live in Greenwich Village and be a part of the Beat Generation, and I wanted to go to graduate school, so I knew that our paths were moving in different directions. For the spring semester, I again ran for chancellor and won.

Sigma Alpha organized a fundraising project for the school called the Flower Sale. Being in the heart of Manhattan, there was a wholesale flower market for the entire city. For a single day, Sigma Alpha bought enough flowers early in the morning and sold them for ten cents to students, faculty, and staff as they entered the one building that was Baruch School. With more than a thousand people entering the building, we made several hundred dollars each semester pestering everyone to give us a dime for a flower. It made the school look a little more beautiful for the day.

I organized one of these flower sales. It took a lot of planning to advertise the day, buy the flowers and find a large group of students to sell the flowers—but it was worth it. Everyone looked great with a flower in a lapel or on clothes. We had to put up with a lot of students who didn't want to part with a dime, didn't want the stupid flower, and just walked past whomever was approaching them. I learned that selling requires persistence and pays off. Refusing to accept no can ultimately make a sale. It requires a hard shell to accept people telling you—NO!

At the end of my senior year, Sigma Alpha took the money from flower sales and hired an artist to make a sculpture. The artist created a bronze sculpture of a beaver, the school's mascot, on a pedestal that we donated to the school. It was a gift from our graduating class of 1960, and I was gratified to see it in the lobby.

It is surprising how life turns out. People you admire when you're young don't always live up to your expectations while others you did not have much respect turn out to be successful. Judging people is one of the toughest calls to make because you never know what people are made of until they go through tough times. Larry was one of those guys who never turned out how I expected him to turn out. I met Larry just after I joined Alpha Phi Omega. He was two years ahead of me, a very confident guy, and very bright. I admired Larry greatly, and he took me under his wing. He was charming, active in extracurricular activities, and eventually became the editor of the Baruch yearbook. One time at a party, Larry took a girl out on a date in his car while I stayed at the party. When he returned, he told me that he didn't want to have sex with the girl; she might have consented, but he wasn't interested. He knew then that he was homosexual, and it came as a surprise to both to him and me. I thought nothing of it; Larry was still my idol. I lost touch with him after he graduated, but forty years later, I found him in Miami. Larry came to the hotel I was staying at, and we met in the lobby for several hours to catch up on our lives.

He arrived with a cane, was poorly dressed, and it was obvious he was suffering from serious health problems. Here was my idol—financially poor and little to show for the promise he had going for him in college.

Larry had given up a serious business career and wasn't making a decent living. I could hardly believe this was the Larry I knew in college, the guy I so admired, the confident, smooth-talking, sophisticated guy I knew. I was sad to learn that even with talent and education, life does not necessarily work out. I didn't sit in his shoes, I didn't know what happened after college, and I did not want to know. I was thankful about how my life was turning out. I had such high hopes for him to be a success in whatever he did, and then he turned out so differently.

I was never a good athlete, but I thought I might try out for a sports team at Baruch. The school did not have a football team, and there were few sports available at Baruch because it was the downtown school of City College. The main campus was uptown at 138th Street, a thirty-minute ride on the subway. At first, I tried out for the wrestling team. I was out of shape and overweight, but I showed up one afternoon to see if I would like it. The coach, a member of the US Olympic wrestling team, asked me to wrestle with another guy who also was out of shape and wanted to join the team. We wrestled for one minute, and then I was totally exhausted. I ended up on top of the other guy, who was equally spent, but that convinced me that wrestling was just too demanding for me. I didn't like the idea of fighting, and I was totally out of shape. That was the end of my wrestling career.

Several months later, I thought I would try out for the fencing team. I had never held a sword in my hand, but I thought my reflexes were good. I took the train uptown and tried out for the fencing team. Again, the coach took one look at me and said that I was too fat for a foil or epee, but I might do well with a saber, the biggest sword of all. I put on the mask and protective clothing and fenced with another more capable guy who told me my reflexes were indeed good. He was impressed at how well I was doing first time out. Then the coach told me that because I was out of shape, I had to run around the quarter-mile track before I could begin my fencing lessons. I tried running around the track on one or two occasions. I quickly knew that getting into shape would take a considerable effort. I had to travel by train uptown each time I went to fencing practice, the opposite direction from where I lived. The commute home would be another half an hour longer. I would also lose my involvement in the Baruch campus by being away from it at another campus. That concluded my fencing career and my involvement in athletics at Baruch.

The head of the Statistics Department was Professor Atkin, an interesting character and a thin man who smoked incessantly. He smoked in class and out of class, and he always had a cigarette in his mouth. He inhaled on that cigarette with a sucking sound he made when he slowly took a deep breath with his lips together. He sucked the cigarette so tightly when breathing in that it made that awful noise with each puff. That sucking sound was totally distracting from learning. In the late 1950s, cigarette smoking had not been conclusively shown to cause cancer, and there was no ban on smoking in classrooms. Other teachers smoked pipes, so it wasn't outrageous for teachers to smoke in class.

Nevertheless, it was a disgusting habit, particularly because I disliked smoking. That sucking sound gave the impression of a man totally addicted to cigarettes. I tried to avoid taking classes with him, but he was the only teacher for some statistics classes, so I had to take them.

Because he was an inveterate smoker and because he was head of the Statistics Department—and a man with a decent reputation in statistics—he was hired by one of the tobacco companies to study the relationship between cigarette smoking and cancer. He made it clear that he was working for the tobacco company to statistically prove that smoking did not cause cancer. I don't know what research he did or what he published, but I knew that he was addicted to cigarettes himself, and he was trying to prove just the opposite.

There was talk at the time that smoking and cancer were related, but Professor Atkin, as a statistician, was convinced that there was no statistical relationship between the two. Here was a full professor, the head of the Statistics Department, who was a habitual smoker, who was supposed to be conducting independent research on a topic, yet he could not possibly be a neutral observer. To suggest that cigarette smoking was harmful to your health would have thrown into question the smoking habit he was addicted to. In all the years that I have been around smokers, I never saw anyone so focused on enjoying every puff as Professor Atkin did. At the time, I was only annoyed at the sucking sound he made on every puff he took, but later in life, as the data became clearly known that cigarette smoking caused cancer, I thought how hypocritical he must have been to sell his professional integrity to a cigarette company when he should have known better. Even in academia there are prostitutes.

In some ways, Professor Atkin reminded me of my friend Howie who smelled his fingers, a mannerism that overshadowed whatever personality he had. The hissing sound of Professor Atkin did the same thing: it created a mannerism that overshadowed whatever he was saying. His smoking created his image, and I just couldn't get past that sound to focus on whatever he was talking about.

At the end of my junior year in college, I again started looking for a summer job, and one of my friends in the neighborhood knew about a busboy job at the Ambassador Hotel in Fallsberg, New York. This was a much bigger hotel than Keim's Hill Top Lodge, so I pursued the matter aggressively. With my previous background as a busboy, I got the job.

The Ambassador Hotel was a major hotel surrounded by other hotels just down the road. The hotel had a large dining room that held about fifty tables that could handle about four hundred to five hundred people. I worked hard that summer and made serious money as tips, a little more than what I had made the previous summer.

I shared a bunk in the back of the hotel with other service people, including the help in the kitchen who ran the gamut from well-paid chefs to low-paid dishwashers. There were several people in my bunk, and with its cramped conditions, I used it only for sleeping at night.

The waiters and busboys were well-educated college kids serving customers. The rest of the kitchen staff was much older and not as educated as the serving staff. Many were black. The contrast could not be greater, and it was clear to me which group would do better in business. This was a perfect example of the difference between where you end up based on whether you are educated or not. The educated staff was out front dealing with customers, making serious money from tips from patrons, while the uneducated staff was in the kitchen preparing the meals and washing the dishes. It struck me that I could end up in the kitchen if I didn't continue my education.

I served the typical table of ten people, covered four to five tables, and was responsible for setting and clearing the tables as well as serving the beverages for them. It was the same responsibility that I had the previous summer, except that the turnover of guests was greater, and there was a broad variety of food. I had a fabulous waiter who was attending medical school. He had a phenomenal memory; he could take the orders of everyone at the table without writing anything down, get each order correctly, and deliver the orders to each person exactly as they ordered it. It was extremely impressive to see him do it night after night, taking a complete order off of a new menu from a table of ten, never write any of it down, and get it all right. It was another feat of photographic memory from a very smart guy. I was impressed. How could I keep up with impressive people? I knew I couldn't do what they did. Still, we got along famously.

I worked hard all summer, up at six o'clock to prepare for breakfast, clean up afterward, set for lunch, take an hour off before lunch, clean up after lunch, get several hours off in the afternoon to rest, and do the same thing for dinner. I was off at about eight at night and could watch some of the shows that played at the hotel; they were decent but not great. One show featured a hypnotist that hypnotized a dozen people on the stage at the same time, told them to look at the audience, and see all the people out there totally nude. The hypnotized people actually believed the audience was nude, and you could see the embarrassment on their faces. The audience loved it, and we all laughed at how people under hypnoses could see things that weren't so.

The summer was not as much fun as the previous summer because I didn't have a girlfriend, and I wanted one. There were no homes around the area where I could meet girls, and the only people I met were the serving staff and the guests that stayed for a short period of time. Most of the kitchen staff was older and uninteresting, and the guests were mostly older people staying for a week or two. The only compensation, and it wasn't as satisfying as having a girlfriend, was that I made a little over six hundred dollars in tips without spending any money. That money kept me in decent financial shape for my senior year in college.

There were three occasions growing up when I was encouraged to complete my education even when I had no desire to do that. On each occasion, I was sure I would never need that knowledge or ever use it. In each case, my parents and my teachers insisted that it would be important to complete the activity because I would never know when it might prove useful.

I wish I had been more forceful about what I wanted to do. I knew what was not my cup of tea. I followed the advice of my family and teachers, but in the end, I think I knew myself better. I didn't have the conviction to stand up to the advice of others, advice that looked reasonable.

This lesson is only clear now: *completion is usually a good thing; it is satisfying, it can come in handy, but it also can waste a lot of good time when other more important priorities should be attended to.* The concept of finishing what you start is imbedded in most of us. It is only recently that I will stop reading a book if I don't like it. While completing an important task is a good trait to have, there are things in life that do not need to be completed because they are no longer fun or not likely to be useful. *Never ask for advice if you know what you want to do.*

In college, I found that 10 percent of the students did 90 percent of the service for the school. The rest had jobs or were not interested. Some of the professors were awful teachers, unprepared for class, and boring lecturers. Some fraternity brothers were not interested in the welfare of the fraternity but interested only in themselves and their close friends. Students cheated on tests and cut classes regularly. And a man I admired so much turned out much later to be far less successful than I expected him to be. *People often don't live up to your expectations.*

We are all human, and perfection is an ideal I strive for and rarely attain. I had to learn not to trust what people said but what they did. I had to give respect only when it was earned and not upfront when I had no idea if promises would be kept. I came to understand that small details make for perfection. In that regard, a bystander observed Michelangelo as he took a long time retouching every detail of a statue he'd been working on for many days and asked why he bothered with them. Michelangelo replied, "Trifles make perfection, and perfection is no trifle." There were few people willing to go that far, and I had to accept the fact that we are not Michelangelo. Perfection is beyond us. Strive for it, but accept a great deal less.

I had to find a standard for judging people. Hypocrisy is found at the highest levels, and that was below my standard. The higher up in authority, the greater that person's responsibility. I expected a high standard from my teachers, a higher standard from the administration and the highest responsibility from my parents. There were a few bad apples, but most often people at Baruch did live up to my expectations.

Throughout my childhood, into high school, and through college, I spent much of my time figuring out what I did not like. I did not like playing organized sports because other guys were much better than me. I did not like certain foods, certain music, much of art, going to bed early, losing bets, making poor grades in school, taking medicine, and dozens of other items. I didn't want to be an accountant, a lawyer, a doctor, or an Indian chief. *You must recognize when it's not your cup of tea.*

Gradually, very gradually, I found what I did like, and that was much more difficult than determining what I did not like. The reason was obvious. If I rejected something, then I did not have to deal with it except on rare occasions. If I liked something, then I was going to be involved with it on a regular ongoing basis. Since I was going to be with it often, it had to be interesting; it had to excite me; I had to find it challenging to keep me interested and excited about it. The more I learned, the more areas I liked because I found them interesting, exciting, and challenging.

Don't go through college; let college go through you. That remark summed up what I looked for in college. I had been a quiet, shy guy throughout elementary school and high school, and I didn't like myself being that way. I wanted to get the most out of college that was possible to get. That's why I was attracted to Alpha Phi Omega. The fraternity was not just out to have a good time but also to serve the school, to be deeply involved in college life, and to produce value for the students and the school. I sucked the marrow out of college, paraphrasing Robins Williams' remarks in the wonderful movie *Dead Poets' Society*. I let college go through me. I threw myself into extracurricular activities in earnest. I became involved as much as I could in college life, and it changed me into a different person. I grew in many ways by learning how to think critically, how to argue, how to speak without being nervous, how to lead, how to manage, how to present myself as self-assured and mature. I threw away the shyness of my youth to become the man I so desperately wanted to be.

Through my ten-year period from age twelve to age twenty-two, I gained confidence in several ways. I found part-time jobs if I looked for them. I could sell myself to a variety of people looking to hire me. When my family knew the person doing the hiring, the relationship mattered a great deal. This applied even when I knew someone who knew the person doing the hiring. When I was interested in a job, I jumped on the opportunity.

I got a job once I had the opportunity to present myself. I didn't know how much competition there was for any of the jobs I applied for, but at the time, it didn't matter. I gained confidence that I could sell myself. Every time I interviewed for a job, I gave the impression that I really wanted the job. I spoke with conviction that the job was perfect for me, I would enjoy doing it, I wanted the job if offered it, and I never argued about money. I wanted to work, and the job being discussed was always the right job for me. That attitude has put me in good stead over my entire lifetime.

Whatever I did, I did responsibly. If I was delivering meat, I got there as soon as I could and made sure the packages were delivered. If I was tying up a package, I learned the best way to tie up a package. I worked on being efficient, and I focused on getting the work done as quickly as I could. If I was on the waterfront teaching kids how to swim, I did the best I could to teach them well. And as a busboy, I did not rest; I set the table exactly the way I was taught and cleared the tables quickly. I learned to stack the dirty dishes in such a way that I could bring as full a load as possible to the dishwasher in the kitchen.

I learned that I could actually start dating, and that girls would be willing to date me. Once I started dating, my inferiority complex diminished considerably, but I still had little experience dating. Having a girlfriend for a summer helped me to get beyond my belief that women were not interested in me.

I also learned the value of money. I had to work to have money in my pocket. When I wanted to buy my first stereo, I had to pay for it with my own money. The eighty dollars that I spent was my own money, and so the stereo became much more important to me because I paid for it myself.

I don't know whether I grew up at the right time when the economy was growing or if I was good at selling myself or if I was just lucky. I still lived at home with my parents, and they paid for my room and board, but I do know that my summer jobs and college gradually increased my confidence that I could find a job and I could pay for myself. One thing was certain—I was much more committed to continuing my education.

Chapter 6

Iowa State University

City College was a very inexpensive school to attend in 1956. Tuition was free except for a ten-dollar per semester student card, and since I lived at home the only real expense for me was books. My parents supported me through college for the few expenses I required, but my father made it clear that he did not believe it was his responsibility to support me beyond college. He wanted me to continue my education if I wanted to do so, but he couldn't afford to pay for it. The only way I could go to graduate school was on a scholarship of one kind or another.

This seemed right to me since I knew my family's finances were not great. And yet, I was determined to get to graduate school one way or the other. I had taken the few math and statistics classes that the Baruch School had to offer, and I didn't know much about the theory that supported the techniques in these undergraduate classes. I had a very superficial understanding of what I was taught. I knew nothing about how to conduct a professional survey or when to use one statistical technique over another. I knew that statistics was essential for medical research, for inventory control, for forecasting, for relating one event with another event, and for many other issues in society, but what I knew was all elementary and superficial. If I was to become a professional statistician, I needed a lot more education. I had to go to graduate school where I could major in statistics, especially mathematical statistics. I didn't know which graduate schools had programs in this subject; I only knew that I had to go on to graduate school to major in statistics.

I approached one of the economics professors at Baruch and asked him for advice on where to apply. He gave me a long list of schools, and I followed up by writing to twenty of them, some of them the very best and some of them good enough to get a good education and more likely to offer me some kind of a scholarship. I asked each about their statistics programs, the courses for a master's degree, and about information on tuition assistance. It was clear that I had to get some sort of scholarship or graduate school was out.

I heard that the US government had some sort of scholarship program that required taking a standardized nationwide exam in mathematics. It was something like the Graduate Record Exam. The winners would receive a substantial amount of money to go to graduate school. I signed up for the exam.

I was frightened about taking that exam. I had one year of calculus with no additional mathematics beyond that. I was up against math majors from great schools all across the country. I was naïve about taking competitive exams like this, and just showed up without any preparation.

In the meantime, I had narrowed the list of twenty schools down to twelve, and they were in some sort of order: Stanford University, University of Michigan, University of Minnesota, University of Iowa, University of Buffalo, and several others. I had eliminated all the Ivy League schools, for I thought I had no chance to get into them, and they would be too expensive even if I did get in. I kept my fingers crossed and prayed that someone would like what they saw on my application.

I took the exam late in 1959 and did not hear about the results until some time in March. A letter arrived, and I opened it with fear and trepidation about what I would read. The letter congratulated me about doing well, not well enough to be a finalist to receive scholarship money but well enough to receive an honorable mention. Honorable mention was nice, but it was like coming in second when the only thing that counted was being first. That was very disappointing, for I knew that now I had to depend on a school to give me some sort of scholarship.

Gradually, I heard from some of the schools I applied to for admission and scholarship. Most either rejected me completely or accepted me with no scholarship of any kind. However, two schools did find money for me: University of Iowa and University of Buffalo. They were not my first choice, but at least I was going to graduate school. I checked with my economics advisor to see which school was better, and he said Buffalo was probably a better choice because I had applied to the wrong school in Iowa. Instead of the University of Iowa, I should have applied to Iowa State University. I was disappointed to hear this, but that is life.

Living in New York City, being very parochial and uninformed, I had no idea of the difference between the University of Iowa in Iowa City and Iowa State University in Ames. I probably thought they were the same school. After checking into the difference between the University of Iowa and Iowa State University, I discovered that the statistics program I really wanted was at Iowa State University, but I hadn't applied there.

And then a remarkable thing happened. I received two letters out of the blue, one from Iowa State University and the other from Ohio State University. Both letters said that they had received information from the mathematics exam that I had taken, and they knew I was an honorable mention, an award they were impressed enough with to invite me to apply to their department in mathematics or statistics. I was thrilled to get these letters, for here was the very school, Iowa State University, that I should have applied to and missed, and now they were asking me to apply to them. I thanked myself for taking the scholarship exam even though I did not win. Now a statistics department wanted me to apply to their graduate school! I concluded that *if you want it bad enough, you will find a way*.

Quickly, I filled out the applications for both schools and sent them off. I waited on pins and needles to hear from them and did not get any response. Finally, it was time to let the two schools that had offered me scholarships know whether I was accepting either of them or not. It was early April in 1960, and I had to make a decision. I didn't really want to go to either school that offered me money, so I put together a priority list of my first choice, second choice, and so on. I went to the bank to get twenty dollars in quarters and dimes to make person-to-person phone calls from a public telephone booth to the chairmen of each of the statistics departments of the schools I had applied to. I called Stanford University first, and the chairman of the department told me that I was accepted into the school's graduate program, but he could not grant me any money in my first year. He said that he probably could find money for me in my second year of graduate school. I thanked him for having confidence enough to accept me, but I had offers from other schools, and even though I truly wanted to go to Stanford, I couldn't afford to pay my way for the first year. I didn't even consider the cost of going to California from New York City or how often I would want to go home to see my parents.

Next, I called the University of Michigan and reached the chairman of the statistics department who quickly told me that I was not accepted. I was unhappy to hear that, thanked him, and moved on to the University of Wisconsin. I was declined there too, and so it went. I did call Ohio State University, the very school that asked me to apply, and I was surprised when they rejected me. I asked myself how it was possible to be rejected given that they had asked me to apply. Only later I discovered that they were more interested in finding mathematics majors rather than statistics majors, but at the time it was a blow to my ego. Finally, on the sixth phone call to Iowa State University, the chairman of the statistics department, Professor T. A. Bancroft, said, "Yes, we will not only accept you, but we will also offer you free tuition and a teaching assistantship that will pay you a few thousand dollars." I was thrilled to hear it, decided right then on the telephone that I would accept that offer, and asked the chairman to send me a telegram to acknowledge the conversation. I then would be able to decline the other offers with some degree of confidence that I had a real offer from Iowa State. It was a lucky break for me—*persistence produces its own luck.*

The next day, the telegram arrived, and I told my parents that I was going to Ames, Iowa, about as far removed from the culture I had grown up in Brooklyn. In Brooklyn, I was living in the heart of the major US city compared to a small university town in rural Iowa. I was living in a very strong Jewish environment, and there were very few Jews in Ames. I was among a strong Democratic New York City population, while Iowa was strongly Republican in its orientation. I knew nothing of Angus cows or farming or growing corn, and all of that was part of being in Iowa. And then there was the requirement to live in a dorm, and that was not a part of my life, for I lived at home during my college years. Still, all of it did not matter—I was going to graduate school.

In planning to go to graduate school without having to pay for it, I started with twenty schools to cover all the bases. I narrowed down my choices to a dozen schools because they fit the curriculum I wanted.

I applied to them all, even though I had to pay an application fee. This was my aggressive approach. *When you know what you want, go after it aggressively.* The taking of the graduate school exam was part of being aggressive even though I had no idea that universities received the results and went after students with honorable mentions. That was lucky for me, for it got me to a school I should have applied to and didn't.

Today, I know high school students are doing what I did for graduate school: picking several schools with at least one of them a safe bet to be sure that they will go to college. I didn't have a safe school in my mind. I had a priority list, but I had no idea which ones would accept me. I overdid it in applying to a dozen schools, but I was desperate to go to graduate school. The strategy worked. It paid to be aggressive when I knew what I wanted.

After I graduated from CCNY, I looked for a summer job once again. One of my statistics professors knew of a summer job with one of his colleagues who had been hired to consult with Kitty Kelly Shoes, a retail shoe store catering to women. He was in need of a junior person to help him organize an inventory control system for the stores in New York. I got the job.

To determine the amount of inventory that a store should carry depends on the average number of shoes sold and the variability in the sales level that is measured by the standard deviation. I was familiar with the Poisson distribution that the consultant wanted me to use because it made the calculation quite simple. Using this distribution, the standard deviation is equal to the square root of the average sales figure. For example, if sales for the week for a given shoe is 16 pairs, then the standard deviation is 4. If you double the standard deviation and add it to the average, then the probability of shoes sales for a week exceeding 24 (16 + 8) is about 5 percent, and that is often the upper bound inventory that a company should reasonably hold with 95 percent confidence that it would not be exceeded. This is what I did for the summer: calculate the average for a shoe size for a given period of time, calculate the standard deviation, and calculate the upper bound number for that shoe size. I did this for every shoe size for every type of shoe, and that required hundreds of calculations. Once I understood the process, it was easy enough to do the calculations. I had no idea if they implemented these numbers and never met with Kitty

Kelly management or anyone else, except the consultant who hired me. It was good money for the summer, but I learned very little about statistics except to become very familiar with the Poisson distribution. It convinced me that while I knew a little about the statistics I learned in college, I still knew very little about how to define a problem or how to find a solution for it.

That September, I found myself on a train to Chicago and then on a bus to Ames. I wrote to my mother that for more than a hundred miles I was looking at Black Angus cows and corn five feet high. Corn and cows, corn and cows, compared to Brooklyn it was quite a difference. Still, it was very exciting going to graduate school. For the first time in my life, I knew I was on the right track for a career, and I was committed to doing the very best that I could.

That first semester was one of the most trying times of my life. I was being challenged mathematically in ways I had never thought possible. I was taking courses on mathematical statistics that required a deeper understanding of calculus than I knew, and I was in class with other students that had much stronger math backgrounds than I had. I had to study the material over and over again to truly grasp it. I was scared I would fail the exams because I was struggling with all these new concepts with a marginal background. I would sit for hours reading the material and trying to do the problems. My intellectual understanding was being pushed to the limits. There was a famous book on probability by William Feller called *An Introduction to Probability Theory and its Applications* that had some of the most difficult probability problems I had ever seen. And the book by Alexander McFarlane Mood that was called *Introduction to the Theory of Statistics* was no easier. I was drowning and I knew it. I wondered whether I was cut out to be a statistician and thought that I could flunk out of graduate school that very first semester.

It was only near the end of the semester that the material seemed to make sense. I was thankful that I was beginning to understand the mathematics behind statistics and that I could solve many of the problems I had struggled to grasp all semester long. When the final exams were over and the marks were posted, I was astonished to learn that I had passed all my courses. It was definitely time to celebrate. I was rooming with Eugene, another Jewish guy from New York who had gone to my same college even though we had not met in college. It was natural that we would room together since we had similar backgrounds and were both statistics majors. I liked to drink gin, but I did not like to drink it straight. Someone had told me that the combination of gin and sloe gin was a great drink, and I started drinking the combination in a fifty-fifty mixture. Gin and sloe gin were the right combination to get seriously drunk. That's exactly what I did the day I found that I passed all my courses. It was the middle of winter, but all of my friends, the half dozen or so first year graduate students, decided that we would pile into a car, go downtown to Ames, and have a celebration at one of the bars. I started quickly with my sloe gin and gin combination in the dorm even before I got into the car and got drunk as a skunk. I don't remember anything about that night, except what my friends told me. They told me that I stuck half my body out of the car as we drove into town, and I told everyone I saw that I passed my exams. They told me I was a happy, friendly drunk and would talk to anyone. When we got back to the dorm, I couldn't even walk up the stairs. My friends placed me up against the wall of the staircase halfway up to my dorm room to rest. I just stood against the wall and gradually slid down the wall to lie down on the landing. They helped me up the stairs, tossed me into my bed, and I slept the entire night through in my clothes. I was a friendly drunk all right, a nice guy totally inebriated and fun to be with, but I don't remember anything at all. I was just glad to celebrate passing all my courses, the hardest semester of my young life, and to tell the truth, no other semester was ever that challenging again.

That first semester changed my life professionally and psychologically. I did not have the mathematical background for such a rigorous program, so I was worried that I might fail. My worries were justified. I struggled day after day, putting in an enormous amount of hours reading the text again and again, struggling with the math, struggling with the problems at the end of each chapter, and scared that the material was too difficult for me. My struggles were not just for one course but for all the courses I was taking as well. I still have the books I used back then in my basement, a testament to the difficulties I was having in mastering the material and the pride I had at eventually understanding enough of it to do reasonably well on the final exam.

I had experienced this learning process before. It was only near the end of the semester after struggling with the material day after day that a solid understanding showed up. It is hard to explain just how that understanding occurs except that it happens after immense effort and frustration. I was unwilling to quit, I wanted to succeed in statistics, and I knew that other students were capable of grasping the material, so I pressed on. It is easy to give up in frustration when the material is difficult, and I was not one to ask for help from other students or the teacher. I just pressed on, working the problems, asking myself what I knew and what I did not know and kept focusing on what I had to understand. Mathematical statistics is not easy, and most people have a difficult time with it, but I knew I had a mathematical gift, and I believed that I was capable of grasping the material. While I had been frustrated in other classes before, I was never challenged as much as that first semester. I was making the transition from a business school with a practical orientation to a business world to a mathematical world devoted to the theory behind the practice. I was being asked to understand the fundamental mathematics that proved the formulas that were implemented in practice, as well as their limitations. That was a difficult transition. I look back on it now as one of the major changes that happened in my life. Iowa State gave me that opportunity, but in the end it was my challenge to overcome, and I am proud of having risen to that challenge. It wasn't easy, and that is why the success I achieved was so meaningful.

That first year at Iowa State, I had an assistantship that required me to take care of the statistics laboratory, a required course for most of the undergraduates. My job was to help students understand the problems they were asked to solve and show them how to use the 10 or 12 column Marchant and Monroe calculators. This was 1961, before the advent of the computer. If you needed to square an X value and a Y value at the same time, which was necessary to calculate the standard deviation, then you put the X value on the left column of the calculator and the Y value on the right column. When you squared the entire number, you got the square of X, the square of Y, and twice the value of X times Y in the middle of the answer. In certain statistical problems, you need all three values. It was a neat trick. Today, the software will do it all for you, but if you want to learn statistics, then you need to do it yourself if you want to understand the process.

There is nothing that builds confidence more than being the teacher in the front of the room teaching students who know considerably less than you know. I knew a great deal more than the students in the room, and I did it for several classes on an ongoing basis. Of course, I had professors to turn to in case I needed guidance. For me, the labs were easy work even though there were thirty to forty students there. Usually, most of the students knew what to do or asked one of their friends, so it wasn't a challenging job. It even gave me time to study for my own classes while the lab was going on, provided no one was asking me for help.

Becoming a good teacher takes time and experience. I wasn't a good teacher in graduate school because I had limited experience teaching. I had learned the material only a few years earlier and had to rely heavily on the book I was using. I did not know what problems the students might have, so I didn't have a chance to work through an easy way to answer their questions. And I did not have the public speaking experience to be able to have fun in class to break up the serious subjects.

The winters I spent in Ames were bitterly cold. I wore an arctic-type jacket with a hood that kept me warm in very cold weather. I needed it. There were a few days when the temperature hit thirty below zero, not the wind chill temperature, but the actual temperature. We had several feet of snow one winter and it was difficult trudging through the icy snow on the sidewalks and the campus. Still, the focus was always on being indoors studying.

The closest Jewish organization was a synagogue in Des Moines, about thirty miles away. There were few Jews on campus, and most of them were graduate students. There were only a handful of Jewish professors too. As a result, I felt totally out of touch with being Jewish and asked my mother if she would send me a care package of Jewish food, which she did. She sent lots of salami, a few knishes, a dozen or so bagels, and that was a welcome addition. With the weather so cold, I merely hung the salami outside the window, and it kept for weeks until it was totally consumed.

After my first semester, several Jewish guys in the graduate dorm decided that we could do very nicely if we left the dorm and rented a house just off campus. Luckily, we found a huge four-bedroom house fully furnished just across from a sorority house, two blocks from campus. The four of us rented the house, and we all moved in: Eugene, my roommate in the dorm, Ernie, David, and me. The four bedrooms were upstairs, and the downstairs had a huge kitchen, a huge living room, a huge dining room, and a porch that ran around two sides of the house on the corner piece of property. With so few Jewish students and faculty on campus, it was nice to have a little Judaism for the four of us.

I don't remember much of the second semester, except that I had made the transition from a business school that did not focus on mathematics to a mathematical statistics department using serious mathematics. The longer I stayed at Iowa State, the easier the courses became because I became familiar with the mathematical techniques required to be a serious statistician. In that sense, I am forever grateful to Iowa State for raising my level of mathematical knowledge, and it served as the transition school on the way to my PhD.

My roommate Ernie worked in the chemistry lab and washed out the various pieces of equipment with ethyl alcohol. Methol alcohol is poisonous and will kill you, but ethyl alcohol is 90 percent pure alcohol or 180-proof liquor. Ernie would bring home a gallon of it, and we would mix it with orange juice and other juices. The punch we made really had a punch. You could get totally drunk on it after only a couple of drinks, and the best part of it was that the alcohol was free. With our large house, we could invite as many graduate students as we knew for a party without much additional cost.

We had a few parties for the sixty to eighty people we knew, and most of them got drunk. One guy was so drunk that he couldn't drive home in his car parked outside our house, and he knew it. He just cuddled up in the car and fell asleep. Somewhere in the night, the police came by, saw him sleeping in his car, woke him up, decided he was drunk, and took him to jail even though he was not driving. He was sleeping in the driver's seat, and that was enough for the police. I guess they didn't want to take a chance that he would drive the car drunk.

Regarding dating at Iowa State, it was difficult to date undergraduate women, and I was not alone. Graduate work required difficult intellectual work and long hours. We had little time to party. In addition, it was difficult to date undergraduate women because the women were from Iowa while many of the graduate students were from out of state. Sorority women especially had no interest in dating graduate students from outside Iowa, and I understood why. We were unlikely to be interested in getting serious, especially a nice Jewish boy like me from New York City. The women preferred men from Iowa, men they might marry and still live in the state they knew, so sorority women wanted to date undergraduate men, especially from fraternities. It was frustrating for most of the graduate students I knew.

Across the street from our house was an undergraduate women's sorority, and we marveled at how attractive the women were. We often saw them walking in the same direction that we were walking. We four graduate students tried to meet some of these women by calling them, by inviting them to our parties, but they never came.

Even though we knew they would not be interested in any of us, we were determined to at least meet one of them. I hit on an idea to send them a huge bouquet of flowers with a lovely poem and a mystery name. We invited one of them to call our phone number. We sent them a second mystery card, and eventually their curiosity got the best of them, and I set up a meeting with one of the women at the Union, the central meeting place on campus. Once she found out that I was one of the graduate students living across the street from her, the conversation ended. Still, it was fun making this happen—a small interlude away from the difficult task of mathematical statistics. As a man, I learned one thing: *with creativity and mystery, a woman will want to meet you.*

One day in the rented house, I was sitting at a desk that had been left in the house. It was a big wooden desk, an old oak desk with plenty of drawers. The desk was empty, but I was curious to see if anything had been left there. One by one, I took drawers out from the desk and looked behind them, thinking that perhaps something had fallen behind the drawer. Sure enough, there was an envelope behind the top left drawer. The envelope was dated 1901 and was addressed to twins that lived in the house we were renting. Inside the envelope was a letter from one of their aunts and enclosed was a dollar bill, a huge greenback dated 1898. The letter stated that the aunt was sending the dollar to the twins so they could each have fifty cents. I had no thought of finding the owner of the letter because the house had be sold and we were paying rent to an agent. Being a coin collector, I was thrilled to find a US dollar so old and a story that went with it. Over the years, I read that letter many times, and each time it brings back memories of living in that house and my days at Iowa State. I still have the letter and the dollar bill, and someday I will frame them.

I had worked each summer since high school for the next year's schooling, so at the end of my first year in graduate school, I began looking for a summer job. Fortunately, the statistics department was well known by corporations looking for statisticians. As a result, I landed a summer job in Kansas City at the Bendix Corporation. I would have preferred to be in the New York area to be able to see my parents, but I went where the job was, and the job was in Kansas City. I drove there in my Chevy, a car I bought used for four hundred dollars, found an apartment with two other guys, and moved in for the summer.

The job at Bendix was to be my first professional job, but in the end, I learned nothing at all for one simple reason: I never did any work. The problem was that Bendix was involved in contract work for the Department of Defense, and I needed secret clearance to work there. I had never been cleared, so I had to work in the "Red Zone" until my clearance came through. The Red Zone was designed so that my boss could come to see me and could give me a vague assignment, but I could not leave the Red Zone.

I saw my boss once or twice a week for about fifteen minutes. He could not give me a detailed problem to solve because the work was classified, so he always spoke in general terms. As a result, I had no real problem to solve, and the amount of work on my part was trivial, requiring nothing more than the conversations I had with my boss. The rest of the time, I read professional articles or studied one thing or another. I was free to do whatever I wanted 90 percent of the time.

Bendix was totally reimbursed by the government for my time, but I thought it was a ridiculous waste of money to have me sit in the Red Zone, essentially doing nothing for the summer waiting on my clearance. I worked at Bendix from May to September and was never cleared. I never knew anything about the work I was to do, I never met anyone except my boss, and I was thoroughly frustrated at not being able to seriously contribute.

I filled out all the detailed questions to receive clearance, which required me to list where my parents were born in Europe, list all the homes that I lived in for the past ten years, and a host of other questions. I thought the clearance process would stop once my job was over, but it continued even after I returned to Iowa State University that fall. Several months after leaving Bendix, an FBI agent showed up in Brooklyn on the street where my parents lived. As my mother told the story, and she loved to tell it, the FBI agent walked over to a group of women who were talking to each other on the street where my parents lived. He flashed his FBI credentials and told the group of women that he was checking on the Lipis family. Could the women say what kind of family the Lipises were? Do the Lipises have a drinking problem or a drug problem? How well do the Lipis parents treat their children? The women merely pointed to my mother who was standing in the group and told the FBI agent, "If you want the answers to these questions, why don't you ask this woman? She is Mrs. Lipis!"

I am sure the FBI agent was a little embarrassed, and my mother always laughed when she told that story. Shortly after that, in February 1962, I was notified by the US government that I received secret clearance. I thought how wasteful the government was in paying Bendix for my summer job and then sending an FBI agent to clear me for a job I was no longer doing. In one respect it was useful. A year later, I needed top-secret clearance and Q clearance for something to do with atomic energy, and those clearances arrived much quicker without bothering me or my parents.

Soon after I arrived in Kansas City, I was invited to a party arranged by my roommates, who also happened to be Jewish. I was thrilled to be at a party of Jewish people my age. I had no real contact with Jewish women for more than year while at Iowa State, and being twenty-three years old, I was certainly ready to be dating. At the party, I walked up to a lovely, attractive woman and introduced myself. She told me later that she was impressed by the simple introduction, "Hello, my name is Allen Lipis. What's your name?" Over the years, I have always been struck at the familiarity that people take by calling others by their first name without knowing them. I always introduce myself by my first and last names because I am more comfortable doing this because I am proud of my last name and because I think a little formality is important in beginning any relationship.

The lady told me her name was Shifra, and we got on so well at that first meeting that I asked her out for a date. That was the beginning of the first serious relationship I had with a woman. Shifra was a beautiful person, easy to be with, playful, intelligent, willing to go to new places with me, and easy to talk to. We had a lot in common, both seriously Jewish, both having wonderful parents, and both interested in building a serious relationship. We spent the entire summer together, taking walks, going on picnics, and talking on the phone.

I had a summer girlfriend in the Catskill Mountains several years earlier, but it was just a summer romance that ended soon after the summer was over. Shifra was a totally different matter. I liked Shifra enough to travel back to Kansas City a couple of times after I returned to Iowa State for my second year there, and Shifra came to my school for a weekend to attend a football game with me. I liked Shifra a great deal, and had I stayed in Kansas City, our relationship almost certainly would have blossomed. However, I had two problems to deal with. The first was the distance. I could not see Shifra often enough to continue the relationship we had over the summer. The summer was not long enough to cement our relationship such that I could put up with the long distance between us. *Long-distance romances don't work.* The second reason was that I had a serious commitment to graduate school. I was now teaching a class on statistics for the first time, and it took a lot of work preparing for that class. I also had my own graduate classes that were demanding, requiring tremendous amounts of time studying outside of class. Finally, I had a master's thesis to write, and that took the most time of all, for I knew nothing about game theory, and game theory was my topic. There was also the matter of passing a language exam and a few other details to be sure I fulfilled all the requirements for my master's degree. I had very little time for Shifra, and reluctantly I broke off our relationship. I felt sad about it, but my education was the top priority. Long-distance romances didn't fit into my plan.

And the end of the summer of 1961, Eugene and I drove from Ames back to New York City to see our parents. It was 1,100 miles and driving at 60 miles an hour took us 24 hours to make the trip. We took my Chevy and switched driving, each of us taking four-hour turns while the other relaxed or slept in the backseat. The trip to New York was uneventful; we reconnected with family and then drove back to Ames. About forty miles from school, having driven for close to a full day, I was driving in the rain while Eugene was sleeping in the backseat. In addition to the rain, I was tired, anxious to finish the drive, and driving too fast for the conditions on the road. As we approached a stop sign, I hit the brakes hard, slid on the wet road and gravel that was there, went through the intersection and swiped a truck going in the opposite direction that had stopped at the stop sign. Had I had a clear mind, I would have taken my foot off the brake, stopped sliding sideways, gained control of the car, and stayed on my side of the road, although I would have gone through the stop sign. My instincts were to stop the car by pressing hard on the brake, and that caused the car to slide sideways, hitting the truck in the front with the back of my car.

I was not hurt, but Eugene bumped his head on the door handle of our car in the backseat; he had no lasting problems. The man in the truck, however, had a lot of glass in his head from one of the windows shattered by the impact; he had to go to the hospital to have the glass removed. I was embarrassed, emotionally upset, critical of myself for letting the accident happen, and relived the event many times. If only I had taken my foot off of the brake, if only I had driven a little slower. If only we had stopped for some rest because I was so tired. It was the worst accident of my life. Like most accidents, that accident did not need to happen. At least I had the presence of mind to go to the hospital where the truck driver was being taken care of and apologized to him for my stupidity. There was nothing he said or could say that was nice, so he remained quiet while I said my apologies.

I had a huge dent in the back left side of my Chevy, and I could not afford to fix it. I did not have collision insurance, so I decided not to fix the car. After a mechanic looked under the car, he told me that the frame of the car was slightly bent, and eventually the differential would stop working and the car would stop completely. He was right. I drove the car very little while finishing my second year in graduate school and then moved to Columbus, Ohio, to start my job. Soon after I arrived, I attended someone's home, and on the way back to my apartment, the car gave out a huge noise and stopped working. I had to call someone to take me back to my apartment. The differential on the car was shot, but the motor of the car was still in perfect shape. I sold the car to a guy I knew at work for ten dollars, and he towed the car home so his teenage son could play around with the motor and the other parts of the car that worked. I was sad to see my first car destroyed this way, but the experience taught me how dangerous a car can be and how important it is to stop when you are tired and not clear minded.

In my second year at graduate school, the Statistics Department asked me if I would teach instead of spending time in the statistics laboratory. I agreed and took on the class on Business Statistics. I had never seen the book though I knew most of the topics in the book since I had taken courses like that at Baruch.

It was fun to be in the front of the room as the teacher, and over time, I think I improved. *Teaching builds your confidence; you have to know the material better than your students.* This is reinforced when your students do well on your exams. You then know that your students are learning, and you helped them. For every hour of class time, I spent three to five hours preparing. I viewed my job as a teacher to make the course as simple as possible, but not too simple. My own studying habits helped a great deal because I tried to simplify a subject to its essence, to understand the basics, and to be sure that I could solve the problems in each chapter of the text. I was teaching business statistics, and the essence of the course was to be able to solve various business problems with statistical techniques.

One incident is worthy of note. I had a desk in an open area with about a dozen other graduate students. I used it to meet a student there. I also kept a notebook in my desk of the students in the class with the marks they received on the tests that I gave them. Some time in the middle of the semester, I gave the class of thirty-five students a midterm exam, marked their grades in my book, and left the book in the front drawer of the desk. A week later, I noticed that one of the grades in the book was changed. The change was noticeable because I could see the real grade below the new grade. It was a poor alteration, and I had to do something about it.

Confronting unethical behavior is not easy. I struggled about what to do. I considered asking for all the tests back. I thought this would be unwise because the student that changed his grade could change his answers on the exam or he could say he lost the exam. I could challenge the student directly, telling him what his grade was, and asking him for his exam to prove otherwise. I was nervous about confronting the student directly not just because I would be embarrassing him but also because I was scared to confront him directly. After all, this was my first teaching assignment. I decided that I would tell the class that I wasn't sure about all the grades, so I was going to read all of them off in class, which I did. I said that if any of you differ with this grade, come see me. When I came to the student whose grade had been changed, I read the original grade, which I knew to be 50 (the grade had been changed to 80). No one challenged any of the grades that I read, so I knew for sure that the grade had been changed. I could have brought the student up on disciplinary charges, but I thought better of it and moved on. I don't recall what that student received at the end of the course; that wasn't the issue. The issue was that I did not like anyone looking for an easy way out of a difficult course. I was not going to let someone take advantage of me, and I did not like cheaters.

I should have confronted the unethical behavior by meeting face to face with the student, asking him for his exam, grilling him on how the grade was changed, and threatening to bring him up on discipline charges to the college for changing his grade. I did not have the courage to do that back then as a graduate student, and it was wrong for me not to do it. That student needed to be taught a lesson, and I let him off the hook by merely putting his grade back to where it belonged.

As a requirement for my master's degree, Iowa State required that I pass a language exam administered by the language department. Each graduate student could pick any book in a foreign language, study any hundred pages in the book, and be able to translate thirty lines selected by the language department at random in thirty minutes. Students were not allowed to take a dictionary into the exam, but they were allowed to take a list of words and their definitions with them from the pages that they studied.

I had taken four years of Spanish in high school, and I was familiar with Spanish, but I had forgotten a lot of my knowledge in the four to five years since leaving high school. I was never very good at foreign languages, so I worried about passing that language exam. My best choice was to pick Spanish for my language exam. Spanish, however, was not considered an acceptable language for statistics since very few statistics papers and books are written in that language. I had a choice to pass the language exam in French, German, or Russian. Naturally, I choose French since it was fairly close to Spanish.

Fortunately, other graduate students were in a similar position, and over time the statistics graduate students hit on a very simple strategy to pass the exam. One easy statistics book in French had been translated by other students, and this was the selected text that all statistics students used to study for their language exam. The text was relatively easy to understand because a lot of the pages had mathematical formulas, and a lot of the words in French were very similar to words in English. I also had a set of translated words page by page to make the test easier.

I studied the book off and on for about a month with and without the translation and compiled my own list of words that I had difficulty with so that I would not be totally confused about the translation. When I was ready, I went to the language department with my book, told them I had studied the first hundred pages, and the professor picked a page at random. The page was not difficult with my word list, and I passed the exam on the first try. I was thrilled, for I thought that this might be the one thing that could hold up my graduation. I was making good progress on my thesis, I had a great professor to guide me, and I knew that I would be able to complete the thesis no matter what.

Computers in the early '60s were huge devices, taking up the entire size of a bedroom, and they were not very powerful. Today's laptop computers are a hundred or more times more powerful than the IBM computer that we used at Iowa State. I had to take a course on computer technology, and I could never write the Fortran programs exactly right to make my software work. One small mistake and the program would not work. If a comma was missing or in the wrong place, the program would not work. I was not detailed enough to get my programs to work, and that convinced me that detailed work, such as writing computer software, was not my forte. I got a C in that class, a failing grade in graduate school, and that set in place my belief that computer science was not one of my strengths.

For my master's thesis, I had a business orientation away from pure mathematical statistics. I wanted to do something in that field. I had never done a serious research paper in mathematics or statistics, so I was very worried that I would not be creative enough to find a topic, let alone do something original. Fortunately, I was assigned to Professor Herbert T. David, a really brilliant man who was doing work in operations research and who consulted to other departments at the university. He was not only patient with his students, but also capable of understanding their strengths and weaknesses. He met with me and suggested that I take on a problem in game theory that had been solved in one form but also could be approached from a different perspective. I knew nothing about game theory, but I accepted the idea because I had no other possibility in mind.

The topic dealt with two opposing planes coming at each other with missiles. As the planes approached each other, the probability of a kill increased. The issue was when to fire their missiles. I dealt with the case where one plane had one missile and the other plane had two missiles. The question was when should each plane fire their missiles to have the greatest probability of killing the other plane? The thesis was called "Noisy Duels as Limits of Game Iterations."

As I write this, it is now fifty years after I finished that master's thesis, and I haven't looked at it since I finished it. I got on the Internet, went to Iowa State, found my thesis, and ordered it from the library. I tried reading it, and I was impressed at what I had written, but I must admit that I don't understand it completely anymore. This is not unusual for me. After I finished a course and passed it with a high grade, I usually forgot much of what I learned. That was true if I crammed for the final exam. There is much that I learned, and a lot of it, sadly, I forgot. *What remains is education.*

To learn difficult material you must be determined and disciplined to struggle with it over time. This is one of the most important lessons that I learned in my life. To master anything difficult you have to put the time and effort into struggling through the learning process. This is true in sports, in math, in writing, in acting, in cooking, and just about anything else you can think of. If the effort is way over your head, you might fail. That's what I felt in graduate school, and I needed discipline and determination to keep going.

The first semester of graduate work in mathematical statistics at Iowa State University was the most difficult learning experience of my life. It is difficult to convey the hopelessness I felt not understanding the books I was studying or feeling completely lost in class trying to grasp what the professor was saying. This was to be my career, not some class I would not care about after it was over. I had to learn the material or flunk out of graduate school. It was that clear to me, and day after day, I was angry with myself for not being able to understand the material. It took great discipline and determination to stay with these subjects when I felt I was in a fog, seeing a glimmer of understanding here and there, but still in a fog of clear understanding. Staying in that fog for months and working for a clear understanding was not easy to do. It would have been much easier to quit, but I am not a quitter and becoming a statistician was very important for me.

Once I overcame my first semester, I had a similar problem writing my master's thesis. I had no idea how to proceed even though I did have an excellent advisor. Still, he did not help me solve the problems I faced. I had to struggle to figure out how to proceed, what might work, try out an approach, and see if that made sense. This is the creative process: thinking about a problem you have no idea how to define, let alone solve. It takes strong determination and discipline to stay with the problem until you find a breakthrough. In quite simple terms, it is what separates those who can from those who can't.

As I neared graduation, I interviewed with a number of excellent companies that came to the campus. I was asked to interview at four companies: IBM in New York, a major oil company in New York, the Office of Naval Research in Washington, D.C., and Battelle Memorial Institute in Columbus, Ohio. I had two major criteria besides salary that I was going to use to determine which job to accept. The first was to be sure I would not be drafted. In the early 1960s, the draft existed though it was after the Korean War and before the Vietnam War. I had been deferred from the draft by going to college and then to graduate school. After graduate school, I would be eligible to be drafted unless I worked for a company involved in the nation's defense and had a job related to national security. The second criteria was to be somewhere on the East Coast so that I could visit my parents and other relatives in New York.

I received job offers from four high-quality companies because I had a degree in mathematical statistics from Iowa State University. That was my union card. *Advanced education is nothing more than a union card. It gets you in the door.* I would not have been considered for these companies if I had not gotten that master's degree. The interviews I went through could not have measured what I knew. There wasn't enough time for that. Rather, the companies relied on my degree to indicate that I had the proper training to do the work they wanted done.

The proof of what you know is what you do after you are hired. If you have learned very little to get that degree, then your lack of knowledge will become obvious. The degree is important, but it is what you know that counts.

At IBM, one of the staff interviewing me asked me a mathematical question that I was not able to answer, and I thought the job there was not a good fit for me. At the oil company, they discussed having me work on a fifty-million-dollar investment, and I was overwhelmed by the number and the responsibility that I would have to take on. I was used to making less than a thousand dollars per year, mostly working during the summer. I had never paid for my education, and ten thousand dollars was a lot of money for me. At college, I was asked what I thought

I would earn annually at the peak of my career. At the time, teachers were making five thousand dollars per year, so I said twenty thousand dollars would be the maximum amount I could hope to earn in any given year. As it turned out, I was off by a huge factor.

The oil company was talking to me about evaluating an investment of fifty million dollars, a number I could not possibly fathom. I was terrified of the thought that I would be responsible, even in a small way, for so much money. I decided I was not ready for such an assignment.

Then I interviewed with the Office of Naval Research, and they discussed having me join a team that analyzed the impact of various weapons. We spoke about kill ratios and other items that dealt with killing people. I came from a culture where life was precious, and while I certainly would serve in the military if drafted, I did not want to focus my professional career on how to maximize the way in which we kill or maim people even if they are the enemy. I considered such a job to be very honorable, but it wasn't what I was looking for.

At Battelle Memorial Institute, I found what I was looking for. The job was to join an operations analysis group of twelve people devoted to helping companies and governments become more efficient. While Battelle was known for its tremendous research capabilities in chemistry, metallurgy, and other sciences, it had a group involved in consulting to various industries. There was a lot of work there for the defense industry. I took the job because Columbus, Ohio, was a lot closer to New York than Ames, Iowa, I could continue my draft deferment, and the job was interesting. My starting salary was $8,100 per year.

Chapter 7

Finding a Career and a Wife

I started at Battelle Memorial Institute in May 1962 and found myself attached to a team trying to improve the railroads. Battelle had sold a consulting assignment to seven major railroads to analyze how commercial traffic moved over the rails. At that time, commercial rail traffic was moving at an average of eight miles per hour, a rather pathetic speed. Part of the problem was that rail traffic moved on a single rail in both directions; therefore, one of the trains had to be diverted to a side track until the other train passed, and then that train could get back on the main track again. Battelle's assignment was to maximize the overall speed of all the trains.

As part of the team, I was given a railroad pass that allowed me to get on any of those seven railroads free of charge. Several times I used it to take an overnight train from Columbus to New York City to see my parents. I paid about eighteen dollars for a sleeper compartment and woke up in Pennsylvania Station in Manhattan early in the morning. It was a nice fringe benefit.

One time, the railroad team went out to Tulsa to view the way in which trains were broken down and reorganized in a train yard. The most interesting part of the trip was meeting the CEO of the railroad—he had his girlfriend with him even though it was clear that he was married. I was astonished that he had a mistress with him and that he would flaunt her to us, seven men from Battelle! He did not know us—we were just working to improve his railroad. I was obviously a naïve guy when it came to women to begin with, and I certainly did not grow up in an atmosphere that either condoned a mistress or had them. For me, it was so alien to my upbringing to see such an open display of infidelity. It made a significant impression on me about the way other people lived. None of my colleagues ever made mention of this, so I don't know how they reacted to see this open display of infidelity. It is still alien to me.

As the newest and youngest member of the team, I had very little responsibility. I would attend meetings, travel to see some of the railroads, and do a few other minor things, but for the most part of the day, I was free to learn on my own. Just out of graduate school with little practical experience, I was at a loss as to what to do. As a result, I read many statistical journals and other technical documents to stay busy, but it wasn't what I thought the job would be like. Over time, I felt isolated, an insignificant member of the team with little responsibility and plenty of time to do as I pleased.

This taught me that *new employees need plenty of guidance or they will be inefficient*. This is a no-brainer. New people need training, often lots of it. Some companies have a formal training program, but small companies can't afford to do that. Regardless, the senior people need to find the time to meet with the new person and answer questions about the assignment. It takes more time than the senior person might want to give, but that is the only way to train a new person.

I found the process frustrating as a new person in the job. I never had enough access to the person I reported to when I had a problem. *If you want your company to be effective, then find the time to help new people on the job.*

I don't want to imply that our railroad assignment was a failure. It wasn't. Our team found that trains were traveling on the same track in opposite directions, and they wrote a program that helped improve the performance of these trains.

I was also involved in another study at Battelle related to antisubmarine warfare and an analysis of multiwarheads. I had no idea about these subjects, but it required top-secret clearance from the military and Q clearance from the atomic energy area. I was happy to work on these subjects, for it guaranteed my military deferment. To this day, I have no idea what I did.

I became involved superficially in a third project related to multiple missile warheads, and that continued my deferment from the draft, but

I never got deeply involved doing anything useful. In fact, I was a junior professional in every way, not given a specific task of significance, and intimidated by the much older and much more knowledgeable people that I worked with. I had no mentor, I was a part of a large team that could do without me, and I was often left out of major decisions that were being made. In short, I was bored and frustrated at the little progress I was making, and it colored my thinking that big organizations can often be this way.

After being at Battelle for one year, it gradually occurred to me that practical problem solving was what I wanted to do, and pure statistics or mathematics, while interesting, was not what I wanted to do professionally. I took a course at Ohio State University on Numerical Analysis and found it to be too mathematical for my taste—though I passed it. Over time, I found interesting mathematical techniques that were recently developed, like dynamic programming and linear programming, and gradually I became interested in the field of operations research, the use of mathematics and statistics to solve business problems. I had no idea about mathematical statistics in college and only learned about it in the middle of my college life, but even then my concept of it was based on a low level of understanding. After leaving Iowa State, I knew what statistics was about. I liked it but did not want to spend my life working in the field, but rather, I wanted to use these techniques to solve practical problems. When I began to understand that operations research was totally focused on using mathematics to solve business problems, I thought that this was a perfect fit for my skill and my interest. I began to think that I needed to return to graduate school to get a PhD in operations research.

The idea of returning to graduate school for a PhD evolved slowly at Battelle. It took well over a year of having little to do, plenty of time to read journals related to statistics and operations research, and time to discuss this with a few colleagues at Battelle outside of my own area. I discovered a book by Churchman, Ackoff, and Arnoff called *Introduction to Operations Research*. Operations research begins with a specific problem, and its main purpose is not to reach a general conclusion but to reach an objective, a solution for that problem, such as reducing costs or maximizing revenue. The objective of science is the development of theories that describes the world while the objective of operations research is the formulation of adequate solutions to specific problems. The system analyst is concerned with finding a better answer, especially for a one-time event, and has a lesser concern with rigorous methodology.

Operations research appeared to be the type of area that suited my talents. I was always a problem solver, and the use of mathematics to solve practical problems suited me more than wanting to be a scientist. I was interested in solving difficult business problems, problems that dealt with finding optimum solutions, problems that were guaranteed to minimize costs or maximize revenue. I was intrigued that I could find an optimum solution for a given objective or find a solution under a given set of restriction. I knew that statistics could be used as part of the solution to business problems, but there had to be more than just that, and operations research seemed like a perfect complement to statistics. I was intrigued with the subject and decided that this would be the way to once again recreate myself by jumping into a new career, somewhat related to statistics but significantly different in the types of problems it could solve.

While my frustration level at Battelle began to build, I was determined to improve my social life. For two years at Iowa State, I never dated. I had no girlfriend except for my girlfriend in Kansas City during the summer after my first year at Iowa State. At graduate school, I rarely spent time with a woman, even just to talk. It was depressing. I was studying so much more than as an undergraduate. I was rooming with three other guys, and they were doing the same thing. Given the loneliness of graduate school in Iowa for two years, Columbus for the first few weeks was more of the same, a lonely existence. The only solution was to get out there and get involved in something important. I was ready to meet a few women, Jewish women, and get back to a normal life again.

However, I knew no one in Columbus, and I thought that I had to get into action if I expected to build my social life quickly. The shyness that I had at sixteen in high school had long disappeared. I had grown in confidence throughout college life. My activities at Baruch had put me in various leadership roles, and all of them had given me the strength to go on to graduate school. I had grown some more at Iowa State, running a lab, teaching a class to undergraduates, and now I had a good job at a first-class research institute. I was ready to show some leadership in my social life.

My first and best idea was to go to the Jewish community center in Columbus to see what was available for single people. I found that there was a Singles Club, but it had fallen into disuse because there was no leadership. There was a database of names of people that were part of the Singles Club, but most of them were in college or working, and no one was actively organizing the club. I thought that this was a perfect opportunity for me—to take on the reorganizing of the Singles Club. By doing so, I would have the opportunity to call all the single people, to meet them, and to restart the Singles Club. In addition, I was told the Singles Club functioned best during the summer when college kids were back from school. Well, it was early, and the college kids were coming home in May for the summer; it would be a perfect time to meet a whole bunch of people.

That is what I did. I got a list of single people that had been part of the Singles Club from the Jewish center and started to call the list. I introduced myself on the telephone, discussed the Singles Club, then asked how it was run in the past, what programs it conducted, and why it was no longer active. Then I asked if the person was interested in reactivating the club, how we might go about doing it, and what the next few steps might be. I also suggested that I was willing to work hard to get things started again and would they be willing to help as well.

All this took several weeks, and slowly my name was being circulated around the Jewish singles my age. I think we had several meetings at the Jewish center to get together, and out of those meetings, I actually met a few women I liked and started dating again.

Judy, who was finishing her junior year at Ohio State, told me that she heard through the grapevine that there was a new guy in town trying to reactivate the Singles Club. We met at the Jewish Center at one of these meetings during the summer of 1962, and I was immediately attracted to her. During the meeting, I asked her to have dessert with me at Emil's, a local restaurant that everyone went to, and that was the start of my relationship with my wife of forty-nine years. We hit it off right away, and we began dating on a regular basis, even after she returned to Ohio State for her senior year.

My wife, Judy, told me many times that she wanted to meet me because my name had gotten around even though she had not met me. There is something to be said about being creative, about having a certain mystery about yourself because no one has met you before. I knew the mystery about me would not last, and the singles group would have gotten started without me being involved. When you see an opening, take it, for it might not last very long. You know the expression, "Strike when the iron is hot." That's what I did after arriving in Columbus. Creativity and mystery to meet women worked again, and that's how I met my wife.

However, I was hungry for a strong social life and started dating several other women too. I had not been dating for two years. I was not sure how long I was going to stay at Battelle—or even in Columbus—and I was unwilling to get involved quickly with one person. I dated a woman named Susan for quite some time but eventually decided that our personalities clashed and gave her up. I dated several other women from time to time, but I always came back to thinking that Judy was the best of the best. She was gorgeous to look at, happy to be with me, warm and responsive to me, smart and confident, willing to spend lots of time with me, and made me feel important. Her charm was impossible to resist.

After several months in Columbus, I started a brief diary about how I felt in general, not just about my social life but about the loneliness of being in a new city, not knowing anyone, and not being able to establish ongoing relationships with men as well as women. I had met Judy by then, but she was back at Ohio State University for her senior year, so we were not dating steadily yet. Here is a short version of the diary I kept back then:

> At the top of my list of attributes that people should have is enthusiasm. I hate a lifeless, dull-witted, slow moving, non-spirited person. Life is too short to make it dull. Passion is as necessary for me as breathing. I like to see it in others. I choose my friends on this attribute. To be happy, you must have enthusiasm, optimism and a desire to enjoy life, however it comes.

> What makes me satisfied? The following is my answer:

> - Feel part of something important
> - Have a few good friends
> - Be wanted as you are
> - Be able to contribute

- Always be learning
- Always desire more
- Be a greater, not a better person
- Be loved
- Be able to choose
- Get better at whatever you do
- Be sensitive to your own world
- Live each day
- Always remember the "Bell tolls for thee"
- Be moved emotionally
- Never be satisfied

Emotional feelings cannot be forced—satisfaction cannot be bought nor sought nor caught. It comes when I've learned something new and good, when I see a job completed successfully, and when I see another person happy as a result of what I have done.

There is a paradox in this satisfaction business. A task finished is a task forgotten. Making progress has a by-product: it creates enthusiasm for plodding along some more.

I despise those who say much in words and do little in deeds; I find despicable those who know nothing yet speak often; I pity those who don't do anything because they can't; I applaud those who try; I help those who want to help themselves; I cherish the friendships of those who have my tastes and beliefs.

I like advice, yet, I like to make my own decisions; I always seek advice—that's not a weakness, that's my strength. My finest attribute is my ability to condense, to seek the heart of the matter, to set out the best possible choices.

To analyze why my leisure time goes by so slowly, one need only say that it is spent alone. What I lack is a good conversation. I like to talk with interesting people about interesting topics. What makes an interesting person? First of all, he or she must have something to say. Nothing is more boring than a complete listener, except perhaps a running from the mouth idiot. Good conversation is the food that feeds the soul, and keeps my ideas healthy. Right now I am starving.

I prefer thinking-type activities and I like to act young at heart. I like industry because of its challenging problems, but I like people, too. I want to contribute to the betterment of humanity. Life brings only a few opportunities, each of which I must capitalize on. Patience and fortitude—keep an eye to the future.

I learned something very valuable from all this: *loneliness is depressing. Get out there!* I took the learning I had at Iowa State to meet women in Columbus, Ohio. I had learned that a little creativity and mystery about me would get me to meet other single people. I had no idea how to do this at first, but it was only a small leap to offer to get a singles group started as soon as possible. With a list of people to contact, the only thing I needed was a little courage to call the numbers and start talking.

The solution to loneliness is to get out there and help someone. Anyone! Then go help someone else. The more you help others, the more your loneliness will disappear.

When I arrived in Columbus, I got in touch with some of the Jewish organizations to see if there were other single guys my age interested in sharing an apartment with me. Somehow I met Marvin, and we agreed to room together with one proviso: Marvin was an Orthodox Jew and insisted that we keep a kosher kitchen. I grew up keeping a kosher kitchen. Although I missed it for the two years I was at Iowa State, going back to keeping kosher was easy for me.

We needed some furniture for the living room, so we bought a couch and matching chair secondhand from an ad in the paper. A man about to get married was selling the furniture. It had a masculine look about it, covered in dark brown and tan. We bought the couch and chair for seventy-five dollars. It was a perfect fit for a bachelor apartment. I mention these two items because they went with me after I got married and for many years thereafter. We covered the couch several times and gave it to one of our children. The couch was absolutely perfect for lying down on it to sleep or for watching TV because it had arms at either end that were tilted just enough to substitute for a pillow. I still miss that couch today.

The chair was even more comfortable for reading than the couch. It was well made, had a comfortable high back, and molded to my body perfectly. We kept that chair and put it in different places as we moved, but it was always used for reading. After fifty years, I still have the chair. When we last covered it, the man who did the job found that in previous renovations the chair was not renovated down to the frame; only a new fabric was put on the old covers. When I saw all of the old covers for the chair, and there were about five of them, it brought back memories of the various places that I lived alone and then with my wife. For the thirty dollars or so that I paid for the chair, I have gotten much more than my money's worth. That chair has become an old friend and still provides comfort to anyone sitting in it.

Marvin found a lovely woman while we lived together, became engaged, and then married. He had lived in the apartment first, so I had to move out so his wife could move in. Naturally, I took the couch and chair with me. I then found another roommate, also named Marvin, who was a professor of Labor Economics at Ohio State University. Marvin was not as observant a Jew as I was, but he agreed to keep a kosher kitchen and we did.

In early 1963, Marvin and I went to services at one of the major conservative synagogues in Columbus. We met the rabbi, and he introduced us to a couple then in their midfifties. They happened to be Israelis, and they told us about their eighteen-year-old daughter. The story they told was that they were now living in Columbus, but their daughter was still in Israel and about to be drafted into the Israeli army for two years. The girl did not want to go into the army, and neither did her parents. The parents said that we could do a good deed if one of us agreed to sign a betrothal document. The document would say that either one of us was engaged to be married to their daughter.

At this time, I was getting serious with Judy and did not want to do it. Marvin, on the other hand, was not involved with anyone and did not ever believe he would get married. He was thirty-two years old at the time, a lawyer and a professor, and he thought he was over the hill for marriage. He thought he would not find a girl his age, for the best ones were married, and he was not attracted to those still single. He believed that women in their early twenties who were attractive would consider him too old to date or to get involved with. As a result, he thought he would do the parents a favor and sign the document given that he was a lawyer. He did that just to be a nice guy, not ever thinking that this was anything more than a favor.

A few months later, after Marvin and I had forgotten about the betrothal, the parents called and invited Marvin to their home to meet their daughter and to thank him in person. Marvin came back to our apartment in love. Even though the girl was fourteen years younger than he was, he felt that she was more mature than American women, and she was exactly what he was looking for. Apparently, the girl felt the same way about Marvin, and they started dating. Six months later, they were married.

This is a perfect example of the famous Jewish remark that *one good deed leads to another good deed*. I have found that one good deed does have its rewards, and it often doesn't take long for that to happen. By agreeing to be engaged to a woman he had never met, Marvin was doing her parents a favor, and he ended up falling in love. The story is wonderful, but the underlying point is that helping others ends up helping yourself.

In a similar way, I came to Columbus and pushed to reinvigorate a Jewish singles group to meet women, but I was also helping others in the process by getting the group going again. By helping others to meet, I was helping myself too and ended up meeting Judy and marrying her.

The first date I had with Judy was to see a play called *Everyone Loves Opal*. We also saw *The Fantastics*. The most memorable line in that play occurs when one of the fathers is talking to the other father and says, "When you plant a radish, you get a radish. When you plant a cucumber, you get a cucumber, but when you plant a child, you never know what you will get." Boy, is that ever so true.

Besides the plays, Judy and I would go for walks in the country or travel to a state park or just hang out at her house or my apartment. At her house, I got to meet her parents, and Judy's mother always had a chocolate cake ready for me, one of my many weaknesses. Her brothers were much younger; the differences in age were great back then—Ronnie was five and a half years younger than Judy, and Michael was four years younger than Ronnie. Today these differences are very slight.

I also got to know where Judy's father worked. He had his own business, a pawnshop on the corner of Oak and Wilson, right in the middle of a poor neighborhood. I had no real interest in the pawn business, but I could see that a decent living was possible loaning small amounts of money at relatively low prices compared to the value of the merchandise left as collateral and then selling the merchandise if it was not retrieved from pawn. The place had a charm of its own, with TVs, electronic equipment, tools, fishing and hunting equipment, luggage, jewelry, and a host of other items. I never really wanted any of the items in the store even though I could have gotten almost anything I wanted at a rock-bottom price or free once Judy and I became engaged.

One memorable occasion with Judy was going to an Ohio State football game. Judy was a senior and had forty-yard line seats. She took me to one of those games. I enjoyed the game, the great seats, and the opportunity to see the Buckeyes in action. The other memorable occasion was going to see one of my favorite comedians live, Joe E. Lewis. I had read the life story of Joe E. Lewis in a book called *The Joker is Wild*. I had also seen the movie with Frank Sinatra playing the lead. Joe E. Lewis had a spectacular wit. I loved seeing him in person. He was always drinking real scotch or something quite strong. One of my favorite lines of his is, "Show me a man with both feet on the ground, and I'll show you a man who can't get his pants on."

As I approached the summer of 1963, I thought it was time to ask Judy if she would marry me. We had been seeing each other seriously for many months, I considered her to be my one and only girlfriend, and I was convinced that we would make a great couple. I was emotionally attached to her, I was in love with her, and I thought that my love would grow even greater over time. We were compatible emotionally, intellectually, spiritually, and physically. I decided that I wanted my parents to meet Judy's parents and asked my parents to come to Columbus, which they did.

Just before my parents were to drive over to Judy's home to meet her parents, my father said to me, "Allen, you know if we are going over to meet the Siegels, that's a serious event. You don't get the parents to meet each other if you are not serious about Judy." I responded, "I know, Dad, and I am prepared to marry Judy, and I believe she will have me." Of course, the meeting went well, and that was a clear indication that the next step was to ask Judy to marry me.

Shortly thereafter, I asked Judy if she wanted to come with me to New York for a nice vacation and to meet my family. We stayed at my parents' home in Brooklyn. On the way home from a nice evening out, I asked Judy if she wanted to see Coney Island and the beach at night. She agreed, so I parked the car, and we walked out on the beach and sat on a lifeguard stand looking out on the Atlantic Ocean. It was then that I proposed to her, and she immediately agreed. It certainly was a romantic spot! I was ready to get married and so was she. We immediately told my parents and Judy's.

Soon after, we traveled to Manhattan, and Judy and I picked out her engagement ring. My brother-in-law, who is a diamond setter, finished the piece, and Judy showed off her engagement ring when we returned to Columbus. Unfortunately, many years later, a thief broke into our house and stole the ring. I replaced the diamond ring with something even nicer, but Judy had an emotional and sentimental attachment to her engagement ring, and nothing could replace that.

One day after Judy and I were engaged, a friend of Judy's father drove up to the pawnshop with a number of original oil paintings in the trunk of his car. Judy and I offered to buy them, and the man sold us the paintings for five dollars each totally framed. Today, the five paintings of the faces of men sit on a wall in our living room. I still enjoy looking at them, and I know they are worth a good deal more than what we paid. Also hanging over the fireplace in our living room is a large winter scene that we bought from the same man that day for about fifteen dollars. We have kept these paintings for almost fifty years and still enjoy looking at them.

My future mother-in-law wanted to make a beautiful wedding at a wedding hall. She knew that many of her friends had weddings there, and it would be cheaper than holding the wedding at a synagogue. However, I insisted on two items: the marriage ceremony had to be held in a synagogue and the food had to be kosher. That eliminated the wedding hall, and so we were married at Tiffereth Israel Synagogue in Columbus by two rabbis: Rabbi Zelizer, the rabbi of the synagogue, and my uncle, Rabbi Philip Lipis, who was the rabbi at Beth El Synagogue in Highland Park, Illinois. The two rabbis were from the same rabbinical seminary and knew each other. Judy admired Rabbi Zelizer while I admired my uncle.

The significant issue was who to invite to the wedding. My parents had no money to put toward the wedding, and I assumed the responsibility for the band, the flowers, and the dinner the night before the wedding. Judy's parents did not have much money either for a major affair, so we argued about who to invite, given that the number of people at the wedding determined to a large extent the amount of money the wedding would cost. Judy's parents argued for their friends and people that were associated with in Judy's father's business while Judy and I argued for Judy's friends. I had very few friends, and most of them were Judy's friends too. Judy grew up in Columbus and had many more people she wanted to invite than I. In the end, Judy and I lost the battle. The Siegels were making the wedding, paying for it, and wanted their friends ahead of Judy's friends. As a result, Judy lost touch with some of her friends who felt slighted because they were not invited to our wedding.

Unfortunately, my mother's brother, Abe, died after surgery four days before our wedding, so under Jewish law relatives could not go to a wedding when they are deep in mourning for a parent or a sibling. For my mother, it was different because she was the mother of the groom, and her presence was absolutely necessary. As a result, very few of my family came to the wedding except my sister and her husband and, of course, my parents. Had we known this, we might have been able to add a few of Judy's friends, but death does not provide advance notice. The total cost of the wedding was about a thousand dollars.

While the planning for the wedding was underway, I had discussed going back to graduate school with Judy, and she agreed that if I really wanted to do it, she would support my decision completely. I then started looking for schools with departments in operations research. There were very few schools that had such a program, but one of them was Case Institute of Technology in Cleveland. I applied there and was accepted to begin the next semester in February 1964. I immediately accepted, so in a little over a month after Judy and I were married, I resigned from Battelle, gave up the apartment we were paying rent month by month, loaded up our cars with our clothes, a few pieces of furniture, small stuff, and moved to Cleveland.

Regarding the opposite sex, *physical attractiveness begins a relationship, but how we act determines the marriage.* Like most men, I was first attracted to women based on their physical looks. My wife was gorgeous to look at, and so were other women. What matters, however, is what is inside of them, what they say and what they do. Anyone can be a beautiful person if they have the right personality, if they have a zest for life, a sparkle in their eyes for other people, and inspire others by the way they interrelate with them.

When I give a toast to the groom at his marriage, I often say that there are two rules for the groom for a good marriage. Rule no. 1 is that if the husband disagrees with his wife, his wife is always right. Rule no. 2 is that when the husband knows that he is absolutely right instead of his wife, see rule no. 1.

For the husband, put your wife ahead of yourself, and for the wife, put your husband ahead of yourself. You can understand this best by reading the famous O. Henry story, "The Gift of the Magi." In it the husband sells his pocket watch to buy his wife a set of combs for her lovely hair, and at the same time, the wife sells her hair to buy a beautiful chain for her husband's pocket watch. That's putting your spouse ahead of yourself.

There were lots of apartments near Case, and we found one nearby on Overbrook Drive, a short distance from the school. At the same time that I was applying for admission to Case, Judy started looking for a teaching position in science in Cleveland. She found one at Glenville High School, located in a very poor neighborhood. As it turned out, there were at most four white students in her school; the rest were black.

We only stayed there for four months, and I found it easy to get back into school again. I hadn't been away from it very long, I was reading professional journals at work, and I had taken a mathematical course at Ohio State University. Given the transition that I went through at Iowa State, the courses at Case were quite straightforward, and I had no trouble grasping the material or doing well.

Judy, on the other hand, was teaching at a very difficult high school. She was teaching science in a school where science and mathematics did not come easy to the students because they did not have the background from earlier classes. In addition, the commitment to gain a good education just didn't seem to be high. During the semester, a black minister was killed by a bulldozer driven by a white man. The man was protesting the location of a new public school, claiming it was designed to avoid integration. This generated a huge protest rally. The school became part of the segregation protest that was going on throughout the neighborhood. To avoid any problems, I drove her and several other white teachers right up to the entrance of the school so they would not have to take their cars and park them in the neighborhood. Judy and many of the other teachers were scared, but the incident passed with no one being hurt.

As I was finishing my first semester at Case, not even four months in Cleveland, Professor Russell Ackoff, the head of our department, announced that he was resigning and moving to the University of Pennsylvania. Ackoff was a senior professor and a consultant to major corporations around the country. Through his efforts, he had consulting relationships with top management at Anheuser-Busch and other high-quality corporations. Our operations research department was bringing in close to one million dollars in consulting, yet he was not receiving the recognition he wanted at Case.

Once Ackoff announced that he was leaving for the University of Pennsylvania, he made it clear that he would take over as chairman of the Statistics Department in the Wharton School. The university agreed that he could change the name of the department to the Statistics and Operations Research Department, and the university would allow him to organize a management science center, another name for operations research, to conduct consulting on behalf of the university. I thought that Ackoff had pulled off an amazing sale to Penn and the Wharton School.

With both of these plums, Ackoff approached the Case faculty in his department, and seven of them decided that they too would resign from Case to join him at Penn. Then Ackoff asked the graduate students if they wanted to leave Case and move to Philadelphia to join the graduate program there. Nine of us decided to leave. Seventeen students and faculty left Case for Penn, leaving a huge void at Case and establishing Penn in the management science and operations research areas. It was a perfect fit to combine the statistics department with operations research, and it turned out to be a major benefit for all of us that made the transition. After consulting with Judy, I became one of the nine graduate students that transferred from Case to Penn.

For me, the decision to go to Penn was easy. First, the faculty that was going there was outstanding, and I wanted to be part of them. Second, it was close to my family in New York City, so my parents could easily come to Philadelphia, and they did. And third, I had wanted to go to the University of Pennsylvania since my high school days. My uncle had convinced my parents to let me apply to the Wharton School as an undergraduate, and I was accepted, but I received no financial assistance. Reluctantly, I had to decline and went to the Baruch School at CCNY where the tuition was free. I had turned down the opportunity to go to a first-class Ivy League school because I could not afford it. Sometimes going in through the back door rather than the front door can be very sweet. Now I was being accepted once again at the University of Pennsylvania in the Wharton School but technically in the Graduate School of Arts and Sciences because the Wharton School had not yet established a PhD program. Nevertheless, I would work and go to class in the Wharton School to get my PhD, and best of all, the cost was free.

Instead of being an undergraduate, I was going to teach undergraduates in the Wharton School in lieu of tuition, and I would even receive a small amount of money to cover my living expenses. It was a reversal of fortunes, a dream come true, and a lucky break. I couldn't believe it. I was sure that God was on my side, that this wasn't just luck but a kindness thrust on me that I had no reason to deserve. Nevertheless, I told Judy that we were moving to Philadelphia, and she was almost as happy as I was. She didn't like the school where she was teaching, and as it turned out, she managed to find a job in Paoli, a very upscale suburb of Philadelphia where she enjoyed teaching a great deal more than in Cleveland.

By the time Judy and I were ready to move to Philadelphia, we had filled our three-room apartment with a reasonable quantity of furniture and other household items. There was much more stuff after six months of marriage than we had after just getting married. We needed a serious U-Haul van to take all of our stuff with us. We had the large Chevy that I owned and the small Corvair car that Judy bought, which served us extremely well.

We rented the largest U-Haul that could be pulled by my Chevy. I thought it might be just enough room to carry all of our stuff, but I was worried. As a result, I measured every large item we owned in terms of length, width, and height. I then measured the inside of the U-Haul and laid out on paper how to pack the U-Haul to get the maximum use of it. I played with various pieces of furniture for several hours until I was comfortable that I had the best packing layout. To save additional money, I asked a couple of my graduate school colleagues to help me lift the heavy stuff into the van. These guys were very accommodating and were a great help, but they were not the best movers. We bumped a few items here and there, especially our new bedroom set, but in the end, it all fit but just barely. I had to hold the TV, the last item to go into the van, with one hand and close the van door with the other; it was that close. There wasn't even enough room for a banana peel when we shut the door. I was thrilled that I had planned it all out on paper.

As we drove to Philadelphia with me driving the Chevy pulling the U-Haul behind me, Judy was really nervous driving behind me, watching the U-Haul sway from side to side as we drove along the throughway. After several hours of watching the U-Haul swaying back and forth, she decided that she had to drive in front of me to stop worrying about whether I would have an accident or not. I knew the U-Haul was swaying from side to side, but my car was steady enough to keep us from having any trouble.

Penn had arranged for us to sleep at a house near the campus for the weekend while we searched for an apartment to rent because we did not want to live on campus. We had too much stuff for a small apartment, and we wanted to have a life outside of the campus. The issue was what to do with all of our stuff in the U-Haul because it would have been impossible to drive to various apartments with a trailer. I had to put the U-Haul somewhere where it would be protected and unlikely to be stolen. After all, everything we owned was in that trailer, we were in a new town, knew no one, and we were reluctant to leave it parked on the street.

Then I hit on a creative idea. I had noticed that within a few blocks from the house where we were staying that there was a U-Haul location filled with empty U-Haul vans that were exactly like ours. We arrived in Philadelphia early on a Sunday morning, and the U-Haul place was closed. Even though we only had a small lock on the back door of the U-Haul van that could easily be destroyed with a hammer, I thought that putting our van on the lot with all the other vans would imply that it was empty like all the other vans. It was an idea borne out of necessity that worked without even having to ask permission because the U-Haul store was closed on Sunday. We did just that. I unhooked the van in the middle of the group of other vans that looked no different from our van and left it there all day and night.

Unless you were a crook and happened to see us unhook our van, you would not have known that our van was filled with stuff. It worked;

no one touched it. We found an apartment during that Sunday. Very early Monday morning, I got up drove my car over to the U-Haul place before they opened, hooked up the van, and drove it to our new apartment. The U-Haul place never knew our van was there. It was a perfect camouflage to bury our van with all the others. I was correct that no one would suspect that among the empty vans, our van was loaded with all of our possessions. It was the perfect hiding place, buried among other empty vans that looked just like ours.

This U-Haul story is one small example of dealing with restrictions, the rules that all of us are told to follow. If you wish to be creative, then understand that *restrictions set the direction for business and life. To be creative, remove the restrictions.*

Restrictions define the standard way to do things. To be creative do not follow the norm, for there is usually nothing creative about following the rules. What if you don't follow the rules? What if you break one of the restrictions that other people follow, like using a different color, or using three pieces instead of one, or doing it at night instead of during the day, or doubling the chemical, or combining two chemicals, or eating six times a day instead of three, or a variety of other possibilities that no one or few others have tried?

Thomas Edison is quoted as saying that he was glad he tried fifty thousand experiments, and all of them failed. He then knew that all these approaches did not work, and that helped him find the one that did work. Creativity is not as difficult as you might imagine once you have an open mind to alternatives. The key is to often drop a restriction or a barrier and ask what would happen if we didn't have that restriction or barrier anymore.

Shortly after arriving in Philadelphia, I decided to get rid of my Chevy because it was difficult to park on campus. I had to commute to school, and I didn't want to look for a parking space each time I got there. I decided that I would sell my Chevy and buy a Vespa motor scooter, which I did. I spent $350 on a brand-new bright red Vespa that held two gallons of gas and got seventy-five miles per gallon. I had to add a little motor oil to the gas, which was not difficult, and learn to drive using a hand throttle and hand brakes, but it was fun. I added a plastic visor to break the wind hitting my face and rode the scooter to and from school all year long in the rain, in the snow, and in cold and hot weather. I could park the scooter right outside the Wharton School, and that made the commute very easy. It was another rule I broke. I would not ride in a car because it was too difficult to park on campus. The scooter was the creative solution.

The classes at Penn went by in a blur. I had only one-year left of classes to take given my master's degree, the classes I had at Ohio State and at Case, and we only had a half dozen or so students in the graduate classes I took. I had a class with Professor Konigsberg on inventory control. He made a remark comparing me to the other students. He said that I may not have the theoretical smarts of the others in the class, but I had an ability to see practical and creative approaches to problem solving that others might not have. That has stayed with me most of my life, and it does reflect one of my strengths.

I did have a course from Professor Ackoff on the history of science, and it was interesting listening to a philosopher, who he was, talk about the science of management. Ackoff was a great lecturer, and I studied his delivery and tried to emulate him as much as I could. One thing he required of the graduate students was to read a five-hundred-page book on the history of science. I tried to read it, found it totally boring, but decided I had to read it to get the essence of the book. For the first time in my life, I was speed-reading a book, moving along at about five times my normal speed. I think I finished the entire book in two days, reading about fifty serious pages an hour, skipping though sections that appeared unimportant and focusing on the few items that were relevant to the class. I was thoroughly satisfied that I could read a difficult text much more quickly than my standard reading speed and still get the essence of the book.

I had another class with another professor that was totally theoretical. I sat in the class day after day totally confused about what the good professor was talking about. I finally concluded that it wasn't my lack of mathematical training that was the problem. I just had a terrible teacher. I checked with the other graduate students, and we all agreed that it wasn't our lack of ability. We just had an awful teacher.

At that stage in my life, I had overcome my lack of confidence in myself, which is critical to doing well in graduate school. I had to conclude that the problem was the teacher, not me. To do otherwise would have decreased my confidence and increased the chances of not completing my PhD. Keeping my confidence up in the face of an intimidating professor was crucial to getting through my graduate program, given my lack of confidence early in my education.

This was an important lesson in graduate school and for any business situation: *remain confident about your ability in the face of the challenges you have to deal with.*

Graduate school was intimating at the beginning, in the middle, and at the end. Getting a PhD demands a great deal from you intellectually. You are supposed to read difficult texts and understand them, deal with complex problems that professors have difficulty with, and write an original piece of research that contributes to the profession. Undergraduate student are not asked to make an original contribution to the field of study, so the transition in graduate school to write something original is not an easy transition.

In graduate school, you are on your own. You study alone, you are required to read many difficult texts to understand the material from several perspectives, and the professors do not usually help you if the material is difficult to grasp. In short, the process can be very intimidating.

You have to fight to stay confident as a graduate student when you do not understand the teacher in class, when the text is too difficult to understand, and when you have no original idea to write about. You must tell yourself that you are capable to do the work and that you will eventually understand the material. It takes strong determination and discipline to stay focused on learning when the learning isn't coming easily. Stay with it, for eventually you will understand what you need to know.

Everything I just said about graduate school applies to business as well: *patience and fortitude!*

During my first year at Penn, I did a couple of consulting assignments as part of the Management Science Center. One of them involved the local telephone company. As part of that assignment, I learned that the fundamental objective of the company was to build its asset base: more equipment, more lines, more phones, more technology, and so on. The reason was that the utility commission that regulates the telephone company allowed the company to make a reasonable return on its investment, something like 6 to 7 percent. Therefore, the more the phone company invested, the more it could make in absolute dollars. As a result, the growth strategy for the telephone company was to keep investing in its equipment, for it could charge more as its investment grew. To increase absolute profits, the phone company had to be continually increasing its asset base by investing in new equipment and technology. This was the right approach in a regulated environment where there is no competition and government regulation is mandatory. Today there are many more choices.

I was dreading having to pass the language requirement at Penn, but luck was on my side. I passed the language requirement at Iowa State. At Case, the school required only a single language to meet the PhD requirement. Since I had passed French at Iowa State, Case accepted my passing of the language requirement at Case. As part of my transfer to the University of Pennsylvania, all the courses taken at Case, including the passing of the language requirement were transferred to Penn even though Penn required two languages for a PhD. Furthermore, the language exams at Penn were much more difficult: no dictionary, no list of words, and no selection of a text. I would have struggled to pass even one of them, let alone two. I had the good fortune to have an easy time of it at Iowa State, then to have it transferred to Case, and then have it transferred on to Penn. It was a lucky break and I took it.

This is the perfect time to say, *it's better to be lucky than smart.*

Being lucky in business or life is not just pure luck. You have to be in the right place at the right time, and that is often the result of sensing that it is the right thing to do, even if you are not sure about why.

You make your own luck by taking action that can make luck happen. Luck usually doesn't happen all by itself. You have to give it a chance to happen, and sometimes it does. Two things are necessary: First, you have to have some foresight to do the right things in advance, giving yourself the chance to get lucky. Second, you have to recognize an opportunity when it occurs. Both require a little bit of risk, but without taking a risk, your chances of being lucky diminish considerably. Life is risk, so get a little courage and confidence and take the risk. The more risk you take, the luckier you get.

If you want another story about why it is better to be lucky than smart, let me tell you about our vacation to Canada. During the summer of 1964, Judy and I took our Corvair to visit her parents in Columbus and then traveled up through Michigan and into Canada. We didn't have much money, so we camped all the way. We bought a small umbrella tent that allowed us to stand up in it and folded up it fit the small trunk of our Corvair. We traveled very light, but we took along our winter coats in case it got too cold at night. Our plan was to stay in campsites that had bathrooms and showers and an electrical hookup. The typical cost per night for these campgrounds was about four dollars, so our main cost was gas and food.

We spent a day on Mackinac Island where cars were not allowed and then went on through Sault Ste. Marie into Canada. Traveling east, we had a grand time seeing Canada for the first time and headed for the Manitoulin Islands, which sit on Lake Huron. The Manitoulin Islands are quite beautiful, so we pitched our tent in the middle of the island. We looked at the various possibilities of getting back to the United States and found that there was a ferry at the southern tip of the island that would take us toward Toronto and Niagara Falls. The ferry schedule, however, was such that it left at 8:00 a.m. and the next one was four hours later at noon. We decided to break camp at six, drive for an hour to the ferry based on driving the forty to fifty miles to get there. We thought that even if it took a little longer because the road was a narrow single lane and not always paved that we had sufficient time to get there.

In the middle of the night, the rain started, and didn't let up. At four in the morning, I woke Judy and asked her what we should do if the rain continued. She said, "Let's follow our plan even if we get wet." The rain continued and got worse, and by six, the rain was coming down in sheets, heavier than ever. Still, we broke camp in the rain. The tent was totally soaked, and we were soaked from head to toe, including our underwear. We stuffed the tent and our stuff into the trunk, and whatever was left went into the backseat. As we took off for the ferry, the rain made the driving hard, the road had plenty of potholes to avoid, and the semidarkness made driving even harder, for the rain prevented the normal daybreak.

Fortunately, no one else was on the road, and we managed to make it to the ferry about 7:45 a.m., just in time for the 8:00 a.m. ferry. However, there was a long line of cars outside the little house that sold tickets for the ferry. I quickly found that the ferry was virtually full, and all the cars waiting to buy tickets would have to wait four hours for the next ferry. Without much thought, I was undeterred, got back into my Corvair, and pulled it up as close to the ferry as possible, thinking that there might be some way to get on the ferry, but I had no idea how.

Just then, the captain of the ferry came down the gangplank and looked at my Corvair. He then said to me, "Is this your car?" I said, "Yes, it is." He then said, "I have room deep in the hold for one small car, and I think your Corvair will just fit there. Put your Corvair on the ferry." I was ecstatic. I rushed over to the house that sold the tickets for the ferry, bought one for my car, for Judy, and for me, and drove my small car onto the ferry. Sure enough, the spot I had for the car was deep in the bowels of the ferry in a small corner, and my Corvair fit there just fine.

Judy had gotten out of the car before I parked the car and went up on the passenger deck. When I got there, it was clear that she was a mess, dressed in a wet parka, with nothing on underneath other than her bra and panties. I went back down to the car, found some dry clothes for her and me, and we changed into them, washed our hands and faces and enjoyed the ferry ride down to the southern part of Canada. We both marveled at the luck we had being the last car on the ferry. I knew that my being aggressive and putting our little car right next the ferry would at least get the car noticed if there was room for it. At that moment, God was looking out for us, and it was better being lucky than smart.

In my second year at Penn, the faculty suggested that I teach a course on business statistics instead of working at the Management Science Center. I was happy to do it since I had taught that course at Iowa State and thought I could handle the course at Wharton.

After the final exam for the class I taught, one student who was failing asked me to give him a passing grade so he could graduate. He told me that my grade would determine whether he would graduate on time or not. I knew he did not deserve to pass, but I did not want to be so tough on him that he would not graduate. After all, I was a graduate student, and I knew what it was like to get a passing grade. I also feared that I could be drummed out of graduate school if I did not pass the comprehensive exam. In short, I wanted to be a nice guy, so I gave him the lowest passing grade that I could. I rationalized. I argued to myself that it is not the grade you get that matters but what you do with the knowledge you gain that matters. Today, I would be more hardened to this type of request, for I know that a Wharton degree is worth a great deal, and it should not be given out lightly. A Wharton degree is a union card; it will get you in the door when other degrees will not.

Near the end of the spring semester, five students were asked to take the comprehensive exam in my department, the exam that determines whether you know the field you are studying. I was one of them. For several months before the exam, I reviewed everything that I had studied, trying to prepare for the most important part of the PhD program. Failure to pass that exam could be grounds for being thrown out of school, and passing the exam would only leave the PhD dissertation. There were four or five difficult problems, and we had three hours to work on them. After the exam, I had no idea how well I had done, but several days later, we were told that three of the five students had passed, and I was one of them. I was elated. The other two were allowed to stay in the graduate program and could take the exam again the next year, but I was elated that all I had left was to write a dissertation, no easy matter as I soon discovered.

Some time after passing my comprehensive exam, I started thinking about a dissertation topic. I had no idea about what to work on, and unlike my master's degree where my professor not only suggested the topic but also worked closely with me, I had no professor to work with and no obvious topic to choose. I had an interest in decision making and found that there was a great deal written on how to analyze investments. I thought that topic could be explored and started working in that area.

I looked for a thesis advisor, and the department suggested Professor Roger Sisson, who proved to be an excellent choice politically, but he made it clear that he had no expertise or interest in the subject. While he served as my advisor in dealing with the other professors that were to evaluate my work, I was alone in having to create an original piece of work. That was not only frustrating but scary as well, and it led me to conclude that *being creative without a mentor is extremely difficult*. A genius does not need a mentor, but most of us that want to be creative need experienced people to guide us in the right direction. Experienced people know what is known and what is not known, and they know how to define a problem so that a less experienced person has a chance to be creative. You create something new by becoming familiar with as much of what is known as you can. The more you know about the subject, the easier it is to define the issues that remain unresolved.

Mentors will be more familiar with a subject than a junior person entering the subject area. The mentor can do a great job explaining to the junior person what is known, what is still an issue or a problem, and how the problem might be solved. If the junior person is really smart, that person might be able to proceed without help from someone more experienced, but it is much easier with a mentor.

The short answer to becoming creative is to work with a master who can train you, guide you, and help you understand how to push the knowledge in the subject matter a little bit further. This kind of mentoring is extremely important in graduate school, but it also very important in business, in the arts, in music, and in most creative areas in life. I found a mentor for my master's degree, but I was entirely on my own for my PhD dissertation.

I found an excellent book that developed a very mathematical approach to decision making under uncertainty by Harry Markowitz. This gave me the idea of looking at the multiple investment decision process when there are not sufficient funds to undertake all the investments at the same time.

During my second year at Penn, I worked on three major activities. First, I taught my class. Secondly, I worked on my dissertation, and third, I worked on building a small replica of the famous sailing ship the *Cutty Sark*. I had to have some diversion away from the mathematics. I could only work on my dissertation for a few hours at a time, and the construction of the *Cutty Sark* was a healthy break from the difficult process of writing an original work in operations research.

The *Cutty Sark* was a famous sailing ship in the mid-1800s. The kit was made out of plastic that required rigging for thirty-seven sails, complete with ropes and pulleys. The easy part was putting the hull together, but the rigging took painstakingly long to put the small pieces of rope through every pulley, glue the pulleys to their appropriate place, and then mount the sails on the masts. It took the better part of the year to put the ship together, spending an hour or two on it several days a week. When it was done, I was proud of it and displayed it prominently in my apartment, then in my home, and then at work. More than fifty years later, the *Cutty Sark* is still with me, a little battered from lack of maintenance but still a beautiful ship to look at. It reminds me of one way to handle a difficult assignment: *when doing challenging work, take a break to refresh yourself.* When I worked on my dissertation, after a few hours I took a break. I couldn't sustain the effort. My relaxation was building my *Cutty Sark*. It took over a hundred hours to finish the ship, and it was a complete change of pace from the mathematics of the dissertation.

After a year of serious scholarship, I had a reasonable draft of my dissertation. It was good enough in my mind to think that I could start looking for a job and finish whatever my faculty committee of five members wanted done after it was submitted to them. Little did I know how difficult the process would become!

I interviewed at M&M Candies in Hackettstown, New Jersey, accepted an offer they made me, and joined them in the summer of 1966. As I was leaving the university, Professor Ackoff took me aside and told me that most people who leave the university before finishing their dissertation never finish. He warned me that the dissertation is the most difficult part of acquiring a PhD, and it was best to stay on campus until it was totally completed. He was right and I was naïve.

Roger Sisson had given me very little advice on the content of my dissertation, but he knew the political process of getting the five faculty members on my committee to sign off on it. He worked on getting the draft to the other four faculty members. This process took months. Two of the five members were in other departments and did not see my draft as a high priority. It took four to five months before I heard anything back, and Roger did not want to give me the comments in piecemeal fashion. I was on hold until early in 1967 when Roger told me that two of them were very unhappy with the draft. One of them thought there was nothing original in the dissertation because it copied much of what Harry Markowitz had written in his famous book. I vehemently disagreed, but one faculty member was adamant. He wanted me to throw the dissertation completely away and start over on a new topic. It took several more months for Roger to discuss how to deal with the situation. Eventually, Roger worked out a compromise where the faculty member resigned from my committee, and we replaced him with another faculty member. The second objection from another faculty member was that there was no real data in the dissertation and no executive summary. This faculty member made it clear that he had no interest in my subject, he would not read the dissertation, he wanted some sort of data analysis, and he wanted an executive summary of the entire dissertation to make his life easy. I had to comply with these ideas even though I was convinced that what I had written was a good piece of work.

Here I was working full-time, I was ninety miles away from campus, and I still had a lot left to do to improve the content of the dissertation. The comment by Professor Ackoff was becoming very clear to me. But I was not a quitter, and I was determined to finish the dissertation; I was not going to be intimidated by two faculty members that had no interest in my subject. All this took the better part of another year to work out, and I began to have serious thoughts that I might not finish the dissertation out of frustration.

At this point, my first child, Pamela, had arrived in September 1966, so I had the extra duties of helping with our newborn. In the summer of 1967, I started serious work once again on the dissertation. I worked on it at night and on weekends, and slowly, the additions took shape. I designed a data analysis that required a software program, paid another graduate student to write the program, and produced a new chapter of original data that turned out to be a unique idea on how to evaluate investments. I wrote an executive summary chapter that wasn't difficult, but it took time. With the change in a faculty member, the subsequent data analysis, and the executive summary, the dissertation took yet another year to complete. It took great discipline on my part to focus on it while I was working full-time, but I got it done.

With all of that, Roger Sisson was a tremendous help; he focused on the politics, and I focused on meeting all of the requirements imposed on me. I didn't like what I had to do, but I had little choice. I was not going to let the whims of a couple of faculty members that I had never met stop me from finishing my degree. It would have been easy to get angry and walk away as many doctoral students do, but I wanted the designation of PhD. I had to put aside my anger, pay to have someone write software for me to create the data analysis chapter, and replace a faculty member on my committee. I worked on the dissertation for two years after I thought I was finished. That is why any dissertation can be a PhD student's hardest hurdle. It isn't easy to produce an acceptable dissertation with no mentor, doing research for the first time, and being evaluated by faculty members who have no interest in the subject you are working on. I worried a great deal about finishing because I was powerless. It took one year after my initial draft to work out the politics of my faculty committee and another year to improve the content of the dissertation. In the end, this did improve the dissertation.

What I learned was *don't fight powerful people*. Every time I fought with a teacher, a professor, my boss, or the landlord, I lost. People who have power don't like being wrong, so if you want to fight with them, you have to do it subtly and carefully. You can win, but it takes time. You have to be nice about how you do it and let them find it acceptable to give in to your request. Often, you do it their way just as I did for my dissertation.

I had a graduate student friend who was smarter than me and thought that he would write his own dissertation without help from an advisor. He produced his dissertation and then presented it to his dissertation committee. They rejected the entire concept and forced him to write a new dissertation on a new topic because he didn't communicate in advance what he was doing. His dissertation committee had the power to do it. This guy was smart enough to do another dissertation, and the second time he didn't make the same mistake.

Whenever you have difficulties with your boss, be careful about how you argue your position. You need his approval. The same thing applies to dealing with the government. For taxes, always produce the detailed documents to support your position if you want the IRS to concede. For speeding tickets, I once won a case by arguing that the police could not have determined how fast I was going. The judge agreed and I won. If you want to argue with people in power, you had better not make an emotional argument but rather have detailed facts to support your position.

One of the great regrets I have in my life is that my father did not live to enjoy seeing me get my PhD. At least he had the opportunity to sit in on one of my classes at Wharton. My parents were impressed as they witnessed me teaching Wharton School undergraduates. He knew, of course, that I was almost finished, but he died at age fifty-nine in July 1968. Our second child, Lori, was born a month after his death in August 1968, and we named her after my father. Two months later, in the fall of 1968, I gave my oral defense of the dissertation, the last item to fulfill my PhD.

Generally speaking, the oral defense of a dissertation is an easy process. Your faculty advisor should not put you through the oral defense until he/she is sure you have a good dissertation and the faculty committee is supportive of your dissertation. In reality, the oral defense should be a time for celebration, a time for the faculty to tell the graduate student what a great job he or she did and send the student off with high praise. That's exactly how my oral defense went.

My oral defense was relatively easy. I only had my five faculty members in the room, I wasn't grilled too hard, I was praised for the original content I had produced, and it lasted about two hours. One faculty member asked me about the objective of the document—why is the research important? I floundered over that question, for I had never really given much thought to it. I remember that question well not just because I had a hard time with it but also because it is a critical question to ask for all research. I took that question to heart and asked that question about all the research I did from then on and to all my business colleagues. In the end, the faculty members did say that my dissertation was impressive and worthwhile, which helped me believe it was a good document. Even today, I believe I produced an original idea about how to measure multiple investment decisions with limited financial resources.

As we neared the end of our stay in Philadelphia, Judy and I had a small issue with our landlord. As part of our rent, we paid an extra five dollars per month for an air conditioner in our living room. We rented the apartment for two years, and after ten months, the air conditioner stopped working. We called the landlord to get someone to fix it, but no one did. We decided that we would hold back the five dollars in rent per month until the air conditioner was fixed, and that amounted to seventy dollars for the fourteen months that we did without the air conditioner.

In our last month, I wanted to use that seventy dollars for part of the rent, but the landlord knew we were planning to leave and insisted on the full rent, or he would evict us from the apartment before we were ready to move, so we paid the full rent. After we left the apartment, the landlord sent us back our one-month deposit less seventy dollars for the air conditioner. Judy and I were furious. We had sent him registered letters telling him that our air conditioner did not work, we had called him several times, and the superintendent for the building knew the problem but couldn't fix it himself. We knew we were in the right, but we were now living in northern New Jersey, and he thought we wouldn't bother him with such a small amount.

He was wrong. I filed a lawsuit in small claims court in Philadelphia for my seventy dollars. A few months later when the case was heard in front of a judge, I drove to Philadelphia and argued the case with documented letters that were sent by registered mail to the landlord. He showed up and called me a "cheap chiseler," but he had no proof that the air conditioner was fixed. The judge found in my favor, and I was elated but only for a day. I had no way to collect the money. I had sued the landlord, so I had to collect from him personally, yet I had no way of knowing where he kept his money, and I didn't want to hire someone to do it for just seventy dollars. Had I sued his company, he might have been forced to get a lawyer to represent his company, which would have cost him more than the seventy dollars, so he might have settled without going to court. As it turned out, I won the case and lost the money. It was a pyrrhic victory, and it taught me a good deal about getting involved in a lawsuit. Even when you win, you can lose. That case taught me that *for civil law, it's never about the principle; it's about the money*. Some people say they are satisfied to win in court for the principle of the thing, and they don't care about the money. Perhaps there are a few people like that. In my experience, however, it's about the money. That's why lawyers take accident cases, class action lawsuits, and many more types of cases. Focus on the money, and you will almost always have the right motive.

If I could tell you one thing about solving a problem it is this: *when you have a problem, be aggressive*. Problems need to be attacked aggressively. If you leave a problem alone, there is a good chance it will get worse. When you need gas in your car, fill the gas tank quickly. When you need cash, get it before you run out. When you have trouble with a powerful person, fix the relationship quickly. Do not leave a bad taste with the person you have offended. When you hurt someone, apologize as soon as possible. Don't wait. Waiting allows the injured person to tell their side of the story, which will not be flattering for you. I was once with my uncle in Israel, and he broke a vase in a shopping market. He immediately offered to pay for it and did. When I owed a dime and didn't pay, the penalty was much worse. When I thought I had a four-hour wait for the next ferry, I was aggressive, and the captain found room for my small car.

In being aggressive, you don't give up your manners. Rather, urgent situations require imagination. Try as many options as you can to solve your problems and deal with them as quickly as possible.

Chapter 8

Learning About Business

I had received a job offer from M&M Candies in Hackettstown, New Jersey, working for Larry Friedman, one of the very first PhDs in operations research. He knew the operations research department at Wharton, and he was looking for an addition to his staff. The other member of the team was Hal, a very bright guy who later rose up the ranks at the company. I was willing to trust that a candy company would have a need for three high-powered mathematical minds with strong operational research backgrounds. I was thrilled because we would live in the New York area near my parents, and the salary was $15,800, almost double what I made at Battelle several years earlier. The PhD was beginning to pay off.

The first thing I discovered was that all the executives except the president and the head of personnel had offices in a large open bullpen. The company did not believe in private offices for the head of engineering or manufacturing or marketing or whatever. These very senior guys had desks just like mine in a large open area so that everyone could see one another. It was a little intimidating to work that way because everyone could come up to you to discuss whatever they wanted to discuss without making an appointment. The assumption was that they had something important to talk about.

There were, of course, a number of conference rooms where private conversations did occur, but in general, you did virtually all of your work out in the open where everyone could see you. Even though the desks were open, I dared not approach someone in a different department unless I had something useful to say to them. Generally, I minded my own business and did what I was asked to do.

This open setting had an impact on my business behavior. It implied *be sure access to management is easy*. M&M Candies was the only place that I ever worked at that had this easy access to management. Every other place had closed offices and personnel that had to be confronted to arrange for an appointment. In some cases, the appointment could not be made at all because I was unknown; in other cases, the appointment was put off for weeks or longer.

In my experience, the smaller the company, the easier it is to meet with senior management. As CEO, keep your door open and encourage your staff to come and talk to you whenever they have something to say. The only time to close your door is when a confidential discussion is taking place, such as a job interview, personnel issues, or legal issues. Otherwise, let your staff pop in to talk about anything. My open-door policy partly reflected what I saw at M&M, but mostly, it reflected my desire to involve my staff in the decision-making process. Senior management needs input from its staff to obtain the widest possible view before a significant decision is made.

The second thing I learned very quickly was that Forrest Mars Sr., the owner of the company, was a fanatic about punctuality and offered a punctuality bonus to everyone. Everyone had to punch their time clock in the morning whenever they arrived. You did not have to punch out, only punch in. That meant everyone, including the president of the company. Every day that you punched in before 8:30 a.m., the start of the business day, the company paid you an extra 10 percent punctuality bonus for that day. Making $15,800 per year and dividing by 250 business days, I was making $6.30 more per day every day I punched in before 8:30 a.m. No excuses were acceptable. It didn't matter if your mother died or if you had a car accident or if you were sick or whatever. If you didn't punch in, you didn't get the bonus. The only excuse was travel on M&M business. In the middle of the winter, senior executives could be seen running over slippery snow at 8:25 a.m. to punch in. If you were late one minute, you were late, and the bonus was not paid. No exceptions. While the extra pay was presented as a bonus, the staff viewed it as a penalty. Nevertheless, for the company, it got the day started on time.

Being on time is always a good thing, but in business, it taught me that *punctuality is good manners and creates efficiency*. My wife is one of the most punctual people I know. From her perspective, if we are late to an appointment by two minutes, we are late. While you may not want to be that firm, being on time is good for business.

A very successful businessman once said that the main reason why he was so successful was because he always arrived at appointments fifteen minutes early. He believed that being there early gave him a significant edge in giving the impression that he was anxious to do business and was prepared, organized, and efficient. This is a good rule for business. I try hard to not miss an appointment. Because you sometimes forget, as I have done, write all appointments down in your computer or notebook. Don't be fashionably late. It is not good manners, and it is not good business.

Whenever I told people that I was working at M&M Candies as an operations research manager, the first question asked of me was what could a candy company do with a mathematical guy like me? The answer I always gave was that we were speculating in the cocoa commodities market. M&M was one of the three biggest companies in the world making chocolate, and cocoa was a commodity that fluctuated substantially. M&M was not buying cocoa at the market price but was doing research to determine where the cocoa market was going in the future, so it could buy cocoa at the lowest possible price for up to two years out in time.

Cocoa is grown in Nigeria, Ivory Coast, Brazil, and elsewhere near the equator. In the 1960s, these countries had poor data on the amount of cocoa that was being grown. Since the cocoa commodity price depends on the supply and demand for cocoa, and the demand is easier to forecast, the key to the price of the commodity was the supply. The question was how to estimate the supply before the rest of the market knew even if that knowledge was known a week in advance.

To estimate the supply before the rest of the market knew, M&M established a sample of cocoa trees in various cocoa countries that would provide an unbiased estimate of the size of the crop relative to the previous year. By counting the cocoa pods on a sample of trees throughout the country, measuring the rainfall in different parts of the country, measuring the size of the cocoa pods during the growing season, and evaluating the canopy of a specific tree, the company could compare the results to the previous year to determine whether the cocoa crop several months in the future would be greater or less than the previous year and by how much. It was a very sophisticated statistical sampling process, well ahead of anyone else in the market, and provided a huge edge to the company in speculating in the market.

The second biggest area that our operations research team was involved in was evaluating where to spend the huge advertising budget for the company. In some markets, we doubled the advertising dollars to measure how much, if any, we increased sales. In other markets, we cut the advertising budget by 50 percent to see if we lost any sales because of it. We looked at what shows on TV to advertise. All this was implemented by the advertising agency, but our department had some say in determining where and how much to experiment and in evaluating the result. Hal did a marvelous study of the various promotions that M&M offered in the marketplace. Over the years, the company had tried different types of discounts, and Hal made an assessment of which ones were the most profitable.

I was asked to evaluate where a new plant might be located to increase the capacity of M&Ms. I had a deadline of one month to do the study. I had to learn where milk was produced, the ports where sugar came into this country, and where union activity was minimal as M&M was opposed to having a union. I centered my effort in the South where union activity was the least organized and recommended several locations, but the study never went anywhere. I worked on assessing the maximum size of the plant at Hackettstown, looking at the total facility and determining how much more production it could achieve with its present equipment in its present location. To do this, I had to assess the various pieces of equipment in use and how much capacity each could generate for each part of the production process.

What I learned and carried with me for the rest of my career was that *any part of the business can be subject to analysis.* You can prepare a cost-benefit analysis on a variety of topics: new products or improvements to an existing service. You can provide a conservative, expected, and optimistic analysis of a situation. Even for a qualitative decision, it is possible to develop quantitative measurements. You can analyze brand loyalty, personnel effectiveness, quality of management, and other qualitative items. Analysis is important and essential to the decision-making process.

However, most decisions are made emotionally, based on personal beliefs rather than strict analysis. Any analysis of the future is based on assumptions. Change the assumptions and you change the results. You need to take into consideration how strongly you believe the assumptions. That often comes down to what you feel in your gut, what experience you have, and what you want to achieve. Analysis is useful, but emotions are powerful in affecting decisions.

One of the most exciting parts of the job was the ability to work with Larry. Larry was brilliant, a junior chess champion, studied under Enrico Fermi in physics, never finished that degree but received a PhD in operations research. He authored one of the very first books on operations research. Larry was a master at data analysis, and I learned how to get the most out of data although I never had his uncanny skill. He loved to take data and plot them, play with them, draw various types of charts with them, put several data sets together, all to explain what was happening. His charts were amazing, but his personality was often hard to take. Larry pushed his ideas too hard, and he often was pushed aside by higher management who did not agree with him. I loved Larry for what he was teaching me, but I could see that he was stuck in his present position because of his personality and unlikely to advance because of it.

Larry's wife, Flo, was an interesting person on her own. When it came to servicing the products she bought that did not work up to her standard, no one was as successful as she was in getting results. She taught me that the best way to solve a problem was to go to the top. One time, her Japanese TV did not work, and she could not get it fixed properly by the local TV repair place. She called the president of Hitachi in Tokyo. He did not receive many calls from irate customers in the United States. After she was finished complaining about how no one could fix her TV, the president said he would take care of the matter. The next day, a vice president of the company called her from Chicago, told her to pack up her TV, and ship it to him. Sure enough, she got a brand-new TV to replace hers.

She called the president of General Electric because her GE dishwasher was broken and told him that she was a user of many GE appliances. A few days later, the president of that division drove to her house in his limousine to see what the problem was and then got it fixed for her. She had more courage than anyone I knew to take on big companies when their products did not work as well as she wanted them to work.

Though often said, there is an important lesson in these stories: *the customer is always right.* Flo taught me not to be intimidated by top management in dealing with your problems. To get a problem taken care of, go as high up in the organization as possible. That's because top management makes decisions happen.

The same thing is true about selling. Get as high up in the decision-making process as possible for the highest probability of success. Lower-echelon people can't make a decision; they go to the decision maker for an answer. Lower-echelon people can veto your proposal before the decision maker knows about it. You want as few people deciding as possible, for the more people the greater the chance that one of them will say no and that will kill your sale. It is best to have only one person to convince—the decision maker. When you're selling, deal directly with the decision maker.

Shortly after I started working at M&M, Judy and I decided that we could not live around Hackettstown. It was too far away from a Jewish community and too far from New York City. I wanted the option of being able to leave M&M if things didn't suit me and have the option of commuting to Manhattan where there were many opportunities. We settled on Morristown area where there was a kosher butcher, a conservative synagogue, and an easy trip to Brooklyn to see my parents.

We rented an apartment in Morris Plains right on Route 10 that took half an hour to travel to work. At first, I tried riding to work on my Vespa, but it would only go fifty miles per hour at maximum speed. It was a long trip by scooter, and eventually I gave it up, sold it to Judy's cousin for seventy-five dollars, and then bought myself an end-of-the-year 1966 Chevelle for $1,800. I should never have sold that scooter; it was fun to ride. Someday, I'll buy myself another one.

In September 1966, our first child, Pamela Hope, was born at Morristown Community Hospital. Judy had labor pains late in the evening, and we hurried into the car to go to the hospital. As soon as I started driving, I realized that I had an almost empty tank of gas and told Judy that I was worried that we might run out of gas before getting to the hospital. I could chance it, but if we got stuck in the middle of nowhere, it would be worse than stopping for gas. Judy was having contractions every five minutes or so and wanted to get to the hospital. She was really upset that I had to find a gas station, which we did find about halfway to the hospital. Instead of filling up the tank, I put in three gallons, knowing that was enough to get to the hospital. There was no problem for the delivery of our baby, but I never heard the end of the extra suffering she had experienced. For years afterward, Judy loved telling the story that in her time to deliver out first child, I had to first stop for gas.

I wanted to be present at her birth, but the hospital was not quite ready yet to let the father in on the birth, so I waited patiently in the lobby until I heard the good news. We had a beautiful six-pound baby girl, and it was very exciting. We had an extra room in our one-bedroom apartment, so we set it up for the baby and enjoyed seeing her grow.

Because I was a coin collector, in 1967 I found that the Federal Reserve was no longer putting silver in any of its coins, and that it would no longer accept silver certificate dollar bills at the Federal Reserve in exchange for actual silver. The last coin with silver in it was produced in 1964. Thereafter, the coins had the sandwich look we have today with no silver in it. It occurred to me that the silver in the coin would become more valuable than the value of the coin, and silver coins with the years 1964 or earlier were still in circulation. Furthermore, M&M had a huge dining room with dozens of coin-operated machines dispensing food and drinks since there was only a very limited kitchen. Every day, the machines were emptied of coins and refilled with food. I asked the guy who emptied the machines if I could look through the coins each day and pay him for the coins that I took. He agreed, as it didn't cost him anything, and it lightened his load. I was giving him a twenty-dollar bill instead of him carrying twenty dollars in coins.

Each day for months, I looked though hundreds of dollars of coins, picking out only the dimes and quarters with mintmarks 1964 or earlier. Over time, these earlier mint marks diminished as many other coin collectors were doing the same thing nationwide. Finally, I decided that the pickings were too thin to continue, and I quit, but I had accumulated just about a thousand dollars in silver coins. Silver was earmarked at $1.29 an ounce, and that price was a fixed standard until silver was allowed to fluctuate as a commodity. Over the years, the price of silver has dramatically increased. In the 1980s, the price rose to twenty dollars an ounce when two wealthy brothers in Texas tried to corner the market and failed. I thought about selling the silver many times, but I always decided against it because I did not need the money. I also thought this could be emergency money: silver coins could be used if paper currency ever failed, which was extremely doubtful, but the thought gave me a small sense of safety. Today, I still have the coins and the price of silver per ounce is somewhere close to thirty dollars, more than twenty-three times the value of the coins. I had to wait more than forty years for that to occur. My investment of one thousand dollars in 1967 is now worth at least twenty-three thousand dollars.

My coin collecting is one simple example that something may have little value at first, but somewhere later *knowledge creates opportunity*. The more you know, the better your decision making will be. This applies to virtually any decision. As a coin collector, I knew what few other people knew: coins with silver will be worth more over time. It was based on Gresham's law that bad money drives out good money. Silver coins would be worth at least what their face value was worth, so I would never lose any money except for a small amount of interest. Even with my limited knowledge, silver had to increase in value over time. That knowledge paid off handsomely though I won't know how handsomely until I sell the coins.

On a much broader level, companies will pay you more money based on your educational level. The more education and knowledge you have, the more you are worth in the marketplace. The more you know as an expert, the more you are worth to people who wanted that expert knowledge. Knowledge is the essential requirement to become a consultant and to sell yourself. Often, the knowledge you have is what you say you have, not what others may think. Confidence in yourself is essential, and that confidence comes from the knowledge you possess.

At the same time that silver coins were going out of circulation, the Federal Reserve announced that some time in 1968, they would stop exchanging silver certificate dollar bills for actual silver. The issuing of a silver certificate by the Federal Reserve meant that $1 of paper money could be exchanged for $1 of real silver at the rate of $1.29 per ounce. I started accumulating silver certificates and had about sixty dollars of them. One of Judy's cousins had also accumulated about a hundred dollars of them, so I offered to take their dollars and mine to the Federal Reserve in New York to exchange them for actual silver. I took a day off and traveled to lower Manhattan and found that the line was two blocks long, four people abreast of each other. I was not the only one doing this. It took two hours to get inside the Fed to present my small number of dollar bills. My dollars were a small amount because in one or two situations I saw silver being wheeled out on a cart; it was too heavy to carry. Large bricks of silver were moving out of the Fed into cars parked outside. That silver represented thousands of dollars in paper money. In terms of the number of certificates I had, it was a small amount.

The Federal Reserve gave out a receipt for the dollar amount they received and told me to return in several weeks with our receipt for the amount of silver they would weigh out for us by then. I asked my mother to take the receipt to the Fed, and she did. I got the silver, sorted the amount in two piles proportional to the certificates I had and what the cousins gave me. Our cousins sold their silver soon thereafter. I kept my silver in a baby jar for years not wanting to get rid of it and not knowing what to do with it.

In 2003, thirty-six years later, my son got engaged, and I decided to take the silver and make it into a silver wine goblet for the wedding ceremony. I could not think of a better use for the silver I had saved for so long. I got in touch with my sister who worked in the diamond industry in Manhattan and asked her to arrange for the silver to be converted into a silver wine cup, which she did. I presented the silver goblet to Leo and his bride, Mimi, and they used it for their wedding ceremony. That justified the reason for keeping the silver so long.

Two years later in the spring of 1968, having worked at M&M for a couple of years, knowing full well that my PhD dissertation was moving along well, Judy and I decided to buy our first house. This was a big decision, for we really didn't have much money to buy one. We had accumulated several thousand dollars and paid off our car loans, but it wasn't enough to make a down payment. About a year earlier, Judy had had a nasty auto accident that wasn't her fault. As she was driving along Route 10 minding her own business, an old man pulled out of a gas station to cross the road to go in the opposite direction from the way Judy was traveling. He hit Judy's Corvair, and she banged her knee quite badly as well as her neck and back. The other car had bad damage too, but no one was seriously injured. The Corvair was totaled, and Judy sued the other driver for negligence.

Judy needed stitches for her knee and went to a couple of doctors for physical therapy on her neck and back. Over the course of many months, the doctor bills amounted to eight hundred dollars. We hired a lawyer and sued the other driver for pain and suffering based on the doctor bills and the long-term impact on Judy. At first, the insurance company, recognizing that the driver they insured was totally at fault, offered to pay our doctor bills. We asked for ten thousand dollars, and they refused. As we approached the trial, there were one or two other offers, but they were still not enough. Our lawyer told us that jury trials in northern New Jersey did not give high-dollar amounts in a case like ours, so we might not get more than seven times our doctor bills or not much more than six thousand dollars. We hoped for more. Finally, the day of the trial arrived, and Judy was worried about testifying, knowing full well that she was the key to our case. In her favor was the fact that she was young, very attractive, and not at fault, but we were not sure what a jury would do. When the judge asked that we get started to pick a jury, the insurance company made one final offer of $4,500. We decided that the risk of a trial for a couple of thousand more was not worth it. We also considered the pain that Judy would go through on the stand recounting the accident, describing her pain, her visits to doctors, and then put up with what could be a nasty cross-examination by the insurance company lawyer. We took the offer, paid one-third to the lawyer, and found ourselves with another three thousand dollars, just enough to add to our savings for a down payment on a house.

We settled on a house in Morris Township. The house cost $30,000, and we managed to amass $7,500 for the down payment. We had seen a nicer house for about $37,000, and we wanted to buy it, but we needed $9,000 to put down on the house, and we just didn't have the extra $1,500 to do it. My parents didn't have that kind of money to loan us, and neither did Judy's parents. Judy's brothers were too young, and my sister didn't have the money to lend either. We were heartbroken to walk away from the bigger and nicer house. We asked the owners if they would take a little less, but they refused.

When I mentioned to Larry at work that I was going to buy a house, he told me not to do it. He thought the market was too high, that this was the wrong time to be buying a house, and I should wait. I told him that

I had to live, that we had another child on the way, that our apartment was too small for two children, and we wanted our own home. Buying the house was to be one of the best decisions of our life, for it led on to the subsequent houses that we bought.

We moved into the house in the spring of 1968, a split-level house with three bedrooms at the top level, a living room/dining room and kitchen on the next level down, a recreation room and garage on the next level down, and a basement with a french drain and sump pump that kept the basement dry by pumping any water out to the stream in the backyard. Eventually, we built a fourth bedroom in the attic. It was a great house on a wonderful street, with a lovely backyard and a small stream that ran year round. We didn't have much furniture, but we were overjoyed to have our own home. Three years later, we sold the house for $44,500, a nearly 50 percent gain.

My first investment taught me what others often said—*buying right is the critical issue for a successful investment.* This applies to buying a house, about buying cars, and about investing in the stock market. An investment in a home usually goes up in value while the purchase of a car usually depreciates. In buying a house, we keep them for a long time and the value goes up over time. For cars, we drive them for years, often until they are not worth much, and then we give them away or sell them for a small amount of money. Therefore, buy the best house you can afford and the cheapest car you are willing to live with.

In August 1968, our second child, Lori Ellen, was born at Morristown Community Hospital. This time, I had plenty of gas in the car, and the hospital let me enter the delivery room. I dressed in a gown and stood behind Judy, holding her hand as she delivered normally. We had a second beautiful baby, and we named her after my father, who had died a month earlier.

Shortly thereafter with little chance for advancement, Larry resigned from M&M to begin a consulting career in commercial operations research at the John D. Kettelle Corporation outside of Philadelphia. The company was doing virtually all of its consulting for the government on various military matters, and Larry offered to start a commercial practice that would enhance the company's growth. Larry then asked me to join him. I talked to Judy about it, and we decided that it would be a great new opportunity, that without Larry at M&M, I did not know what I would do, and that I liked working with him. We complemented each other even though he was much more experienced than I. I left M&M knowing that I could have had an excellent career there, but I preferred smaller companies and consulting seemed exciting.

What I was to learn over the next several decades in business was that *small companies are more interesting businesses*. I have worked for large companies and small ones, and I prefer small companies. First and foremost there is more chance of promotion in a small company. There is less competition and a better chance to grow by doing multiple tasks instead of being pigeonholed in one area of the large company.

There is a greater chance of substantial ownership of a small company than a big one. Your stock options in a big company are insignificant to the overall ownership of the company while your stock options in a small company can be 5 percent or more depending on how valuable you are to the company. In a small company, you often work directly with the president or the owner whereas in a big company you may never get a chance to meet senior management or have them judge the quality of your work.

Small companies exist because they are better, more customer oriented, more efficient, and more effective than large companies. If it weren't true, big companies would drive small companies out of business. Big is not better; it is merely bigger.

Chapter 9

Consulting and Citibank

I joined M&M Candies in the spring of 1966. I left in the winter of 1968 to join the John D. Kettelle Corporation. As a start-up division to conduct operations research consulting for commercial organizations, Larry and I were isolated from the military consulting that was the main part of the company. In addition, we both lived in the Morristown area, away from Paoli, Pennsylvania, where the company was located. We would drive to Paoli, but most of the time, Larry and I were with clients.

The first major client we sold was the National Sugar Refining Company in Philadelphia. There were two great assignments I was involved in. The first was negotiating the quality of the sugar purchased from large ships arriving from sugar producing countries in the world. Typically, raw sugar has from 97 to 99 percent pure sugar, the rest being other ingredients removed in the refining process. The percentage of pure sugar in the raw sugar varies from ship to ship depending on the processing that occurs in the country producing the sugar and the refining process used there.

The percentage of pure sugar contained in raw sugar is calculated by chemical analysis.

To keep the buyer and the seller honest, samples of raw sugar are taken from various parts of the ship and split into three equal parts. It is then given to the seller, the buyer, and a neutral firm. Each firm does its own chemical analysis and submits it in a sealed document. For each sample, the three results are compared, the two closest percentages are averaged, and the third estimate is discarded. This is done for each sample, and then all the samples are averaged to obtain the overall percentage of pure sugar for the entire ship. Discarding one of the parts in each sample that is farthest away from the other two keeps the buyer and the seller honest because if they cheat too much, their estimate will be discarded.

Our consulting assignment was to evaluate each seller's cheating percentage to determine how much National Sugar could cheat and still have their estimates in the average, discarding the seller's estimate. The problem was a bidding strategy, somewhat like game theory, where you could cheat a little to gain an advantage, but not too much. Eventually, if the buyer keeps winning, the seller probably lowers his estimate to gain the advantage, and that drives the fudging toward no fudging at all, provided both buyer and seller are rational. So long as the seller is cheating, however, the buyer can save money by cheating just a little less. It requires a constant analysis of each seller to know how much to fudge each estimate.

The second problem was much more straightforward. The company had a series of warehouses that maintained its supply of various sugar products that it produced. The company had no inventory model to determine how much inventory to carry for each product at each warehouse. In addition, National Sugar could ship the sugar products by rail or by truck, and the tradeoff had not been studied.

I worked on these problems for several months and concluded that truck shipments were preferred to rail shipments because of the speed of the trucks and the flexibility it provided to handle small replenishments. My most important contribution, however, was the development of a mathematical inventory model that estimated the sales for each product at each warehouse based on previous sales, weighting the recent sales more heavily than sales farther back in time. The model was quite sophisticated mathematically, using some of the operations research training I was familiar with as well as new material I had to learn from textbooks.

National Sugar liked the solution and wrote the software to implement my model. It was an immediate success as it lowered the inventory and reduced the amount of stock outage at the warehouses. Larry thought the solution was elegant, encouraged me to publish the model and the results, but I never did. Ten years later, I heard from Larry that the model was still in use at the sugar company, a pleasant surprise, and a tribute to the power of operations research methods when properly used. It was very satisfying to solve a business problem, work out the mathematics on paper, have it programmed into a computer system, and see it work in operation. It was even more gratifying to learn that the solution remained in operation for more than a decade. *Analytical tools are powerful business weapons.*

As a start-up consulting division serving the corporate community, we were doing quite well for being in business for one year. In the fall of 1969, Larry told me that the rest of the firm, however, was downsizing because the firm's government business was not doing well as a result of the recession then going on. I was surprised to learn this because Larry and I were busy with contracts at Hamm's Beer and National Sugar. I had my head down, focused on serving our clients and nothing else. I had no idea what Larry had in mind except that he told me to hang loose, and he would try to determine a proper strategy for us.

Several weeks later, Larry told me that he had decided to pursue other interests outside of the company, and he was working on four opportunities. I then asked him whether those opportunities included me, and Larry, to my very great surprise, told me that two of the four opportunities included me. I was surprised because I thought we were a team, that we had left M&M Candies as a team, and that it was unreasonable to not include me in his new opportunities. Larry apologized in his own way, saying he just wasn't sure which ones would materialize, and he wasn't sure which ones he would take. I then asked the obvious question, "What about me?" He said, "I think you should start looking on your own, and I will keep you abreast of what I decide." That conversation didn't please me at all. I liked Larry; he was a great mentor, we were a strong team, and I didn't think he would leave the company without me. Now I knew that I couldn't be sure.

After talking with my wife about what to do, it was obvious that I had to start looking for a new job without depending on Larry. I got in touch with an executive recruiting agency, and they were interested in me. After sending them my resume, they called in two weeks to say there was a perfect job opening at Citibank. I was definitely interested.

I had always had an interest in the financial marketplace. I had aggressively studied how to invest in the stock market, finance was of great interest to me, and my PhD dissertation was on how to optimize investment decisions with limited amounts of money. In a short period of time, I interviewed at Citibank, they liked me, and I liked the job. The job I was offered was to become assistant vice president, the lowest official level at the bank, at the salary of twenty-five thousand dollars per year.

I approached Larry shortly thereafter, told him I had a job offer at Citibank, and asked him once again what his plans were. Larry was vague on what he was going to do. That convinced me that I had to accept the job, and I told Larry that. He grudgingly agreed that I was doing the right thing in the face of his uncertainty, and we both departed upset that we would not be working together in the future. Several years later and on many occasions, Larry told me that he had made a bad mistake not keeping us together. I felt the same way back then, and my opinion has never changed. Reluctantly, I resigned from J. D. Kettelle and accepted the job at Citibank. That decision was the most important decision in my professional career, for it set me on a course that established my career for the rest of my working life.

Before I describe my career at Citibank, there is one important story about Larry worth telling. Larry and I were in New York City around New York University and Greenwich Village. It was springtime, and there was a great art sale going on. Artists were on the sidewalks and in Washington Square Park displaying their own art, some of which was gorgeous. We decided to browse the art.

Larry became fascinated with a huge five-foot-high and three-foot-wide oil painting of a Spanish flamenco dancer. The lady was gorgeous; the colors were brilliant. It was a first-class work of art. Larry asked the price and was told it was for sale at $1,400. Larry looked at the painting, asked me for my opinion, and we both agreed that it was worth buying. Larry loved to negotiate, however, so he asked the artist if he could make an offer. When he was told yes, he said to the artist, "Look, I like the painting, but I can't spend $1,400 on it. I don't want to embarrass you with a very low offer, so would you consider a low bid." The man said yes, so Larry offered four hundred dollars. The artist said quite forcefully, "No way!" Larry and the artist continued to negotiate, but Larry would not budge. No matter what the artist did in lowering the price several times, Larry did not move off the four-hundred-dollar price.

As we were about to walk away, Larry told the artist, "Here's my card and phone number. If you change your mind, give me a call." Several days later, the artist did call Larry and agreed to the four-hundred-dollar offer. By then, Larry had lost interest in the painting and turned him down. I thought Larry was foolish doing that, for the painting was a steal at that price, but Larry was a stubborn man. There is no cure for stubbornness. But more importantly, I learned for the first time that *in negotiating you don't need to come down a small amount from the offering price. You can be aggressive with a ridiculously low offer.*

When I joined Citibank in 1969, it was a very exciting place. John Reed was then senior vice president in charge of all operations for the bank, reporting to Bill Spencer, the president of the bank, and Walter Wriston, CEO. Reed argued that the bank was similar to a production facility, for it processed millions of pieces of paper, and it could be managed as a production facility, just as cars are managed during their production process. As a result, he hired a man from Ford to manage the check-processing operation located at 111 Wall Street.

To support the move to a more efficient operation for check processing, lending, and the new credit card operation in Jericho, Long Island, Reed organized an Operations Analysis Department to evaluate these operations and to suggest improvements. I was hired to be one of the four senior men in Operations Analysis, a group of twenty-four people. My boss was also Larry (not the same Larry I worked for at Kettelle and M&M), who reported directly to Reed. Although the concept of the Operations Analysis group was to have four groups of six people each, five supporting people reporting to a senior person, the reality was that I undertook projects on my own without much help and reported to Larry and Reed on my progress.

My training as a consultant had taught one important lesson. *Take your marching orders seriously. Put the client first.* Do not put your own needs ahead of the client. I focused on grasping the problem, defining it carefully, and only then looking at potential solutions. This was the best way to achieve the objective the client wanted to achieve.

My first assignment was one of the most interesting of all as it set out a path I was to follow for the rest of my professional career. Citibank had an established credit card operation on Long Island well ahead of the other major banks in New York City. Manufacturers Hanover

Bank (Manny Hanny) and Chemical Bank, two of the other major New York banks, had just established ESBA, the Eastern States Banking Association. ESBA was a cooperative credit card venture of several major banks established to process credit card transactions for all of them. ESBA was new to credit card processing, and Reed suggested to both Manufacturers Hanover and Chemical that Citibank might be willing to jointly process for these two banks if they were interested.

Each of the three banks had political motives for wanting to participate in a study of the costs of credit card operations by Citibank, ESBA, Manufacturers Hanover, and Chemical. Reed thought it was a long shot to expect the other two banks to let Citibank process their transactions since they were major competitors. He wanted, however, to prove to his boss that Citibank was more efficient than the other New York banks, thus looking good inside his own bank. I did not know this and thought there was a chance that all three banks might want to work together. I was naïve about the motives of senior management and took what I was told as the real objective: to determine which system was cheaper and to suggest how they might work together.

Manny Hanny and Chemical also had other motives that I only appreciated later. They wanted to learn how Citibank operated their operations in order to improve ESBA. They had no desire to have Citibank do their processing, but they did want to learn how to make ESBA more efficient. A study of Citibank's operation would help them to do that.

Each of the three banks provided two analysts to generate a study group of six people to conduct the analysis. I was selected as the lead person from Citibank and, within a short period of time, became the lead person for the entire team. I had stronger analytical training, Citibank had the better operation, and I was open to sharing and working together as a team. The Manny Hanny and Chemical staff provided knowledgeable people about their own operations and were willing to let Citibank take the lead because they believed this would produce more information for them.

I lived in Morristown, fifty miles west of Manhattan in New Jersey, and had to travel to Jericho to visit the Citibank credit card operations fifty miles east of Manhattan on Long Island. Driving by car through Manhattan would have been a disaster. The best way to go was over the George Washington Bridge, across the Bronx, and then out to Long

Island. The hundred-mile ride took me two hours to get there one way, a formidable trip on a regular basis. The trip to ESBA was a little closer on Long Island, but it too was a major drive. In short, I spent a lot of time in my car, leaving just as my two young children were getting up and arriving home just as they were going to sleep.

Because the study group had the support of the senior management in their respective banks, we had access to any data we needed even though much of the data was confidential. We spent several months on the study, and I pulled together most of the data that was provided to us. The results were impressive for Citibank, for it was processing credit card transactions at one-third the cost of ESBA. Citibank had much more volume than ESBA, and credit card operations are volume sensitive, and have economies of scale. In addition, ESBA was quite new to the credit card processing business, it was processing much less volume, and justifiably did not have the sophistication that Citibank had.

I was a good analyst new to Citibank, trying to prove myself on my first major assignment, willing to cooperate with everyone. I was focused on doing a good job of analysis. I had no idea of the politics behind the study or the objectives of Reed, let alone the other senior bankers from Manny Hanny and Chemical.

During that credit card assignment, I was isolated from Citibank. I was traveling outside of my office in Manhattan, so I was immune to much of what was going on in my group. I rarely spoke with Larry but he would hold a group meeting weekly, and I attended them to let the rest of the group know my progress. As we approached the end of the study, Larry sent another guy from my group down to help me prepare the final report. This guy informed me that he had no idea what he was going to do, and we both agreed that it was being done simply because Larry did not trust me to do a good job. I did not know Larry well enough, but I quickly determined that he trusted no one. Larry was paranoid about everything. He had to check and double-check on everyone and everything. I had never worked with anyone so lacking in trust. In short, he wanted a spy in my midst to inform him whether I was going to produce a good report or not.

Once I understood why the other guy was to work with me, I told him to get lost. I was confident about my ability, I didn't need help, and he would slow me down. I told Larry to leave me alone, to trust me, and I would produce a good report, which I did. After I left the bank, I heard that Larry was first promoted to head the Information Technology Division and then fired by the personnel department because there were too many complaints to personnel about the way he verbally abused the people who worked for him.

In my experience, straight A students often end up working for people who had average grades in college. The reason is that these people work well with senior management, work well with colleagues, and can identify excellent staff. Larry, my boss at M&M Candies, was brilliant but had an arrogant attitude that came across to management. He often was right, but top management didn't like the way he argued. Larry eventually realized that he would never be promoted and quit. Larry, my other boss at Citibank, was paranoid about people. His lack of trust forced him to check up on his staff again and again to be sure that they were doing a good job. He was brilliant too. In fact, both Larry's were PhDs, but their personalities got in the way. Too many people disliked them, and neither of them could move into the top management ranks. *In big business, the people who reach the top must not only be great strategists but also have strong interpersonal skills. You need both.*

Once the study was completed, Reed took me with him to meet his boss. It was the first time I was to meet the president of Citibank. I was nervous, but the meeting went extremely well. Reed was proud to tell his boss how efficient Citibank was in its credit card operations compared to its competition, and I was pleased that he was pleased. That told me that I had established my credentials with my boss's boss, and that eventually led to a new career a year later.

My first assignment at Citibank was a major event for me. I learned about the credit card business from one of the best-run credit card operations in the business. I met senior management at Citibank and two other New York banks. I learned about cooperative bank operations at ESBA, and I found that I could analyze complex bank operation issues. Most importantly, for the first time in my life, I was working in the payment systems industry and liked it. I had the skill to contribute, the industry had major growth potential, and that made problem solving fun, exciting and important. I knew I could make this a career because I enjoyed doing this kind of work.

I had two other assignments at Citibank. I was asked to analyze the retail lending operations, but it never amounted to much because I didn't spend much time on it. I also became involved in check-processing operations, and this helped to establish my knowledge there, the largest payment system in the world.

In 1969, Citibank was using Burroughs equipment for its check-processing operation, and IBM wanted to displace them. I did an analysis of the two systems and concluded that there was not sufficient benefit to make the change. In addition, several of the analysts in my group began to study the entire check-processing operation, from the receiving of the checks from tellers in branches right through to the preparation of customer statements. It was a complicated process, so we constructed flowcharts of the work for all the steps that the processing of the check took, such as, the encoding process (putting the dollar amount on the check), the handling of a deposit when it is out of balance, the capture of the checks, the handling of rejects when a check is ripped or cannot be read, and so on.

It wasn't easy to do this work for several reasons. First, we didn't know the process, and each person working there only knew a small part of it, and they often didn't want to take the time to explain what they knew in detail. Secondly, there were very few people who were willing to explore new ways to improve the process. My group was interested in improving the process, but we didn't know the process well enough to know the implications for any improvement if the process was changed. Finally, the check-operating group wasn't interested in working with us, for they viewed my boss as a thorn in their side, critical of what they were doing instead of working in a cooperative fashion.

The check processing people did not want to be viewed as running an inefficient operation, so they viewed us as critics rather than being there to help improve what they were doing. Our view was to embrace change, not to find fault but to improve the process. So long as senior management made our view clear to the operations people, we thought that that would be sufficient to gain their cooperation. However, if senior management was not clear about the reason for the analysis, then the operations people would see us as evaluating them and their operation to make personnel changes if necessary. The first way was positive for the operating staff while the second way was threatening for them. Only senior management could set their mind at ease, and my boss did not know how to do that.

It is important to gain the trust of the people who work in the function you are analyzing. *Your client must believe your objective is future improvement, not judging past performance.* Otherwise, your client can stonewall, tell you nothing, make it extremely difficult to understand the process, and avoid discussing problems that need to be addressed. When people believe you are there to hurt them, to point out their inefficiencies, and to report that to management, you must gain their trust. You are not there to hurt them but to help them improve, and that is not easy. This was an important lesson to learn because it affected every consulting assignment I did during my career.

Because operating people did not support our efforts, I felt frustrated trying to understand the process, and then think through how the process could be improved. Part of the reason was my own ignorance of a complex system, and part of it was the unwillingness of the operations people to work closely with us. I was slugging away at a big system with no support from the top to make this a cooperative effort with operations. This study was completely different from the credit card study where support from the top of the banks made everything easy. Nevertheless, I was learning check processing in detail, and this was contributing to my payments-system knowledge.

Joining a consulting firm gave me the first chance to lead in a business situation. I had to sell myself to people in senior positions, analyze the problems I was asked to solve, and sell the solution to those senior people. I worked hard to be the leader I was supposed to be. *Consulting is good training for leadership.* At Citibank, I was also thrust into an internal consulting role. I had to assess an operation and make recommendations to senior people. It required dealing with people who questioned what I was doing. I had to not only lead in doing the work but also lead in selling the results. It was excellent training. Consulting is a demanding position, but it pushes you to be the best you can be.

In early 1971 my boss invited me and another staff member to go with him to Casa Grande, Arizona, for a one-week T-Training program. I had no idea what T-Training was, but when your boss invites you to join him, you accept. I was told that this was about personal improvement. I would be in a group of fourteen people at my professional level, no one from Citibank would be in my group, and I could be myself. I would be able to see how other people saw me so that I could understand myself better, and this could lead to my own personal improvement. When we arrived at the T-Training program, the leaders informed us that there were not enough attendees for three groups, so there would only be two groups. Since Citibank had three people, I was asked to join my boss in his group—not exactly the right solution for me—but it was the best the program had to offer.

I had dealt with my boss for more than a year. I thought I was competent at Citibank. I believed that he thought highly of me though he mistrusted everyone. I decided that I would be myself in the group, regardless of what my boss might think afterwards. I was determined to get the most out of this training and acted naturally the entire week, even disagreeing with my boss on a couple of occasions.

It didn't matter to my boss what I did or how I acted, for he was literally hated within the first hour that the group started working together. Here is what happened. The group leader began the first session by pointing out that he was there to help us understand ourselves. We would find out more about ourselves by working with people we did not know, me excluded, and this would show us whether we were leaders or followers, whether we could convince other professionals of our ideas. Since we would be intimate with each other for a week and probably never see each other again, we would have no other motive than to be honest with one another.

The group leader then shut up, sat in the room with us, and said nothing. The fourteen attendees then spent the better part of an hour, moving from one topic to another, offering ideas of what to do next, who should be in charge, why they were here, with no apparent agreement on anything. Finally, in frustration, my boss stood up, grabbed a piece of chalk, went to the blackboard, and tried to take control of the meeting. His motive was good: to organize the group into a set of objectives, to determine what we wanted to achieve, and to set out an agenda for our group. While his motive was fine, his approach generated a series of nasty comments that he was taking over the group, that he was trying to dominate and dictate the discussion, and that he was unwilling to give up the chalk to anyone else. The other dozen people jumped all over him for his arrogance, his control, and his insistence that an organized agenda would be preferred over the meandering that we were doing. He was roundly criticized while I just sat there listening. I was totally transformed by what I was hearing about my boss. I knew he was not liked for his dominating attitude, for his desire to control, for his lack of trust of others, but I did not realize how quickly he could generate hatred about himself. Because I was unwilling to let my boss dominate me, I didn't realize how he could come across to others. It was an enlightening moment in my professional life.

The rest of the week was a blur. I tried to contribute, and I did. I learned a lot about myself: that I had confidence in my professional ability, that I could hold my own intellectually with men being paid more than me, that I could get along with people I had never met, and that I could convince them that I could help them. The first hour with my boss, however, convinced me that I had to find a different boss.

A few months later, in April 1971, my boss invited me out for dinner after work. I had never been invited out for dinner by anyone at Citibank, so I knew something was up. At dinner, he told me that there was a study going on at Georgia Institute of Technology in Atlanta that dealt with the future of electronic banking. The man in charge of the study, a professor at Georgia Tech, had died of a heart attack, and there was no one to finish the study. I later learned that the professor was Paul Han. The Federal Reserve Bank of Atlanta was paying Georgia Tech to perform the study, and the bank had no one to finish it. As a result, George Mitchell, then a governor of the Federal Reserve Board, asked Reed, whom he knew well, if he could find someone at Citibank to finish the study and continue on to the next phase. Reed met with my boss, and they decided that I was the right guy to complete the assignment.

My boss asked me if I had ever been to Atlanta, and I told him that I had never been in the South, except to go to Miami when I was a kid. He asked me to speak with my wife, and if I agreed to go, then Citibank would pay for the trip and pay to rent a house for a year, the expected length of time to finish the study. I would remain on the payroll at Citibank, and I would fly back to New York every month to update him and Reed. Finally, I should leave my house in New Jersey vacant and pay the mortgage because the bank would cover my living expenses in Atlanta.

When I mentioned that I had a five-year-old who would be starting kindergarten in the fall, my boss said that I should find a good school for her, and the bank would cover the expenses because he did not believe the schools in the South were as good as the schools in New Jersey. I was not excited about moving anywhere, let alone a city I had never been to almost a thousand miles away from my mother and the rest of my relatives. I agreed to get back to him as soon as I spoke with my wife.

When I told Judy about the offer, she was positive about moving there but concerned about her pregnancy; she was about to enter her ninth month. We spoke about the difficulty of finding a new doctor in a strange town, about finding a place to live, about moving furniture, about finding a Jewish neighborhood and a synagogue, and about leaving Morristown, a place we liked, and the friends we had made there. We both thought, however, that it would be a nice adventure, an opportunity for my professional growth, and I was not very happy working for my boss. We knew that Citibank would take good care of us financially and that it would only be for a year. Little did I know!

We moved to Atlanta around May 11, my birthday, three weeks before our son, Leo, was born. Judy and I were thrilled at having a healthy new baby, but for different reasons. We did not want to know the sex of the baby beforehand, and if the baby was a boy, Judy did not like the person who would perform the circumcision in Morristown. He had a poor reputation for circumcisions, and Judy was reluctant to use him. When Leo was born, Judy was happy that we were in Atlanta, and she would be able to find another person to do the circumcision. I was happy that I had a boy to carry on the family name. There were few relatives named Lipis, and none of them with that last name were having male children. Leo would be one of a very few with the Lipis name, and I wanted the name to continue.

Citibank had a relationship with Trust Company Bank in Atlanta, and they had a man who helped important clients take care of personal matters when they moved to town. Judy and I flew down to Atlanta a few days after we agreed to the assignment, and the Trust Company man took us around to various parts of town showing us houses to rent. After visiting several of them, we settled on a house in the northeast part of town. The house was quite large, and we decided that we would rent furniture for the large den since we did not have such a room in our Morristown home. Judy spoke with her gynecologist in Morristown, and he recommended a doctor in Atlanta. She was satisfied that he would serve her and the new baby well. I was given an office at the

Engineering Experiment building on the Georgia Tech campus with enough room to add a sizeable group of people to undertake the rest of the study for the next year.

In a short period of time, we had help from the moving company to pack up our furniture, kitchen stuff to maintain our kosher home, our clothes, and most of the rest of our home. We got our two young girls ready for the trip, arranged for a moving company to deliver our stuff in Atlanta just after we got there, closed up our house, and flew to Atlanta. The moving company delivered our cars to us a few days later.

To avoid having to take all of our possessions for just a year and then to bring them back to New Jersey, we boxed a lot of books and other items we didn't need and put them in our basement. I had a large collection of statistics and operations research books, and Judy had cookbooks and books from her college days. We also had a large collection of fiction and nonfiction books. We didn't think we needed them all in Atlanta, and the house we rented didn't have the bookcases to put them all in. In short order, we found ourselves nicely settled in Atlanta, and I started my new career in electronic banking.

Chapter 10

Atlanta Payments Project

Before I could sink my teeth into the work ahead, Judy was fast approaching her due date. I had asked her whether she preferred to have our baby in New Jersey with her existing doctor and then move to Atlanta or move to Atlanta before the baby was born and deal with an unknown doctor. After a brief discussion of the pros and cons of each, she decided she would rather move first, take her chances with a new doctor, and organize the house in Atlanta before the baby arrived. It was a wise decision because we had plenty of help all along the way. The moving company packed our stuff and delivered our furniture on time in Atlanta. We had help from Trust Company finding a house to rent, and we didn't have trouble renting furniture for the large den, which didn't exist in our New Jersey home.

By the end of May 1971, the house was in relatively good shape. I was working on finishing part 1 and part 2 of the Federal Reserve study with a couple of graduate students at Georgia Tech. I was also in touch with Brown Rawlings, the senior vice president and key person at the Federal Reserve Bank of Atlanta who was controlling the study, along with the chairman of the Industrial Engineering Department at Georgia Tech.

In late May, the weather in Atlanta is gorgeous. Since I had been playing raquetball in Morristown and needed the exercise, I was out playing with some of the graduate students on June 1 when Judy had a doctor's appointment. Judy seemed fine when I left for work, but when she showed up at the doctor's office for her regular appointment the doctor examined her and announced that she was dilated seven centimeters and needed to get to the hospital immediately. In fact, he took her there himself.

The doctor's office called my work number to let me know, and one of the graduate students ran out to where I was playing to tell me to get to the hospital immediately—the baby was coming. I rushed to my car and arrived at the delivery room about half an hour before Leo was born. I was happy I made it, but it was close. Our first child took quite a while to deliver, our second child was much faster, and Leo took less than an hour. I was thrilled to have a boy to partially even out our family since I was outnumbered with three women.

Being an observant Jew, we had to have a bris (ritual circumcision) in Atlanta without knowing anyone. We had not joined a synagogue, but an Orthodox synagogue was close by. When I went there, I was told that the only mohel in Atlanta, the person that performs the ritual circumcision, had just moved to Israel, and there was no other mohel in town. Judy and I did not want to use a Jewish doctor to do the circumcision; we wanted a mohel who was trained to do this as a profession. We were told that such a mohel existed in Birmingham, Alabama, so I called him and he agreed to come. Cantor Ostrovsky drove the two-hour one-way trip, we paid him seventy-five dollars for his efforts, and he did a perfect job.

My only regret was that we had so few people there. My mother, my uncle, and my sister came for the occasion, and Judy's parents were there, but we didn't have more than a dozen people in total, and half of them were not Jewish. A bris is a great celebration, and in my culture, it is open to everyone. We didn't know many people to invite, and I was caught up with taking care of my two young girls, helping Judy to adjust to our new home, and dealing with a new assignment at Georgia Tech. Nevertheless, I looked back on that occasion more than once as the omen for a wonderful way to start a new life with a new baby in a new city with a new job.

In 1982, a decade after I began my work in Atlanta, the *Atlanta Business Chronicle*, the Atlanta business newspaper, had a cover story about the Atlanta payments project, summarizing how it began. Here are some excerpts from that story:

> About 1970, Paul Han, a Georgia Tech banking professor, came
> to the Fed with the bold idea of researching the possibility of

electronic funds transfer. No paper would be involved. There would be no room full of check sorters. There'd be no trucks, no airplanes hauling boxes of checks from city to city.

The man Han approached at the Atlanta Fed was Brown Rawlings, then senior vice-president. He became the dean of payment systems research. Han envisioned a marriage of computer technology and the need for efficiency. Having witnessed firsthand the basic inefficiency of traditional paper-based money transfers, Rawlings endorsed the study proposed by Han and became its patron. The Atlanta Payments Project was born.

Brown Rawlings recommended that the Fed provide funds and office space for the research such a study would require. Rawlings campaigned for and nurtured a study of how money would move from payer to payee in the future. It is because of Rawlings that Atlanta became electronic banking's equivalent of Renaissance Italy.

Han died in 1971, stricken by a cerebral hemorrhage, while driving through the Tech campus. Rawlings needed a replacement. He was Allen Lipis, a 31-year-old assistant vice-president at Citibank when his boss loaned him to Georgia Tech to replace Han.

When I returned to work, I found that the first two parts of the study for the Federal Reserve were virtually completed. These two parts dealt with the present payment systems in Florida and Georgia based on a survey of the financial institutions there. There were five hundred charts and tables that had been produced based on these two surveys. What remained was to organize them into some sensible format, write an introduction to each document, and publish them. Since no one else seemed to know what to do about finishing the documents, I took the charts and put them into sections, deciding which ones would come first, second, etc., for each section. That didn't take very long, and then I wrote an introduction to the exhibits. The whole process took a month or two to complete using several graduate students at Georgia Tech.

At that point, I told the Federal Reserve and Georgia Tech that the first two reports were finished, completing the work of Paul Han. This was relatively easy to do as the exhibits only needed to be organized. Nevertheless, Brown Rawlings was impressed, and asked me to take on the next phase at its project director. I did not realize it at the time, but there was someone at the Federal Reserve Bank of Atlanta who also wanted to take on the role of project director. He was responsible for the entire planning department at the Atlanta Fed. Later, after he left the Fed to start his own very successful company, I learned that I had been selected over him.

The next part of the study, phase 3, was to deal with the future of electronic funds transfer. This was an area few people knew much about, one which would require significant knowledge of the existing payment systems as well as an ability to imagine what the world of electronic banking might realistically look like. The project had to be led by people who understood bank operations and had the experience to make the leap to the new world of electronic banking. The conclusion I came to was that we needed bankers, not graduate students to undertake the study. *Always get the best team for the job.*

Reluctantly, I informed Georgia Tech that we would need less graduate students. I then met with Rawlings at the Atlanta Fed, discussed my plan, and he agreed that this would be a sensible strategy and gained the approval from Monroe Kimbrel, then president of the Atlanta Fed. Kimbrel immediately sent a letter to the CEOs of the five major Atlanta banks asking for their help. He made a comment to me at the time that I have tried to follow in my professional life: *keep the letter to one page.* Many corporations insist that a memo be one page. It is an important thing to remember, as it requires the writer to summarize the issue, explain it succinctly, and make the request clear. Kimbrel was a master at it.

After the letter was sent, Rawlings and I made the rounds to the five major banks to see if they would support our project. I had met with the president of Citibank only once, and now I had the chance to meet with the CEOs of the five biggest banks in Atlanta or someone they designated. It was exhilarating for me given that I had been a lowly assistant vice president at Citibank.

Four of the five banks responded positively and agreed to provide not just one analyst, which we requested, but two of them to join our staff for a four—to six-month period. They would help to do the study while remaining on their bank's payroll. The banks included Citizens & Southern National Bank, First National Bank of Atlanta, Trust Company Bank, and Fulton National Bank. The fifth bank, National Bank of Georgia, didn't have the quality staff we required, so they agreed to pay a sufficient amount of money equal to the expense of providing two staff people for the six-month period. In addition, the Atlanta Fed agreed to provide three of its analytical staff to the study. Finally, I had sufficient money from the Fed to hire a permanent staff and three outside consultants if we needed them, which we did.

Some time in the late summer and early fall of 1971, I met each of the bankers from the banks, the analysts from the Fed, and discussed what they might do when they joined me full-time on the study. The first man I met was Bob Clayton at C&S National Bank, and after we spoke, he looked me in the eye and asked whether he would be on the study or not. I liked him, of course, and immediately agreed, but it was the first time that I recognized that I was really in charge of the study and had the power to direct the people who served on it even though they did not report to me.

As I quickly discovered, the Atlanta banks offered the study a fabulous group of people. Bob Clayton went on to become a senior cash management expert at C&S and stayed with the bank as it went through several mergers to become NationsBank and then Bank of America. Jimmy Jarrell at Trust Company Bank stayed involved in payment systems for most of his professional career, later joined me at Payment Systems, Inc., and became the president of the National Automated Clearing House Association. Bill Adcock at Fulton National Bank started his own consulting firm in payment systems with Anne Moore, focusing on payment-system marketing research. George Budd at the Atlanta Fed went to work for the C&S in a very senior position in bank operations. Each of these people became the nucleus of the Atlanta Payments Project, and we have stayed in touch for more than thirty-five years. We get together a couple of times a year to renew our friendship and talk about old times.

There was another man from the Atlanta Fed that impressed me, and that was Michael Hosemann. In his early career, he had been a priest and married a woman who earlier had been a nun. They were a terrific pair. Every time I was with them, their faces lit up as though they were happy to be alive and thrilled to be with me. It wasn't me that lit them up. That's the way they were. Michael worked on one of the most difficult aspects of our research: float. He looked at what impact electronic funds transfer would have on the speed at which checks might clear, which was an important contribution to our work.

Michael improved my writing with one idea. After reading my writing, he mentioned that I always wrote in the past. I didn't understand what he was talking about. He then showed me in my own words that I was always using the past tense, using such verbs as *was* instead of *is*, *produced* instead of *produces*, *suggested* instead of *suggests*, *determined* instead of *determines*, *hoped* instead of *hope*, *developed* instead of *develops*, and so on.

He pointed out that *writing in the present tense has tremendous power*. It implies that it is happening now, not in the past, which is yesterday's history. This was very insightful on his part, and it had a huge impact on my writing. I found myself changing the past tense to the present tense as often as possible. That one idea changed me as a writer, and I am very grateful that I had a Michael to show me the way to become a better writer. I tried to hire Michael many times, but he was established in other assignments. I miss having his advice.

I was also fortunate to hire Bill Moore, a Harvard Business School graduate, and we worked together for eight years, well beyond the Atlanta Payments Project. I interviewed a number of other people for the job, but in the end, Bill Moore was my best choice, and I was right. Bill was very bright, an excellent writer, a guy who never got angry and always spoke from a rational perspective. He was a perfect fit for me because he would often get me to reflect on what I wanted to do or what I wanted to say. In all the years that we worked together, I cannot recall a time when we had a difficult time resolving an issue. Bill often questioned my approach, forced me to reevaluate what I wanted to do, and always improved the result. We were a great partnership.

As we were completing the phase 1 and phase 2 reports, I had a chance to meet the head of the secretarial service group at Georgia Tech. I liked her professionalism and her personality and hired her to handle administrative matters after the completion of the phase 3 report. Mary Floyd was a jewel, extremely competent, and she went on to join First National Bank in the microcomputer department, teaching the bank how to use personal computers when they were just emerging as a major force in banking. Finally, I needed a couple of outside consultants to support what we did not know, so I hired my former boss, Larry Friedman, from M&M Candies. He had a brilliant mind, and I knew he would be able to provide an outside perspective on what we were doing. Also, I wanted to pay him back for being my mentor.

With a group of seventeen people, we called ourselves the Atlanta Payment Project. Bill and I were paid by Georgia Tech as were the consultants. The bankers were paid by their own banks because they would return to them after the study was completed. Georgia Tech, in turn, billed the Federal Reserve Bank of Atlanta, and the Fed billed Citibank for my salary.

Once the major Atlanta banks were committed to the study of electronic funds transfer (EFT), they decided that they needed a senior group of bankers to oversee what we were doing and to review the recommendations that would flow out of the study. The California banks had such a group, called the SCOPE Committee, the Special Committee on Paperless Entries. The Atlanta banks called their group the COPE Committee, the Committee on Paperless Entries. I would often comment in a speech that Scope was the name of a mouthwash and Cope was the name of an aspirin, so the California banks were merely improving their breath while the Atlanta banks were solving a headache.

Once a month, the COPE committee would meet, and I, along with some of the other team members, would bring the senior bankers up to date on our progress. The most exciting thing we worked on was the analysis of the Automated Clearing House (ACH), an idea the California banks had developed. The idea was to build an electronic network that would be the equivalent to an electronic check. The ACH, however, would not only be able to debit a checking account as a check does, but it also would be able to accept credits to a checking account, such as a direct deposit of payroll, a social security deposit, and other credits. The California SCOPE Committee had already developed the framework for such a system, hired Touche Ross to write the software for their IBM computer, and was willing to sell their software for fifteen thousand dollars to other banking groups to promote a nationwide ACH system.

The phase 3 study began in September 1971 and concluded in February 1972 with the production of a six-volume 1,300-page document. It was the first comprehensive look at how electronic banking could develop in the United States, and it was widely disseminated. Volume 1 provided an executive summary of our work, volume 2 dealt with the system design and analysis of batch systems (payments that clear once a day overnight), volume 3 dealt with the system design of an online point of sale system, volume 4 dealt with market research that we completed, volume 5 dealt with the various issues related to float (money that can be used because of delays in the clearing and settlement of a transaction), and volume 6 dealt with the legal considerations associated with electronic transactions.

To take on such a massive and original effort, we divided the project into independent sections with periodic reviews to assure there were no gaps when the sections were combined. With one to three people in charge of a particular area, each group met on its own and, from time to time, presented their thinking to the overall group, gaining comments and advice from them. In addition, we set aside an entire day several times during the project to allow each group to present their progress, so that we would not lose track of the overall plan and be able to determine if an important issue was not being dealt with by at least one of the groups.

This is basic project management. There are two critical steps to break the project into distinct pieces such that they don't overlap and yet cover all of the parts of the project. The first step is to make each section as independent as possible of the other steps. This may not always be obvious. The second step is to select the right people to take on each piece. These people need experience for the part they are given, leadership to manage their part of the project, and the personality to deal with the other leaders of the other pieces.

The review process is very important because it identifies which pieces of the project are falling behind, which leaders are not doing their job, and whether there is overlap or missing parts of the project that no one is doing. Quite often, an overlap is useful as it allows two groups to tackle the same issue. This can provide a choice as to which solution is best.

At the time, none of us appreciated the significance of what we were doing because we were focused on doing a good job. However, as time progressed and as our work started to take on a structure, several important people outside of Atlanta came to hear firsthand what we were doing. I was impressed when Reed, my boss's boss at Citibank, took a day out of his busy schedule to get an update on our progress on his way back from a meeting in Florida.

The fundamental thrust of the study was to design an electronic funds transfer system (EFTS). We believed that the benefits of such a system could simplify and streamline paper processing systems, reduce personnel and processing costs for banks and businesses, provide consumers with new and improved ways of making payments, and provide a means of orderly growth in the payment system.

As the study progressed, it became clear that the ACH could become a major activity, so we focused heavily on all the issues related to its implementation. At the end of the study, we produced the following conclusions and recommendations:

1. Checks will continue to be the mainstay of the payment process.
2. Direct deposit of payroll, electronic bill payment, and debit cards could eliminate 30 percent of the total check volume.
3. A central clearing mechanism is needed to process electronic payments.
4. We should support the ACH effort begun by the California banks.
5. The Atlanta Federal Reserve was the best entity to run the ACH for the Atlanta area.
6. Membership in the Atlanta ACH should be as broad as possible by including all the banks in Georgia.
7. A debit card would be an effective mechanism for purchases at the point of sale. Such a system would allow for the verification that sufficient money was in a checking account for the acceptance of a check at the point of sale.
8. A debit card system is a major investment, but it can be very profitable.
9. The Atlanta computer network for debit cards should be controlled by the commercial banks as a joint venture.

The COPE Committee accepted our report, agreed to support the ACH effort, and asked the Federal Reserve Bank of Atlanta if they would run the ACH for them. Rawlings got the Atlanta Fed to agree to the request and obtained agreement from the Federal Reserve Board in Washington, D.C. That was easy to obtain because Governor Mitchell, vice chairman of the Federal Reserve Board, was substantially behind the movement toward electronic banking.

Getting the Federal Reserve to operate the ACH not only saved the banks from developing the ACH service but also *used a widely respected organization to promote the idea*. The Fed first promoted the idea for Georgia, but other parts of the country began to get organized and the banks in these areas generally asked the Federal Reserve Bank in their area to run their ACH. With the Federal Reserve behind the idea, the ACH became a major new electronic banking service and eventually connected every financial institution in the United States. It would not have happened without the support of the Federal Reserve—both in running most of the ACH's and promoting the concept.

Government involvement in business has a duty to be fair and open and to set standards so that all the profit making firms have equal access to the services being provided with the same set of procedures for everyone. By providing access to their service, *government involvement can speed up implementation, set a common standard, and will require all players to abide by the same set of rules, but it reduces innovation and profitability*. Innovation occurs when there is competition, so whenever possible, avoid having the government be the only one offering the service.

That's what happened with the ACH in the United States. Once the Federal Reserve was asked to run most of the ACH's in the country, they offered the service to all financial institutions, forced a single standard for clearing and settlement on the industry, and priced the services to everyone without distinction. By homogenizing the service, the Fed made it difficult to make a sizeable profit by offering ACH services because most of the financial institutions could compete on an equal basis, driving down the price to clients and reducing profits.

With the study finished and presented to the COPE Committee, Reed approached me to return to Citibank. He had received an excellent report on our progress from the Atlanta Fed, and he offered me four different jobs at Citibank. I was torn between returning to New York with the possibility of working for a man who might one day become the CEO of one of the greatest banks in the world or staying in Atlanta at the start of what I thought could become one of the major changes to the banking industry, electronic banking. Both opportunities were exciting, and I was pleased to have a choice. The deciding factor turned on family issues. I had my mother and other family members in New York, but Atlanta was a great place to live. We had begun to make great friends, Atlanta was cheaper than New York, had a better climate, an easier commute to work, and we could buy a bigger and probably nicer home. The final factor was that I was my own boss in Atlanta while in New York I would be thrown back into the politics of a major New York bank, not as pleasant an environment as I thought Atlanta would be.

When I turned down Reed's gracious offer and told him I decided to stay in Atlanta, he wrote a strong letter to the Atlanta Fed about my decision. He said that he had been gracious to the Fed and had provided a person to the Fed for one year. He expected that the Fed would return that person after the one year was up. He did not expect that the Fed would steal that person away. That showed a lack of good faith on the part of the Fed. In return, the Atlanta Fed wrote him back that they did not steal him away, but rather the Atlanta banks had made me an offer to work for them. The Fed had nothing to do with the offer, and they were prepared to return me to Citibank. The issue was with the five major Atlanta banks. They had decided to offer me a job to stay on as their project director. I knew Reed would be angry, but I had to do what was in my best interests.

Sometimes you get lucky and find what you're looking for. *One good idea can launch a career.* Other people may search for a lifetime still looking for the perfect job. What I found was payment systems. It suited me, it challenged me, and it paid well. There was, fortunately, much going on that made my job interesting and often exciting. *The choice as to whether I liked what I was doing or not depended first on the assignment, second on my boss, and third on whether it would produce something useful.* I found all of that in the new world of electronic banking. I have no secret on how to find an idea to launch a career except to broaden your outlook, do as many different jobs as possible, and be open to new opportunities. The broader the net you have, the greater the chance of capturing your career in that net.

As with many other choices that I made throughout my life, I often thought of the famous poem by Robert Frost "The Road Not Taken." The poem ends, "Two roads diverged in a wood, and I, I took the one less traveled by, and that has made all the difference." How could I know what the road would have been if I had returned to Citibank? There was no telling. Reed did go on to be a very successful CEO of Citibank, and he took quite a few people along with him, making their careers successful. I had the chance to become one of them but took another road. I could have gone to Brooklyn Tech high school but took another road. I might have borrowed enough money to go to the Wharton School as an undergraduate but took another road. I might have selected another graduate school than Iowa State but selected it. And I might have decided to hang on with Larry when he was changing jobs but decided on Citibank. I had many choices along the way, and I took the road that seemed the best choice at the time. The roads were the less traveled roads, going to Iowa from Brooklyn, staying with the Atlanta banks instead of Citibank, and this made all the difference. I would be faced with these decisions many times more in the future, and each time, I took the road less traveled by, and they all made the difference.

With my decision to stay in Atlanta made, I threw myself back into moving the ACH forward in Atlanta. The need to stay at Georgia Tech was over, so the Atlanta Fed offered me an office in their building. There was an office on the fourth floor set aside for the Fed examiners that showed up once a year for a week to audit the books of the Fed. For the three years that I was there, I moved out for a week each year while the examination was taking place, but outside of that, I had my own office at the Fed. Although I was not an employee of the Fed, I had access to the officer's dining room and parking privileges in the parking deck at the Fed. I had the best of both worlds: I was treated as an officer of the Federal Reserve Bank of Atlanta without the responsibilities. I had easy access to Rawlings whenever I wanted it, I had my own staff, and I would attend COPE Committee meetings once a month to bring them up to date on our progress. In short, I had a small but important empire, and I felt like I was my own boss.

Once the ACH decision was approved, the Atlanta Fed purchased the ACH software from the California banks. Since it was written for IBM equipment and the Atlanta Fed had Burroughs computers, it took several months to convert the software to run on the Burroughs computer. In the summer of 1972, the software was ready, and the US Treasury was also ready to test the concept of direct deposit of social security payments.

While the software was progressing, the Atlanta Fed and the COPE Committee decided that we needed to educate the banks and other financial institutions throughout the state about the benefits of the ACH. I was empowered to produce an ACH presentation that I could give in various Georgia cities to explain the ACH. With the Federal Reserve behind the effort, we organized a series of meetings in six to eight cities in Georgia: Savannah, Macon, Valdosta, Albany, and a couple of other cities. If the Fed asks for an audience with a bank, they usually get it, so we had great turnouts at each of these presentations, and many questions were asked about what the banks needed to do to participate. For me, it was great fun traveling the state, meeting local bankers, being the center of attention, and beginning to feel that I had made the right decision to stay on in Atlanta.

The Treasury wanted to test direct deposit of social security payments in Florida where many more retired people lived, but the Florida banks were not ready—they had not organized an ACH yet. We had traveled the state of Georgia, and the Atlanta Fed believed that the Georgia banks would be a better state to test social security direct deposit. As a result, Georgia was used as the first test of social security direct deposit, and it worked beautifully.

In addition to traditional ACH services, Jimmy Jarrell created the concept of bill check. It was a simple idea. On a bill sent to the customer, the customer merely indicates his bank and checking account number on the stub, writes the dollar amount he wants to pay, signs, and returns the bill as an authorization to the biller. The biller transforms the information to an ACH format and sends the information through the ACH for clearing and settlement. From the first authorization, the biller can store the customer's bank and account number its system, so that future authorizations only need the amount of payment and a signature. The biller can then fill in the bank and account number of the customer stored in the biller's system.

C&S National Bank implemented bill check for more than a decade, and it was very successful. Without promotion by anyone in the industry, no one else saw fit to do it, although it was a wonderful idea to get consumers involved in not having to write a check. *It is not sufficient to have a good idea. The graveyard is full of good ideas. You need to promote it by people that other people respect.* Eventually, bill check was eliminated by C&S as online bill payment became the more standard approach to electronic bill payment. Nevertheless, bill check was a unique idea that helped to move consumers one step closer to electronic funds transfer.

While the Georgia ACH was progressing, the Atlanta Fed decided that they would publish the phase 3 report for $150 to get it out to the broad banking community as the report was beginning to gain wide-scale acclaim. Bankers were coming to Atlanta to visit me to find out what we were doing. With quite a few visitors, I proposed to the COPE Committee that we organize a conference at one of the local hotels, invite any banker that wanted to know what we had accomplished to come to the conference by registering for it, thereby providing a source of income to the COPE Committee to maintain the ongoing efforts of the Atlanta Payments Project.

When the COPE Committee agreed, we organized a two-day conference, put together a nice brochure and a large mailing list. We invited people around the country to come, and the turnout was immense. We had a paid attendance of 632 people, $140,000 in revenue and cleared a cool net profit of $110,000 after expenses. This became the war chest to pay my staff and me for the next several years. The COPE Committee and the Atlanta Fed were thrilled to have such a huge turnout and received the recognition that they deserved. I was thrilled that our work had received such wide-scale recognition and that we had put Atlanta on the map as one of the leading research places on electronic funds transfer.

Throughout my three years after the publication of the phase 3 report, I was a "hot person" on the bank speaking circuit. I was invited to speak at many conferences about what was going on in Atlanta regarding electronic funds transfer. Georgia was the second ACH in the country, and other areas of the country, such as Boston and Minneapolis, were in the process of establishing their own ACH. Everyone wanted to know about the ACH, how to implement it, what policy issues needed to be addressed, how to gain wide-scale acceptance by financial institutions, and how to market those services to consumers and corporations. In March 1974, in recognition of the need for a comprehensive document about the ACH, the Atlanta Payments Project produced the first major document on the ACH, entitled "Automated Clearing Houses: An In-Depth Analysis."

Naturally, we sold the document, and it sold quite well, perhaps several hundred copies for several hundred dollars a copy. It added money to the COPE Committee to pay for continuing our work.

After the phase 3 report was completed and the Atlanta banks were committed to establishing an ACH, they asked me to continue our work on the design and development of a point of sale system. That became the phase 4 report. The phase 4 report was all about an online point of sale system for debit and credit cards, especially debit cards. The study was entitled "A Technical, Marketing, Organization and Cost Evaluation of a Point-Of-Sale Terminal System." Bob Clayton from C&S stayed on for the phase 4 effort, but many of the other bankers from the phase 3 report returned to their banks. The banks, however, continued to support the phase 4 project with other staff. In addition, IBM supplied a person to work with us, and we hired Don Leonard from TRW to work on the system design. Don eventually left TRW and joined me at Payment Systems, Inc., heading up the consulting division on the West Coast. And, of course, Bill Moore and Mary Floyd continued on as part of my permanent staff.

To appreciate the study, which was completed in January 1973, bank credit cards were just being implemented, there was no nationwide credit card network, banks were issuing their own credit cards, ATMs were just being installed, and there were no regional ATM networks and certainly no national network. Debit cards did not exist. In addition, there was no organized way for merchants to verify the balance on a check before it was accepted for payment.

As such, the phase 4 report evaluated four payment services:

- Check Verification—allowing the merchant to verify that a customer's check was drawn against available funds.
- Bank Credit Card Authorization—authorizing a customer purchase made with a bank credit card
- Bank Credit Card Data Capture—authorizing a customer purchase made with a bank credit card and electronically capturing the transaction data for posting to both the customer's and the merchant's accounts.
- Debit Card Funds Transfer—authorizing a transfer of funds from a customer checking account to a merchant checking account,

and electronically capturing the transaction data for posting to the customer's and the merchant's accounts.

The conclusions from the study indicated that the system was technically feasible, it could be marketed to merchants, the services would be acceptable by consumers, there were no legal barriers to its implementation, and the profit potential could be substantial. The system, however, like most new payment systems, had a chicken-and-egg problem. Merchants would sign up for the system if many customers would use it, and consumers would use the system if many merchants implemented such a system. The difficulty was that both had to happen at the same time. Merchants wouldn't sign up for the service without a significant consumer base, and consumers wouldn't use the system if there were only a few merchants implementing it. To establish the system in a significant way would take several years or more, yet there was a substantial investment up front. The profitability of the system would take time, but it would provide a substantial return down the road as the volume built over time.

When the phase 4 report was completed, the COPE Committee supported a second conference to explain that report. While the turnout was not as big as the first conference, it was big enough to produce another substantial profit.

The *American Banker* ran a front-page story on December 5, 1972, on the Atlanta Payments Project, written by Phillip Brooke, the lead payment system reporter for the paper. The first few paragraphs of the story are worth repeating:

> A technical research study initiated here with little fanfare three-and-a-half years ago has materialized into a detailed design for the most ambitious electronic funds transfer project yet attempted in the nation's banking industry. The design, created by an assortment of commercial bankers, Federal Reserve officials, academic research specialists, consultants and lawyers—an interdisciplinary team known as the Atlanta Payments Project—is a blueprint for a multi-faceted, consumer-oriented payments system for this sprawling metropolitan area. The project here is a big gamble. If it proves successful, the system stands the chance of being adapted by the commercial banking community

for use in other major metropolitan areas. If it fails, it will have been a costly experiment. Regardless, though, the volumes of information already gathered and the combination of new services being explored by this group represent a major contribution to payments system development in this country. Thus, even at this stage, before its full research had been completed, the Atlanta Payments project is gaining a reputation as the most significant cooperative endeavor in the new era of electronic money.

As a result of the revenue from the conferences that we held and the reports that we sold, the Atlanta banks never had to write another check for the next three years while the Atlanta Payments Project remained in business. The reports we sold and the conferences we held paid for all the staff and consultants we hired throughout the Atlanta Payment Project's existence. I was beginning to think I could make a serious living in the payment system business.

Even with all the publicity that the Atlanta banks were receiving, they naturally did not want to invest in a point-of-sale system without knowing just how long it would take to recover their investment. It was an easy decision, therefore, for the banks to ask the Federal Reserve Bank of Atlanta if it would be willing to operate an Atlanta point-of-sale switch for the all the Atlanta banks, thereby relieving the banks of that expensive burden. In 1973, this was a creative idea because the Federal Reserve had not become involved in credit cards or anything related to plastic card processing. The Fed was involved in the payment system for check processing, wire transfers and now the ACH, so the idea was not farfetched.

The Atlanta Fed was anxious to support the Atlanta banks, they had always had an excellent relationship with them, and they had spearheaded the idea of processing ACH payments. After serious deliberation, the Atlanta Fed agreed that it would be willing to put up a point-of-sale network switch for the Atlanta banks, which was a major milestone, but the Atlanta Fed insisted on gaining the approval of the Board of Governors to do it. As a result, a single document was prepared for the Fed Board based on the phase 4 report, along with a proposal from the Atlanta Fed to indicate the extent of the Fed's commitment.

For months, the proposal went nowhere at the Board of Governors. My staff and I, the COPE Committee, and the Atlanta Fed all waited for a reply. My group was on hold awaiting the Board of Governor's response. Finally, Jimmy Jarrell, one of the members my group, arranged for us to meet with Senator Sam Nunn from Georgia who had been his fraternity brother at Georgia Tech. We flew to Washington, D.C., explained our situation, and asked him if he could move the Federal Reserve Board along to reach a decision. I wasn't sure if this was such a good idea, but we had waited for more than six months, and it was time to get a decision one way or the other. The odds of a yes from the board diminished the longer we waited, and there might be other options if the Fed declined to put up a switching and processing center, the centerpiece of our point-of-sale system.

Finally, the Board of Governors responded that they did not believe it was in the best interests of the banking industry to become involved in a point-of-sale system. Rather, the banking industry should take this on. As a result, the Atlanta banks backed off from their enthusiasm because they did not want to put up the money themselves. They might have done that together if they could have figured out how to cooperate with one another. That was difficult for the banks to do, for they were competitors.

To make matters worse, while the Atlanta banks waited on the decision to run a switching and processing center for debit cards, First National Bank of Atlanta was busy planning its own program to guarantee checks for grocery stores and other retailers. They took much of our research and figured out a system they could offer merchants to verify the acceptance of a check at the point of sale. The bank called their service Honest Face. It was a neat idea. A customer was given a plastic card that carried the name *Honest Face* on it. Any customer from any bank could get an Honest Face card by signing up at a merchant, say a grocery store. The Honest Face card did not need to know the checking account number of the customer nor the bank the customer did business at. It only needed the customer's information, such as name, address, telephone number, etc.

When the customer presented a check at the point of sale, the customer was asked for her Honest Face card. When presented with the card, the card was swiped through an Honest Face terminal and sent to First National Bank. The bank merely verified that the Honest Face card did not have any previous bad checks associated with it. The check was never verified, only the Honest Face card. So long as the Honest Face card never had a bad check presented with that card, the check was authorized as a good check for the merchant. For this service, the merchants paid a fee. Once a bad check was written with an Honest Face card, that card was blacklisted, and no more checks could be authorized with that card until the customer made good on the bad check with the merchant. Merchants would let the Honest Face system know when the bad check was paid so the Honest Face card could be removed from the blacklist. Finally, if the merchant wanted to have the check guaranteed, then a higher fee was charged, and First National Bank accepted the problem of collecting from the customer on a bad check instead of the merchant.

First National Bank saw an opportunity to launch Honest Face alone because they believed this new service would be more profitable done alone than cooperating with the other Atlanta banks. *In business, competition trumps cooperation.* The profit motive undermines cooperation.

US banks will work together on operational issues because they do not believe it undermines their ability to compete. They will not, however, work together on anything related to revenue, first, because it violates antitrust laws and, second, because it will impact their ability to make a profit. British banks, on the other hand, believe that cooperating even on operations will affect their bottom line. They are not as willing to cooperate because there are only a handful of major banks. The key issue is whether cooperation impacts the firm's ability to make more profits or not. When profits are impacted, cooperation will not occur.

Had the Federal Reserve agreed to run the central switch for an online point-of-sale system, it is unlikely that Honest Face would have been implemented by First National Bank of Atlanta, but that did not happen. Even more important, if the Fed had become involved in running a point-of-sale switch, they would have sped up the growth of debit cards in the United States by perhaps a decade because debit cards did not take off in growth until the 1990s, fifteen years after the Fed's decision not to participate in operating a point-of-sale switch.

When the Fed declined to participate at the point of sale, it had a devastating impact on my work. We had put together a marvelous plan to implement a point of sale system that would not only encourage debit cards but also would authorize credit cards and verify the account balance when a check was presented at the point of sale. My team was counting on a long-lasting project related to point of sale developments, for the ACH could not sustain my team alone.

Honest Face destroyed the cooperative effort among the banks. Since I was the project director of the cooperative effort, it was obvious that my time as project director was coming to an end with one possible exception. That exception was whether the other four banks would decide to continue to work together to compete against Honest Face by bringing out their own point-of-sale system. In that event, I would still have a job working with the other four banks on its implementation strategy.

In my concern to keep my job and the cooperative effort going, I made a call on William Matthews, the executive vice president at First National Bank. Matthews was a very competitive man, super smart, knowledgeable about EFT and banking. He made it clear that his bank was committed to Honest Face as a competitive service and did not want to work with the other Atlanta banks.

At first, the other four banks considered implementing a competitive service to Honest Face. Our team did some work on the assignment, but it became obvious rather quickly that it would be expensive, that two systems in the market at the same time would take extensive marketing dollars and split the revenue. In the end, the four banks decided to wait to see how well the Honest Face system did, and that put the last nail in the coffin of the Atlanta Payments Project. It was time for me to move on, much that I enjoyed every minute over the four years that I was involved with the Atlanta banks.

The most natural thought that occurred to me was that one or more of the five banks that I had worked under for three solid years would want me to join their staff. We had proven ourselves more than once, we were well-known entities, and we had a depth of knowledge that few others had. We could easily have fit into a number of areas, including strategic planning, operations, credit cards, cash management, and the world of electronic funds transfer, then a fledgling enterprise. No one bit, no one approached Bill or me, and I was surprised. While no one said a word or implied it, I could only think that I was Jewish, and there wasn't a single Jew at any high-level position at any of these banks. If any of this was true, and I had no way of knowing, the most optimistic thought I could think of was that if I was given a position at one of the banks it was likely that the opportunities for advancement would be limited. Perhaps the members of the COPE Committee knew this and did me a favor by not offering me a position. They knew that my chances for advancement would be limited by my religion, and they wanted me to do better than be frustrated at their bank.

The Atlanta Fed, however, felt a strong obligation to me. They had gotten me to Atlanta, they had seen firsthand that we had put Atlanta on the map not only in terms of the research that we did, but also in implementing the ACH before virtually anyone else. Rawlings felt a strong commitment to my welfare, and I will always be in his debt.

As we were winding up the affairs of the Atlanta Payments Project late in 1974, Rawlings invited me into his office and offered me the job of senior vice president in charge of operations at the Federal Reserve Bank of Philadelphia. He had checked into various positions around the Federal Reserve, and they needed someone with my type of skill at the Philadelphia Fed. I was impressed, went up to Philadelphia, met with some of the senior people there, and concluded that it was a very good job, something I could do well. But it required me to move from Atlanta. In the four years that my wife and I were in Atlanta, we had grown to love the city, we had joined a synagogue, made friends, we had purchased our own home, and our older children were well established in Jewish schools in Atlanta. It would be hard to leave, and I looked for another alternative that could keep me in Atlanta.

I was also determined to find a home for my two staff: Bill and Mary. I wanted to keep my staff together because they were loyal to me. *If you are loyal to your staff, then they will be loyal to you.* I had spoken to both of them, and Bill was willing to chance coming with me if I could find something suitable for both of us. I was determined to do so because I remembered what happened to me when I was working for Larry, and he told me that some of his opportunities included me and some didn't. I did not want to do that to Bill. Bill and I were a great team together, and I felt loyal to him. Sometimes a team makes it much easier to find a new career. I never considered doing anything else. Loyalty has its advantages in more ways than one. Wherever I ended up, I would find a position for Bill. That was crystal clear in my mind, and I made it crystal clear to Bill.

On the other hand, Mary was not as willing to be at risk. She was married, needed to work, and wanted something less risky. As a result,

I approached C&S about hiring her, and they immediately agreed. As our first-class administrative assistant, she was a real find for anyone. She was smart, organized, pleasant to deal with, and efficient. There was nothing in the administrative area that she could not do, especially when it related to technology. Later, Mary joined First National Bank of Atlanta in the microcomputer department when personal computers were just beginning to emerge and proved that not only could she master the technology but she could also teach it to most of the bank. I think of her often, and while Bill and I see each other on a regular basis, we both miss not knowing what happened to Mary.

Since I had spoken at many conferences, I looked around for a consulting firm that would suit my skills. I had spoken at a couple of conferences sponsored by Payment Systems, Inc., (PSI) owned by Dale Reistad. Reistad was one of the early pioneers in electronic funds transfer. He had worked at the American Bankers Association responsible for the National Operations & Automation Convention, one of the largest banking conventions in the United States. He then started his own firm, launched a monthly newsletter on payment systems, and then had the very creative idea of launching PSRP, the Payment Systems Research Program. PSRP was launched in 1974 with four meetings a year and six research reports dealing with the future of electronic banking. He was struggling to get enough members into the program to make it profitable, and it was costly to pay outside consultants to write the six reports per year that his program was committed to produce. Since I had spoken at two of his conferences, I knew Reistad well enough to approach him about running PSRP. I thought I could not only save him money on producing the research reports, but I also had a small staff that could match the quality of the reports he was producing, if not exceed them in quality. I also thought I could help him grow the program since I was becoming known in the industry for producing quality research, and Atlanta was considered a leading edge city for electronic funds transfer.

Reistad was very interested, but since he was located in New York, he wanted me to move there. I countered that Atlanta was my home, I wasn't going to move, I had access to leading-edge developments in Atlanta, and my staff all lived in Atlanta. Finally, he agreed that I could stay in Atlanta, take Bill Moore with me to the new firm, and become senior vice president of PSI in charge of research and consulting, which included the fledgling PSRP.

I was elated that I could pull this off. The salary was a good bit more than I was making working for the Atlanta banks, and I was staying in Atlanta. I was in charge of an electronic banking program in a field that I had come to enjoy, my boss was in New York far enough away to not bother me too much, and I had a chance to help grow the company. I thanked Rawlings at the Atlanta Fed for going to bat for me, but I was taking another route, joining PSI so I could remain in Atlanta. Shortly thereafter, I went looking for office space in downtown Atlanta because I wanted to remain close to all the major banks in town, and they were all located in the center of town. I found space in the Equitable Building, a huge building a few blocks from all the banks. I thanked the Atlanta Fed for the help they had provided me, signed a lease, and moved into the Equitable Building.

Ten years later when the *Atlanta Business Chronicle* reviewed what the Atlanta Payments Project had accomplished, they wrote,

> When the study was published in 1972, the results drew international recognition. As a result of the study and the work that followed it for more than a decade, the city's electronic banking research community became recognized throughout the industry as the foremost colony of payment system futurists in the nation. Atlanta is a city Northern bankers have looked at to scope the future shape of retail transactions. The city is famous among bankers for its leadership in electronic payments, one of the most important and controversial topics in the industry today.

Chapter 11

Payment Systems Inc.

I started working for Payment System, Inc., (PSI) in early 1975 with a small staff of Bill Moore and one other person. I was determined to change the nature of the Payment System Research Program (PSRP) from producing research reports written by outside people to producing high-quality documents written by my staff. The savings from no longer paying outside consultants was used to hire quality staff to write the reports internally.

Through the late 1970s, payment systems were going through huge growth spurts. The ACH was moving along slowly, and different parts of the country were organizing, implementing, and growing their own ACH services. To organize a nationwide set of new products and standards for the ACH, the National Automated Clearing House Association (NACHA) was founded. Bank credit cards were beginning to show substantial growth and beginning to overtake the retail and gas company credit cards that had been in place for decades. Individual bank credit cards merged into two main systems: Interbank, which later became Master Charge and eventually MasterCard, and BankAmericard, which became Visa.

In February 1975, the PSRP membership stood at fifty organizations with substantial revenue. For the membership and prospects for membership, we issued the first PSRP bulletin that outlined what we intended to do with the PSRP program for that year.

In April, Dale called me from New York to tell me that he had sold PSI to American Express. I was both surprised and elated. I liked the idea of working for a small consulting firm; it was a step up from being an entrepreneur at the Atlanta Payments Project, it had more stability, but was still quite risky. American Express was a premier company worldwide, it had tremendous stability, it added to the prestige of PSI, and it would offer me more stability and more mobility in my professional career.

In a letter to stockholders dated April 11, 1975, PSI announced that it had reached an agreement with American Express whereby American Express would purchase the assets and liabilities of PSI. The transaction was consummated in July of that year. While I had no stock or stock options in PSI, Dale negotiated a stock option agreement for me to obtain American Express stock over a five-year period. That sweetened the deal for me, and I supported the acquisition totally. American Express announced that PSI would continue to retain its identity, and that PSRP would be operated as in the past, and they were true to their word.

As a result of the acquisition by American Express, I announced in April to all the members of PSRP that I was looking to add to the staff. Several months later, in July 1975, I announced the addition of new staff members: Anne Morgan Moore and Richard Speer.

Anne had worked at Fulton National Bank for nine years as a strategic planner in payment systems and wanted to leave the bank for a chance at consulting. She had a strong background in market analysis and EFTS implementation. She turned out to be a terrific hire and an excellent writer and researcher, who stayed with PSI for many years.

Rich had wanted to work for me in 1971. I suggested that he needed more experience. After working for First National Bank of Atlanta, then First Union in Charlotte, and finally for two years at Union Planters in Memphis, I thought he was ready to join us. Once he knew that I was looking for staff, he approached me once again, and this time, I was convinced that he could make an excellent consultant, not just to write research reports, but also to build a consulting practice. Rich was an aggressive, ambitious man who presented himself as one of the smartest people in the business, an excellent strategy for a consultant. He had a way of suggesting to a prospect that they needed him to solve their problem, and without him, they might have a great deal more trouble internally with their management. He was attracted to building a consulting practice for PSI, which he did over several years.

As a separate event, PSI organized an EFTS library in New York to maintain books, documents, periodicals, articles, and slides that were all available to PSRP members. Eventually, the library was moved to Atlanta to be near the staff. In its day, it was an enormous asset to the company and was the most complete library on EFTS that I ever saw.

With American Express now owning PSI, I was worried about what the banks in PSRP would think about paying a subsidiary of American Express, a company they might believe was a competitor of theirs. We had many discussions about this, but the die was cast and my group was going to be a part of American Express regardless of what I thought. Our strategy was quite simple. We made it clear to all our clients that American Express would take a hands-off policy regarding PSI. Our subsidiary would be independent in running PSRP and our consulting practice. American Express was true to its word. Not once in the nearly four years that I worked there did American Express ever get involved in the policies that affected PSRP or our consulting practice.

Reistad was interested in being a part of American Express not only because he obtained American Express stock for his small company but also because he believed he could move up in the American Express hierarchy. Unfortunately, it became obvious over time to American Express management that Reistad was a dreamer, a visionary when it came to business. He loved technology and would show up at PSRP meetings with some new technology gadget that he believed could transform the payment system in one way or another. He was enamored with the future.

People like Reistad, who are entrepreneurs, can grow a company up to twenty to thirty people and still manage the process from start to finish. The entrepreneur is a hands-on person, driven to create the idea for a product, involved in every detail of it, and committed to selling it personally. The entrepreneur has a passion for his products and is often unwilling to let go of control over any aspect of the products he/she sells. The entrepreneur is not just the creative force behind the product, but the manufacturer, the salesperson, and the administration to be sure the product makes a profit.

It is a different matter when it comes to running a company like American Express with hundreds and thousands of people. In that environment, senior managers are dependent on all kinds of staff, and the entrepreneur will have to give up being an entrepreneur for becoming a strategist, for handling people well, and for dealing with financials. It requires a different personality, a different mind-set, and a different set of interests. Small companies survive on creativity and innovation. Large companies survive on strategy, managing people, and focusing on financials. *Entrepreneurs for small companies do not make good choices for senior management at large companies.*

Reistad had one idea after another. It was up to me and my staff to figure out whether we thought it was a good idea or not. Often, we would have the complete agenda set for the next PSRP meeting, and then Reistad would call me to say he wanted to insert another presentation into the agenda because he viewed that subject as "hot," and the industry wanted to hear about it. Quite often, we would make the change partly because it was a good idea and partly because he was the boss. On the other hand, we would often find one excuse or another to put off the subject, either to the next meeting or kill the idea completely. I was still trying to find my own limits within the company, and I did not want to fight with my boss on every idea he had. Gradually over time, I took more and more control of PSRP and made Reistad suggest his ideas much more in advance of the meeting or in advance of doing some research report. In this way, I somehow managed his creativity.

Shortly after being acquired, the Travelers Checks Division at American Express asked me to play a role in helping to set their strategy. At the time, American Express had just developed standard packages of traveler checks for its customers in denominations of three hundred, five hundred, and one thousand dollars. There was also a great deal of concern about Visa and MasterCard offering travelers checks through their banks, one of the major ways that American Express offered its checks.

As part of my assignment, I sat in on senior management meetings with Jimmy Robinson, CEO of American Express, and Lou Gerstner, head of TRS, Travel Related Services, which included the credit card and travelers checks divisions. For me, it was heady stuff. I was involved in senior management activities even though I had no say in the matter. Still, I was in the room and that mattered greatly to me. Eventually, Gerstner became vice chairman of American Express, then left to become CEO of IBM, and then CEO of RJR Nabisco.

I look back on the fact that I worked under John Reed, who became CEO of Citibank, Jimmy Robinson, who was CEO of American

Express, and Lou Gerstner, who became CEO of IBM. These were three powerhouse men who had much to contribute to the financial industry, and I had a chance to observe and learn from all of them. Each of them had an impact on my career. However, they barely remembered me. Many years later, I said hello to Reed after he spoke at a banking convention, and I doubt that he recognized me. After Robinson left American Express, I had a chance to present an idea to him. I think he had only a small inkling of who I was. And at a bank convention twenty years later, I attended a cocktail reception for Gerstner. After he spoke at the convention, I spoke with him one on one. He had written a book called *Can Elephants Fly?* about his experiences at IBM, and I wanted him to autograph it. When I told him that I worked for him, he asked me if it was at American Express, IBM, or RJR Nabisco. He had no recollection of me though I remembered him well.

This taught me that *subordinates not only remember you well but can also recall what you said and did on a given occasion while you, as the boss, may not remember the incident at all.* It was important to those personnel because their careers depended on the decisions of top management. On the other hand, senior management has hundreds, if not thousands, of people working for them and could not possibly remember everyone's names or even their faces. To Reed, Robinson, and Gerstner, I was at best a vague recollection and probably not remembered at all. It was just the place in the organization that made the difference, and not a reflection of your skill, talent, or results.

At that time, traveler's checks were being offered by Citibank, Bank of America, and Barclays Bank. American Express was dominant in the business, Bank of America was in the process of exiting the business, and Citibank was second in market share behind American Express. The major concern at American Express was that Visa and MasterCard were both about to enter the traveler's checks business with traveler's checks of their own, which is why Bank of America was leaving the business, having been the major force behind the Visa brand. American Express was concerned about Visa offering traveler checks to five thousand banks nationwide, thereby undermining the American Express brand, for American Express sold their travelers checks through the very same banks that Visa was targeting.

In order to slow down the implementation of the Visa Traveler Checks implementation, Citibank decided to sue Visa on the basis of antitrust laws. The argument that Citibank made was that they were one bank and Visa was putting together hundreds, if not thousands, of banks to put Citibank out of business. Visa was putting together a conspiracy to undermine Citibank's traveler's checks business by having so many banks working together under the Visa label. At American Express, we relished the lawsuit, wished Citibank would prevail, but stayed above the fray. I had no idea about antitrust law, I was minding my own business working with American Express, and we had no contact with Citibank whatsoever.

Shortly after the Citibank lawsuit against Visa, Visa countersued Citibank and American Express, claiming that they were working together in a conspiracy to prevent any other bank from offering its own traveler's checks, which Visa was proposing to do. That was a clever strategy on Visa's part even though there was absolutely no substance to their case. Shortly thereafter, I received a call from American Express's law firm on Wall Street to inform me that I was identified by American Express as one of its employees involved in their traveler's checks strategy. The law firm informed me that I would be required to undergo a deposition by Visa lawyers to determine whether I had any involvement with Citibank's traveler's checks.

My first emotion was bewilderment. I told the lawyers that there was no truth at all about working with Citibank on anything, let alone a conspiracy with them to defeat a Visa strategy. Why in the world would anyone think that I was involved in it, or whether American Express would work with Citibank on a conspiracy to defeat Visa? It made no sense. The lawyer said it didn't have to make sense. It was a lawsuit, it needed to be dealt with, and I was involved in it.

My second emotion was anger. I had done nothing wrong, I was doing my job, I was helping American Express and no one else, and I had a relatively narrow role in the overall traveler's checks strategy. I didn't work in the Travelers Checks Division, I was in a subsidiary in Atlanta, I came up to New York a couple of times a month, and I had no thought of helping anyone other than American Express. I was angry at becoming involved in an antitrust lawsuit I had no idea about, and it would take a considerable amount of my time to review the five hundred pages of traveler's checks material that was in my possession. My lawyer explained that conspiracy is a criminal offense and is punishable by a jail sentence, so I had better be well prepared for the deposition that I was going to face.

That immediately raised my third emotion: fear. Was it possible that I could end up in jail? I had done nothing, absolutely nothing wrong. I knew nothing about Citibank's traveler's checks, and now I was involved in a conspiracy lawsuit. I thought through everything I had done many times, reviewing all the meetings in my mind, and there was nothing illegal about any of them. I was doing an honest job with high integrity, acting as a consultant to American Express. I had done nothing wrong. And yet, the lawyers might find something, something I might have done, something I did not understand that would get me in trouble. Could it be possible that I could go to jail? The thought haunted me for days, and I kept telling myself that my fear was groundless. But I had five hundred pages of notes, and I had forgotten what was in all of them.

The lawyer told me to study the five hundred pages I had in my possession related to the American Express traveler's checks strategy even though none of it related to the lawsuit, and none of it dealt with Citibank. He told me that I would have to come to New York for one solid week to be prepared by his law firm prior to the deposition.

Once I started to study the pages, I had my fourth emotion: uncertainty. I did not remember everything that was written on those five hundred pages. Some of the material in my mind was vague, I had completely forgotten about the context of what was written on some of those pages, and some pages contained material that others had written. The more I studied these pages, the more uncertain I became. Fear kept returning because I did not recall everything in the detail that existed on those pages. I needed coaching.

Once in New York with my lawyers, I spent an entire week with three lawyers, six to eight hours a day going over the five hundred pages that I was to be grilled on. The lawyers asked to me to explain the trivia on every page that was confusing, and that caused yet another emotion: inadequacy. My lawyers drilled me again and again on what I would say on this question, on that paragraph, on this trip to Florida, and so on. They suggested every possibility that might indicate that I was conspiring with Citibank, and they listened to my explanation about why that was not possible or not true. In the beginning, my explanations were open to interpretation, and I felt inadequate in answering all their questions.

As we approached the end of the week of preparation, my answers improved because my memory improved, and I felt more and more confident that I could deal with any question the Visa attorney would ask me. At last, the final emotion showed up: confidence. I knew I could confidently deal with any question.

A week or so later, I went through the real deposition in a lawyer's office in Manhattan. The Visa attorney grilled me much more gently than my own lawyers, and the deposition was a breeze. I was fully prepared, totally confident, and the Visa lawyer did not drill down into the five hundred pages as much as my own attorneys had done. I was relieved that the ordeal was over, that the Visa attorney had found nothing remotely associated with a conspiracy or a violation of antitrust laws. The deposition was nothing more than a fishing expedition, and the attorney had found nothing and probably expected to find nothing. I was forced to suffer through a deposition in a case that wasn't going anywhere.

Before I was deposed, I went through six major emotions. I went from disbelief to anger, to fear, to uncertainty, to inadequacy, to confidence in becoming prepared. It was a lesson I learned through experiencing it myself. The process taught me the difference between good lawyers and mediocre ones. I had the best in the business, and they prepared me exceedingly well. They took the time to go over every page with me, drill me on every question that might come up, anticipate what the deposing lawyer might ask me, and make me feel totally comfortable with material I had long forgotten. It was a process I took with me: *as a witness in a lawsuit, be completely prepared, especially when the stakes are high.* It is the only way to be sure that justice is served.

The case went on for several more months and was finally dropped by both sides. Citibank could not prevent Visa from offering traveler's checks to its member banks and merely wanted to delay the introduction by a year or more. American Express and Citibank had not worked together in any sort of conspiracy. The lawyers were doing their jobs, but there was no case for either side, and all the lawyers knew it.

In the late 1970s, ATMs were also showing substantial growth. Initially installed at the branches of individual banks with their own logo and serving only their own customers, the banks began to recognize that they had to be a part of a regional network of ATMs to provide greater geographical access to their customers. Regional ATM networks were becoming prolific with eventually over a hundred separate networks. The banks knew that all these networks could not survive, and there were discussions about national networks. International ATM networks were yet to come. The ATM card was just an ATM card since the development of debit cards was also yet to come, but there was much discussion about them. Prepaid cards existed in Europe, but there was little usage in the United States.

There were early developments in home banking. The internet did not exist for banking yet, and even personal computers were not in the banks, so home banking was being tested by calling operators at the bank, by using touch-tone telephones after calling the bank, by using the cable network on TV and other specialized products, like Videotex being developed in Canada.

On the corporate side of the bank, developments were also underway, with products like wire transfers. The banks had organized the Bank Wire to compete against the Fed Wire. Retail lockboxes for large numbers of checks of small dollar amounts and corporate lock boxes for small numbers of checks of large dollar amounts were being offered to speed up the collection of checks by having them processed in many locations.

Banks had not really begun to merge and were generally confined to branches in the one state where they were organized. However, new branch designs were smaller, containing only one or two staff. There was a huge discussion as to whether an ATM was a branch and needed regulatory approval.

Check processing was showing substantial growth, and there was serious concern about how to handle the huge volume growth that was expected over the next five years. With the settlement of a check dependent upon the physical delivery of the paper check to the payer bank, there was a great deal of emphasis on float—the time it took to deliver the check from the depository bank to the payer bank.

In short, electronic funds transfer was a hot topic for bankers—for the vendors serving the banking industry and for government regulators. It was the perfect time to have a Payment Systems Research Program, and we made the most of it. Year after year, from about seventy members in 1975, the program grew and peaked at about a hundred or so members in 1979, the last year that I was in charge of it. At its peak, the revenue from that program brought in close to one million dollars annually, and it became the place to be if you were involved in electronic funds transfer systems. That is not to say that the major industry conferences offered by the bank associations, like the Bank Administration Institute and the American Bankers Association were less valuable than PSRP. They were merely different. The industry conferences were trade shows with huge exhibit halls, and attracted thousands of people to see the latest in technology. The speakers at these conferences were often limited in the amount of time they had and often would not go into the detail that we could provide at our PSRP meetings. PSRP focused on quality research and in-depth discussions, while the industry meeting focused on the vendors in the exhibit halls, big industry names and many breakout sessions for more complete coverage. Serious players and more serious discussions were what we emphasized, and it worked so long as new developments were underway, and there were plenty of them.

From the 1970s onward for the next four decades, electronic banking had legal and regulatory changes, technology innovation, and huge changes in the nature of competition. It had all the elements that made for a great consulting career as banks and other financial institutions developed new products, installed new technology, and focused on reducing costs. There were opportunities galore, and it made for a very exciting place to be. *Consulting does well when there are companies with legal and regulatory changes, technology developments, plenty of competition or substantial profit opportunities.* The more change there is, the more need there is for expertise, and that justifies hiring consultants. For consulting, seek out areas where change is occurring—those areas always require expertise.

In January 1976, I hired Robert Cady as vice president of marketing for PSI. Bob had worked at Addressograph-Multigraph for several years and had the responsibility for the development and marketing of the company's point of sale terminals and minicomputer systems. Bob had been an early member of PSRP, and we had gotten to know each other quite well from his attendance at our meetings. I was thrilled to have him, and we became good friends as well as excellent professionals working together. Our relationship blossomed over time, and when I left PSI in 1979 to start my own company, Bob joined me as a partner.

In 1976, PSRP became even more ambitious and began to run several workshops and programs throughout the country. PSRP members received ten complimentary copies of the *PSI Newsletter*, a subscription service that was written by the PSI staff, bulletins covering late breaking news stories related to EFTS, one-page summaries of the documents, and meetings for senior management. Our staff was available to consult on EFTS planning and implementation projects, including feasibility studies, market research, strategic planning, and economic analysis. All told, it was a very busy schedule full of meetings, reports, and consulting, and I loved every minute of it. I was involved in the most progressive developments going on in EFTS, and it was very exciting meeting the leaders in the industry, hearing their stories, and writing about them. We were also contributing through our own original research and analysis as to where the industry was and where it was going.

In 1976, PSI opened a third location in California. We had determined that the only way to do serious amounts of consulting to the West Coast banks was to have a consulting group on the West Coast.

To provide a perspective on the world of electronic banking in 1976, I found excerpts from a speech that I delivered to the EFT Conference of the Illinois Bankers Association in February 1976. It was published in *The Magazine of Bank Administration* in June 1976. Excerpts from that speech are given below:

> EFT (Electronic Funds Transfer) is here to stay. It is growing, the equipment industry is prepared, a very sophisticated technology exists, financial service institutions of all kinds are experimenting with a wide variety of services, regulatory agencies are providing substantial support to EFTS (Electronic Funds Transfer Systems), and finally, the public is beginning to find these EFTS services more and more acceptable.

> There are EFTS events on the horizon that will entirely undermine the need for traditional branch banking, events that will provide a mechanism for competition through electronic technology that will compel bankers to deal with EFTS as a threat to the very basis of the way they do business today.

> In the government/regulatory area, it is clear that most regulatory agencies are strongly encouraging EFTS developments. The Justice Department is looking for the private sector to take the initiative in EFTS developments. That is why it was opposed to the Federal Reserve and the Federal Home Loan Bank

Board operating point of sale systems. Governor Mitchell of the Federal Reserve System has warned bankers not to depend on government protection from competition. This statement is being echoed in many quarters, and it is beginning to show up in actuality. In December 1975, the Senate passed The Financial Institutions Act of 1975, and sent the bill to the House of Representatives. The section of the bill that affects payment systems includes:

- Repeal of a 42 year-old prohibition on payment of interest on demand deposits, affecting both businesses and individuals. The change would not take place until January 1, 1978, however, and could be delayed until 1980 if the Fed wishes.
- Authorization for the first time of issuance of credit cards by S& L's, mutual savings banks and credit unions.
- Blanket access by any depository institution to the clearing and settlement facilities of the Fed.
- Authority for mutual savings banks to convert to Federal charters in the 17 states where they now operate.
- On December 16, 1975, the House joined the Senate in passing legislation permitting the expansion of NOW accounts (Negotiable Order of Withdrawal—another name for a checking account) to all 6 New England states. Massachusetts and New Hampshire financial institutions have been offering the accounts under a special exemption since 1973. These powers were extended to banks and thrift institution in Connecticut, Vermont, Maine and Rhode Island.

Paying interest on demand deposits through NOW accounts and providing thrifts with third party payment powers and credit cards might not happen this year, maybe not even next year. But that does not mean that such things cannot happen soon. There is a very strong trend in the Congress to provide a more competitive balance of power between the banks and thrifts. And there is an even stronger concern, as I read the Congress, to provide more customer convenience, increased customer service and greater protection to the consumers than ever before. Branch Banks no longer have the same degree of control over retail banking they once had. The McFadden Act of 1927 provided Federal regulation on branching that deferred to state law. The concept was originally designed to keep national banks competitive with freely branching state banks, but its effect has been to hold national banks to state limitations.

So long as the national banks tried to expand their delivery system through branches, they could be contained through state regulations. But the rules are changing, because the technology is changing. Technology is making our definition of a branch obsolete. Customer bank communication terminals—CBCT's (an early name for ATM's)—are not deemed branches, says the Comptroller of the Currency. Remote Service Units—RSU's (another early name for ATM's)—are not deemed branches, says the Federal Home Loan Bank Board. The issue of whether CBCT's are or are not branches is one of the hottest EFTS issues presently facing banking. The answer to that question will, to a large extent, determine the future direction of EFTS, and, in fact, the future direction of retail banking.

To my knowledge, four different decisions have been reached by four different federal courts on the question "Is a CBCT a branch?" In Washington D. C., a judge ruled that accepting deposits, credit and debit card transactions and guaranteeing checks are all illegal through a CBCT, because such services constitute branch banking. In Illinois, a federal judge said that accepting deposits and making loans were illegal, but cash withdrawals and check guarantee services were legal. In Colorado, a judge decided that only deposit taking was illegal. And finally, and most recently, a federal judge in Oklahoma upheld the Comptroller of the Currency's interpretation ruling that CBCT's are not branches for even deposit taking.

We now have four different opinions, and it is clear that they will be resolved only by the US Supreme Court or by Federal legislation. Most experts agree that it will take at least a year to get a definitive Supreme Court ruling on the CBCT question. While it is conjecture as to how the Supreme Court will view this issue, it is fair to suggest that the recent Supreme Court decisions in favor of the C&S National Bank in Atlanta could be somewhat enlightening. The Supreme Court said that the C&S Bank Holding Company actually fostered competition rather than stifled it when the bank holding company helped form five banks and maintained close ties with them. The court majority opinion noted that the banks were "sponsored" by C&S at a time when Georgia state law prohibited branching outside of a city.

Let me quote the Supreme Court's key conclusion: "To characterize these relationships as an unreasonable restraint of trade is to forget that their whole purpose and effect were to defeat a restraint of trade. Georgia's anti-branching law amounted to a compulsory market division" and made suburban and rural areas "a captive market for small unit banks."

The same argument will be made with respect to CBCT's. Do CBCT's foster competition or stifle it? If the fundamental purpose of prohibitive branching statutes is to restrain trade, and if CBCT's open up trading areas to additional competition, then it is very likely that the Supreme Court will support the legality of a CBCT.

At present, the merits of a CBCT have been argued on the technical question of whether EFT services can be construed as accepting deposits, making loans or cashing checks. But at the Supreme Court level, it would appear that the broader issues of restraint of trade, of customer convenience, and in the public interest will be of greater significance in determining their legality.

Justice Department Action

To further advance this theme, let me summarize briefly five major points made by Thomas Kauper, Assistant Attorney

General in charge of the Justice Department's Antitrust Division in recent testimony before the House Banking, Currency and Housing Committee.

1. **Competition.** In the area of competition, the Justice Department concluded: "that many of the existing limitations on financial institutions should be altered or eliminated if those institutions are to be expected to meet the present and future needs of our society. Greater reliance must be placed on competition in a free marketplace and less on direct government regulation.

2. **Interest rate ceilings.** In the area of interest rate ceilings, the Department concludes that: "Interest rate regulation has not been completely effective in reducing cost pressures. The slight rate advantage of thrifts over commercial banks has not offset the overall disintermediation caused by low deposit rate ceilings; the housing sector has thus suffered with the financial sector."

3. **DDA (Demand Deposit Account—checking account) interest.** With regard to the prohibition on paying interest on demand deposits, the Department concluded that this prohibition is being gradually rendered meaningless by the use of such devices as NOW accounts, non-negotiable third party payment services and, in the future, EFTS.

4. **Market specialization.** With regard to having financial institutions specialize in specific areas by enforced regulations, such as the housing area by thrifts or checking accounts by commercial banks, the Department believes that this has not worked well in the past, and the "development of EFTS, improved money management techniques and NOW accounts in thrift institutions are likely to decrease the practicality of government-imposed institutional specialization.

5. **Restrictive entry.** And finally, the Department concluded that geographic market restriction "should not be imposed by

government unless the public interest clearly requires it." In the Department's opinion, "the public interest does not require nearly so extensive a limited entry policy as is currently contained in state and Federal regulation of the financial sector."

The Future of Retail Banking

I summarized Mr. Kauper's remarks because I believe that the future of retail banking is in these decisions. The financial industry is becoming more competitive. Regulation Q was recently extended, but it has not been an effective way to channel funds to the housing industry in high interest rate periods. It is only a matter of time before we will all be paying interest on some form of demand deposit accounts. Thrifts continue to gain new services, and many of them are planning marketing strategies based on full service financial centers. And restrictive branching statutes will be subverted by the advent of EFTS. The development of remote automated teller units and point of sale terminal systems will provide a more convenient way to do banking for the customer than the existing branching network.

Once POS/EFT (Point of Sale) systems are established, it will be far easier for banks to compete in the marketplace than ever before. Bricks and mortar branches costing upwards of $500,000 to establish, being fixed in concrete with absolutely no mobility, will be unable to compete with highly mobile terminals costing $1,000 or less to install. Banks will be able to experiment with point of sale locations. If one location doesn't work, the bank can try another. The cost to change the location will probably be less than $100 with a call to the local telephone company. The point is that instead of having the customer come to the bank at the bank's convenience, the bank will come to the customer at the customer's convenience.

EFT has been characterized as an evolutionary process. It will be evolutionary in terms of time, in terms of volume, and in terms of generating profits. But it is revolutionary in terms of bank policy and bank planning. It is revolutionary in terms of bank commitments and marketing strategy.

I believe EFT is the future of retail banking. I believe regulatory reform will occur this year or next. I believe thrift competition is very real indeed. I believe that CBCT's and RSU's are not branches, that they will not fall under the branching statutes, and that they are more convenient to the public than the present branches. These are the future directions for retail banking—and EFT services are leading the way.

There is a rather famous quotation from Shakespeare's Julius Caesar that applies here, "There is a tide in the affairs of men, which, taken at the flood, leads on to fortune." The tide in banking today is EFTS. It is not at the flood stage yet. But EFT is growing; the EFTS tide is moving forward, and those financial institutions that are participating in this development are doing so because they believe at the flood stage they will be prepared to take full advantage of the situation.

In 1977, I met Stan Rifkin, one of the members of our California staff. Stan had dinner at my home, and I found him to be a bright guy, but I knew little else about what he did or about what the other staff did in California. Stan became quite famous a year or so later, committing the largest single fraud then in the history of banking and went to jail as a result. Based on the way I heard the story and the details I found on Wikipedia, Book Rags, and other spots on the Internet, my company had a contract with Security Pacific Bank to evaluate the corporate payment systems of the bank and develop a backup system for the bank's wire room. As a consultant to the bank, Stan had access to the wire room at the bank.

Stan learned the transfer procedures used for a wire transfer and knew that the bank wrote down the daily transfer code in the wire room. In mid-October 1978, he made his way into the wire room, saw the code, memorized it, and walked out. He also knew a corporate account with millions of dollars in it. Acting like a banker, he then made a few phone calls at the bank and had $10.2 million dollars wired out of that corporate account to Irving Trust Bank in New York for the credit of a bank in Zurich, where he had already set up an account.

Before the transfer occurred, Stan flew to Zurich and set up a transaction with a Russian import export dealer in diamonds using his account at the Zurich bank. After the wire transfer, he flew to Zurich and picked up 43,200 carats in diamonds from the Russian dealer, which he purchased for $8.1 million. He then managed to smuggle the diamonds back into the United States. Five days after the wire transfer, he began to sell the Soviet diamonds. First, he sold twelve diamonds to a jeweler in Beverly Hills for twelve thousand dollars.

Shortly after the fraudulent wire transfer, Security Pacific discovered the missing money and called in the FBI to determine who might be the crook. The FBI had identified Stan as a potential suspect who had access to the codes, were looking for him, and believed he might be the crook.

On November 1, a couple of weeks after the fraud, Stan traveled to Rochester, New York, to attempt to sell more of the diamonds. He said that he had received diamonds as payment for a West German real estate deal—and he wanted to sell the diamonds for cash. Before the guy had a chance to act on Stan's request, he saw a news item on television describing a multimillion-dollar bank heist in Los Angeles. The story named Stan as the possible thief. The guy contacted the FBI.

Not knowing the FBI was after him, Stan flew to San Diego to spend a weekend with an old friend. He informed his friend that he planned to surrender, but he never had the opportunity to give himself up. By then, the FBI knew from the New York guy in Rochester which calls to record from Stan. On November 5, Stan called the guy in New York. The conversation contained information that allowed FBI agents to track Stan to his friend's address in California.

Stan surrendered without a struggle. He turned over evidence to the federal agents: a suitcase containing the twelve thousand dollars from the Beverly Hills diamond sale and several dozen packets of diamonds. Soon after, Stan was released on bail and got into more trouble with the FBI. He had begun to target Union Bank in Los Angeles using the same scheme that had worked at Security Pacific Bank. What he did not know was that someone involved in the scheme was a government informant who had set him up. Stan was arrested again on February 13, 1979. Tried on two counts of wire fraud, Stan faced the possibility of ten years imprisonment. He pleaded guilty and, on March 26, 1979, was sentenced to eight years in federal prison. In its day, it was the largest bank fraud in history.

The kicker in the story is that Security Pacific Bank was given the proceeds of Stan's sale of diamonds and the remaining amount of diamonds. Security Pacific sold the remaining diamonds and made a handsome profit on the deal. The diamonds were worth about 50 percent more than the money Stan stole from the bank. To this day, it still bothers me that I worked with a staff member at my company that was willing to destroy his integrity for money, even a lot of money.

In 1977, Jimmy Jarrell joined PSI, along with Ronnie Bennett and Diane Morris. As one of the original members of the Atlanta Payments Project, Jimmy and I had a mutual admiration for each other. He was a fun guy to work with and would tease me mercilessly, so when he became disenchanted with his growth at Trust Company Bank, I added him to our staff at PSI. He was a great addition. Ronnie was added as a strong research associate, and Diane took care of many of the seminars and conferences that we held. We also added Melinda to the Atlanta staff. Melinda came from the Federal Home Loan Bank Board with knowledge of their regulations. She also was a wonderful addition to our staff and focused on scheduling and participating in PSRP workshops. I was building a very strong staff.

In 1976 and 1977, we built a strong business for PSI. In 1976, the total Atlanta revenue was eight hundred thousand dollars and contributed 89 percent of the profit for the company. We had fifty-eight full-time members of PSRP. In 1977, there were sixty-six full-time members of PSRP contributing $700,000 in revenue, $275,000 in consulting revenue, and another $240,000 from an annual symposium, a summer educational program on the basics of EFT, and other programs. Business increased by over 50 percent.

It is difficult to find a good product, something the market will pay for that is profitable. When you find it, *focus on growing a good product aggressively before launching something new.* This was the case for PSRP. We had created a wonderful program to address the early developments of electronic banking, and the financial industry liked it to keep up with the latest developments—and there were many of them.

In 1977, Peter joined PSI from American Express. He had been working in the credit card area, had taken an interest in PSI, and Reistad agreed to add him to our staff. Peter, of course, was located in New York with Reistad, and both of them had little to do in running the research and consulting business that I controlled in Atlanta. Nevertheless, both of them inserted themselves into my area on a regular basis. After all, they had little else to do since American Express was not interested in spending a lot of money on new PSI developments. American Express kept PSI to protect their existing American Express products. This kept both Reistad and Peter frustrated over the lack of financial support they were getting from the management at American Express.

This was understandable because I did not believe any of the ideas that Reistad or Peter created had a real chance of making serious money. As a result of their frustration, they devoted a lot of time to reviewing my business, making suggestions as to what research we should do, what speakers we should get for our conferences, and in what directions we should proceed. It was annoying to constantly put up with their suggestions—some good and some ridiculous—but Reistad was my boss and Peter was someone I had to respect. He was interested in finding something useful to do to justify his job.

At the same time, Rich Speer was building his own consulting practice. He was winning consulting assignments and beginning to add staff to focus on consulting, independent of the PSRP group. In 1977, I had a desire to be home more regularly. Pamela was eleven years old, Lori was nine, and Leo was six. I wanted to be home at night as much as possible to be with my family. Rich's consulting business required a great deal more travel to clients and a lot more time away from family. I had much less interest in the consulting part of the business and focused on PSRP.

I would meet with Rich from time to time to monitor the consulting business, but I let him alone to a large extent, and he was doing quite well. I had serious concerns, however, about him as a team player. He was secretive, ambitious, and rarely told me what was going on unless I asked him. When I asked him about the consulting assignments, I often received short answers; I did not know the consulting projects in detail. Part of the problem was my own doing. I did not want to visit clients for the start of a project or for the completion and presentation of the final report, so I was giving away control of the consulting area by largely avoiding it. One day, Don, who was head of the consulting practice in California and worked with Rich on consulting assignments, called me about Rich. Don and I were close because he had worked for me on the Atlanta Payments Project several years earlier; I trusted him and knew the feeling was mutual. He told me that I should not trust Rich, that Rich was speaking poorly about me, that he was undermining me to Reistad and Peter, and I should consider firing him. My gut told me that he was right, that Rich could not be trusted, but he was growing the business, and it would be difficult to justify firing him based on his results.

I thought about what to do with Rich and concluded that there were three choices. I could find a way to fire him, but then I would have to find someone else of his quality to take over the consulting practice, and I did not have such a person. I certainly did not want to do it myself because I wanted to be at home with my family as much as possible. Second, I could leave the consulting business as is, with Rich reporting to me, but I did not like Rich undermining me, and I did not appreciate having Peter asking me about the consulting business when he did not have responsibility for it. Third, I could give Peter responsibility for the consulting practice. That would get Peter out of my hair, remove Rich from my control, eliminate the need for me to travel, and get me focused on what I liked doing, which was running PSRP.

In a meeting with Reistad and Peter, I suggested that Peter take over the consulting practice and have Rich report directly to him. Both Reistad and Peter were surprised to hear this suggestion. However, they both immediately agreed to it. Peter was thrilled to have something serious to do, and Reistad did not really care because he was focused on trying to find an important assignment within American Express, which never happened.

It was the worst decision that I made in my entire professional career. I was giving up an important source of income, I was not dealing with my subordinate who was undermining me within the company, I was giving control to someone else, and by doing so giving away a lot of power I had within American Express. In addition, I was now allowing both Rich and Peter to work together to undermine my power within PSI, giving them more influence with Reistad and others about the direction of PSI and my role in it. I had enormous power when Rich worked directly for me, and I could justify continuing to control consulting, for it was located in Atlanta and Rich worked just down the hall from me. By giving away control over Rich, I was giving up any possible way to fire him, I was giving him more opportunity to talk poorly about me, and I was giving Peter more influence than he deserved. In short, I was undermining myself within PSI and within American Express.

PSI was under the control of George Waters, an executive vice president at American Express. George was a straight-shooting, brilliant guy who understood people, dealt with Reistad and Peter regularly, and knew me from the various times I would come to New York on American Express business. I had a professional relationship with him, but I never was forceful enough with him to discuss the difficulties I was having with Rich, nor the constant insertions that Reistad and Peter were having in the business I was running from Atlanta. I was too immature to understand the politics of clashing personalities or the desire to succeed in business by undermining others rather than succeeding by producing results. If I had the ambition to run PSI, get rid of Rich, Peter, and Reistad, I might have succeeded by going to George to explain how little Peter was doing and how Rich was undermining my authority. I knew that George had his own assessment of Reistad, and I did not have to say any more about him. However, I was not built for this type of attack, undermining others, playing politics, and fighting for control by hurting other people, even if they deserved it. It was not who I was or what I wanted to be.

The most important lesson I learned was *do not give power away to people you do not trust.* Trust was more important than expertise. That is why new CEOs that come into a company bring in their own staff, people they can trust, even if the existing staff is capable. Finally, I needed to listen to what people I trust tell me. They often know more about situations that I could possibly know.

In the end, the decision to turn over consulting to Peter was my own undoing. It increased the amount of insertions into my business, it decreased my power within PSI, and it forced me to evaluate whether I wanted to continue at PSI with three strong personalities continually evaluating my every decision. If I knew then what I know now, I am sure I would have fired Rich, found a good replacement for him, and moved on. Back then I didn't have the stomach for it. I thought I could continue to do my job without having to put up with Rich and his ambitions. I thought Peter could contain Rich and leave me alone to do my job. What I didn't realize was that instead of getting rid of one bad apple, I had taken on two of them. It was a really bad mistake short term, but it forced me to quit and start my own company. In that sense, it turned out to be one of the best decisions in my career. It increased my desire to own my own business. It forced me to start and run a profitable company and that told me that I wanted to be an entrepreneur first and foremost.

In early 1978, I was becoming unhappy at PSI even though I was involved in most of the PSRP programs and consulting to American Express on either traveler's checks or its credit card. At the PSI Symposium at the end of 1977, we added an exhibit area to the conference that attracted a nice group of exhibitors. At the annual symposium in April the next year, we announced the PSI Spotlight Program for $950. This was the typical brainchild of Reistad and Peter, and we spent considerable time discussing it internally. It was a hard sell to someone in the bank because it offered a program not for one person but for an entire department. Unless we found a senior person in an organization committed to EFT, the program would be unlikely to find a buyer. I thought it was a stupid idea, and it turned out to be just that because very few sales were made.

As another example of what I had to deal with, we planned a symposium at the Hyatt Regency Hotel in New Orleans. Reistad decided that he wanted to have an unusual brochure in the form of a paper bag. The brochure had to be light brown to look like a paper bag, had to be perforated at the top, and had to have a list of groceries on the inside cover. The grocery bag had nothing to do with the symposium as the titles of the sessions dealt with legislation, card services, NOW accounts, corporate EFT, telephone bill payment, consumer acceptance, credit unions, standards, and the future of the payments industry. There was one session over a two-day period on retailers and supermarkets, but it was not the focus of the symposium. I fought hard to change the brochure to something more suitable to the overall thrust of the conference and lost. I produced the brochure as requested, didn't like it, thought it was inappropriate, but I wasn't in charge. It was just another item on the list of why I couldn't stay at PSI.

The lineup of speakers included introductions by me and a keynote address by Reistad that covered the past, present, and future of EFT.

However, I was upset and unhappy by all the bickering over the production of the brochure, the addition of the Spotlight Program, and the small exhibit area, which I opposed. I did not want to compete with the major bank conventions that focused on exhibits as their major attraction. Still, we had to have one because Reistad wanted one. I wanted to compete on the quality of the presentations, and on that score, we were tough to beat.

When you no longer enjoy your work, find another job. I followed this advice most of my life. It is not always easy to do because jobs are not always available, and many people don't have the luxury or ability to find another job easily. Nevertheless, it is the right thing to do, and anyone unhappy in a job will not be doing it as well as a happy person. The happy person feels committed to the job, will come in early, stay late, and do whatever is necessary to fulfill his or her responsibilities. When you are an unhappy person in a job, there is a lack of commitment to the assignment, a lack of passion, and a lack of desire to work hard. When you are unhappy, don't wait, don't hesitate, and don't rationalize about there not being another possibility. Get out there! Start looking for a job you can enjoy.

In the middle of 1978, I decided to leave PSI and start my own company. I had many sleepless nights thinking about it. I was leaving a solid job with a solid income. I was in a stable position with plenty of revenue to support me, but I wasn't happy dealing with the politics I faced on a regular basis. I had George Waters to turn to, but it wasn't my style to fight for control of the company. I wasn't in New York where George had his office, and Reistad and Peter were there and had George's ear regularly. I wanted to leave, but I had never started a company. If I started my own company, it would begin with no revenue and no support from a major company. I was plenty scared.

I kept telling myself that I was an entrepreneur at the Atlanta Payments Project. I had developed a creative approach to studying EFT that turned out to be a major success, I had the support of the five major banks in town and the Federal Reserve, and I knew how to conduct research. I had found ways of bringing in revenue for that group through seminars and selling our research, so the banking industry was willing to pay for what I knew. And yet, I never had to worry about making a profit or making a payroll because the banks and the Fed would pay for any mistake I made. At PSI, I had the backing of American Express; I would receive a salary no matter what I did. If I quit, there would be no one to pay my staff or me except through my own ability to sell research and consulting to the banking industry. I would be totally on my own, totally dependent on creating proposals and products that the banking industry wanted. This would not be for a few months but for years—for the rest of my professional career. Could I be capable of continually finding issues that the industry wanted to know about and would they be willing to pay for answers? I wasn't sure that I could deliver on that easily or with difficulty or at all.

I was scared. I had a wife and three children. I had mortgage payments. I had only enough money to sustain me for a year. There was no big cushion to fall back on. My father was deceased; my mother had no money to lend me, and neither did my in-laws. And none of my relatives or my wife's relatives could bankroll me. I was totally at risk, and the prospect didn't sit well with me. I worried about this day and night for six months until I bit the bullet and struck out on my own.

The decision was made easier when I approached Bob Cady to join me. He was selling PSRP and consulting for PSI. He readily agreed to join me, and we agreed that I would own 60 percent of the business, and he would own 40 percent. I wasn't willing to give in to a fifty-fifty relationship because Bob worked for me and I wasn't willing to give away control. With 60 percent of the ownership, I was totally in charge, and I wouldn't have to put up with an argument about what would be done or even risk the chance that my partner would undermine me. I had enough of that at PSI, and I wasn't going to live with that any longer. I was going to be my own boss and swim or drown. Still, I worried day after day until late in 1978 when I announced that I was leaving PSI. Since I had no legal contract with PSI or American Express, I was free to do whatever I pleased. The same was true for Bob. We had no ties, no noncompete agreement, and no worries about staying in the payment system area. I did not announce my intentions because I was going to remain in the same business as the company I was leaving.

Surprisingly, American Express did not want me to leave. George invited me up to New York to discuss how I might be able to remain a part of American Express. At that point in time, I opened up to George, explaining the difficulties I was having with Rich, with Peter, and with Reistad. George listened intently and told me he would get back to me, which he did in a couple of weeks. He proposed that I leave PSI, move to New York, and join the American Express credit card division to be part of the team responsible for its credit card strategy. I was very familiar with the American Express card, I was knowledgeable about the competition, I had contacts with banks throughout the country, and American Express sold its credit card through many of the major banks I knew. I was a known resource when it came to doing excellent research.

However, I did not want to move back to New York. I was well established in Atlanta, my children were going to Jewish schools that my wife and I liked, my wife and I loved the synagogue we were involved in, and most of all, I wanted a shot at becoming an entrepreneur. I was worried, but I also wanted the opportunity to succeed or fail on my own. I thought I could do it. I had met hundreds, if not thousands, of bankers through the Atlanta Payments Project, the many speeches I had given at major conventions and the hundreds of bankers and vendors that came to our PSRP seminars. I knew that I had a great opportunity at American Express, but I also knew that if ever I was going to own my own company, now was the time. I could not turn that chance down. I thanked George profusely, resigned, and left PSI at the end of 1978 to start my own company, Electronic Banking, Inc. (EBI).

Chapter 12

Electronic Banking, Inc.

Bob and I decided to leave PSI in February 1979 to start our own company; we named it Electronic Banking, Inc. (EBI). It was an appropriate name because that was exactly what we expected to do in the new firm.

We found a nice location a couple of miles from my home to avoid having to travel to downtown Atlanta. Our business was not geared for Atlanta or even Georgia but for banks, other financial institutions, and vendors serving the banking industry. I set myself up in a corner office and got down to work.

Although I had controlling interest in the company, I cannot remember a time when I disagreed with Bob. We normally deferred to each other based on our relative enthusiasm for a project. If I was dead set against something, then Bob accepted that. If Bob was strongly for something, then I trusted him enough to go with it. For the most part, we worked well together.

In 1979, there were many new products and services under development, just getting started, or experiencing substantial growth. There were many unknowns with different banks trying different approaches, all making substantial investments in electronic banking. Payment system fees were a substantial part of the revenue stream for a bank, and electronic banking fees could enhance that revenue. In addition, electronic banking had the potential to reduce operating costs by eliminating paper processing.

Bob and I decided that we would launch a program focused on telephone bill payment. This was an easy decision because there was so much going on regarding electronic bill payment, and none of it was successful enough to dictate the correct path for the industry. Computers were not yet in banking, and the Internet was not in existence. Bill payments were made by speaking directly to a person at the financial institution or by using a touch-tone telephone. Other approaches were using a cable box at a television set. In addition, the savings and loan industry was ahead of the commercial banks in offering a telephone bill payment system, so our major clients that we served were trying to decide how and when to enter the telephone bill payment market. All this made it an easy decision to offer an industry wide multiclient program. We called it the Home Banking Society.

In May 1979, the *American Banker* carried the following story:

> Atlanta—Electronic Banking Inc. here is undertaking a 10-month multi-client research project on telephone bill-paying (TBP) in an effort to establish itself as an information clearing house and leading source of consulting in that field.
>
> EBI, formed several months ago by Allen H. Lipis, former head of research at PSI, believes its 3-part national research effort will fill a void that has developed despite the fact that nearly 200 financial institutions in the US, including institutions as large as First National Bank of Chicago and Mellon Bank, offer telephone bill payment services.
>
> Even without a formal marketing program by EBI, several organizations have already subscribed on the basis of preliminary prospectus. The program is priced at a $4,800 fee and includes all study modules, original research, nationwide surveys, and attendance at conferences to be held during the course of the study. EBI has booked over $100,000 in business.

In its first three months of operation, the company met its bookings and revenue projections. The client list of EBI represented the top organizations in the financial industry, including the Federal Reserve, the American Bankers Association, the Electronic Money Council, and the Bank Administration Institute. Citibank and Chase Manhattan Bank were also clients.

The Telephone Bill Payment Study (TBPS) was mailed to a test market of more than a hundred key organizations. Ten had committed, representing a $48,000 revenue commitment. The goal was twenty subscribers. EBI expected to hire two people bringing the EBI staff to six people.

In May, billings of more than fifty thousand dollars almost doubled April's billings. At that point, I started to take a salary. EBI was mentioned in over a dozen articles in trade publications as a result of an intensive PR campaign. Executive luncheons were held to introduce our research project. Several consulting projects were delivered, which received good reviews. Having added staff, we needed at least a hundred thousand dollars additional consulting revenue to continue the current pace. Product development was lagging based mainly on my ideas.

In July, the Telephone Bill Payment Study generated $140,000 in business based on forty-five members. Total business for the year was nearly three hundred thousand dollars. The company exceeded its initial projections by 150 percent. The basic outline for the next study was defined. The study dealt with check truncation and called for two hundred thousand dollars in revenue.

In August, consulting generated a small amount of work because there was no active marketing. Employee six and seven joined EBI. Plans for the check truncation program began with a draft prospectus. We also decided to hold the first annual Electronic Bill Payment Symposium in November.

In September, the first deliverables for the TBPS program were produced. The TBPS program continued under a new name, the TBP Society. Allan Gural joined the staff as employee eight. Cash flow of thirty thousand dollars per month was necessary, but half of that was expected over the next two months.

In November, we prepared the 1980 budget, which called for $750,000 in revenue to assure a reasonable profit. This would double our 1979 business. In December, the TBP Progress I meeting attracted 125 people and established our ability to put on an excellent conference. Consulting reached $42,000 for the month, a record. However, product releases were too late because bank commitments for the coming year are often made in the fall. In February 1980, the end of our first year in operation, EBI booked over half a million dollars and had a profitable first year. The check truncation study was off to a good start with ten members.

The 1980 plan had two projects: the TBP Society and check truncation. Two major meetings were planned and a university series. Each project had a brochure to introduce the study and each project would have a product manager and an ad in the *American Banker*. Product development focused on educational products, fielding a publication, and designing a new product for 1981. Consulting had to be more organized into a real business line. Budgets had to be monitored more closely and each project tracked for its man-hours. Advanced planning would produce less crisis situations and reduce outside costs. The budget anticipated $800,000 in revenue, and the 1981 plan was to reach $1.1 million in revenue. We expected to grow the business without borrowing from a bank.

For the full year in 1980, the company had revenue of over seven hundred thousand dollars. The TBP Society had forty-seven members, and the check truncation study had twenty-four members. The company also launched a telephone bill payment program in Canada and held two symposiums on telephone bill payment. However, profits were only $23,000.

In 1981, EBI was going to continue its existing programs and launch a branch study, an electronic cash management program, an educational program, and Home Payment Service '81. As business improved, I turned to some people I knew in Atlanta who might be interested in working at EBI. One of them was Tom Marschall, who worked at the Federal Reserve Bank of Atlanta. In 1978, the Atlanta Fed was working on a national survey of check processing, a study to follow on to the original study I worked on when I first arrived in 1971. Rawlings had decided that another study of check processing would prove useful for the industry, and Tom was developing the survey questionnaire and its nationwide implementation.

I offered to work with Tom on its development as a courtesy to Rawlings. I was knowledgeable about the first survey and knew the survey's limitations. Tom was very bright, easy going, and a brilliant analyst. When I approached him to join EBI, he agreed and became an excellent hire.

When it came to evaluating banking people I knew as potential employees, I thought they were either too expensive, not knowledgeable about consulting and the research work we were doing, or generally not suited to a consulting type atmosphere. I decided to turn to the academic environment. Emory University was a great school, so I advertised there for people with strong writing skills, analytical ability, and a desire to do original research. I found Jan, a political science professor, and she joined us. She quickly introduced me to another of her political science professors, and I hired Al, a terrific guy, smart, entrepreneurial, and able to take on virtually any project we had. He then introduced me to another woman, a professor in the history department, and I hired Gayle. She was another brilliant person, who had the capability of writing analytically on virtually any topic. All three had PhDs. In short, I built a great staff of analytical writers and taught them payment system knowledge as they needed it, but in the main, they all picked it up on their own.

Bill payment was something they all did, and paying bills by telephone was not rocket science. Consumer research was survey research that many of the staff was familiar with from their academic backgrounds. Summarizing material from a variety of sources was just another area that academic people were excellent at. In short, I preferred adding analytical writers with liberal arts degrees to my staff. They could be taught payment systems more effectively than taking people knowledgeable about payment systems and teaching them how to write as a consultant. That is not to say that payment system people do not write well, but it was much easier going from a liberal education to understanding payment systems than it was to take payment system people and turn them into analytical consultants.

Shortly after we began EBI, I learned that the major part of the consulting staff at PSI, my old company, was fired in a single weekend. It occurred because Bill Moore, my previous colleague, guessed that Rich Speer, the head of the consulting practice, was planning to start his own business. Bill found a filing for a new company Speer & Associates at the State of Georgia.

Bill informed Peter about this, and Peter seemed to dismiss this information as posturing by Rich. The truth was that Rich had approached a number of the people working under him, and five of them had decided to leave en masse to begin their firm. Peter apparently knew about what Rich was planning to do and did nothing about it. He kept American Express in the dark.

Bill then went up to see George, the senior vice president at American Express, informed him what he knew and what he suspected. George immediately flew down to Atlanta, confirmed what Bill told him, and fired all of them on the spot. When George also found out that Peter knew what was happening and did nothing about it, George removed him from PSI, and Peter returned to American Express. Peter left shortly thereafter. Several months later, Dale resigned from PSI and moved down to Florida, leaving PSI without a clear leader. After the whole affair had ended, with Rich, Peter, and Dale all gone, George asked First Data Resources (FDR), then a subsidiary of American Express, to take control of PSI.

A few months later in 1979, Bill Esping, then CEO of FDR, asked to visit with my partner and me at our office. He wanted to talk to us about PSI. When Bill arrived, we met in a small conference room next to my office. He got straight to the point: would I be willing to come back to be the CEO of PSI? He told us that he wanted to give us PSI. The focus was on us taking over PSI. He said that PSI was losing money, and American Express would continue to absorb the losses.

Bill said he knew my reputation and that we would protect American Express's reputation. The idea was to make this transaction as soon as possible. We would be responsible for the current operating costs, a small amount of debt, and the current year's revenue would accrue to us. Bob was thrilled at the time. He was sure we would say yes in principal and meet several more times, probably up in New York, to work out the details. We would double in size, stun the banking world, make our first acquisition on favorable terms, and take on several successful banking programs.

While Bill wasn't interested in buying our company, I could not see any other way to run PSI and EBI except to combine them since they were essentially in the same business. I could incorporate EBI into PSI, taking all my staff with me, and combine PSI and EBI into the first-class consulting and research firm it once was. Further, I would be guaranteed that whenever American Express wished to sell PSI/EBI, I would be the one that it would be sold to.

I had just one problem. At the time, EBI was generating two hundred fifty thousand dollars in revenue, and we had worked extremely hard to launch the Home Banking Society as well as build a relationship in the market that led to consulting and research beyond the Home Banking Society. I wanted some recognition for this effort and proposed to Bill that American Express pay fifty thousand dollars in cash for EBI to merge EBI into PSI. I thought this was a trivial amount of money, but it recognized the business we had built from scratch. Bill refused and said that it just wasn't possible to pay anything in cash for EBI, but that we would have a chance to own both EBI and PSI down the road.

Bob and I discussed the need to get some recognition for the fledgling company that we had created, and both of us concluded that we needed to get paid something for that effort. After all, we not only had two hundred fifty thousand dollars in revenue and a strong client base, but we were also likely to make a small profit. We both didn't think that fifty thousand dollars was a lot of money for what we had achieved. It was recognition for our work; it was compensation for bringing two hundred fifty thousand dollars in revenue to PSI and American Express as well as a quality staff and the likelihood of a larger profit. We weren't asking for much, and I wasn't willing to accept a merger with PSI for absolutely nothing at all. It was upfront compensation for our efforts.

After a few preliminary questions, I told Bill that I didn't think I could do this without American Express putting up some money for any contingencies that might arise since we had not looked at the numbers in detail yet. I wasn't talking about a loan or a line of credit, but a fee for combining the companies. I mentioned fifty thousand dollars. Bill then said, "We are giving you PSI. We aren't going to pay you to take it. We're absorbing all the costs." I persisted that we needed a small amount of money from American Express for our success. I was in negotiation mode, but Bill was in no mood to negotiate. He thought he had made a very generous offer, and when I asked for a little bit more, he repeated what he had just said, "I'm giving you the company and you want money? I've obviously made a mistake." He got up and left the office, very upset at me, and that killed the deal.

Bob didn't think it was the time to negotiate. He thought this first meeting was executive to executive, that I should have agreed to the big picture, and then worked out the details. He knew we would know more over time to make a more knowledgeable decision. Bob saw the offer from Esping as not only a growth and revenue opportunity but also an ongoing sweetheart relationship with American Express, a consulting bonanza. He thought my early negotiation as inappropriate timing. Bob expected me to treat Esping's offer as a magnanimous executive handing out a gift with the details to be hammered out later. I was new at this type of negotiation, and Bob and I did not discuss what to do beforehand. Bob expected me to listen, agree to whatever he wanted us to do to keep American Express satisfied, and then later, after we became more knowledgeable, either accept or reject the opportunity.

In considering a deal to be acquired, do not reject the initial offer; explore how to make it work to your satisfaction and reject the offer when all alternatives are unacceptable. Only later did I realize the legal effort it takes to make an acquisition. I was only focused on my needs and not on what American Express's needs were. Esping never told me why there would be no upfront payment, and I never pushed him hard enough to get the answer.

With more experience and more flexibility, there could have been many other possible approaches with Esping that might have worked. I could have asked for a higher salary or stock options. I never explored how or in what way I would eventually own the combined companies that I would run. The payment I demanded upfront stopped the negotiations.

It is better to continue negotiating to try to reach a mutually beneficial agreement instead of being fixated on a set of conditions that the other side cannot accept. Explore how to make the sale work. Take the time to explore what the other side is willing to do. There is no telling what another approach can do to resolve an impasse. Do not be too quick to assume the worst, to conclude that the deal is too risky and stop negotiating. You still might end up in the same place unwilling to take the risk, but don't conclude that until you have thoroughly explored all of the possible options. I stopped too soon. Negotiations should be explored thoroughly before walking away from a deal.

I have often thought what might have happened if I had taken the offer. I might have asked for an American Express stock option in place of upfront cash or a larger salary or a bonus plan. This was a case of not thinking outside the box—of not being able to find a solution that would satisfy both American Express and me. I was too stuck on a preliminary position that American Express could not accept. It was the road not taken, and there was no telling what might have happened. If I had one regret in my career, this was it.

American Express ultimately sold PSI to the Tampa-based outfit that Dale had joined. Dale raised the money to buy the company with money from his investors down in Florida, so Dale once again had control of PSI late in 1980. Selling it to Dale made sense for both parties.

Had I agreed to merge EBI into PSI, Dale would not have gotten his company back, PSI almost certainly would have remained with American Express for a bit longer, and in the end I would have had a much bigger company than EBI. It almost certainly would have changed the direction I had to take with EBI a year or so later.

Once Dale had PSI back, he called about the possibility of merging EBI into PSI. Again I was interested enough to discuss this, for I could work with Dale alone so long as Rich and Peter were out of the picture. To begin the discussion and to impress Dale with the quality of my staff, I decided to take Al with me. Al had become a terrific researcher with a great personality, and he was capable of impressing anyone. Dale was impressed with Al, as I knew he would be, and when our negotiations broke off because Dale had no money to buy EBI, he offered Al the opportunity to head up the research at PSI.

I should have known better. I did the same thing ten years earlier when John Reed at Citibank had lent me to the Atlanta Fed to run the Atlanta Payments Project and the banks asked me to stay in Atlanta. I should have known that once Dale got to see the qualities in Al, he might do the same thing that the Atlanta banks did for me, which was to offer him a job. I should have left Al in Atlanta or gotten Dale to agree that he could not hire any of my staff for a one-year period once we started negotiations. I didn't put any restrictions on my employees then or since. I didn't think it was useful or fair, but that didn't mean I had to show Dale one of the best employees I had. The mistake was taking Al with me. I could easily have negotiated with Dale without him. I was really pissed off at Dale and told him so, but it didn't matter. Al left EBI for PSI, eventually ran PSI, and built a great reputation for himself. I felt the loss at EBI, and I could not understand why Al left. I thought EBI was a better company than PSI, but only later did it occur to me that Al could not take over my job, but he could take over Dale's job. Later, I admired him. At the time, I was just plain angry at the loss.

Earlier, I described the Honest Face system, a point-of-sale terminal check guarantee service implemented by First National Bank of Atlanta. The Honest Face system was the brainchild of Bill Matthews at the bank, and Matthews had moved on to become the CEO at Union Planters Bank. Matthews wanted to own the Honest Face system, but he knew that his old bank would not sell it to him. He thought of us, since he knew us from his days in Atlanta. Either he or his chief financial officer called my partner to ask me if we would consider taking on the Honest Face operation.

Bob and I talked about buying Honest Face. I was pretty negative about it at first because I had no experience in running a system. Bob, on the other hand, did have experience with the system, and he had discussed having the key operating guy at Honest Face continue to operate the system under our control. When the bank indicated that they would sell the system for two million dollars and the price was firm, I then agreed to explore the possibility.

We, of course, did not have two million dollars to invest in such a system. If we borrowed that kind of money, it would be an enormous risk. However, I knew that Matthews had developed Honest Face, and he might be interested in helping us buy Honest Face and eventually own it through us.

When Bob called Matthews to arrange a meeting in Memphis, Matthews told him that we should come up to see him and we would work something out. In Matthew's office, we explained the deal as he paced around the room. He said there would be no problem to arrange for a two-million-dollar loan, and he offered up front that it would be an interest-only loan, and the bank wouldn't require us to personally sign for the loan. Honest Face would be the collateral for the loan.

When I asked him how much the business might be worth, he didn't know and didn't care because it would be owned by EBI, with Union Planters funding the investment. In this way, EBI would be at risk, but Matthews could gain control of Honest Face. I assumed that eventually Union Planters might want to buy Honest Face and run it directly. That buyout was not made clear, and I never pursued it.

We went back to Atlanta and looked at the numbers again. More than anything, I was worried about running an operating company, and being on the hook for two million dollars. For me at that point in my life, the risks looked enormous. EBI was a start-up operation, and neither Bob nor I had a lot of money. Even if I did not have to personally sign for the loan Union Planters would give us, I thought my small net worth would be totally at risk for a business that Mathews and Bob wanted more than I wanted. Bob came from a company environment that produced hardware and software, and he knew a lot more about running that kind of business than I. Did I want to be at risk for two million dollars in a company that I did not know much about, in a business that I knew only from a consulting perspective, and which might be eliminated over time as electronic banking became more widely established? The risks were just too great. I didn't have the courage to take on that kind of opportunity, and besides, EBI was doing just fine. I had enough entrepreneurial spirit to start my own company but not enough to bet on something much bigger and more removed from what I knew.

Bob was still interested in making the deal, running it for a time and then selling it for a profit. We agreed to go further and meet with First National Bank of Atlanta. The meeting occurred at the Capital City Club in downtown Atlanta. Tom Williams, the CEO, attended with another banker.

At the meeting, I agreed in principle that we wanted to buy Honest Face, but I said that their price was too high. I suggested that the price should be about $1.2 million. The bankers asked me what the basis was for that price, and I said that I didn't know what the risks were and would sooner or later have to buy new equipment, so the company wasn't worth what they were asking.

The bankers got up and said, "I thought we had a deal. I can see that we don't have one. Let's go." At that moment, I was happy. I didn't really want to do the deal. Everything was rushed, and it didn't fit my expertise. This was different from the deal with Bill Esping to take over PSI. There I wanted PSI but screwed up the negotiation. For Honest Face, I should have said no thanks instead of offering an unacceptable price, but I was young and inexperienced.

Several months later, the bank sold Honest Face to a European company for about two million dollars in cash, and the rest of the price was based on future earnings. A few years later, Honest Face faded into oblivion as check-guarantee services were replaced by debit cards, making the need for guaranteeing a check much less of a value to a retailer.

In 1981, Jeffrey Kutler, then the main writer on payments systems at the *American Banker* newspaper, approached me with an idea for a monthly magazine on payment systems. I immediately liked the idea because in addition to an ongoing research program, we could start a newsletter with perhaps the best writer on payment systems in the business. In many ways, it fit what I wanted to do with EBI: build quality reports, avoid huge amounts of travel, and deal with the critical issues in payment systems. The magazine would do just that, and it would be another ongoing source of revenue.

In discussions with Jeff, we agreed on a salary, agreed that he could remain in New York City, and agreed that he would do virtually all of the writing and publishing while we would do the marketing from Atlanta. We called the publication *Transition: The Journal of Financial Service Strategy*. The first issue came out in July 1981, and it immediately generated a major problem for me.

The Federal Reserve Bank of Atlanta had just published its 1979 check-processing results based on a nationwide survey I had worked on with Tom Marschall. It was a big deal for the industry, for it estimated the number of checks written in the United States, a number that was elusive to get. It involved canvassing a random sample of banks and other financial institutions that had checking accounts. Different groups had different estimates, and it appeared that the Fed study had the definitive answer. Jeff was determined to have the lead story in the first issue of *Transition* magazine deal with the Fed study, so he flew down to Atlanta to interview several of the staff at the Atlanta Fed about it.

The cover story of the first issue was entitled "Check Volume Growth . . . Whose Number Is Right?" The conclusion of the story was that the prediction of the check's demise was overblown, and the results of the study's core conclusions seemed to be solid. Indeed, the study held up over time as a definitive piece of research. However, there were several statements in the lead story of the magazine that Bill Ford, then president of the Atlanta Fed, took great exception to. Out of courtesy, Jeff sent a draft of his article to the Atlanta Fed, and Ford blew his stack when he read the draft. He called me on the phone and told me in no uncertain terms that the article could not be published because it maligned the Atlanta Fed. I then read the article again in detail and discussed this with Jeff. Jeff told me that there was nothing wrong with what he wrote, that Ford had gone beyond the data, and that he stuck his neck out in making speculative projections for the next decade when the survey was not designed for this. The research was only designed to document the 1979 period. Nothing in the survey suggested anything about the future, yet Ford insisted on doing just that, and it upset the staff at the Atlanta Fed.

I concluded that the real issue was that Jeff was questioning Ford's speculation, as was some of the Atlanta Fed staff that worked on the study. I couldn't tell Ford that directly, so I called him back and told him that we reviewed the article, and I would not change it. He then insisted on seeing me and came to my office. Here I was, a start-up company with not much revenue, and the lead story of the first issue of a new magazine dealt with the speculation of the president of the Atlanta Fed. The president of the Atlanta Fed was coming to my office to insist on meddling with the press. I had a great relationship with the people at the Atlanta Fed, they were a mentor for me when I came to Atlanta, they gave me an office in the building and treated me as one of their own, and I had come to have tremendous regard for the people who worked there. I certainly didn't want to piss off the president.

Still, Ford pushed me hard. He insisted that I either change the article to remove the "negative" statement about his Fed or delete the article completely. I had to decide to either support my new editor or cave in to the Fed's demand. I weighed the decision for most of the day before Ford arrived and decided that I was dealing with freedom of the press. The ethics of that outweighed whatever problems I had with Ford even if he was a powerful Fed president. So after Ford ranted and raved about the changes that had to be made in the article, I told him I had read the article carefully, I had discussed the matter with Jeff, and we both felt that the Fed was not maligned, that the article was truthful, that freedom of the press was an issue, and I would not overrule Jeff. Ford stormed out of my office and saw to it that I was persona non grata at the Atlanta Fed so long as he was president. I did not receive a lick of work from the Atlanta Fed for years until Ford finally resigned and moved on. I think it was one of my finest hours. I put ethics ahead of business.

In choosing between acting in the best interest of the business or acting ethically, choose ethics. It would have been easy to put business ahead of my own ethics because I was a small company, and the Federal Reserve was a good client. I knew I would suffer by going against Ford, but I had to stand up for what my editor believed to be fair as well as what I believed was at stake—freedom of the press. I knew that no business with the Atlanta Fed would occur so long as Ford was president. I considered that and still decided that my ethical beliefs came ahead of business considerations. It took several years before we could do any business with the Atlanta Fed again.

Over the years, I have reviewed that decision in my mind many times, and it has given me the courage to put ethical considerations ahead of business considerations on a number of occasions. I may have lost business because of the decisions that I made, but I sleep well at night knowing that I could not live with myself if I did otherwise. It is just that simple.

A year or so later, *Transition Magazine* was sold to the *American Banker*, and Jeff returned to work for them again.

When I left PSI, I focused on the subjects I knew best, which were the evolving world of new payment systems, such as home banking, ATMs, ACH, and debit cards. I had asked various people for advice on how to start a company, and the general answer I received was to focus on my strengths and on what I knew best. We launched the Home Banking Society, then a program on check truncation, and that was sufficient for the first couple of years of the company. However, as time went on, serious problems began to emerge that put the company in jeopardy. In some sort of order of importance, they were as follows:

A partner in a new business is comforting, but be sure you have the right one.

I thought I had the right partner in Bob. He was a preeminent salesman, and I believed that I could handle the rest of our business: product development, consulting, and administration. On paper, it looked good, but I soon discovered that the company was too dependent on me for product development and too dependent on Bob to sell. We needed to do both to grow the company. So long as both partners were successful at what they did, the company was in good shape. Once one of us failed, the company failed. I didn't want to sell, and Bob didn't want to do product development. There was just too much that depended on a single person.

All the owners of a new business should be multifaceted—to be able to sell the service and to deliver it. It's what makes being an entrepreneur difficult. A single owner has to be able to sell and deliver, and partners should also be able to do both. It is only over time as the business grows that partners can specialize because other staff members can support both the sales and operations parts of the business.

The first products of a new business must generate a sizeable market and a sizeable profit. The first two products of EBI were successful and did carry the company for a couple of years. During that period, the focus was on revenue growth and not on profits.

The emphasis on growth is critical to establishing a business, but we put too much emphasis on it by hiring excellent staff and not enough focus on making a serious profit. Growth and profits are needed to sustain the company, especially when a small company is not well funded. Because we focused on adding staff and generating revenue, the level of expense increased substantially without any cushion for a downturn. The result was that the profit in the first few years was minimal, and with no real capital to start the company there was always a concern about cash flow. The emphasis on profits is not to get rich but to build a cash cushion to carry the company in the event of a shortfall in revenue. If a product failed without a cushion of cash to carry the company, we were at the mercy of our finances. A failure of the revenue stream to support the growth of the payroll put the company into jeopardy, and that eventually happened.

Without a sizeable profit, the firm was totally exposed if the next product failed, which it did. It would have been much wiser to grow more slowly with much less people, and put equal emphasis on both growth and profits. Had we done this, we might have been able to withstand a decline in revenue without having to sell the company.

For small companies, cash flow is critical to staying afloat.

I can't emphasize this point enough. Small businesses fail often because they run out of cash. I started my company with no cash at all and built the company on the cash flow we received from selling multiclient programs because clients paid for them up front when the program was getting started, and not after the program was completed—as is the case with consulting. up-front cash flow will allow a company to grow into a million dollar business on a shoestring of cash. While this is exciting, it also puts the company at great risk for any type of failure. The bigger you get, the more at risk you are for one small failure. That failure can bring your company down. It did that to mine.

It is more prudent to build your company more slowly and focus on preserving cash. I learned from my first company that cash flow is critical not just for success but also for survival. I never forgot this lesson.

Multiclient programs require perfect timing in the marketplace.

The key to any multiclient program is that it has to have perfect timing in the marketplace. If the program is too early, the potential members will not see the need to join the program because they won't see it as necessary. If the program is too late in the marketplace, then potential members will be involved with other consultants or committed to a direction they don't think they can change, so they will not see the program as necessary. Timing is critical. However, once you get a multiclient program to launch, which is never easy, it can continue for many years and is a source of stable revenue to support a consulting firm.

Our focus was mostly on multiclient studies and not enough on individual client consulting.

Multiclient studies are wonderful products if they are launched, and that depends on picking the right study and marketing it aggressively. The first two studies—Home Banking Society and check truncation—were two successful launches, and they maintained the company's growth for several years. As the staff grew, however, there was an increasing need to define additional multiclient studies, which depended on me to create them. At the time, NOW accounts were a big issue, and eventually I decided to launch a multiclient study on it. The problem was that I was a year or more late. NOW accounts were growing in 1980, and I was launching the program in late 1981 when many other consulting firms were already in the market. The result was that we had few clients interested in the program, and it failed to launch. With lots of revenue riding on that launch and with several months of effort spent on it before giving up, there was a huge hole in the revenue stream while expenses continued to mount.

Not all great ideas have a market.

Discuss a new idea first with your staff, then clients, then sell the idea to them with a definitive price tag. If that succeeds, build a strong marketing plan to develop the idea aggressively. My company failed to do this for all of its products and ran into trouble because it did not follow this roadmap. The key is to cut your losses quickly if the idea does not have a market but not too soon, for an idea needs time to germinate. Often the idea receives a lukewarm reception, but over time, it gathers a more positive response. You have to give it a real test, pushing it hard before you reject it. The only problem is that when you have a boss or a partner with lots of ideas, you don't have the resources to take them all through the rigorous process to see how acceptable they all are to the market. Sometimes, you just have to go with your gut.

Hiring professionals without experience in the company's field of concentration restricts the growth of the company.

I initially hired excellent professionals composed of research people, not consultants. These people did not have the experience in the field of consulting that we were focused on. We had a wonderful staff for multiclient studies who could do excellent research, but most of them were not knowledgeable about the technology that drives payment systems. We could conduct market research studies, competitive analysis, and evaluate vendors, but we rarely were invited inside our clients' business to fix their problems. So long as I could bring in research business, they could do the work. This put a huge emphasis on me to define the studies to be launched and on my partner to sell them and for both of us to find consulting assignments. The staff I had was too inexperienced to bring in new business. That reduced our ability to attract serious consulting assignments from a bank or a vendor, and it put all our emphasis on multiclient studies.

For a small staff, it is possible for the owners to manage an inexperienced staff and be successful. After five to six people, the demands become too great, and it is necessary to add experienced staff from the field of concentration to be able to bring in new business. To continue the growth of a company, there has to be a balance so that staff with experience in the business can mentor the inexperienced staff. In my case, there was an imbalance between experience and academic professionalism. By the time I recognized the problem, it was too late and I had to sell the company.

The staff grew too quickly.

Bob pushed hard to grow the company and convinced me that we should hire bankers that could sell consulting studies as well as sell multiclient research. As a result, we hired John Domer from Mellon Bank, and another man from a Savings Bank in New York. They were expensive hires, and they of course, focused on selling the NOW Account program that was being launched. They were too new to jump into selling consulting, and so the combination of additional expensive staff with no revenue to support them put the company into a serious cash flow problem. We just couldn't continue with that level of staff given the failure to launch the NOW Account program.

We focused on future payment systems, not on present payment systems.

Multiclient programs usually focus on the future, on an unresolved issue that many in the industry face. The study attracts clients who want to know what to do in the future. That is fine if you can define industry issues early on before they are resolved. That approach doesn't deal with existing payment systems that have their own issues, such as credit cards, check processing, cash management, ATMs, and ACH. At the time based on my experience, my focus was on new products and new services, and not on existing payment systems. It was a big mistake. It was too limiting, and inevitably, I picked a topic that the industry did not have an interest in because I was late getting it to the market. If I picked an issue that was too far into the future, the industry would not be interested because it was not relevant. Too late or too early makes it difficult to find multiclient programs that sell.

After killing the NOW project, and as chief product designer, I settled on a new multiclient product called the Electronic Branch, yet I was still delivering last year's multiclient project by spring. By the time we had our project designed in late summer and Bob went to our "angel" clients to bring in enough revenue to guarantee that we would at least break even before we mounted the marketing campaign, our clients told Bob that another company, Synergistics, had released a similar program, and they had signed on to it. Bob should have had that market intelligence, but he didn't. He wasn't doing his job of keeping track of what was out there. If he had, we could have done something differently. Without the income from that project and with it being too late to start another program with the bank's budgets set, we spiraled down.

In hindsight, of course, we may have done something else, but our decisions were based on what we knew at the moment. The real key was capital. Without reserve capital to carry the company after a small setback or capital to expand, the company was at a severe disadvantage.

In spring 1982, it was painfully obvious that we did not have the revenue to support the staff that we had. We had revenue of just over one million dollars for the year, but our expenses exceeded that. I told Bob that we had to do two things quickly: reduce our sales staff and look for a company to acquire EBI. He reluctantly agreed because we were running out of cash, we had no line of credit at the bank, and I didn't want to put our personal assets on the line to get one. We dropped our new salesmen, and Bob found Bank Earning International (BEI), a growing consulting firm in Atlanta interested in acquiring our company. While Bob and I had no real interest in selling our company, we had little choice.

BEI sent Bob Ivey over to check out our books, and he found them in good order and recommended that BEI take us over without paying a single penny for the acquisition. I reluctantly agreed. In September 1982, EBI was acquired by BEI and set us up as a separate division. BEI kept me on as president of that division and offered to pay me the same salary that I made as CEO of EBI. I did not want to go back to working for someone else. I knew I wanted to be my own boss, but Bob and I had failed to strike a balance between growth and profits. We lost the company because we grew too fast, did not focus on being profitable, and did not have enough capital to sustain a small setback. It was unfortunate but necessary to salvage the company and support the staff we had. The BEI acquisition provided jobs for them, for Bob, and for me. As BEI found out after the acquisition, there were several hundred thousand dollars of bills to pay that we could not pay, and that would have forced us into bankruptcy.

Chapter 13

Bank Earnings International

In 1976, Jim Cotton and Jerry Eickhoff founded Bank Earnings International (BEI) to consult to the banking community on earnings improvements. The consulting company grew rapidly and was one of the fastest-growing companies in the United States in terms of revenue. It was selected by the Federal Reserve Bank of Atlanta as one of the best-managed companies in the southeast.

BEI assisted its clients in the implementation of changes and enhancements to their systems and programs to bring about projected improvements. These earnings improvements included virtually every banking discipline, including retail banking, fee income, mortgage and commercial lending, trust services, data processing, research, capital generation, and review and disposition of nonearning assets.

BEI's consulting business was much broader than electronic banking, and I learned to *go where the money is*. The company focused on the biggest services in the bank: lending, credit cards, mortgages, check processing, and trust services. They were not interested in blazing new territory, but rather working on earnings improvements—substantial improvements that usually were a result of high-volume operations with large staffs. It was a totally different model, and it produced a totally different profit. The answer is to go where there are large volumes and excessive staff. In that regard, old established services will generate more revenue for a consulting firm because they have more volume, more staff, more bureaucracy, and more opportunities for improvement.

BEI offered a contingency pricing arrangement under which the consulting fee was based on a percentage of the actual measured annualized earnings improvements. Flat fees were also offered based on the number of man-weeks of work similar to the way other consulting firms priced their work. A contract proposal was based on an initial study of key areas of concern. Based on that assessment, BEI proposed to save the institution a certain amount of money based on that initial study and gained approval from the institution to proceed based on that earnings improvement. If the results proved out, it would be a win-win for BEI and the financial institution.

Some people will argue that cost determines the price. Determine your cost first and then add the profit margin that you expect to the cost to obtain the price. BEI never followed that model. Rather, the company *set the price based on what the market could bear* and then determined how to make a profit with the revenue that flowed from that price. BEI had high consulting rates because their process-improvement assignments could justify the rates. The same was true about contingency pricing. The rate was based on the benefits that resulted from improving the process. Banks and companies have lots of money to spend when they perceive the value for their organization. The issue is convincing the buyer that what you have will be more valuable to them than their cost to hire you.

The consulting team undertook studies in such areas as float, check processing, platform services, teller operations, branch operations, trust services, loan services, data processing, bookkeeping, and fee income. In each case, the consultant would rely heavily on specific interviews, on-site observations, task analyses, and workflow evaluations, an understanding of the marketplace and their own banking backgrounds. Recommendations would then be formulated, proposed, piloted, and implemented. The fee paid by the financial institution would be a percentage of the annualized savings produced from the consulting assignment.

In 1984, BEI began providing consulting services and assistance in connection with the establishment of de novo (new) financial institutions. It literally would help a client raise the money to start a bank and take the new bank through all the regulatory procedures necessary to open the door of the bank. It would also help to find the appropriate location for the bank, including help with hiring the staff.

BEI also took advantage of the recession in the 1980s when the banking industry had foreclosed on homes, acquiring real estate owned that was no longer bringing in any revenue. In 1985, BEI began providing financial institutions with consulting services and assistance in targeting and evaluating nonearning loans and assets in the real and personal property areas. The company established PEI, Property Earnings International, for the review and disposal of nonearning assets, specifically real property, and provided consulting services for the conversion of these nonearning assets to earning-asset status. After analysis and review, each property was outlined for the most advantageous method of conversion to an earning asset, which resulted in earnings improvement for the financial institution. This included organizing an auction to sell the various properties to the public.

Here was case in point: *launch a new program when the market needed it, and then find the expertise to manage it.* When you perceive a new market for a service, get into that market as quickly as you can. Find the expertise inside the company to take on this new service or hire the expertise from outside the company. With smart people, they can focus on this new service and build the expertise over time. A new service is a new revenue stream, and this has to be the emphasis for a company. This is an effective strategy, even when top management in the firm may not know the area. You must rely on your staff to bring or acquire the expertise and to build the business into profitability.

Over time, I recognized that it was important to *focus on a broad array of services.*

In my first company, I only felt comfortable consulting on services that I knew well. Across the broad spectrum of possible consulting activities, I only had expertise in a small area. I recognized at BEI that senior management did not have to have the expertise to offer a new set of services but depended on one or more of their staff to have the expertise that was needed. I did not have enough confidence in my staff at EBI to do this because I was hiring research people who did not have the expertise to consult on a banking area. I was limiting the growth of my company by focusing only on what I knew and not hiring other banking experts in areas that I did not know, but where consulting opportunities existed. If there is a need for services in a particular area, find the expertise and depend on them to grow that part of the business. It takes trust in others to make this happen.

One of *the hallmarks of BEI was that they established joint ventures with other much larger companies* serving the banking industry piggybacking on their expertise. One of them was EDS, the software and consulting firm that Ross Perot began. EDS offered an outsourcing service whereby they would take over and run the operations of a bank or savings and loan association under contract. Once the contract was signed, BEI would conduct an earnings-improvement assignment to improve the EDS operations. This produced a more efficient operation for EDS while generating a ready source of consulting revenue to BEI. There were other joint ventures with First Nationwide Network and Hogan Services Corporation and, eventually, with American Banker.

These joint ventures consistently generated revenue that would not have occurred otherwise. A joint venture requires an open mind—an ability to think about products beyond the company's limited expertise. It requires thinking on a grander scale and finding a partner that has a similar vision. BEI started new ventures from scratch, added their expertise to a larger firm to help both of them make a sale they probably could not make otherwise, and acquired companies to grow their business. While it is reasonable to grow organically, joint ventures should be explored seriously with the openness and encouragement to find ways to do them instead of finding reasons to dismiss them.

I started at BEI as an employee instead of the majority owner of a company. It was not an easy transition for me. I no longer was the ultimate decision maker; I had to listen to people who were younger than I, made more money than I, and believed they were smarter in business than I. It was a drastic change in my work habits, but I made the best of it. I did what I had to do, and that was to put on a positive face, be agreeable as much as possible, and become a team player.

What helped a great deal was having taken a program called the Forum. The Forum was a personal improvement program that forced me to think about what I said and what my attitude was about what happened in my life. For me, it was a life-changing event because it exposed me to how I came across to people and how other people came across to me based on what they said. I had been briefly exposed to this type of people analysis many years earlier when I was at Citibank, but I had forgotten much of that over time. The Forum brought people issues front and center, forced me to evaluate what I said and helped me to understand people based on what they said. The result was that I could frame my language at BEI to be as positive as possible, to make the best of my employee status, to speak as a team player, and to focus on doing the best job I could. I worked very hard on that attitude and maintained it right up to the time I resigned from BEI more than five years later.

At BEI, I decided that I did not want to go back to consulting. I had a research bent, and I did not want to leave my home on Sunday to spend four days at a client and return home on Thursday even though consultants did not have to come to the office on Friday. In 1982, my children were sixteen, fourteen, and eleven years old. This was an important time, and I wanted to be at home for them as well as for my wife. BEI's consulting business was different from the EBI business that I had. EBI was more of a research company, doing research, running seminars, and writing reports on the payment system industry while BEI was solving problems onsite for specific clients. Both consulting businesses were useful, but onsite consulting the BEI way was very profitable, much more profitable than the research business I had begun.

Eickhoff, the partner that focused on marketing and sales, decided initially that EBI would offer a new syndicated research study, and he picked the topic. He knew that the banking industry had mixed feeling about the role of the Federal Reserve in the payment system, for the Fed regulated the industry while it was a major player in it and, as a result, often competed with the largest banks. Eickhoff proposed that we launch a study called "The Role of the Federal Reserve in the Payment System." I fought against such an idea because I knew that banks buy syndicated research when they believe it offers benefits to them that they can put to use. I had failed to launch my own syndicated program on NOW accounts because the banks saw no benefit to them for participating. While a study on the role of the Federal Reserve might find that the Federal Reserve should not be doing what it was doing or change some regulation or fee, it did not have an immediate impact on the banks that would be paying for the study. Eickhoff was my new boss, so I supported the idea to the fullest and put on the best marketing effort that we were capable of doing. Nevertheless, I thought the banks would not pay for such a program.

We held a preliminary meeting to explain the new program, and a sizeable number of banks showed up to hear what we had to say. We presented the program, Eickhoff spoke eloquently about what we offered, and then the banks asked the critical question, "What's the benefit to my bank?" When no hard-hitting answer was possible, the bankers there could not see how they could gain management approval to participate, and that killed the idea. It also turned Eickhoff and BEI off to syndicated research for the next year or so. In turn, it also gave the management of BEI the feeling that they had overpaid for EBI because even though they acquired the company without paying for it outright, the accumulated bills at EBI amounted to almost three hundred thousand dollars. When I found out that the EBI bills amounted to that much money, I was thrilled that BEI had bought us because it provided jobs for all my staff, including Bob and me. It would have been a real mess to have closed EBI down and perhaps ended up in bankruptcy.

Once the syndicated research idea was dead, Eickhoff approached me with the idea of growing our consulting business. He suggested a significantly higher revenue goal and offered me a fifty thousand dollars bonus if I could achieve it by the end of the fiscal year. I immediately accepted and went about the business of growing our consulting revenue, along with the existing multiclient programs that we had. Bob joined me in those months to also bolster our business, and slowly it began to grow. At the end of the fiscal year, we did reach and exceed the goal. I was happy that I could rise to the occasion, that I had enough contacts in the business that continued to hire us to do consulting, and that I could produce under pressure.

When I reminded Eickhoff of his bonus commitment, he demurred. He told me that he did not expect to pay that huge amount of money because he did not realize that BEI had to pay three hundred thousand dollars in expenses for EBI. I told him that he had assigned Bob Ivey to check our books in advance of acquiring the company, and that decision had nothing whatsoever to do with meeting the revenue he set for me and the fifty-thousand-dollar bonus that was associated with meeting that goal. Reluctantly he agreed, and after several months of nagging him for the money BEI eventually wrote me a check for that amount.

The two partners of BEI had apparently paid $140,000 each to EBI to pay off EBI's debt, and they carried those payments as loans to EBI, which they eventually paid off several years later when the company went public. It was a personal expense for them that turned into a tax deduction, which is why it was annoying to Eickhoff when it came time to pay me my fifty-thousand-dollars bonus. He thought he overpaid for my company and didn't think I deserved to get a huge bonus—even though one thing had nothing to do with the other.

Somewhere in 1983, shortly after beginning work at BEI, I had the idea of writing a book on electronic banking. No book on the subject existed, and my work over fifteen years had accumulated a huge amount of material that would make the content of a book on various payment systems easy to compile. I approached two excellent writers on my staff, Tom Marschall and Jan Linker, and they agreed to work with me on the various chapters for the book. We split up the chapters, and slowly the book began to take shape.

I was worried about getting the book published, but I knew that John Wiley & Sons was in the business of publishing technology books like the one we had in mind. I approached the company with the idea by laying out the various chapters for them, along with a marketing plan as to how to sell copies of the book. John Wiley readily agreed to publish the book, so we worked in earnest to get a decent draft ready. This took about a year to complete since Tom, Jan, and I could only work on it part-time. Most of the effort was completed while working at BEI, so I felt obligated to approach Eickhoff about whether Tom, Jan, and I could split the revenue or whether the revenue would go directly to BEI. Eickhoff's view was that the money should go to BEI since we worked on the book on company time; reluctantly I agreed.

John Wiley sent the draft of the book to several people in payment systems for a critical review. They had many comments to make, the most important one being that the book did not take a position on electronic banking. I agreed with that comment because we wrote the book as an educational book, explaining how the systems worked, along with various marketing studies that would help the reader understand the issues the industry faced in moving forward. We did not want to promote a given service, but rather to explain what they were and the issues that made the service complex to implement, and difficult to justify economically. After incorporating the comments from the critics into the book and gaining approval in writing for the various charts and exhibits that were in the book, the book was published in 1985. Over the next few years, the book sold quite well, selling close to ten thousand copies, a decent result for the technology book that it was. John Wiley had agreed to pay the authors 15 percent of the revenue, and with the book priced at about $10 per copy, that amounted to about

$15,000 to BEI. If I had split the revenue with Tom and Jan, each of us would have received five thousand dollars, not much for the effort we put into the book. Nevertheless, it was a significant achievement. And since I was the first author on the book, any search of the Internet on electronic banking will produce my name associated with the book. The book is no longer in print, and the material in the book is way out of date. I could update the book, but that would be a major effort given the enormous changes in payment systems that have taken place since then.

It wasn't long before the old EBI staff knew that research was a secondary effort for BEI, and the most important way to grow the company was to become a payment system consultant, knowledgeable about a bank's process and capable of producing earnings improvement while onsite for the client. Some of the EBI staff, like Tom Marschall, were very capable of doing that type of consulting, but other members of the staff did not have the banking background or a desire to do that kind of consulting, so they gradually left BEI for other opportunities. Bob Cady was mainly involved in marketing and sales and focused on launching syndicated research. He often clashed with Eickhoff, who was more interested in growing the company through joint ventures, acquisitions, and new products. Bob was not the type of person that would fit nicely into Eickhoff's short—or long-term objectives, so Bob left BEI within a year of the acquisition of EBI for other opportunities. In short, EBI was dismantled within a year after its acquisitions, and while I did eventually launch a major syndicated research program, it was not the major activity of BEI.

In 1984, microcomputers were just entering the banking industry. Financial institutions were buying computers but did not know what to do with them. There were fledgling PC departments in banks to teach their staff about working with a computer because they were complex to use effectively. Software using Windows did not exist, and the user had to know a series of commands to use the computer. Still, applications were popping up all over the bank by a few computer savvy nerds. Several people at BEI suggested that we should take advantage of this opportunity by launching a syndicated research program on the profitable use of computers within the banking industry, and it naturally fell to me to organize such a program.

Eickhoff was concerned that we might not be able to launch the program alone and suggested that we joint venture with the *American Banker* because they could provide free and powerful advertising of the program through their daily newspaper. Personally, I felt very capable of launching the program alone, but I agreed with my boss that the *American Banker* would certainly provide a wider scope to our marketing efforts. Eickhoff and I flew to New York, met with senior staff at the paper, and quickly worked out an agreement that they would advertise the program with a full-page ad. I would work with their marketing department to prepare the ad as well as develop a huge mailing list to send out the prospectus that described the program. Since the research effort would be conducted by BEI under my control, BEI would suggest a fixed fee to do the work, and the remaining money after expenses would be split fifty-fifty between BEI and the *American Banker*.

The launch took place in 1984 with a price of $2,750 to participate by a given date and after that date the price went up to $3,750. The price of the program was set to appeal to a large number of financial institutions so that a hundred or more would participate. The program was a tremendous success and garnered 210 participating institutions in the project in its first year. We developed a market research questionnaire that was sent to hundreds of financial institutions, asking them about what they were doing with their computers. We summarized the results of the research into a written manual entitled *The Profitable Use of Microcomputers in the Financial Industry*. In the first year of the program, the revenue totaled over $500,000 and after BEI's research fee of about $200,000, the *American Banker* received about $150,000 for its marketing effort.

With such a success, we decided to continue the program for a second year and received renewals from a little more than half of the first year's participants, about 110 members. The second report was entitled "Microcomputer Solutions" and focused on case studies of what computers were being used for in financial institutions. Since the revenue was under three hundred thousand dollars and the BEI fee was substantial, the profit for the *American Banker* was significantly less than the first year. As a result, Eickhoff and the *American Banker* decided that we would not continue the program for a third year although I was ready to do so without the *American Banker*. Had we known how powerful the computer would become in banking, we might have had the opportunity to continue the program with onsite consulting, with economic justifications for various banking services, with benchmarking comparisons among the participants, with technology issues, and a variety of other issues that bankers wanted answers to. We just weren't that smart, and a brilliant multiclient program was laid to rest and never resurrected.

With the microcomputer study complete after two successful years, it was time for me to find another significant place in BEI if I was to stay there. In 1985, there was not enough revenue from the old EBI firm for me to remain as its president, and I was assigned to Bill Williams, then head of BEI onsite consulting. I liked Bill a great deal and thought he was good man. He was intelligent and capable of running the consulting staff that was the main source of revenue for BEI, but I did not want to get on planes, be out of town, and go back to the consulting I knew I could do but didn't want to do. I looked around the company at what I could do that was useful and decided that I would create a formal marketing department at BEI, for it did not exist and the company needed one.

For the large variety of consulting services, there was no formal brochure for each of the many areas that BEI was involved in, so I took on the assignment of writing, structuring and printing about twenty such brochures for use by the BEI sales team and consultants. A senior consultant from each consulting area gave me a rough draft of what they wanted to say in the brochure, and I and one associate under me edited the material, printed it, and added it to the family of BEI brochures. This took considerable time to do, but it was a necessary part of growing BEI.

There was another important structure that BEI put in place: *senior staff must do the selling; they don't always need to do the work.* BEI hired bankers who knew the business and could size up a situation quickly as well as write a good proposal. They could talk the talk and even walk the walk if they had to since clients like to meet the people who will do the work. They could also persuade the prospective client that they understood the problem, they had the resources to improve the situation, and they could propose a price for services that was commensurate with the benefits. However, once the contract was signed, the senior staff tried to move on to the next customer but stayed in touch with the client to provide assurance that the work was being done professionally. In this way, senior people could be more productive by continuing to sell after a contract was signed as others on the staff could do the work. Nevertheless, a senior staff person had to not only make the sale but also review the work and show up at client meetings, especially for the final report to assure the client that the work had the stamp of approval of senior management.

In reviewing the various consulting assignments that BEI was doing, it was clear that the more profitable assignments came from a *focus on large-revenue assignments*. EBI's revenue was often based on small-revenue assignments, making it difficult to make a large profit although the profit margin was acceptable. The real profit came from large revenue assignments that could be completed efficiently. With an efficient staff and a complex proposal to a client, a large-revenue assignment can be plus or minus fifty thousand dollars or more. While the money is important, the client is always more interested in a good result. With a good result, the price of the contract becomes much less important because the value that flows from a good result far exceeds the cost. A good result for a client will justify the cost the client pays, and the bigger the project, the more chance there is to achieve a very good result.

In addition, I took responsibility for the BEI booth and cocktail parties that BEI held at the three major banking conventions that the staff attended annually. The most memorable cocktail party that I organized—and perhaps the most successful one I ever attended—was held in New Orleans in November in the mid-1980s. The American Bankers Association was holding a convention for the presidents of the independent banks in the country, and several thousand senior bankers were attending. The major banks that had strong close relationships with these smaller banks were holding cocktail parties of their own, and we had to compete with these cocktail parties. It was no easy assignment. Still, it was important for BEI staff to meet the attendees and for them to know about BEI. While BEI had a large client base, the company was not known at the majority of these smaller banks, let alone known by the senior management there. I was tasked with the job of holding a cocktail party that would attract as many of these senior bankers as possible. I asked for a budget for the cocktail party and was given $25,000, a lot of money at that time for a cocktail party.

Several months before the convention, I got in touch with a number of excellent caterers in New Orleans, figuring they knew how to put on terrific parties given it was one of the great party cities in the United States. I had several excellent proposals, and decided on the most dramatic proposal of them all—putting on Mardi Gras in November for our cocktail party.

The result was tremendous. We sent out invitations with a small ceramic mask, and it had a dramatic impact on the wives of the bankers. They convinced their husbands to go to the cocktail party. We had over five hundred people attend the cocktail party, picking them up by private bus from their hotels and later returning them that way. The party was held at a huge warehouse that contained the various floats used in the Mardi Gras parade, which made the location interesting. As they entered the warehouse, a black church choir singing with enthusiasm greeted the bankers. The jazz band marched into the warehouse playing all the time and throughout the evening. And finally, near the end of the evening a local high school band of a hundred strong in full uniform marched into the event to blow everyone away. It was quite an evening, and throughout it all, a large number of BEI staff introduced themselves to the bankers.

It was, of course, hard to tell what lasting impact that cocktail party had, but BEI made a lasting impression on many bankers who attended, and the growth of the consulting practice continued unabated thereafter. It was the New Orleans caterer that had the masterful idea, and I also cannot take credit for the growth of consulting after that. Certainly that cocktail party had an impact on a lot of bankers. These senior bankers didn't know us, but thereafter back at their banks, they were willing to sit through a presentation of what we did, and the cocktail party made those presentations easy to arrange. Since getting in the door is the first step in making a sale, the $25,000 cocktail party was quite a success.

To provide a quantitative picture of the growth of BEI, the year ending June 30, 1983 produced $9.1 million compared to $5 million in 1982. That included over five hundred thousand dollars or more in EBI revenue for the nine months that BEI owned EBI during that fiscal year. In 1984, the revenue jumped to $11.2 million, and after I became the head of marketing in 1985, it rose to $13.9 million.

At the end of 1985, BEI had 160 full-time employees, with 108 of them project managers or consultants, 17 engaged in marketing and sales, and 35 engaged in administration. I was listed as EVP and president of EBI. I made \$132,000 for the year, much of it from a company-wide bonus plan.

BEI had a bonus pool for the consulting staff. This was a powerful incentive because the company *shared the profits with the staff*. Almost every one of the consulting staff participated, and we anxiously looked forward to hearing the results and sharing in the success of the company. This was in addition to raises for select members of the staff who deservedly did outstanding work. Sharing the profits of the company requires the company to be transparent about the overall results of the firm, which might undermine the confidentiality that some owners may want about their profits. However, it has the enormous benefit that every staff member is concerned about revenue, costs, and profits of the company. This far and away is more valuable than protecting the confidentiality of the company's results.

Besides sharing the profits with the staff in the mid-1980s, BEI management decided to sell their shares to key employees. The shares were evaluated at a market price that could only go up over time because BEI was doing extremely well. To avoid giving away control of the company, these *employee shares were sold to employees without ever giving them control of the company*. Employee shares were class-B shares exactly the same as class-A shares of the owners except that class-B shares didn't have a vote. This allowed the owners to share ownership with the staff while staying completely in control of the company.

The most important event while I was at BEI was the acquisition of Lifetime Communities. Lifetime was a real estate holding company in Florida that owned and developed residential communities in California, Colorado, Florida, and New Jersey and had extensive experience in selling distressed properties. Lifetime had only a few employees and had little in the way of growth opportunities since the real estate market was not growing. With Lifetime in the real estate market with little prospects for growth, its stock was stuck at about six dollars per share.

On the other hand, BEI had strong growth opportunities and strong management. Since Lifetime was a publicly traded company and had huge tax loss carry-forwards, BEI was interested in merging with Lifetime. The carry-forwards expired from 1989 through 1999 in various amounts, but they totaled just over \$92 million. That meant that

BEI earnings for the foreseeable future would be tax-free. This was a huge benefit, and at tax rates of over 30 percent, the value to BEI was worth over $27 million. This was a windfall for the owners of BEI.

Not everyone was happy with the merger in the stock market. Richard Lilly at the Raymond James stock brokerage company wrote a scathing research report on the merger entitled "The Squandering of One of the Best Tax Advantageous Vehicles of the American Corporate Scene—A Classic Case of Managerial Naiveté Together with a Blatant Disregard for Stockholder Well-being." The theme of the report was that the merger would lead to onerous dilution of Lifetime stock, a less than timely use of a large tax loss carry-forward, and the sacrifice of a rare opportunity to otherwise find a better company than BEI to merge with. His conclusion was that Lifetime stockholders would stand to be literally raped. He believed the merged shares would head down to five dollars a share.

Lifetime agreed that while they would acquire BEI, the management of BEI would run the merged company, and its headquarters would be in Atlanta. This appeared to be a win-win for both companies, especially for BEI. At the time of the merger, the stock had risen to almost twelve dollars per share. BEI employees had stock at $3.58 per share and those shares would receive a little more than 1.5 shares of Lifetime, so at $12 per share, their $3.58 investment was now worth about $18.

The merger took place in May 1986. Technically Lifetime Communities bought BEI, but BEI management took control and changed the name back to BEI. BEI shares now had a public market. Before the merger, BEI class-A shares were controlled by Eickhoff and Cotton, while class-B shares had no vote and were given to the other employees. In this way, the two partners controlled BEI completely. After the merger, the two partners still had a substantial amount of shares to control the merged company.

As a result of the merger, I no longer could produce a simplified and inelegant annual report. BEI was now a publicly traded company, and as the head of marketing for the firm, I focused on producing professionally printed first-class annual reports, with photographs of the senior executives. The 1986 report ended with the following statement from Jim and Jerry, "BEI is not high tech, but rather high talent." I concurred.

In 1987, the annual report restated BEI's 1986 revenue from $13 million to $71 million because of the merger and then presented the 1987 revenue as having declined to $44 million. The net income per share, however, went from twenty cents in 1986 to eighty cents in 1987. Part of the reason for the revenue decline was a 12 percent drop in bank consulting as well as the write-down and decline of sales of Lifetimes' real estate. The restructuring of the consulting area produced three major regions for clear accountability: independent sales strategies, a focus on long-term revenues, and a reduction on holding company overhead.

It was at that point in my stay at BEI that I concluded that I would not be able to contribute as productively as I had in the past. The company was moving out of the bank consulting business that I loved, and I thought I should begin to consider other alternatives. While I had no idea what those alternatives might be, I was convinced that I was an entrepreneur at heart, that I wanted to be my own boss, and that I had learned a great deal at BEI to take another shot at running another consulting firm more profitably than the first one I failed at. I just needed to find the right opportunity while I continued to be as productive as possible at BEI.

Two other activities made my last few years at BEI bearable. The first was that the trust consulting group at BEI was interested in launching a multiclient study. Since I was very knowledgeable about how to do that, I worked with them to produce a good prospectus and then worked with them on getting the program off the ground.

The second area that became quite interesting for me was getting involved in a check processing fraud case for Valley National Bank in Phoenix. Bob Sabeck, executive vice president at the bank, asked BEI to provide an expert witness to help defend the bank against a bank customer that was suing the bank, claiming that the bank was negligent in not catching the fraud that occurred on the customer's account. I spent a fair amount of time in Phoenix with the law firm gaining an understanding of the legal issues, reviewing the case, and working on how to present the problems any bank in the mid-1980s would have in finding fraudulent checks. I considered how to get a jury to visualize the number of checks that were processed in the United States. I estimated that in 1985 there were 46 billion checks written by consumers, corporations, and government. Using six inches, the length of a check, the annual volume of checks would amount to over 4.35 million miles of checks in a year laid end to end. That would be equivalent to having these checks go to the moon and back more than eight times. Furthermore, if a clerk could file one million checks per year, a reasonable number for a clerk, it would require 46,000 clerks to file all the checks written annually, significantly more clerks than existed at the time, causing an increase to the banking industry of seven hundred million dollars.

The real argument was that there were very few forgeries found by clerks or anyone else in the bank. The reason was that there was one forgery in every 2.5 million checks back then. It was like trying to find a needle in a haystack. It was mission impossible to find it. If you were filing one million checks per year, a filing clerk would see one forgery about every three years. That forgery is in a clerk's hands for about six seconds, and then it is gone. The clerk then would have to wait on average another three years to see another forgery. Over the three years, the clerk would be productive on average for two seconds a year in finding a forged check. That is the futility of signature verification. The filing clerk was the only one in the bank doing the job of verifying the customer's signatures on the account.

Eventually, the case was settled out of court, but I had hit on a new career for myself: becoming an expert witness in payment systems. I had the right credentials, a PhD, the president of my company, a strong research background, and a pioneer and expert in payment systems. While it was the only legal case I was involved in at BEI, it became a specialty for me after I left BEI.

I would be remiss if I did not say something about Bob Ivey. Ivey was a close personal friend of Eickhoff. They had grown up together, and Ivey was very highly regarded at BEI not because he was a friend but because he was very bright, very analytical, and an excellent marketing man. He was an all-around first-class consultant, which is why he was sent to analyze EBI before it was acquired by BEI.

Ivey was also in excellent physical condition. He was a strong runner and prepared to run a marathon. At an executive BEI retreat, he ran ten miles to keep in shape for the marathon to come. I say all this because in about 1984, Bob Ivey contracted Lou Gehrig's disease. No one could believe that Ivey who was in such amazing physical condition could get this disease. He was a very religious Christian and often told me that God had a reason for giving him this disease that he and his family did not comprehend, but he continued to believe in the Lord. As the illness progressed, he insisted on working for as long as possible. Near the end of his ability to work, he and I were invited to make a speech in Texas to one of BEI's clients. We prepared a slide presentation, and I had the honor to help him in and out of planes, get him to our client, help him on and off the elevator, and get him to the client without them knowing his condition. Once he stood up, he could speak quite well, use the clicker to move to a new slide, and gave a first-class presentation even though the disease was strongly affecting his ability to walk and hold anything that weighed much at all. Ivey was determined to be a class act and act professionally as long as possible. This was the last time he ever spoke professionally. Shortly thereafter, he was in a wheelchair and gradually deteriorated physically. All of the BEI team, me included, were saddened by his death. I will always remember his will to live, his determination to remain the professional that he was until it was impossible to do it any longer.

Once I moved away from individual consulting and research to take on the job as head of marketing, the management of BEI decided that I would not receive individual raises even though I certainly participated in the bonus pool for the entire staff. I recognized that this was inevitable because BEI rewarded those consultants that brought in revenue or managed large profit-making projects. I was doing neither of them. Still, I was content to focus on marketing because it provided a lot of freedom and very little travel. I was not rich but had a decent salary to be able to spend more time at home with my family rather than make more money and travel to clients several days a week.

When we first moved to Atlanta in 1971, Pamela was not yet five and was enrolled in a parochial kindergarten. Thereafter, she attended a private Jewish day school, and Lori and Leo followed suit. All three went on to the private Jewish high school, and all the schools had significant tuition fees. To cover their tuition expenses, I gradually sold my American Express stock that I received by working for the company during the 1970s.

In 1984, Pamela went to New York University. In 1986, Lori entered Emory University, and Leo followed her in 1988, skipping his last year in high school. All these first-class universities had substantial tuitions, but Leo's tuition was slightly offset by becoming a National Merit Scholar. To pay for their college tuition, I sold my BEI stock. This covered most of the tuitions.

When Pamela was in her last year of high school, I offered to prepare her to take the SAT test for college. She asked a couple of friends to join her, and that got me started on teaching high school kids how to prepare for the SAT national exam. After a few sessions with them, I thought I could do a credible job for the high school my children attended and offered to do it as a service to the school without accepting any pay. The small fee that was charged was donated to the high school.

After several years, it became obvious to me that SAT preparation could be a real business opportunity. Stanley Kaplan and the Princeton Review were writing SAT preparation books and offering SAT tutoring nationwide. My results were impressive—I had increased SAT scores one hundred points on average. For Lori, who did poorly on her first SAT test, I worked with her twice a day for a month, and her score jumped three hundred points, enough to get her into Emory University, clearly demonstrating that she was smart, and I was a capable teacher. I had analyzed dozens of actual SAT tests, and I had written my own two-hundred-plus-page book on SAT preparation. As a result of several years of tutoring several hundred high school students, my wife and I decided to establish a formal SAT course under the name of Educate America.

For the last few years that I was at BEI, Judy and I expanded beyond our kids' high school to offer SAT preparation to high schools in Atlanta. We obtained names of juniors and seniors in various Atlanta high schools, sent them a mailer, and called them on the phone to offer our course. We charged slightly over three hundred dollars for the course, which was less than the competition. We arranged to meet at churches around the city, paying a small fee for a classroom early on Sunday mornings, the only time for me to teach the class. We held ten classes for an hour and a half each and timed them to end near the scheduled date for the SAT test. Over the many years that I did it, first with my own kids, then at various high schools before leaving BEI, and then after leaving BEI, I taught about a thousand high school kids. The money was not great, probably under ten thousand dollars annually, but I loved teaching SAT preparation because it produced definitive results. I could tell how good a job I was doing by asking my students to provide their test results to me. I continued to produce one-hundred-point increases in results, which was a substantial increase and most of the students were satisfied.

Every so often, I would meet with Cotton and Eickhoff about my future. They saw value in the marketing I was doing, but as time went on and the company grew beyond bank consulting, it was clear that individual segments of the company were doing their own marketing. I knew from 1987 onward that I was marking time at BEI, that my contribution was less important, and the only way for me to continue with BEI was to go back to consulting and the travel it entailed. I didn't want to do this as an employee for BEI, so I began to look for alternative opportunities. I wanted to run my own company again.

All the while that I was at BEI I made up my mind that *as an employee be a team player*. I was not happy giving up ownership of my company to become an employee. I could have had an awful attitude about this, but I followed my father's attitude that it was my responsibility for what happened and I had no right to complain about it. What I said was a reflection on me and no one else, so I could be satisfied or unsatisfied according to what I thought and what I said. I had to be a team player to survive in the company as well as enjoy what I was doing. So long as I was happy being an employee I would be satisfied, and I was totally in charge of that. It was a lesson worth taking with me not just at work but in everything I did in life.

Nevertheless, *there is a time to move on.* The time to leave a company is when you are no longer happy about what you are doing or when you believe you are not or cannot contribute as expected by management. Staff with lower salaries leaves a job to increase their income. Professional people leave because they are unhappy and unsatisfied. Their decision is emotional, not monetary. I overstayed my time at BEI and didn't leave when I was no longer happy doing what I was doing. I spent a lot of time at my company. It was a significant part of my life. But once my job was no longer satisfying, I thought about leaving. I didn't enjoy coming to work; it was time to move on. And that's what I did.

Although Bob Cady had left BEI several years earlier, we stayed in touch because he wanted to go back in business with me again. Some time in 1988, he mentioned that he was discussing the possibility of going into business with Steve White, who had joined Payment Systems in 1979 just before I left the company. Steve had founded a company called Global Concepts, Inc., to consult on payment systems, and he was working on his own. He was using his wife, Sherry, to manage the finances of the company. I did not know Steve at all, but I was interested.

Over the latter part of 1988, Steve, Bob, and I met several times to discuss how the three of us might work together. In the end, Steve decided that he was fine to be partners with me but uncomfortable with Bob. Steve knew Bob's skill was marketing, something he did not believe we needed because we would be selling ourselves. Steve also liked the idea of continuing Educate America under Global Concepts, and eventually we decided to be fifty-fifty partners under Global Concepts, and I would bring my book and Educate America into the company as a tradeoff with the furniture and other assets that Steve had bought for the business. I started working there in December 1989 after resigning from BEI. The resignation was amicable enough. Cotton and Eickhoff knew I had to do something different from what I was doing. They wanted me to go back to consulting, and I didn't want to do that. The best thing to do was to resign and move on to other opportunities.

Chapter 14

Global Concepts: Partners

While I wanted to leave BEI to start my own business again, I had serious concerns about leaving a well-paying job for another start-up company with no guarantee of revenue. There were other concerns. I wasn't sure that I wanted a partner again, and yet I wasn't ready to risk being in business alone. I wasn't happy with either choice, and in the end, I took the safer approach—taking on a partner even though I did not know my partner well.

I thought about not leaving Bob Cady out of the partnership. Bob was a good friend, a decent partner, and someone I knew well. It was surprising to me when Steve told me that he did not want to be partners with Bob. I was willing to take Bob into our partnership, but Steve was adamant, and it was either work with Steve without Bob or start a company on my own. I could have partnered once again with Bob, but I thought that Steve was a better choice because he already had an ongoing business with contracts; Bob didn't. I also thought that Steve was not only a good salesman but also a good consultant. Bob was sales oriented and not as knowledgeable about payment systems as Steve—extremely important for a consulting business devoted to payment systems.

Nevertheless, I had concerns about Steve. He was one of the five consultants who left with Rich to start Speer & Associates, and I did not like the way Rich operated. While I did not want to brand Steve with the same personality that Rich had, I still had misgivings about

Steve coming from that environment. I wondered whether his ethics and his integrity would stand up to the high level I held for myself.

I had other concerns unrelated to Steve. I did not have a great deal of cash to sustain me in a new business. My children were twenty-two, twenty, and seventeen years old. One was entering graduate school, and two were at Emory University. The tuitions for them were significant, and I had used up a great deal of my assets paying for their education from kindergarten on up. I still had several more years to go paying college tuitions. My daughters would get married someday, and weddings would not be cheap, and my wife was asking me about my planning for retirement. I had no decent answer for her. Going into a new business with only enough cash to sustain the family for six months was a serious concern, but I wanted another shot at my own business.

I also had a concern about Educate America. Judy was doing the marketing and sales for the SAT classes, and I was doing a good job delivering the product on Sunday mornings at various church locations around Atlanta. The classes had decent attendance, we were charging less than the competition, but the revenue was small compared to what I knew we could make consulting to banks. Steve was generous in accepting my SAT book and material as my contribution to our fifty-fifty partnership. On the other hand, he was only offering the furniture and fixtures, which did not have a revenue stream, while my SAT course did even though it was small. Yet another concern was whether I could really grow the SAT business and do bank consulting at the same time. When consulting picked up, that concern was well founded.

Finally, the major concern was the way Steve wanted to handle our partnership. He insisted on having one decision maker while I was comfortable with joint decision-making, splitting the decisions according to the partner's areas of expertise. We never discussed splitting up the decision making because Steve pushed hard to be the final decision maker as CEO, and I agreed to be president. I did that because I was comfortable with my ability to stand up to Steve on anything that did not sit well with me. I thought that there would be little to argue about when the business was small and focused on growth. I had done well working with Bob, and I had stood up well against the two partners at BEI. I felt comfortable letting Steve be the CEO, for I could fight for what I strongly believed in whether Steve liked it or not. In short, I was willing to take on a partnership with a man I only knew by reputation because

I did not want to continue working where I was. I did not want to start a new company alone, and I knew that my partner was not only good at sales but could also deliver bank consulting in the field I wanted to work in. It was a risk I was willing to take.

Steve knew of a good lawyer named George Fox, who put together a buyout agreement for us. The essence of the agreement was that we were fifty-fifty partners, that Steve was CEO and I was president, and that either one of us could offer to sell his share of Global Concepts to the other. The person who wanted out (partner A) had to state that he wanted out of the business and then make an offer to the other partner (partner B) that was fair and reasonable. If the offer was too high, then partner B could sell his ownership of the business at the high offer. If partner A's offer was reasonable or low, then partner B could buy partner A's ownership at that reasonable or low price. If partner B wanted to counteroffer, then partner A had the right to either sell his ownership to partner B or buy partner B's ownership of the business at the new offer being made. In this way, the partner making the offer is forced to make a fair and reasonable offer, for the other partner can either buy or sell the offering partner's ownership at the offer being made. While this is a good approach in theory, it doesn't always work out in practice; it is a good starting point toward separating the partnership.

Since Steve's wife was already in the business and my wife was selling Educate America, my wife entered the business as well. I had never had my wife involved in my business affairs, and while I thought it was acceptable for her to help me in Educate America because it supplemented the income I was receiving from BEI, it was another matter to have her directly involved in the main consulting business that Steve and I were starting. Judy is extremely capable at whatever she takes on. That was not the issue. The issue was that I was not fully in control, and inevitably, Judy would have to be evaluated by Steve and his wife, Sherry. I did not want to hurt my wife's feelings if things did not work out.

For several months, Judy focused on Educate America, making a small amount of revenue. During that time, Steve and I began to sell our consulting services and managed to win a number of contracts that dealt with the evaluation of ATM locations, ATM networks, and ATM profitability. Steve was a master at this, for he had done these kinds of evaluations at Speer & Associates. My only concern about them was that we often took previous material from another assignment and inserted it in the reports instead of writing a unique report for each client. I was used to writing a report from scratch, and Steve was content to borrow material from a previous client for the new client. This bothered me since it wasn't my style, but I thought it was acceptable given that the borrowed material was from a previous report that Steve had written.

I almost immediately found a contract that required me to work as the acting CEO in Atlanta for Michael Lafferty, who lived in England and who owned a number of banking newsletters that were written in England, Ireland, and Atlanta. Michael wanted me to join his company, Lafferty Publications, as the US CEO, controlling half a dozen financial newsletters that were produced in Atlanta. I thought that it was a nice safety net for me in case consulting with Steve did not work out, so I suggested that I work as the acting CEO on a part-time basis for six months, and then we would reevaluate whether I would join his company full-time. I thought the odds of my giving up my new ownership in a consulting firm were remote, but it was something I could not totally dismiss.

I had the luxury of a backup when I started Global Concepts. I could have continued Educate America as an SAT preparation course, or I could have joined Lafferty's company as CEO in the United States. In both cases, it was comforting to know that I had backup jobs in the event that my consulting firm failed. This was especially useful for me, for I had failed to succeed with my first company.

On the other hand, it is often more important to have no backup. This means that failure is not an option, and you must work as hard as you can to make the one company you have succeed. I was fortunate that GCI got off to a great start, and I could dismiss the backup options at the end of six months in my new consulting firm. *When starting a new business, a backup may be comforting, but you should operate as if no backup exists.* It is best to put all of your eggs in one basket and watch that basket carefully. That is what entrepreneurs do. Focus all of your energy on that basket to make it prosper.

In the meantime, for Lafferty Publications I launched a new newsletter on electronic banking in the United States, managed the Atlanta staff, and met with Michael and his partner, Vera Vaisova, when they came to Atlanta on a quarterly basis as well as speak at one or more of Lafferty's banking conferences in Europe, another major activity of the company. As it turned out, Vera had worked for Citibank at the same time that I worked there, and we had met back then. That helped to solidify my relationship with Michael.

Together with ATM consulting and being president, I had little time to really focus on Educate America. After about six months, Steve and I decided that the consulting business was off to a good start, and Educate America was not bringing in enough revenue to justify continuing the business. As a result, we shut down Educate America, and Judy took on other assignments of an administrative nature.

In many ways, I loved Educate America. I was teaching high school kids to get ready to take the SAT test, and I knew I was a very good teacher for that. Had I focused on that as a real business, I believe that I could have competed with Stanley Kaplan, Princeton Review, and the others in the business. The problem was that I was doing all of the teaching, and that is not how to grow a business. At the time, I did not have the vision to hire other teachers or to aggressively market the program although my wife was doing an excellent job signing up students for my classes. In short, it was a sideline business that complemented my bank consulting business, but I never had the time, the vision, and the commitment to make it into a serious business.

Once it was clear that I could make serious money in bank consulting once again, I gave up on Educate America because I couldn't start two businesses at the same time. Since *it is difficult to start two businesses at the same time, pick the most profitable one.*

Today, with over thirty years more experience, I know I can do it now. But back then with limited experience, the only possibility was to shut it down. I had to stay with the business that was growing, making serious money, and had prospects for the foreseeable future.

After a year or so, Steve approached me to say that he no longer thought it was a good idea to have either of our wives in the business. I was totally surprised by this statement, for our wives were doing a good job fulfilling various administrative functions and earning their paychecks. Steve felt that the business was growing, and as long as it remained a family business, it would undermine the other employees that we had hired. I had a totally different view. I was comfortable with family in the business. I believed that Judy and Sherry were doing a good job and saw no justification for firing them. Steve disagreed adamantly and insisted as CEO that he should make the final decision. It was the first time that we had a major disagreement, and I was unwilling to tell my wife that she had to leave the business. Finally, and with great reluctance, I agreed that if Steve really wanted to do this, then he would have to do the talking to both wives. Steve did talk to both women, and as I predicted, my wife was extremely upset. She did not understand why her being asked to leave the business was justifiable, and I agreed with her. On the other hand, I felt I had to support my partner's decision even though I could see no good reason for doing so. It turned my wife off to Steve, and she never said a nice word about him from then on. Once Judy was fired, she left the company, but Steve's wife stayed on for quite a while. This incident was a wake-up call for me about sharing decision making with Steve. He was not a compromising kind of guy, and I should have known this early on when he insisted on one final authority and wanted to be that person.

After our wives left the business, we continued our partnership for a while, but it was never the same for me. I could no longer let Steve make decisions for the both of us; I wasn't sure that he would consider my point of view, especially when it differed from his own.

In conjunction with the departures of our wives from the business, we hired Anne Sullivan to do the accounting, handling anything related to the office, and generally deal with anything related to finance. Anne became proficient at many administrative tasks and stayed with the firm until her retirement.

As part of my arrangement with Lafferty, I was responsible for hiring new staff to launch one or two new newsletters on payment systems. After looking at a variety of resumes, I settled on Steve Ledford, who was working for the Bank Administration Institute (BAI) in Chicago. Ledford had grown up in Atlanta, wanted to return home, and had a strong background in payment systems. After interviewing him, I was convinced that he was very smart, a strong writer, and knew a lot of people in the payment system industry—all excellent qualities needed to launch a new payment system newsletter. We hired him at Lafferty Publications.

In addition, a young man with a degree from Stanford University applied for a job as a writer. He had no experience, but his earnestness, his desire to become a writer, and his strength of character impressed me. I had a good feeling about Tom Murphy, and even though he had no background in payment systems or banking, I decided to hire him.

I offered him a starting salary of $15,000, a measly salary even back then, but Tom accepted the job. Over time, he became a terrific addition to the Lafferty staff.

I also got to meet the existing staff at Lafferty, an impressive group of writers and researchers. Among them was a women named Rebecca Poyner Burns, who wrote on payment systems. I was impressed with her skill at writing excellent stories. She was a quick study on almost anything, and she had an even-handed personality that put people at ease when talking to her.

I mention these three people because one by one, I hired them to join Global Concepts. After six months at Lafferty, I concluded that my heart was in bank consulting, and I wanted to grow my own company. Business was good, we had plenty of consulting work, and we needed additional staff. I met with Lafferty, told him that I would not give up my own company, and ended my consulting relationship with his company. I could not in good conscience continue to work for him when I knew I was not interested in joining his company.

A month or two later, we approached Rebecca Poyner Burns, offered her a raise in salary, and she joined Global Concepts. Several months later, Ledford joined Global Concepts, and eventually Tom came as well. Working with Lafferty gave me the opportunity to hire three people, test them on payment systems, see their work up close, and then hire them for my own company. Fortunately, I did not sign an employment contract with Lafferty, and I had no restrictions on hiring Lafferty staff. After discussion with Steve about the ethics of hiring staff from a company that I was consulting to, we both concluded that there was no ethical violation and that we owed it to the people to let them determine where they wanted to work. In the end, each of the three people we hired wanted to work with me at Global Concepts. Each of them went on to wonderful careers not just at Global Concepts but also beyond that. Rebecca stayed at Global for several years and then left for the publishing business, her first love, and eventually became the editor of *Atlanta Magazine*, one of the really outstanding magazines in the United States. She also published three books.

Tom stayed at Global for about ten years, becoming a first-class writer and researcher on payment systems, and left to manage a yoga company in Atlanta. Tom was one of only two people I knew who was capable of studying a problem in great detail, developing the entire outline of the report he was to write in his head. He did not need to write anything down on paper or in a computer until he had all the facts straight and all his questions answered. Then he would crank out a first-class report from his head from start to finish. Some of these reports were thirty to fifty pages long and even longer. Since I was not capable of doing this and most other consultants wrote their reports in sections, it was impressive to see the way he worked. It was a feat few others could do.

Finally, there was Ledford. Steve was brilliant, a summa cum laude graduate, and extremely capable of taking on any payment system assignment. Over time, he became the most knowledgeable person at Global Concepts on anything to do with payment systems, and he built a national reputation for himself as the consultant of choice on assignments for the most prestigious clients we had. He eventually became my choice to take over Global Concepts when I sold the company.

We also hired Lee Thrasher, one of the few people on our staff with a banking and sales background. Lee was responsible for growing the business, especially the forums we ran, and he was also asked to help grow the consulting business. After a few years, it became clear that Lee was better suited for a vendor than our consulting firm, so we parted amicably, and Lee went on to continue his career as a vendor to the banking community.

During the 1970s and early 1980s, I was often asked to speak at major banking conventions. At BEI, I was off the speaking circuit and wanted to get back to it to promote Global Concepts. In conversation with Unisys about my new company, I mentioned that I would be interested in speaking at one of their private conferences. Shortly thereafter, they invited me to speak at their payment conference in St. Paul de Vence outside of Nice, France. I was thrilled to be invited. It was an opportunity to get my name in front of potential clients. I spoke on the consumer research we had conducted on payment systems.

The highlight of that conference was the last speaker, Denny Farkas, then director of payment systems for Unisys. Denny spoke about a new technology for check processing called image technology. He said that check processing could be made much more efficient by capturing the picture of the check and processing the image instead of the paper check itself. He described how the process would work, that it would substantially change the flow of the check through a check processing operation: it would speed up the process, reduce costs, offer new products, and generally revolutionize the entire check processing business. I was immediately taken by what Denny said, and even though I knew nothing about image technology, I could see that Global Concepts could help the industry move forward with this new technology. I came back to Atlanta with the idea of launching a new multiclient product for our company, which we called the Image Forum.

Steve did not like the idea for a number of reasons. First, he knew very little about check processing. He was more focused on plastic cards, on ATMs and credit cards; check processing was not his area of expertise. Second, he was not enamored about multiclient programs. He argued that they were hard to launch, and unless they reached a sizeable number of participants, they would not be profitable. I argued that no other consulting firm was offering image technology consulting since the technology was so new. Therefore, we had a chance to get in on the ground floor, beat our competitors to the market, and establish ourselves as a leading consulting firm in image technology. At the time, this was all speculation on my part. It was a strategic initiative, and it all depended on how attractive image technology was going to be for check processing and how well we implemented my idea. Steve conceded that he would allow me to launch the program, but it would have to be my baby while he attended to other consulting. I agreed. As later results proved, I was right on the money.

My initial idea was to hold four meetings a year with a report at each meeting. Each meeting would last for a day and half, ending in the afternoon on the second day. In late 1989, I started the Image Forum. The major vendors, like Unisys, IBM, and BancTec, all supported the idea, for the Forum would help educate their clients on the use of image technology. A few of the large banks with research staffs joined because they had the money, the staff, and the interest to explore how image technology could be employed throughout their organization.

The first few meetings had twenty or so people attending. At first, we turned to the vendors to explain the technology, to show why the technology could improve various banking operations. We also asked the vendors to ask their initial banking clients that had successfully implemented image technology to speak at our meetings. Because image technology was more advanced in nonpayment system areas than in check processing, we split the presentations between image technology in check processing and image technology in other parts of the bank. We invited potential clients to attend the meetings and to receive copies of everything we produced for that meeting to evaluate whether their organization would become a member. After the first year, we decided that four meetings was too much and reduced the meetings to three per year. We also had learned enough by then to define a series of reports that we would do not after each meeting, but before each meeting. We decided that our best course of action was to produce a report on image processing for each meeting, a book with all attendees, speakers and their presentations, and a summary written after the meeting. This was sent by email to the attendees and key contacts, so the summary could be distributed within each organization.

For multiclient programs, there is always a need to reach a critical mass of participants so potential customers can convince themselves that the group is not only viable but also has leading edge players that can provide the best information on the subject. It takes time to accomplish this because it is a chicken-and-egg problem. Clients will join the program with the right players, and the right players join only when other right players join. You have to tell prospect A that prospects B, C, and D are ready to join if prospect A will join and then tell prospect B that prospect A, C, and D are ready to join if prospect B joins, and so on. Once the nucleus is established, the program sells itself provided the subject matter is of interest to the participants.

Within six months of marketing the Image Forum, we had enough of a nucleus to know we had a reasonable success, and the program would be profitable. As we grew in terms of revenue, Steve hired an old friend of his to join our firm, Steve Bacastow. In turn, Bacastow had worked with Jenny Johnson and recommended her highly. We hired her, and she was a perfect fit to grow the Image Forum. She was not only a consulting professional, but also had strong communication skills with clients, building close working relationships with them and even friendships beyond a strictly professional association.

At the end of our first year, I was happy with the result. We had a couple of dozen organizations in the Image Forum, and it was beginning to make a profit. The prospects for continuing growth were excellent. In addition, we were learning not just about image technology but also beginning to really understand the check processing business, one of the largest systems in the world and certainly one of the most complex businesses to really master. While all this was going on, Steve stayed away from this effort and continued to focus on other consulting related to plastic cards.

At the start of 1990, Karl Sammons, one of the key players in image check processing at Unisys, approached me with the idea of launching a similar program for the banks and vendors in the UK. While the volume of checks in the United States far exceeded the volume of checks in the UK, the UK was processing about five billion checks a year, and that volume was certainly big enough to justify image check processing. In addition, Unisys had a strong presence in the UK and wanted to educate bankers there to convince them that the technology would save them money too.

I told Karl that I had no idea how to approach the banks in the UK: no office there, no knowledge of cheque (they spell *check* that way) processing in the UK, and no contacts at the banks or other vendors. Karl proposed that Unisys would help me. He arranged for me to work at the Unisys office in London and got me a list of key people for me to call on at the banks. Furthermore, he arranged for me to work with Gail Bishop, a Unisys marketing person in London, my contact while there. Beyond that, I was on my own. I thought about the idea, discussed it with Steve, and he agreed that it was my call. I thought it was worth the effort, not knowing how long it would take or how successful I would be.

In early 1990, I flew to London for a week and met with Gail. I couldn't have found a more enthusiastic person to work with. She found me a place to work, a phone, added to the list of bankers to call, and I got to work calling them. It was quite difficult at first, for no one knew me or Global Concepts. I often had the wrong person, and I had to speak to several people before I found the right person in check processing that might be interested in a forum on image cheque processing. The real advantage I had was that we already had an existing image forum in place in the Unites States, we had four major reports on image technology, and we had a number of American bankers who had spoken at the US Image Forum, had good presentations, and wouldn't mind coming to London to give a presentation there.

I spent a week every month for six months in London trying to launch the program. No one wanted to join at first until they could see what I had in mind. To satisfy that need, I organized a one-day program by bringing one speaker from the United States, along with Unisys and myself to discuss the benefits of image check processing. The event was held at a Unisys location, and a small but influential number of bankers attended. The program was decent and generated a little more interest. A couple of months later, I found an expensive restaurant in the center of London and invited the decision makers to lunch with a short presentation thereafter about what the image forum might do for UK banking. It, too, was a reasonable success. When we reached the summer of 1990, I concluded that I had been to London a week every month for six months, that I had approached the major banks in England and Scotland, and that the cheque processing vendors serving the UK market were aware of my efforts. In addition, I had also approached a few of the large building societies that had cheque processing operations. It was time to either make the image forum in the UK a reality or call it quits.

The key player at Barclays Bank was David Cartwright, who was then responsible for cheque processing at his bank. He was in the early stages of negotiating with IBM to install their image check processing system. After I told Cartwright that I was near the end of my rope in trying to get the Image Forum UK started, he suggested that we have a meeting in September at Barclays to decide what to do, and he would invite the right people to the meeting. I gave him my list of interested people, he added additional people that he knew were important to the decision, and in September, I showed up at Barclays ready to give my pitch for the Image Forum UK. When I arrived, I thought that the meeting would begin as American meetings tend to do. It was about three-thirty in the afternoon, and Cartwright, in wonderful British fashion, had arranged for tea and cookies to be served. While I was geared up to be serious about the business at hand, Cartwright showed me how a civilized UK business meeting begins in the afternoon. Naturally, I was at the disposal of the bankers and had tea with everyone else, but I didn't enjoy the delay. I was nervous and ready to get started.

Once the meeting got started, I spoke without notes and indicated the strong level of commitment that my company would put behind the program, our willingness to organize the meetings, our ability to invite American bankers to come to London to speak at their meeting, and our pledge to write Image Forum UK reports that were based on cheque processing in the UK, totally independent from the reports we wrote for the US Image Forum. Finally, I said that the minimum number of organizations that I had to have to start the Image Forum UK was ten participants. There were about twelve or thirteen organizations in attendance, including Gordon Gove from the Woolwich Building Society, along with several of the major vendors. After I spoke, several of the bankers spoke positively about the need for such a program, especially Gove. He made it clear that his organization would welcome such a program, and all the while, I was sitting on pins and needles not knowing how the vote would turn out. Near the end of the meeting, Cartwright asked for a show of hands for participating in the Image Forum UK, and ten hands went up. I was thrilled and excited to see that after a tremendous amount of time, my efforts had paid off. It was the biggest and longest sale I had ever made. I knew that Steve would be ambivalent about the result, for he had not participated at all, yet it would contribute handsomely to our revenue. I thanked all the people in the room for having confidence in my company and in me, that we would get started in 1991, and that we would be in touch with them all very shortly. I left the meeting with the realization that image technology was going to change cheque processing, that Global Concepts would be at the center of understanding that technology, that I now had an international company, and I could sell.

At about the same time that I was working on launching and establishing the Image Forum in the United States and in the UK, Steve sold a contract to Visa to study the launch of their debit card program. It was a very exciting project because we were working directly with the senior management at Visa. Visa invited some of their largest Visa credit card banks to work with us on assessing a Visa debit card: how to present it, how to price the interchange fee, and how to assess the potential fraud that might result from it. Steve and I would spend several days each month at Visa at their headquarters in San Mateo working on a variety of issues. I spent time with the Visa banks trying to assess the potential fraud impact that might occur from a debit card. We used an interesting technique asking each bank to estimate the size of the fraud without telling any other bank. Then we presented the results to the group and asked them all to reassess their estimate in light of knowing everyone else's estimate. The idea was to try to force the outliers both on the high and low side to converge toward the center, thereby reaching a general consensus. That did occur, and we concluded that debit card fraud requiring a PIN at the point of sale would be less than credit card fraud, which did not require a PIN, but higher than ATM fraud, which could only be used at an ATM and did require a PIN. This, of course, was no real surprise, but it did produce a small percentage range for debit card fraud that was useful in thinking about pricing the debit card interchange fee, the fee that the consumer bank pays to the merchant bank.

A Visa person shared an interesting comment that I try to follow, especially when starting a new consulting assignment. She said that she never speaks at staff meetings, for when she is speaking, she never learns anything because she already knows what she is going to say. On the other hand, when she listens to others, she learns many things. This woman was not shy or reserved, and she would speak up forcefully when she had something to say. Still, she had the emotional control to contain her speech and take in what others were saying long before she ventured an opinion. It was politically astute and intellectually smart.

In addition to the Visa business, we had a growing business in electronic banking. We won a contract with Security Pacific Bank to evaluate their ATM losses, and Bacastow did an outstanding job identifying thirteen different places in their ATM network where potential losses were occurring. One example was that the bank offered up to five hundred dollars in cash based on a deposit made at the ATM even if the only money in the checking account was the deposit itself. A crook could have a balance in his account of twenty-five dollars, deposit a check for a thousand dollars in the Security Pacific ATM, and then withdraw five hundred dollars. The bank allowed this for marketing purposes, assuming there was a legitimate thousand-dollar-check being deposited. The problem was that crooks would not even put a check in the deposit envelope. The envelope was empty, and once opened at the back office operation of the bank it was then obvious that there was nothing to cover the five hundred dollars withdrawn from the bank except the twenty-five dollars in the account. Since it was relatively easy to open a checking account at the bank, a crook might have multiple names, multiple addresses, and multiple checking accounts. At the time, the losses from crooks were in the millions of dollars. Our consulting efforts not only identified where the ATM problems existed but also worked with the bank to fix most of them. It was a great assignment, and we were well paid for doing it.

We also had assignment at Citibank, at Mellon Bank, and at Total Systems in Georgia. Each of these assignments was significant in terms of our revenue, and in total, GCI was doing over five hundred thousand dollars in consulting business. In addition, the Image Forum in the United States was generating almost one hundred fifty thousand dollars in business and would renew strongly. I had single-handedly launched the Image Forum UK for 1991. I had gotten over the conflict with Steve, business was good, and the company was on a roll. I looked forward to the growth of our partnership.

Nearing the end of 1990, we had a staff of ten people, including Steve and myself. At a strategy planning meeting of us all, it was clear that Steve would be responsible for electronic funds transfer and data processing consulting while I would be responsible for image technology, check processing, forums, and marketing research. Even though Steve's area was producing the largest amount of revenue at the time, the Image Forum UK would produce sizeable revenue, and the Image Forum US would very likely renew strongly. I viewed Steve as being an excellent salesman, a good project manager, and capable of handling the administrative side of the business. I was strong on product development, sales, and cost control. I could handle the financial part of the administration. I believed we were a good partnership, we had a growing company, and I looked forward to a continuing partnership.

I say this because one morning at breakfast with Steve, he shocked me when he told me that he wanted to leave the company and requested that I buy him out. I summarized that meeting at the time, and it reads as follows:

On the morning of November 26, 1990, at the Marriott Ravinia Hotel near Perimeter Mall in Atlanta, Steve White requested that I buy his entire share (50 percent) of Global Concepts, Inc. He said he was tired of consulting in banking, wanted a new challenge, and would move out of the company as owner.

I said I was interested in buying Steve out but wanted time to analyze the present business and its future prospects. Steve suggested the following terms:

1. Fifty thousand dollars in cash plus payment of one year's annual salary at the present rate of $12,000 per month in take-home pay.
2. Payments to be spread over one year to ease the cash burden on the firm.
3. He wanted his desk, chair and credenza, and a few reports—leaving all originals.
4. He would return his Mac computer that cost the firm $12,000.
5. He would sign a noncompete clause for clients based on a specific list.

I indicated that this was a complete surprise and needed time to evaluate his offer. I told him that I would give him an answer in a couple of weeks, realizing that this was a very quick decision. The buy-sell agreement that we signed at the start of our partnership required me to respond to an offer within thirty days.

Steve had just signed a two hundred fifty thousand dollars five-year leasing agreement for our office. I told him that it wasn't fair of him to sign the lease if he knew he was going to leave the firm. The lease was a good one in terms of cost per square foot, but we could have negotiated for less space if I knew he was going to leave or at least have had that option. He said that he did not know what he would do, but he wanted to have the option to begin a new career, and he would remain in his present home in Atlanta. He suggested that we get in touch with our lawyer about our buy-sell agreement and work up an analysis of the financial condition of the firm. He also indicated that he would be willing to stay on as a consultant to the firm and bring in business for at least one year to assure the stability and growth of GCI at a consulting rate to be established. I replied that maintaining the growth of the firm would be a key area for him to help in, but that I was concerned about the detail in his non-compete agreement. We agreed not to inform employees or people in the industry about this until the buy-sell arrangement was completed.

The next day I informed Steve that I was much more comfortable about buying him out, but I would need time to do due diligence. I suggested that Bacastow was a concern because he was so close to Steve. Steve said that he had not spoken to Bacastow, that he was a man of integrity, and that he believed Bacastow would stay on with Jenny for the immediate future. Steve indicated that he would do nothing to encourage Bacastow to leave but rather encourage him to stay and that he hoped all employees would stay on to maintain the growth of GCI.

Two days later, Steve and I had yet another conversation about him leaving GCI. He said he was willing to stay on in a sales capacity one to two days per month to ensure the company's growth. He suggested that I talk with Bacastow as a critical employee to be sure he would stay with GCI. Steve reiterated that it was to his benefit and mine that Bacastow stay with GCI so that the company continued to do well. That would ensure that he could get his money out. I told Steve that if he called on banking clients, it might be difficult to continue with that client once Steve left GCI. I asked him to spell out his future business to ensure there was no conflict. He did not answer my question, but suggested that he could sell for GCI exclusively for at least four months. He was also willing to discuss some sort of contingency payment depending on the success of the firm since the firm was having success in growing its business.

In addition to that, there was a second discussion that day. Steve argued that he signed the lease before making his offer to be bought out because he thought I would hold up signing the lease if I knew he was leaving. He thought the lease was good regardless of what happened to him. I thought to myself that he was acting arrogant and manipulative.

Steve then said that he would be flexible on the fifty thousand dollars in cash, but he wanted a one-year buyout. That was his best offer. If I did not like the one-year deal, he was prepared to buy me out. Even though he was prepared to buy me out, he reiterated that he did not want to be in the consulting business for another three years, and if he were forced to do that, then he would look to sell the company. He made it clear that he would be making his salary elsewhere that year besides the money from the buyout. He made the point that the right time to sell is when business is good, and business for GCI was good. His final point was that I either accept his offer as is or modify it. If I modified it, then he wanted the right to accept it on either the buying or selling side as our legal agreement resolved a fifty-fifty partnership. He concluded that he would only modify his position if the firm were in serious financial stress, which it wasn't. He expected me to borrow the money to pay him off, and he would continue to operate in the business as a full partner until a decision was reached.

I now had a serious dilemma, and I was scared. Steve wanted to leave the company, and I wanted to stay at the firm, yet he was prepared to buy me out if I modified his offer, which I did not like. I didn't want to give him any chance to buy me out. That was crystal clear. I was worried about what would happen after Steve left, for the bulk of the consulting revenue was due to his sales efforts, and we had a number of major consulting assignments that he was managing, along with Bacastow, who I thought would quit to join Steve since they were close personal friends. I didn't know exactly what Steve wanted to do in his new company, and I was also fearful that he might end up competing with me regardless of the noncompete agreement he would sign. The state of Georgia had right to work laws that might make it difficult to enforce a noncompete agreement, and I didn't want to go to court to argue the point even if I won.

On the other hand, I didn't think that paying close to two hundred thousand dollars was reasonable, plus interest, plus his office furniture, and whatever else Steve had in mind. While it was possible that the firm would be doing close to one million dollars in revenue, it was not likely that the firm would do that without Steve. Without Steve, we might drop to half that amount, and the profit of two hundred thousand dollars this year might drop to one hundred thousand dollars next year or even zero. I was convinced that the company would suffer significantly with Steve gone, and if Bacastow left, that would hurt even more. The image forums were strong, but they would only generate about $250,000, and I needed a significantly higher amount of consulting, which might be much more difficult without Steve and Bacastow. I didn't think that paying two hundred thousand dollars or more in a year was justified.

I needed advice. I spoke with my wife, and she was very positive about the divorce. She didn't like Steve, and thought I could manage nicely on my own. I spoke with a good friend of mine, Leonard Epstein, and he gave me excellent advice. He said, "Have patience. Steve wants out and is in a hurry. You are not in a hurry. Time is on your side. He will negotiate his offer if you wait. Don't make him a counter offer and don't accept his offer. Simply wait. Time will produce a better result for you even though you don't know what it is." I took that advice to heart and did nothing for several weeks, telling Steve I was considering his offer and would respond shortly but never did. It was the best advice for this situation though I had no idea what I was going to do. I only knew I was not going to give up the business to Steve.

After three weeks of not responding, Steve approached me with yet another offer. This offer focused on what he called inequities. He proposed that there were unequal assets originally contributed to the business partly because we had shut down my Educate America business, and these inequities needed to be resolved. The inequities focused on our initial investments, invoices that were pending before I joined GCI, American Express payments on both of our credit cards, insurance premiums that were different, unequal payments to our retirement accounts, a computer bought for Steve and not for me, etc. He wanted to add/subtract the net of all inequities to the selling price. Steve still wanted $50,000 in cash and $12,000 per month for a year, but instead, he proposed a payment of $250,000 in place of that, excluding the inequities. In short, he would accept $250,000 plus or minus the inequities.

Steve proposed three payment options. Option 1 was payment in full up front. Option 2 was fifty thousand dollars up front and twelve equal payments at 10 percent interest, guaranteed by C&S National Bank in an escrow account. Option 3 was twelve equal payments at 10 percent interest but not guaranteed. However, if the payments were delinquent for ninety days or more, he would receive 50 percent of GCI stock back and he would return as CEO, and he could sell his 50 percent ownership of GCI to anyone he wished.

Regarding a noncompete agreement, Steve said he would sign a one-year noncompete agreement, but he still wanted to consult to GCI companies for a maximum of two days per assignment. He viewed these as personal consulting days to senior management, and not large-project consulting. He also wanted to consult to companies outside of GCI's scope. He would refer all project work that was more than a two-day assignment to GCI. He would not subcontract with firms that competed with GCI. He would not hire Bacastow or other key GCI employees. He would subcontract to GCI at $1,200 per day. He would pay GCI a 10 percent commission on any work GCI referred to him, and GCI would pay him after he left the firm a 5 percent commission for consulting leads and a 10 percent commission for closing the contract for GCI. If he violated the noncompete agreement, he would forfeit all revenues to GCI that were obtained in violation of the noncompete agreement.

Steve also proposed that he take his table, chairs, credenza, bookcase, a two-drawer filing cabinet, and copies of any materials he needed, but he would not take the originals. He would leave on January 31, 1991. He would still participate in helping to set GCI's strategy in a two-day offsite meeting, and he would participate in the Image Forum if required. Finally, he assured me that he would make every effort to get Bacastow to see the merit and potential of staying at GCI long-term.

I will not bore you with all the concerns that this proposal raised. I knew that if I bought Steve out, I would end up with complete control of GCI. I could put my vision in place, and I had a great staff to do it. I had strong revenue growth now and in the future, a good reputation, and I liked what I was doing. The concerns I had dealt with were: assuming the responsibility to run the company, a heavy cost to pay Steve, the risk of a downturn in revenue, the strong possibility that some employees would quit, and I was depending on Bacastow, who would leave regardless of Steve's promise. The bottom line was that I had to assume the marketing and sales effort to really grow the firm.

In addition to all that, I had to negotiate every line with Steve to reach some compromise. In early January, our lawyer wrote out a letter of intent that simplified the buyout. The letter of intent said

The price for Steve's 50 percent ownership is $250,000 plus or minus the inequities. The maximum value of the inequities is no more than fifty thousand dollars, so the maximum price is three hundred thousand dollars. The inequities dealt with the initial investment, the accounts receivable prior to the partnership, Steve's computer, payments to our retirement accounts, and individual life insurance and disability insurance for the year 1990, $10,000 on the signing of the buyout contract and $10,000 per month until the $250,000 plus or minus the inequities was fully paid, (this was better than $12,000 per month), and interest at 5 percent on the unpaid balance paid monthly. This cut the 10 percent interest rate that Steve proposed in half. Payments were to be made on the first of the month with a 5 percent penalty on the unpaid amount if not paid by the fifteenth of the month. Prepayment is acceptable at the discretion of GCI.

GCI would pay Steve's medical insurance, life insurance, and disability insurance with the total cost deducted from his monthly payment. This was a big win, for Steve wanted to add that to his monthly payment. The noncompete agreement would prevent Steve from taking any existing GCI contracts. If this occurred, the value of the contract that Steve took would be deducted from the buyout price. This implied that Steve might compete with GCI, and I was worried that this might happen.

Steve would not hire Bacastow and four other identified employees. If that occurred, then the last annual compensation paid by GCI to that employee would be deducted from the buyout price. I still thought that Bacastow would leave. Steve could compete but only as a one-person consulting company. He could hire whomever he wished so long as he did not compete with GCI. This definitely kept Steve competitive with GCI even though Steve argued that these assignments would be only very small consulting contracts. The burden was on Steve to determine whether he was in violation of any noncompete. The reality was that the burden was on me to monitor what Steve did in his new company.

Steve could take his office furniture, and GCI would pay $1,200 per day to use him as a consultant. GCI would pay a 5 percent commission to Steve for contracts he finds but not subsequent contracts, and Steve could copy any report he wanted. Once Steve left, I had no intention of involving him in anything that we did.

We would notify existing clients once the buyout agreement was signed, and Steve could do the same. I believed that GCI had to notify the clients first since they were our clients. Again this implied that Steve might want to compete with GCI.

What I described above was only a letter of intent. It was not the final agreement but a description of what Steve and I settled on. I was happy that I was the buyer and Steve was the seller, and I knew that we could cover the ten thousand dollars per month payment so long as business kept up in a reasonable way. Through all of the negotiation, I had several thoughts about why Steve wanted to give up his partnership. There were three reasons.

First, Steve needed to have complete control of the company, and he was losing that. I didn't realize how important total control was for him because it wasn't important for me. I was reasonably self-assured and believed that most decisions in business could be based on compromise and still turn out well. I believed that other people were like me, a naïve view I had growing up, and a view that I carried with me most of my life.

I was rarely in control, learned to give it up not just in business but also in my personal life although my wife often thinks otherwise. Steve just didn't want to share control of the company with me, and I suspected this applied to anyone. It was so important to Steve that he was willing to walk away from a company that had terrific prospects for financial and personal success. It was his loss.

Second, I had developed a completely new product line—forums, which Steve had never run—and he knew that I could run them better than he could run them. I had run the Payment System Research Program while at PSI fifteen years earlier when he was just joining PSI, and he knew that was my specialty. I suspected that he did not want to have me control these forums alone, and inevitably that would happen.

Third, the forums focused on image technology and check processing, two areas Steve knew nothing about. If they grew in importance to the firm and that was likely, then he would not be the kingpin in all of our consulting. He would be second best to me and to others in the firm as we built our own expertise in these areas. In suggesting that he wanted to sell his ownership when the firm was in good shape, he implied that he was a major contributor to that growth, and he didn't want to wait to see his contribution diminished as forum revenues grew along with check processing consulting, all of which did happen.

Even after Steve and I signed the letter of intent, there was much that needed to be done to complete the purchase of his ownership. I thought it could take quite a while to negotiate the inequities, and I was in no hurry to do it. I kept thinking that time was on my side—patience and fortitude, as Fiorello LaGuardia, the mayor of New York City, was fond of saying. About a week or two after signing the letter of intent, Steve approached me yet again with another offer, and this one I liked better than all the previous proposals. He said he was in a hurry to complete the deal. He wanted to get on with his new company, and he was willing to take a lot less money if I paid it up front with less noncompete restrictions on him. He proposed that I pay him $125,000 in cash up front, that he would not compete against any existing business we had, and he would not directly approach any employees at GCI to work for him.

By then I knew the business he was trying to develop. He wanted to start a consulting business to CEOs and other top management to be their mentor. He would get paid on a daily basis or on retainer. He did not want to consult on payment systems unless it was of interest to top management, which was unlikely. He initially presented his new company to me as a one-man company, but it gradually dawned on me that it would be difficult to undertake his idea without some staff.

My initial reaction to this new offer was to jump on it immediately. It cut my payment to him by 50 percent, it severed any ongoing relationship, and I had the cash in my company from our small profits and early payments to our forums. While I worried that the noncompete was virtually nonexistent with this proposal, I accepted the fact that he was trying to start a new business that would not compete with me. I also believed that he did not need any of my staff to launch his new business. I accepted his offer, we signed an agreement for the sale of his ownership, and I paid him his money on the day we signed and sealed the deal.

I learned three important things from the breakup of our partnership. The first was that *legal agreements seem definitive, but it is a starting place for negotiations*. I had little training in legal matters, except for the purchase of my homes. I took for granted that legal agreements were definitive and negotiations thereafter were not possible. The negotiations with Steve opened my eyes to the fact that a legal agreement is not the end of negotiations, but the beginning. It is very expensive to go to court, even if you are likely to win, so it is often the better strategy to negotiate out of court and settle the matter.

In the case of Steve wanting to sell his 50 percent ownership in GCI, he legally had the right to force me to buy him out at his offer or he had the right to buy me out at the same offer. I didn't like either prospect and waited. He then made a second offer and then a third offer, and on the fourth offer or so I finally agreed to his proposal. No formal offer was ever made in writing. We just talked about what he had in mind. Once we agreed, we put it in writing with counsel, and even then, Steve came back to me with yet another offer, which turned out to be the offer that settled the matter. The legal agreement was never the final answer, but it started the negotiation process.

The second thing I learned was that *when negotiating with an impatient person, patience is an advantage*. It has to do with how quickly the other person wants to make a deal. Impatient people will suffer in a negotiation because they are likely to accept an offer from the other side just to finish the deal. Patience is a benefit in the negotiation process. I have lost a couple of deals by waiting, but by searching for a win-win for both sides you end up with a better result than trying to finish the deal quickly. Steve was in a hurry to settle his ownership of GCI, and I waited him out and got the better result.

The third thing I learned was *when separating a partnership, make a clean break.* If you are divorcing, then make a clean break and move on. In Steve's case, I could see more negatives for him staying involved in my company than positives. I didn't want his advice any longer, I didn't want him to know my clients, I didn't want him to have access to my staff to convince them to leave me to work for him, and I didn't want to pay him when I could get my staff to do the work he would be doing.

Within two weeks of the signed agreement, Bacastow quit GCI and did not say where he was going. Then Gwen quit, along with Jennifer, a young administrative person that was related to Steve. Within a short period of time, I discovered that all three of them had joined Steve's new company. I immediately called him to complain about it and told him that he could not solicit my employees even under our loose noncompete agreement. Steve said that he did not solicit them while they were employees. They quit first, and each was looking for a new opportunity after they quit. He did not encourage them to quit. They just quit. When they were looking for a new job, they called him and he did need their help, but that was only after they quit and only after they called him. As a free person having quit GCI, Steve argued that he wasn't violating the noncompete agreement by hiring a person looking for a new job.

I never believed in noncompete agreements, especially in a state like Georgia where there are right to work laws, making it difficult to put teeth into a noncompete agreement. A noncompete has to be limited in the areas it covers and in its duration. I have lost good people for failing to require a noncompete of my staff, and that did hurt, but I don't know if that would have prevented these people from doing what they did. Noncompete agreements are considered important by large firms, especially technology companies. Given the many issues I had to deal with regarding competition from employees leaving my company, *noncompete agreements are important because of the cost of a lawsuit.* I should have put them in place for my staff.

I thought all of what Steve said was bullshit and told him so. I reminded him that he said he would do everything in his power to convince Bacastow to remain at GCI, and he did just the opposite. I didn't care about the other employees leaving because I probably would have let them go anyway. However, the loss of Bacastow hurt, and Steve and I had discussed this possibility many times. My respect for my ex-partner dropped substantially, and I made a mental note to remember this type of behavior if I ever had to deal with him in the future.

While I have no proof of this, the evidence suggested that Steve spoke with Bacastow in advance of the last offer he made to me, and Bacastow probably told him that he preferred working with Steve rather than staying at GCI. Almost certainly, Gwen did the same, and Jennifer would have wanted to work for Steve, for she got the job through him. Knowing that Bacastow would be quitting and joining Steve, along with the others, Steve did not want a strong noncompete arrangement because that kind of noncompete would require Steve to pay me Bacastow's annual salary and the other two salaries, about a hundred thousand dollars. This would put Steve at risk if the payoff to him occurred over a year or two-year period. In addition, it could lead to a lawsuit for much more than that, not just in legal fees, but also on the lost revenue that GCI might incur. To get around this problem, Steve proposed an immediate payment for the entire amount, a weak noncompete, a story that Bacastow quit first and then called Steve, and a substantial cut in the total payment to make it my first choice. Steve was betting on the future of his new company and was willing to take a lot less of a buyout in order to get Bacastow and Gwen as employees. He thought it would be a win-win for him and his new employees. I would pay less and take the deal, and he would be able to start his company with three employees from GCI without worrying about abusing a noncompete agreement.

At the time, I thought it was unethical and I still do. It hurt to lose Bacastow, but the rest of the staff that stayed supported me, and they were an excellent staff. We did lose momentum as a company for the next two years as we refocused our business on check processing, image technology, and forums. There was, of course, some consulting, but it wasn't on the same scale as when Steve was selling. We did not continue to do the large credit card or ATM projects that we did under Steve because we were growing our business in a different direction.

Finally, the reduction in staff meant a reduction in expense, so even though revenue declined, so did our expenses, and that still produced a small profit for GCI.

Steve leaving Global Concepts took only a few months, yet it changed the entire direction of the firm. During that period, the entire company was not very productive. The staff knew what was going on, and they had to determine what they wanted to do. While Bacastow and the two others quit to join Steve, the rest of the staff was convinced that I could run the company by myself, and they provided a positive perspective that I would get over the loss of Steve and Bacastow.

Because the company was doing well financially, because the US Check Forum received a lot of its revenue up front, and because the separation occurred early in the year, the company had sufficient funds to pay Steve his money without my having to borrow a penny. I did not know whether I would have to put my own money in later in the year or not, but I believed that the company would continue to succeed in terms of revenue and profits. Once the agreement with Steve was signed and done, I was elated to be the sole owner of Global Concepts and looked forward to being my own boss once again.

I had two partners in business, and both of them had strong points and weak points. I suppose the same applies to me too. I knew Bob quite well before we went into business together, for he worked for me at the Payment Systems. I knew he would focus on selling and on growing the business. However, he focused too much on growing the firm and not enough on making a profit. I was taken in by our own success and believed that growth was inevitable, which surely it was not. I was not strong enough to contain the focus on growth to also focus on making a profit.

With Steve, I didn't know him well, and it was only over time that I realized that he needed to be in control. Nevertheless, Steve was a great partner for starting a consulting business. He could sell and he could do the consulting. I wanted to continue my partnership with Steve, and we would have been great partners if Steve had been willing to share the decision making with me. In the end, he wasn't willing to give up control, and that hurt him. I bought him out of our business cheaply, and the business grew considerably once we got over his loss. There's no telling where Global Concepts might have ended up if we had stayed together. In sum, *if you want a partner in business, be sure you know the other person well.*

Chapter 15

Global Concepts: On My Own

Once Steve left Global Concepts, I was now on my own, and I had to reassess where I wanted to take the firm. All businesses want to stay current with developments in the marketplace, which is why consultants are useful for them. To be useful, consulting requires continuing expertise on the latest developments. More than that, expertise generates new products and services, and this generates new revenue sources. *Expertise creates new businesses.* My firm had to continue its expertise in payment systems to stay busy and be profitable. Our specific area of expertise was check processing, and I focused on becoming the most knowledgeable consulting firm in that arena. As a result, we had many opportunities to create new products: forums, benchmarking, simulation modeling, research studies, and onsite consulting.

I began by focusing on syndicated research programs, especially as they related to check processing and image technology because a *new technology is a perfect place for a syndicated research program.* Over a thirty-five-year consulting period, I had great success with syndicated research, another name for a multiclient program. Wherever there was new technology, like image check processing, the Internet, and electronic banking, the opportunity for syndicated research was crystal clear to keep the industry informed of the latest developments and to have industry people present to one another. Launching these programs had basic requirements: a good idea and proper timing. It could not be the entire direction of the company, but it was the place from which I knew I could build a very successful consulting company.

The major problem in getting the UK Image Forum started was finding some organization in London that would handle the administrative part of it. We needed to have someone find a location for our meeting, accept reservations for those attending, prepare the extensive meeting book for all attendees, and generally deal with other administrative problems that might come up. I approached a number of consulting firms in the UK believing they might undertake doing this level of effort in order to stay in touch with the participating organizations that would be coming to the UK Image Forum. Coopers & Lybrand Deloitte agreed to be our administrative company, and they did it gratis for the contacts that the Image Forum generated for them. I didn't know who their clients were but suspected that many of the banks were their clients, and this was a service they were doing for them.

The first meeting was held at Latimer House, a wonderful meeting facility, on April 2-3, 1992 with six of the twelve UK banks participating as paid members, along with a number of vendors and Woolwich Building Society. I was not content to begin with only paid participants, so we invited the check processing players to attend, and many of them did. Including the eleven speakers and the three Global Concept staff, there were eighty-two people in attendance. With that level of attendance and the quality of our speakers, the meeting would be a smash hit—and it was. It was only a matter of time before participation would increase. We just needed to keep the quality of the meetings at the same high level as the inaugural meeting.

Throughout much of 1991, Leo, my son, now twenty and a senior in college, lived in London and focused on growing the UK Image Forum. We also added a woman from our Atlanta staff willing to spend a few months in London to help market the forum. Gradually the Image Forum increased in size and in attendance.

After about two years of running the Image Forum UK with Coopers & Lybrand Deloitte, we were approached by APACS, the main banking association in the UK. They recognized that our Image Forum had become the major conference on check processing and wanted to support it as the administrator. They proposed paying one large fee for all of the twelve commercial banks in the UK, holding meetings at their facility, and handling all of the administrative functions for the meetings. We thought this was a splendid idea, a win-win for them and for us. We thanked Coopers & Lybrand Deloitte for their support and switched to APACS. From then on, our working relationship with APACS was excellent. They were efficient, connected to all the banks, willing to copy reports for us, and effective in getting out emails for all of our meetings. While Global Concepts gave up some control over negotiating with each individual bank, it made it easy to renew the program year after year. So long as the program continued with APACS and the banks, the vendors were sure to renew as well because our meetings provided a perfect opportunity for a vendor to be with their clients or potential clients for two days in an informal setting. Vendors rarely got this type of opportunity, and they knew it. We only had to convince APACS of the value of our program from year to year to continue the forum.

From the mid-1990s until the early 2000s, the volume of cheques in the UK continued to drop, but there was sufficient volume to continue the forum. In the mid-1990s, we changed the name of the forum to the Cheque Forum UK with three meetings a year. This coincided with the name change of the US Image Forum to the Check Forum in the United States. In line with the US Check Forum, each UK meeting had a report on UK image check processing, a meeting book with all attendees, speakers and their presentations, and a summary written after the meeting that was sent by email to the attendees and key contacts so it could be distributed within each organization. It was never difficult to get an American banker to come to the UK to present what their bank was doing with image check processing because GCI paid for their travel expenses. For these bankers, a trip to London with most of their expenses paid made for a nice vacation as well as a chance to learn something about UK check processing.

Eventually as cheque volumes declined, we reduced the number of meetings to two a year, and then to one meeting a year, and in 2006, the forum was cancelled because the volume of cheques in the UK had declined from its high-water mark of about five billion cheques per year to under two billion. There just wasn't enough volume or new ideas worth discussing anymore. The forum was about leading-edge developments, and there was very little of that. The only new idea was how to eliminate cheque writing completely, and that was under discussion. Finally, the really knowledgeable cheque processing people that not only loved the business and knew the process in great detail were replaced by less knowledgeable people who didn't care about preserving or growing the business but focused on reducing costs. Innovation was no longer a priority, and it didn't make sense to continue with a forum that focused on innovation and technology when there was little or none going on. The cheque business was dying in the UK, and the only concern was how to keep costs down and get out of the business.

When innovation dies or there is a lack of interest, consulting and syndicated research die. For stable businesses, management does not need a great deal of advice. When business is declining, there may still be a need for consulting to determine what to do to remain profitable, but at some point, the business is so low in terms of revenue or volume that it can no longer justify hiring consultants. The focus is not on growing the business or even making a profit, but rather, just getting out of the business altogether.

Once Steve left the company, we had a significant drop in consulting business related to plastic cards. We had enough consulting work to complete the assignments we had, and that paid the bills for the first half of 1991. While that was going on, I was focused on seeing that the two image forums continued to do well—and they did—but the revenue from them was not sufficient to carry the staff. We needed additional work to break even, let alone make a significant profit. I had to reduce our costs to get through this transition period, and the only major cost area was salaries.

Once it was clear that new business was not as strong as it had to be, I temporarily cut salaries for the entire staff. Recognizing that lower-paid staff could not take as large a cut in salary as those with larger salaries, I cut my salary by 25 percent, cut senior staff by 15 percent and the administrative and junior consulting staff by 10 percent. Everyone knew that I was doing this for the survival of the company, and there were no outward complaints to me about it. This was not pleasant for anyone, but it had to be done instead of firing anyone. We just didn't have the revenue to sustain the higher salaries, and the overall reduction amounted to about fifty thousand dollars.

Before Steve left, we were generating about one million dollars in annual revenue. Although four people left reducing salaries, it wasn't sufficient to offset the shortfall of about three hundred thousand dollars in revenue. We were selling some consulting, but not enough, and it took a couple of years to hunker down with the smaller staff, refocus on the new areas of the business, and get the senior staff that had done the work to also call on prospective clients to sell consulting. This took time, but I had the right staff, and over time, it worked out. We could easily have had a more serious problem if the remaining staff had not been able to find their own work. The cut in salary lasted for about eight to nine months, and then there was enough work and revenue to return to full salaries.

One of the biggest ideas we had during this period was to organize the Atlanta Cash Card Study. The Olympics was coming to Atlanta in 1996, and we believed that issuing a new plastic card for the Olympics would be a grand idea. The concept of a smart card was being explored in the United States. It was a plastic card containing a computer chip imbedded in the plastic. The computer chip has enough security in it to allow a customer to put cash in the chip and use that cash to pay for small purchases at merchants that had a terminal that read these cards. The terminal removed the cash from the card, stored it in the terminal, and then sent the information to the bank that issued the card for payment. The bank that issued the card initially removed the amount of cash from the customer's checking account when the bank issued the card and set that cash aside for payments to merchants. While the idea to launch these smart cards was for the Olympics, we envisioned that once established for many merchants in Atlanta, cash cards could continue for Atlanta thereafter, and set a standard for other cities to follow. The beauty of starting the idea for the Olympics was that the card would be a memento of the Olympics, and the banks that issued the cards would make money by selling the cards and keep the cash that remained unused on the cards after the Olympics was over.

We prepared a prospectus for the program and convinced eight companies to participate: American Express, Bank South, Coca-Cola, Diebold, Georgia State University, IBM, MARTA, and VeriFone. It was an excellent group, but only one of them, Bank South, was a major bank in Atlanta. We were missing Bank of America, Wachovia, and SunTrust. Without them, the study was interesting, even exciting, but unlikely to be implemented for the Olympics or Atlanta, so I thought. As it turned out, the study was not only interesting but also provided excellent data on how to implement a smart card for a city as well as provide the economic justification for undertaking the effort.

After the study was completed, we presented the results to our clients and wrapped up the study. A couple of years later as we approached the Olympics, the major banks in Atlanta did offer a smart card for the Olympics. They were a unique payment mechanism because the pictures on the cards were of Olympic athletes. These cards did not allow the customer to put cash on the card but, rather, were sold with a certain amount of cash on the card to begin with, such as a five-dollar card, a ten-dollar card, and a fifty-dollar card. The pictures were lovely, and some of the cards were never used, merely bought to remember the Olympics or to give as a gift to someone back home. After all, people were coming to the Olympics from all over the world. I have no direct evidence that our study led the way to these Olympic cards, but we did the research long before the cards were issued. We put no real restrictions on the use of our research, and the clients we had could easily have shared that information with the banks that launched their Olympic smart cards. I hope we had some impact. The shame of it was that after the Olympics was over, the smart cards were no longer accepted at merchants, the terminals were removed, and the concept of a smart card for a city like Atlanta was dead. It was exciting for a few weeks and then was gone with the wind.

The concept of a smart card was being explored in the United States although it was well established in Europe. The most powerful group associated with smart cards was the SmartCard Forum, a large group of banks, vendors, and others interested in the various aspects of smart cards.

There were fifty to seventy-five member organizations, and they charged a fee to be a member. As part of their membership, meetings were held regularly and research was conducted on the use of smart cards as well as the technology, economics, and legal issues. In 1995, the SmartCard Forum through its Multi-Application Committee issued a request for proposal (RFP) to conduct market research across ninety major merchants nationwide to assess their interest in smart cards.

Global Concepts submitted a proposal to the SmartCard Forum to conduct this Multiple Application Card Merchant Market Assessment. We were extremely qualified to conduct such a study as we had completed a similar study in Atlanta for the Atlanta Cash Card Group two years earlier in support of developing a prepaid card for the 1996 Olympics. We proposed two primary objectives for this research: to assess the level of merchant interest in prepaid cards and other related applications, and to understand the factors that would drive merchant acceptance of prepaid cards. We proposed that the most effective way to determine the viability of the prepaid card concept was to go directly to the merchants, conducting interviews with a representative sample of them.

The research outlined in the RFP required five onsite interviews from the top ten merchants in nine industry segments. We argued that it would be very expensive to complete since these merchants were located throughout the country. We proposed interviewing merchants, bankers, vendors, and senior executives through telephone appointments. Properly organized with a competent professional doing the interviews, we knew we could produce equally good results more quickly, more efficiently, and with less hassle than onsite conversations. After an extensive review of our proposal in a very competitive situation, we won the contract to complete ninety interviews and prepare a final report for a hundred thousand dollars.

It was an excellent contract for us, and we put some of our best people on the telephone calls. We used two people per call, one to ask questions and conduct a dialogue with the merchant, while the other person took detailed notes. It made for a great way to explore the questions we wanted answers to while giving the merchant a chance to ask us about the topic since we could pass on the knowledge we were gaining from the other merchants we were speaking with.

Before we started any interviews, we met with the Merchant Committee of the SmartCard Forum. We discussed the questions in detail, in most cases actually wrote out the exact wording of the question and gained agreement that this questionnaire would not be a yes-or-no question, but a dialogue with the merchants to gain a real understanding of what they thought about the various aspects of smart cards, including how interested they were in putting such a smart card in place for their own company. With approval of the Merchant Committee of the SmartCard Forum, we conducted the interviews over many months. One of the strongest researchers on my staff, Tom Murphy, wrote an excellent report. He went way beyond merely summarizing what he and others on my staff had heard but produced a series of exhibits. These exhibits were scatter diagrams, and their explanations showed where each merchant group was in terms of their interest in various aspects of smart cards. It was a brilliant analysis with one problem: merchants were not generally interested in smart cards.

The committee accepted the report and paid us all the money for it. I thought we had a great contract totally completed. Three months after delivering the final report, a member of the Executive Committee of the SmartCard Forum, the equivalent of the board of directors, called to tell me the report was unacceptable, that the report had to be rewritten, and insisted that we could not do it. We were asked to turn all of our notes over to another competitive company, and they would rewrite our report. I knew the SmartCard Forum would not like the report because retailers had little or no interest in smart cards. That didn't sit well with the SmartCard Forum because they were in the business of promoting smart cards, not discouraging them. As a company with integrity, we had no other choice but to tell it the way we heard it from the marketplace.

The discussion of what to do about the report went on for weeks with the Executive Committee of the SmartCard Forum insisting that we could not rewrite the report while we were unwilling to let any other firm do it. In fact, we could never get the Executive Committee to let us know exactly what was wrong with the report. I knew we had written a first-class report. I read it several times, and I was impressed with the quality of the interviews and the analysis. I believed the only reason why the Executive Committee wanted to have some other firm write the report was because it was so negative on smart cards. I wrote a letter detailing my disagreement with their position and sent it to one of the members of the committee.

After I wrote the letter and had much discussion with the Executive Committee, I agreed to rewrite the report with another excellent researcher on my staff, but the results were still negative on smart cards. The Executive Committee then insisted on getting part of their money back. I refused because we not only completed the report but also wrote it twice and I was losing money on the contract. I didn't believe that I could turn our notes over to any other company because we had agreed that all conversations were confidential and we had to protect the identity of the respondents. In the end, the SmartCard Forum and I disagreed on the quality of the work, and I understood their position. I don't think they ever published the document, and now more than a decade later, I can say that smart cards are still not in use by retailers or bankers. Our consumer research was accurate, the client didn't like the result, and that's just the way life turns out sometimes. That's why you do research: to find out what companies think about the future and what the public is likely to do.

Relationships are difficult when there is bad news to report. I learned that *delivering bad news to a client has serious risks, and sometimes the messenger gets the blame*. On the few occasions when I had to deliver bad news to a client, my company suffered. The SmartCard Forum did not want to hear that retailers did not like smart cards, and they did not want to publish the results even though time proved our work to be right. The president of the Atlanta Fed did not want to hear that he was overplaying his own bank's research when the research was not designed to be a projection. When I held the line on what my staff did, when I put my integrity on the line and stood up to my clients, when I put principle ahead of practicality, I suffered. If I had to do it over again, I would have done it the exact same way because my ethics will not let me to do otherwise. I understand why others put practicality over ethics. It is better for business. It is a judgment call as to whether your ethics will allow you to put business ahead of ethics. I can't.

There was another consulting firm in Atlanta named McGarvey Ross that focused on lending, an area our firm knew very little about. At a conference, Ross and I discussed the possibility of working together on a multiclient program that came to be known as benchmarking. Benchmarking in the industry is focused on an apples-to-apples comparison among a group of similar functions across a number of participants, sharing the way the process flows, their costs, and their efficiencies. The reason why clients are willing to share their process and financial numbers with each other is because it doesn't involve pricing or revenue, which is illegal, but focuses on operational improvements. This is not as direct an approach to earnings improvements as BEI did with onsite consulting, but in some ways, it was even better. Instead of relying on consultants to tell the firm what it could do to improve, the benchmark identifies expensive parts of the process relative to other competitors as well as promotes a discussion on how the process could be run more efficiently.

As a result of our discussion, McGarvey Ross and GCI decided to offer a benchmarking program in consumer lending. McGarvey Ross knew consumer lending extremely well, and we knew how to run multiclient programs. Within a short period of time, we had signed up eight to ten major banks in consumer lending, and there was sufficient money to split between the two consulting firms to make the project worthwhile.

As it turned out, consumer lending is complex, and not every participant does it the same way. For example, the loan application may be filled out in the branch or at a separate location. The decision on whether to grant the loan may be made at the branch or a central location. The processing of the loan could be done centrally or in some distributed fashion. And even the payment process and the collection process can be different.

As a result of those differences, McGarvey Ross wanted to focus on the flow charts for each participant, pointing out the differences. They believed that understanding the various flows of the process would allow them to identify the most efficient ways of conducting the consumer-lending function. We believed that the best way to benchmark a process for consumer lending was to measure the costs of each part of the process, standardizing them by calculating various ratios, such as the cost per loan or the number of loans processed per person. We wanted to quantitatively measure the process while McGarvey Ross wanted to qualitatively measure the process flow. We argued about it several times and finally decided that we would do both. But since McGarvey Ross knew the business better than we did, the focus ended up being more on process flows than on costs.

Nevertheless, the project ended well even though we had a difference of opinion on the quality of our staffs, the focus of the assignment, and the presentations to our participants. Most of the differences were internal to the two consulting firms, so the clients never did know about our different approaches to benchmarking. After the benchmarking program was completed, I decided that we didn't know enough about consumer lending to make it a continuing business. On the other hand, McGarvey Ross created Benchmarking 2000 as an ongoing multiclient program on consumer lending for their company. That program went on for many years, and I was a little envious. It was the first time that our firm had studied the benchmarking process, and I knew that we had an approach to benchmarking that could become another major product line. We just had to find an area that we were expert in, and it didn't take long for that to happen.

As part of my commitment to the employees that remained, I continued the firm's policy of paying for all of the medical coverage of all the employees. Over time, this became a huge benefit as medical insurance went up substantially. As a small business, this was an important benefit for new and old employees, and it constituted an important advantage for the staff to remain at the firm. With a young staff, the need for disability insurance was minimal, so it was not offered. Life insurance was offered with coverage equal to the employee's annual salary. This was inexpensive to provide and not considered to be very important for the staff as most of them were not married and did not even think about the possibility of dying.

On the other hand, our 401(k) retirement program was important to the staff because the money could be sheltered from immediate taxes, and the money could be invested in a variety of stock market programs. At first, the firm matched twenty-five cents on every dollar an employee contributed up to 4 percent of their salary, but over time the matching was raised to thirty cents on the dollar and, eventually, thirty-five cents on the dollar.

I also instituted bonuses that we set on the basis of each individual achieving certain goals. Bonuses can be tied to performance, but it is difficult to set out performance goals in advance. It is also difficult to determine who contributes the most when the staff helps each other. Some employees made their goals easily, and some had difficulty. That was partly because it was difficult for me to set goals that were equally easy or difficult. As a result, some of the employees who made their goals early would help the other employees make their goals. There was no loss for the ones who made their goals, so they helped the others having trouble. After a couple of years, I decided that individual goals were not doing what they should be doing, that we were a small enough company and everyone should be pulling in the same direction together. I set up a bonus structure totally dependent upon the overall profitability of the company. The best solution is to *tie bonuses based on bottom line profits*. The benefit is that it aligns the staff with the same objectives that management has—to maximize profits. It also minimizes objections to selling the company since senior staff having company ownership stands to benefit from the sale.

The staff has to accept the accounting practices of the firm, which have to be fair and reasonable. That means the owner cannot take an unreasonable salary and cannot put expenses on the books that are unjustifiable.

By tying the bonus directly to the bottom line profits of the company, you have to be open about how profitable the company is, and it makes everyone pull together in the same direction to make the company as profitable as possible. This is more valuable than trying to keep the profits of the company confidential. I was willing to live with full disclosure to the staff for the advantage of having them all focused on making money for us all.

Initially, I set the bonus for all employees except me to be a percentage of the annual profits of the company to be paid out at the end of the year around Christmastime. Having everyone working on increasing profitability was a win-win for them as well as for me. I paid a bonus in early July, however, based on the first six months of profits and deducted that from the annual bonus paid in December. The bonus began as 20 percent of the profits, moved up to 25 percent, and eventually reached 30 percent. The bonus was split among the employees proportional to their base salary, so it became important for employees to get a raise annually not only to increase their base salary but also to increase the proportion of their bonus. It turned out to be the right kind of a bonus for my small consulting firm, and it consistently produced very high profits.

The last piece of the benefit package that was offered to key employees was stock options. I defined the value of the stock much lower than I thought the market value was and gave a few employees the right to buy stock from GCI at that low price. They couldn't sell the stock. The only way they could turn the stock into cash was to leave the company forcing the company to buy back the stock or wait for me to sell the company, which might take quite a while. The stock the employees owned was class-B stock, equal in all respects to class-A stock, which I owned, but class-B stock could not vote. I had seen this done at BEI and copied the idea so that I would have complete control over the company without minority stockholders being able to vote.

While stock options were okay, the employees requested a way to sell their stock back to the company if they needed cash, and that led to the implementation of SARs, stock appreciation rights, to replace the actual stock in the company. All employees with stock options converted them to SARs. This gave key employees a way to sell their shares back to the company when they needed cash for personal reasons. It also avoided minority stockholders.

After our work with McGarvey Ross, I knew that the concept of benchmarking was extremely useful for banks and other firms. I was anxious to apply benchmarking in an area that GCI had some expertise. Several years later, we had such an opportunity. In 1994, Chase Manhattan Bank asked if we could compare their check-processing operation to their competitors. The senior management of the bank questioned whether Chase was operating efficiently, and the best method of comparison was to measure the operations of other major check processing banks against Chase's numbers. Chase was willing to pay for the entire benchmarking program, so all we needed to do was to find a handful of banks willing to share their numbers, and those banks would receive the results free of charge.

After approaching several of them, a number of check processing banks were very interested in knowing how well they compared. They agreed to participate, and we organized the first check-processing benchmark in over a decade. The results that each bank received were their numbers compared to the average of the group while we provided Chase with the individual results of each bank. In all cases, the names of the banks were kept confidential, only identified by bank A, bank B, bank C, and so on.

The results did show that other banks were more efficient than Chase, but it was because Chase provided some services within check processing that other banks did not provide. In addition, New York had higher wage rates than other parts of the country, and we provided the results in two ways—the actual results and results modified by cost of living rates from city to city—so that a more accurate comparison could be made.

All of the banks were associated with the Bank Administration Institute (BAI) as BAI had become the major bank association dealing with check processing issues. Apparently, the banks in the Chase benchmarking study indicated to BAI that they wanted to continue a check benchmarking study, and in 1995 BAI issued a request for proposal to consulting firms to work with them in launching such a benchmarking program. Naturally, we were extremely interested in pursuing this opportunity. After the BAI and a committee of bankers reviewed all the proposals and presentation by the competitors, we were fortunate to win. I remember quite vividly presenting our credentials in Chicago to a formidable group of bankers, explaining what we did for Chase and indicating the quality of our staff. We also had the tremendous advantage of having a check forum in the United States and England to indicate that we really understood the check-processing business. All of this helped to win the contract.

Although we won the contract, there was great skepticism about whether we were capable of producing a benchmark program that would be meaningful for the bank participants. The reason for this skepticism was that a decade earlier, Peat Marwick & Mitchell, a major consulting firm, tried to implement a benchmarking program for check processing, and it had never lived up to its potential. It was difficult to obtain an apples-to-apples comparison because individual banks process checks differently and the process is complex. Recognizing this issue, my staff believed that the only authentic and accurate way to obtain apples-to-apples comparisons was to be very detailed in defining each element in the benchmark. This would require bringing the participating banks together for several days to determine first what metrics would be meaningful and, second, to define those metrics as clearly as possible. When we did this, not all of the banks initially agreed on what metrics to get or exactly how to define them, but after much discussion a final determination emerged. For example, when it came to the cost of a particular function, we all agreed that the total all-in cost was the most appropriate measure, and that included people who were on vacation, people out sick, substitutes, replacements, and part-time staff. It also included all fringe benefits. The argument that won the day was that the bank had to pay these costs, and thus, they should be a part of the comparison. The bank had control over these costs, and if they were too high, the bank might change its policy if it so desired. If one bank's ratios proved to be best, then that bank might be able to explain what it did to achieve that result even if other banks could not do what the best practice bank did. Still, it would be useful to know what might be done in the future if management wanted to reduce its cost.

There is much that has to be done right to make benchmarking a success for participants. When done right, however, *benchmarking is not just profitable in its own right as a service but it also provides a deep understanding of the process being benchmarked*, it provides best practices that may lead to other consulting assignments, and it provides access to very senior management at the participant organizations who desire to know how well their company is doing relative to the competition.

In addition, a benchmarking study can continue for many years after the company establishes the first benchmark, for the participants are now convinced that your firm can be trusted to maintain the confidentiality of the data, that you have mastered the benchmarking process, and no other firm has your expertise. Benchmarking the same process can be performed annually, semiannually, or on some other time schedule, but the firm that establishes the benchmarking process has the upper hand in continuing the program against all competitors.

Benchmarking is not an easy process to implement because it places significant requirements not only on the firm doing the benchmark but also on all the participants. There are six major issues that must be addressed, and if they are not done well, the benchmark will not turn out well. Benchmark ratios must be defined, each element in the ration must be defined, data must be gathered, gathered data must be reviewed, best practices must be explored, and finally, onsite presentations must be made.

These benchmarking programs continued on year after year in check processing because they helped the participating banks understand where they could improve their operation. The benchmarking results showed that there were opportunities to provide bonuses for operators with high production rates, proper ways to implement image statements, comparisons on how best to present the image of a check to an operator, how best to handle image reject repair, how to increase earnings with items that were sent to the wrong bank, and so on. With a complex system like check processing, there are many areas where improvements are possible. So long as participants do not see one another's operations as competitive and are willing to share their best practices, a benchmarking program can have benefits for participants year after year.

Several years after Steve left GCI when business was back growing again, we decided to increase our staff. We interviewed a young man named Dave Stewart just out of Grinnell College in Iowa. Dave was the kind of guy I was always willing to take a chance on even though he knew nothing about banking or payment systems. Dave was confident, a bit unpolished but outgoing, smart, and a leader. I could have looked for staff at an Ivy League university and found similar type people, but from Grinnell I didn't have to pay as much of a salary. A number of smart young college graduates might eventually leave GCI for an MBA or to join a larger firm or for some other reason, so it made sense to pay lower salaries to begin with. We kept the winners by giving them large salary increases as they proved themselves and implied that they wanted to make a career at GCI. Dave turned out to be one of those winners.

Shortly after Dave arrived, he approached me about starting a forum focused on using the Internet as a payment technology. This was the mid-1990s, and Internet banking was just beginning. Bill payment from home had gone through many technology changes and still had not caught on very well. In the 1970s, home banking was expensive for a bank because it required a person at the bank to talk directly to the consumer about what bills were to be paid. In the 1980s, touch-tone telephone banking didn't work well either, and neither did banking over cable television. From 1975 to 1990, home banking was a failure even though many different programs were tried. The Internet, on the other hand, had the promise of changing failure into success. Dave suggested that since we already had forums on check processing why not launch a forum on the use of the Internet for home banking. I thought the idea was ingenious, and I agreed to give it a serious effort as I had done to launch the check forums several years earlier.

Before Dave's suggestion, I had tried to launch a new forum called the Internet Financial Services Program with Dale Reistad, my old boss from the 1970s, but it didn't work out. We had a few meetings, but the revenue from the effort did not justify continuing the program. Dave's idea was to focus entirely on the Internet for banking and to launch the program by getting the key players involved that drove the Internet. They understood the technology better than anyone else. Dave and I flew to California and met with several of the technology companies involved in the Internet, and the reception we received was encouraging. Their position was that they would support an Internet forum if we had sufficient support from the banking community. If we could announce having some of the major Internet players supporting our Internet forum, then that would be a very positive incentive for the banks to participate.

After several months of negotiations with key Internet players, we were happy to announce that Edify, First Data Resources, MasterCard, Microsoft, VeriFone, and Zenith Data Systems were members of the Internet Forum, and we were also having serious discussions underway with IBM and Sun Microsystems. The Internet Forum was launched in June 1996 and continued for the next ten years beyond my retirement. It followed the successful program that existed for our check forums.

New technology drives innovation and *innovation drives consulting and syndicated research*. Innovation can also occur from new laws and new regulations as well as brilliant marketing campaigns. Most companies want to innovate to be different from their competitors to be better than their competitors. The world is always changing, and it requires consultants to stay current with the changes and even be ahead of them. The Internet is a good example. You then have something to offer to the markets you serve.

As I look back on the launch of the Internet Forum, I am struck at how stupid I was to have missed launching such a program twice before. At EBI in 1981, I had launched the Home Banking Society when banking from home was in its early infancy. It was a good idea then, but we focused on producing only research reports without getting the membership of the program together to discuss them in detail. I had learned in the mid-1970s that research with meetings was the successful model but did not implement that at EBI. Then EBI was bought by BEI, and the concept of a multi-client program died for several years until I again launched a study of microcomputers for the banking industry in conjunction with the *American Banker*. I still didn't understand how valuable a forum would be on the use of personal computers in banking. And I certainly did not perceive that the computer connected to the Internet would provide the technology to really launch home banking successfully. I had several opportunities to become the early leader in Internet banking and didn't have the foresight to see the possibilities down the road. It took more than a decade to get back into the home banking business, and it might not have happened without a young college graduate like Dave bringing up the possibility because he had used the Internet throughout his college career. Sometimes you are too far in front of the technology to realize its power, and sometimes you are too late in getting into the game after the technology is well established, and other consulting firms are way ahead of you, taking advantage of the situation. Timing is everything, but foresight is even more important.

Sometime around 1995, I concluded that we had successfully changed the firm's consulting practice. Instead of focusing on electronic banking, on ATMs, and plastic cards, we were focusing on check processing. While all of the services were payment systems, there was a huge difference between the new plastic card world and the old world of processing paper checks. In addition, the company no longer had to worry about the firm's cash position or profitability. We were growing a very profitable company. It was time to hire more experienced staff familiar with check processing. We needed individuals who had the experience to enhance the more junior staff who could do the research and run forums but did not know check processing from the inside of the bank.

We first hired Jay Mahaffey, a man who was running the check-processing operation at the Federal Reserve Bank of Atlanta. In turn, Jay knew Michael Fisher, also at the Federal Reserve Bank of Atlanta, who was also very knowledgeable about check processing. We hired him too. By then, I had reestablished a good working relationship with the Fed in Atlanta, and I was a little concerned about hiring two of their excellent staff. I checked with the Fed and they did not object, so Fisher joined us. Dave also knew of a good friend of his from Grinnell, who was ambivalent about going to graduate school to major in mathematics. Dave thought he might consider joining us. I liked Todd McGuire immediately. While Todd did not have a check-processing background, he was very competent in building models, and as soon as he joined us he took naturally to the intricacies of check processing, especially working through the analyses of our check-benchmarking program. In a short period of time, Todd became very knowledgeable about image check processing and could handle almost every consulting assignment in check processing that showed up for our firm.

To round out our banking expertise, John Mateker joined us from the banking industry. He was knowledgeable about payment systems and retail banking. Together, this team along with our existing senior staff comprised an extremely powerful group of consultants on payment systems, but especially on check processing.

With a consulting staff really knowledgeable about check processing, I was taking a page out of the BEI consulting book that I had seen almost a decade earlier. In addition to the research we were capable of and our ability to run forums, benchmarking, and research studies, we were now capable of going onsite to a particular bank to undertake intensive consulting associated with a bank's particular problem. Jay spent several months onsite at Barclays Bank in London dealing with the implementation of their image check-processing system. Steve was hired by APACS to work with them on the implementation of IBDE, Interbank Data Exchange, the system that allowed UK banks to send the clearing of their check-processing work electronically before the paper check arrived. We did an evaluation of the image check-processing systems used to store images at both First Union Bank and First National Bank of Atlanta when they merged to determine which system was best. We evaluated the ACH system for Visa and suggested they get out of that business, which they did. And we conducted many, many more assignments for individual banks involved in check processing and the ACH, assignments we were not capable of if we just had smart people from college because they did not know the payment system world from the inside.

Finally, we hired Karl Sammons, who had been in the banking industry for decades at Unisys, to help on our sales strategy. Karl convinced the company to undertake a benchmarking program to analyze the retail and wholesale lockbox business, which we did quite successfully.

While I did focus on hiring staff who had a background in payment systems, I continued to hire junior staff who had no background in payment systems as well. These people were smart, communicated well, and had a passion for consulting and research. We hired John Crofoot, a PhD in Middle Eastern history from the University of Georgia. We hired Marcy Ellis, a recent college graduate, and over time, she took on more and more challenging assignments until she ran the Check Forum. We also hired Scott Anderson, a summa cum laude graduate from the University of Georgia, who produced a remarkable set of research reports over time but eventually left to go to law school. Not all of our hires were successful, and those who weren't left the company on their own or were asked to leave. However, the success rate of those without a banking background was better than 50 percent, and it helped to keep our salary expenses down while allowing ample opportunities for junior staff to move up the company if they were successful.

In 1996, the lease that Steve signed was up, and it was time to either renew the lease or move out. I thought the market for owning our own office was good, so I hired a real estate agent to find us a new office. I figured that the rent we were probably going to pay for a new office would cover the mortgage payment on an office I would own, and it turned out to be the case. We found a condominium about as far from my home as our previous office, nestled in a small office park. We bought the entire building, renovated the office to suit our needs, and moved in. There was enough room to add a couple of additional staff, and it suited our needs for about three years.

I separated the ownership of the condo from the ownership of the business so that selling the business would not affect the ownership of the condo. My wife was given ownership of the condo, and she collected the rent from GCI, paid the bills associated with the condo, and generally did all the bookkeeping for it. I could have set the GCI lease at any price I wanted, but I believed that we had to stay with a rental rate that was close to the market price for a number of reasons. The first was that it was the ethical thing to do. Second, we were paying a portion of the profits to employees, and a high rent would reduce their profit sharing, which they would have known about and complained about. The third reason was that the impact on my taxes was negligible. In spite of a reasonable rent, there was enough to pay the mortgage and taxes and still have a little left. Over time, the condo increased in price, so that when we sold it four years later, I made money on the sale.

Unfortunately, I could not find another building to buy after we sold the condo. The market had changed, and the cost of buying my own building went up considerably. In addition, I wanted to move my office closer to my home, which narrowed the choices available in the market. I was then making a decent living, and a short commute was more valuable than making money in an office far from my home. Had I not been making serious money, I might have made a different choice.

Still another idea occurred to my staff in the mid-1990s. The Check Forum in the United States dealt with the large variety of check-processing services. One such area was cash management, the check-processing services usually made available to major corporations. Banks had a separate department in the corporate side of the bank that dealt with payment services to corporations, such as wire transfers, lockbox services, ACH for payroll, and a host of other services. The only time that cash management bankers got together was at cash-management conferences organized by corporations to discuss their cash-management issues. At these conferences, the banks were the exhibitors because they were selling their services to the attendees, the corporate treasurers, and controllers of these companies. This was a competitive environment, so no discussion could occur among the bankers themselves. This provided an opportunity for GCI to organize a cash-management forum for the bankers and vendors to those banks, without having their corporate customers being present.

When a group of companies has nowhere to go to discuss their industry, a multiclient program is a likely possibility. When we discovered that bank cash managers had nowhere to go to discuss what was going on in their industry, the Cash Management Forum was born. In 1996, we launched the Cash Management Forum. It was an immediate success. The major banks had no other outlet for discussion of the issues they faced in their business, and they were willing to talk about what they were doing with two caveats. The first was that we would not promote the forum to their customers, which was easy enough for us to do, provided we had enough banks to constitute a profitable forum. The second issue was that we would stay away from pricing to avoid antitrust problems, and that too was easy enough to do because the speakers at the forum were the bankers themselves, and they would certainly police what they said.

Once we had ten or so of the major corporate cash management banks in the forum, the rest of the banks that had cash management services joined. In terms of getting a forum started, this one was the easiest one to launch because we had a reputation for running excellent forums, the need for such a forum was great, and the cash management part of the bank usually had the funds to pay for such an activity.

John Crofoot took naturally to this forum even though he had no knowledge of the area whatsoever. John had tremendous communication skills and stayed in touch with virtually all the participants on a regular basis. In time, he became intelligent about cash management, reading books on the subject, speaking with his participants, involving himself in all the presentations made at his forums, and writing research papers on cash management from time to time. John made the Cash Management Forum a great success, and it was a sad day for GCI when he announced that he was moving to Constantinople, Turkey, to begin a new career there.

The Cash Management Forum was in continuous operation at GCI for more than a decade. The bankers themselves help drive what they want GCI to do in terms of research reports and speakers at the meetings, which is why it has been so successful. There must be plenty of opportunities like this in other industries and in other countries. Once you find a good idea for a forum that meets an unfulfilled need, it is relatively easy to persuade the people in that group that you can organize meetings and reports that serve their needs.

At BEI in the mid-1980s, I served as an expert witness for Valley National Bank in a check fraud case that was settled out of court. At GCI, we were known for our knowledge of check processing, so we began to get requests from lawyers to serve as an expert witness for the banks they were defending. The check-processing people recommended us, and since I was the resident PhD, CEO, and had experience as an expert witness, I usually ended up serving as the expert for our clients.

Over the intervening years, I served as an expert witness in various fraud cases, especially check fraud cases, and helped to set the standards by which the bank would be judged in court. The expert's role is to serve the court and determine whether the defendant bank acted with ordinary care in a commercially reasonable manner. The majority of cases dealt with signature maker fraud, forged endorsements, or check alterations. In a signature fraud case, the signature of the maker of the check is forged and deposited in the crook's account. This is often an inside job whereby the legitimate signature is copied by a crook that has seen the legitimate maker's signature many times. If the signer of the check has a stamp made of his/her signature, the employee crook can use that stamp illegally to sign a check made out to that employee or anyone else the crook wants to pay. The crook then fixes the books of the company so the check will be difficult to detect.

In the forged-endorsement case, the check received at the company is stolen, and the endorsement on the back of the check is forged and deposited into the crook's account. In ingenious cases, the crook establishes an account resembling the payee on the check to make it look like a perfect match between the payee on the check and the crook's account. An example is to take a check made out to Oppenheimer for the Oppenheimer Fund and open an account in the name of Oppenheimer Management or Oppenheimer Associates. The check will look acceptable to a teller when deposited into the account with a similar name.

The third case of an altered check occurs when a legitimate check is stolen before it is mailed or from the mail. The payee is erased chemically, and the crook's payee is substituted, depositing the check in the crook's account. With billions of checks written annually and millions of small businesses, fraudulent checks occur on a regular basis, but they constitute a tiny fraction of the number of checks written.

In addition, we handled check procedural cases, usually associated with whether the check was returned from one bank to another in a timely fashion. The Uniform Commercial Code sets the period when a check must be paid or returned for a variety of reasons. The rule is that the check must be physically presented to a bank for payment, and that bank has until midnight of the day after the check is presented to either pay it or return it. A late returned check does not have to be accepted by the depository bank. This occurs when a crook presents a check for deposit and then removes the money from the account before the check is returned to that depository bank. If the check is returned late, the depository bank can refuse to accept the check because there is no money left in that account, and the paying bank is stuck with the loss instead of the depository bank.

The law in the United States requires a bank to use "ordinary care" in processing checks, and the decision as to whether the bank is negligent and liable for the loss or not hangs on whether the procedures of the bank are commercially reasonable. The answer to that question usually rests on an expert witness evaluating what the bank did, comparing what that bank did to what other banks do. If the comparison is commercially reasonable, the bank is not negligent and is not liable for the loss. The loss is then the responsibility of the plaintiff, who is usually the account holder on which the check was written. There is also a time limit in notifying the bank of the fraudulent check. The longer the customer takes to notify the bank, the more likely it is that the customer will not be able to recover the funds from the bank.

To determine whether the bank used ordinary care in processing the fraudulent check, I concluded that the judgment of the bank's procedure had to rest on what it did for all of its checks, not just the fraudulent check at issue because banks cannot be expected to catch all fraudulent checks. The plaintiff's argument is simply that the bank is liable because it did not catch the fraudulent check. I argued that if the overall procedure of the bank was commercially reasonable, then the bank could not be held liable for not catching the fraudulent checks at issue. To do that, I established a series of ratios that I used to compare the procedures of the bank involved in the case to other banks. Obtaining these ratios was not easy as banks do not release this type of information. I was able to gain this information because we had excellent contacts at virtually all the major check processing banks in the United States. From time to time, we would issue a questionnaire asking for this information, and the banks usually were kind enough to provide that information to us because of our relationship with them.

In 1997, Carreker, a major bank consulting firm much bigger than my firm, proposed to merge with Antonori, a software company serving banks. Denny Carreker, the CEO of Carreker, asked me to meet with him at a restaurant in Atlanta, and I agreed. I had known Denny for many years since he began his career at the Federal Reserve Bank of Atlanta, and we had met often at various banking conventions. At the restaurant, Denny offered me the opportunity to have GCI merge with Ron Antonori's company in a three-way merger. Denny argued that adding my firm to the two other companies would produce a first-class consulting and software company serving the banking industry. The commitment was to first merge the companies and then go public with a huge stock offering. I asked what role I would have, and Denny told me that he would be the new CEO and chairman, Ron would be the vice chairman, and I would be in charge of all research. I was flattered and somewhat interested in the idea, but I didn't like Denny's management style, and he would be running the company.

Denny had a very strong personality, and I thought it would difficult to get what I wanted if he disagreed with me. I had worked for those types of people in the past and did not want to do it again unless the value of the proposition was so overwhelming that I could not say no. Denny concluded the conversation with the proposal that if I wanted to move forward, then Ron Antonori would negotiate the merger with me. I thought about the matter for a few days and concluded that I really didn't want to merge my company into Ron's and Denny's companies, but I would do so if they could provide a number of assurances to me.

I drafted a letter detailing what I would need as assurances going into such a merger.

The conclusion that Ron got, and it was the one I wanted to give him, was that I wasn't really interested in giving up control of my company, and the offer they wanted to make to me would not be sufficient to get me to change my mind. The idea of being acquired was dead on arrival, and I was happy about it.

A year or so later, Carreker/Antonori went public, Carreker and Antonori made a lot of money, and eventually, Ron quit the company and retired. I suspected that he couldn't work with Denny either. This was an opportunity I was glad to pass up.

For several years, I wanted to give a speech on the value of the check as a payment service to the banking industry. Over time, this became important to me, for I thought that the payment system industry was continually focused on various electronic banking services that were growing. There was always a great deal of good being said about credit cards, debit cards, ATMs, Internet banking, cash management services, and the ACH. These services were always being presented, praised, and promoted, and yet the paper check was the biggest payment system in the United States and, indeed, in the world. Paraphrasing Rodney Dangerfield, a comedian that often said he got no respect, the check got no respect.

In 1997, when the check was near its peak in terms of transaction volume, the American Bankers Association asked me to address a major convention on payment systems, and I was given the chance to speak about the check. This was the golden opportunity I had been waiting for, and I spent considerable time writing out the speech. At first, I titled the speech "In Homage to the King: Long Live the Check." As I continued to give the speech after the first presentation, I shortened the title to simply "The Check Is King," and it became an instant hit within the industry. I say that because for the next two years, I was asked to give that speech again and again to virtually all of the payment system conferences that took place. I gave the talk about a dozen times, and each time I changed the talk to meet the time requirements of the speech, yet it was the same talk. In time, I became associated with that talk so much that people who heard it and recognized me would greet me not by saying, "Hello, Allen," but by pointing at me and saying,

"The check is king" and then smile. Because the industry associated me with that speech, I have provided some of the highlights of that talk below:

Highlights from my 1997-1998 speech
"The Check is King"

When I was asked to speak about the future of the check, I quickly accepted because I want to say some things about this subject to this payment system audience for years. We have a tendency to emphasize the new, the fashionable, and the outrageous while taking for granted the ordinary and the traditional. We have a tendency to flog the ordinary because it is so ordinary.

Little minds are interested in the extraordinary. Great minds are interested in the commonplace. Some take the ordinary for granted, and others feel it is their right to criticize it. Even more, we believe it is our duty to improve it. It is the American way; it is the way of progress. As Charles Kettering once said, "We work day after day, not to finish things, but to make the future better . . . because we will spend the rest of our life there."

And so at the outset of my career, I followed the American way of emphasizing and building the new and the fashionable, criticizing the old and the ordinary. That process led from one thing to another for decades until I realized that for twenty-five years, I had been trying to kill the king. I have not been alone. For twenty-five years there has been a massive conspiracy in the United States to kill the king. I have been one of the leading conspirators, and I dare say that many of you in the audience today have also been part of that conspiracy to kill the king.

Today I am here to ask the king for forgiveness. It was a ridiculous idea twenty-five years ago, and it is a ridiculous, foolish idea today. It is a ridiculous idea because we cannot kill the king, and we have been trying very hard to do it. It is a foolish idea because the king is a benevolent king, and all his subjects are prospering. The king has the Midas touch; the king makes money—lots of it for everyone.

The king I am talking about is the check. The check is king; the paper check is king. After cash, the most efficient payment system in the world is the check! There is not another payment system anywhere in the world that processes more volume, more quickly, more efficiently, and more conveniently than the check. The check has been king of all payment systems for more than three decades, and all we ever do is talk about killing it by reducing its volume, by replacing the paper check with electronic funds transfer systems. Some people have been proclaiming the big lie, that the check is inefficient, costly, and out of date. That's a load of claptrap. In the South, politely we would say, "Sir, you are mistaken"; in New York, they would say that's a bunch of bull. Here in this audience, I am sure you would have a much more colorful expression.

Last year, McKinsey & Company delivered an excellent study of the US payment system and spoke at a payment system conference. With regard to the check, they concluded that US banks generate $39 billion from checking accounts, and this subsidizes the branch network. Over 50 percent of the revenue is from free balances. Seven billion dollars is from return check fees—at risk if the check disappears. Further, McKinsey concluded that electronics does not provide cost relief in the near term—although it may do so in the long term.

For a payment system, check processing is old, but not out of date. If a thing is old, it's a sign that it was fit to live. The guarantee of continuity and longevity is quality. That surely is check processing. There is no royal road to anything; one thing at a time and all things in succession. That which grows slowly endures. That is the check! It endures. The facts are indisputable, and I will say it again. The check is the most efficient payment system in the United States and in the world. Period.

Killing the payment system king has been the fashionable discussion since I arrived in banking in the late '60s. In the early part of my career, we were all trying to establish new electronic banking services, and it seemed sensible to go after the king because we all believed intuitively that electronic banking would be more efficient than paper processing. Paper processing was thought to be inefficient because of the need to shuffle paper one piece at a time while electronic processing was thought to be efficient because it required less people, avoided using paper, and was, if nothing else, electronic.

In the 1970s, leading proponents of electronic banking talked openly about the cashless/checkless society. The government promoted electronic funds transfer, EFT, as a more efficient payment system than the paper check, which was predicted to have rising labor costs that would make paper much more expensive than electronic banking. The theory put forward was that paper costs would inevitably rise as inflation rose while the cost of electronic banking would decline as transaction volume increased and economies of scale occurred.

In the 1980s, there were many predictions that the paper check would reach its peak. Experts were positive that direct deposit of payroll would replace the check, that ATMs would eliminate the need to write checks for cash, that point-of-sale credit cards and debit cards would eliminate check writing at the point of sale and home banking would put an end to writing checks at home. Corporate checks would also be eliminated by electronic services.

I was involved in many of these projects, and we were all trying to kill the king. We were working to put the check out of business. But the king of payment systems has taken on all comers and still remains king. The check has increased its transaction volume over the past twenty years more than all electronic banking services combined.

I will put to you a very simple proposition why the check remains king. Those of us who believe in the check, who make our living from processing checks or improving the efficiency of the check have felt the heat of competition for many, many years from many, many internal and external sources, and we have responded to those threats in dramatic and very competitive fashion. We know that a major part of the battle for payment system superiority will be won in how efficiently we process an item. The threat of electronic banking strengthened the nerves and sharpened the skills of those in check processing. Our antagonist has been our protagonist. The check had to improve or decay. There was no other choice.

Check processing has been focused for decades on becoming more and more efficient and you can see the results today. The paper check clears nationwide in the United States in two days or less, error rates have dropped, productivity has increased, systems have become more efficient, vendors have improved the technology, and customers continue to be pleased writing checks.

The stubborn resilience of the paper check has some important implications for senior managers, some who have misplaced priorities. Strategists tend to support existing processing systems with only basic operational budgets while they devote the big marketing money to electronics. Banks go out of their way to encourage customers to use direct deposit for their paychecks, to visit ATMs instead of branches, to try out home banking on their personal computers. Meanwhile, banks seem to neglect marketing the check—which is, after all, the more profitable product—while underfunding projects aimed at making electronic services more efficient.

A better strategy might be to invert priorities, backing the paper check product with marketing muscle and reinvesting more operational money into electronic payments to bring the costs down. The check is such a well-established product that marketers give it little attention. Perhaps familiarity has bred contempt. Perhaps marketing people believe the check is a dying product and not worth their time and attention. That would be serious mistake if it were true. When MasterCard and Visa bash the check in TV commercials, which occurs daily in the United States, the check should at least counterattack with all the benefits that a check provides. When is the last time you saw a TV commercial selling the benefits of check writing? Have we all lost faith in the check? I hope we are not killing the king because we have a love affair with electronics, even when an electronic payment may be more costly to process than a paper check.

We have lost sight of thinking of checks as products that people and companies pay for because checks provide a very valuable service. We have lost sight of the many revenue streams that checks provide to banks, from cash management fees from corporations, from transaction fees from customers, from monthly fees for the account, from nuisance fees for overdrawing the account, and from collection fees for failing to pay when the check is presented for payment. The revenues streams from checks are enormous, yet banks have lost sight of them because the check is not considered a stand-alone business. No entrepreneur would ever do that.

The second problem is that check people are not defending themselves against the public relations onslaught that the check is inefficient and electronic banking is the future of money. When MasterCard attacks the check and cash because they are old technology, when Visa attacks the check as being slow and flabby, when consultants tell you the Internet will be the next great payment system, when the government says they will mandate the replacement of all paper check processing, the check must defend itself. Who is defending the check? Who is speaking for the greatest payment system in the world? Who is defending the king? Surely, I cannot be the only one. No one is speaking on behalf of the check. No one. The king is beginning to die from neglect. The check gets no respect. I'll tell you whom we need to get to speak on behalf of the check; it's the comedian Rodney Dangerfield; he always says he gets no respect.

Three men were laying brick. The first was asked, "What are you doing?" He answered, "I'm laying some brick." The second man was asked, "What are you working for?" He answered, "I'm working for fifty dollars a day." The third man was asked, "What are you doing?" He answered, "I am helping to build a great cathedral."

Most people in operations are just laying brick, doing their job, and not thinking about the future. Many of the vendors are just selling their product and not thinking about the future. Some of us are this third man. We have been laboring for decades creating the future, and we have built a great cathedral called the check-processing system. And as a result, the American public has a love affair with writing checks, and the banking community has done everything in its power to make the check the ubiquitous payment instrument it is. The check is a measure of the trust the American economic systems give to its customers; it shows the high level of morality we have in business and the culture of our people to do business on a handshake.

The check is not going down a beaten path. Beaten paths are for beaten men.

Competition has forced the king of the payment system, the check, to defend his throne, and the king will not go down without a fight. The king has a ten-year strategy, not for mere survival but to remain king.

The check has undergone continuous refinement driven by very clever vendors and bankers. Some bankers are calling it "electronification of the check." The world is divided into people who do things and people who get the credit. Check-processing people belong to the first class, the people that get things done. Certainly, there is less competition there. Check processing is not some out-of-date Model-T Ford, but a very sleek, streamlined racing car that is improving every year.

Women write most of the personal checks while men prefer to use credit cards. I continue to be amazed at the men I meet at conferences like this who tell me they rarely write checks. Women are the check writers because they are the shoppers and the bill payers. If you intend to reduce check writing, you will have to convince women to stop writing checks. Ask your wife how quickly she is prepared to give up check writing.

For the check, we know that low prices have caused millions of customers to write billions of checks, and the efficiency of the check processing system is the result of the need to make a profit at the low prices banks charge. In that respect, the check follows the Henry Ford model of putting marketing first to create volume and then producing an efficient payment system to meet the marketing requirements. But with regard to electronic banking services, we have not yet put these services through a competitive ringer to squeeze out all the inefficiencies they have. They are still considered the "fair-haired boys" that need time to grow and mature, and the betting is still on the future.

The fundamental point is that we have squeezed out the inefficiencies in check processing, and we are under severe pressure to continue to improve, but we have not done the same thing with our electronic banking services. Until we do, and we have a long way to go, the check will remain king.

While the check may be the most efficient payment instrument, that's only part of the story. Let's look at the revenue side of the business. How does the check stack up there? Well, that's a very complicated question because we have to consider who gets credit for the deposits in a checking account. I think it can be successfully argued that without check writing, we would not have very much of the customers' deposits. Most people open accounts today to write checks and view electronic banking as a value-added service. It is check writing that opens the account, and that's why we call it a checking account, not an ATM account or an electronic banking account.

Checks generate a very substantial fee income for returning unpostable checks, most of them for NSF, non-sufficient funds. Typically, the return rate is ½ percent of the checks, which amounts to returning more than three hundred million checks annually. Using reasonable industry prices, the annual revenue from returning checks is seven billion dollars. That is a lot of money.

The only major threat to the check is the check itself. Like the Roman Empire, the check will collapse by its own inefficiencies if we become too complacent or do not undertake the appropriate steps to keep the check the payment instrument of choice for consumers and corporations.

I want to be perfectly clear about my feelings regarding electronic banking services. I want electronic banking services to succeed, and my fervent hope is that they will replace the check over time. Let's judge them by results. Thomas Edison said, "Results! Why, man, I have gotten a lot of results. I know several thousand things that won't work." Still, I believe in electronic banking, and I believe these services can be delivered very efficiently. But I want this to happen on a level playing field without making the transition mandatory and without the hype and mystique of some futuristic, unproved, electronic solution. I want the check to have the opportunity to remain king of the payment system if it can.

I want to make this perfectly clear too. There is nothing evil about processing paper and nothing intrinsically good about processing electronically. The paper check is not hell, and EFT is not heaven. Paper processing is not inherently inefficient, and electronic banking is not inherently efficient.

Today it is just the opposite. The check has brought us the most efficient payment system in the world. The check supports the collection of enormously cheap deposits that makes banking the profitable business it is. The check has given the banks control of the payment systems in the United States, and that provides a franchise and a monopoly that should not be taken for granted.

Who can compete with check processing? No one. Who will compete with electronic processing? Everyone. If we get rid of the check, we may undermine our own need for existence because lots of companies know they can process electronically. Why should we give up the franchise and the control that goes with paper processing until we have to? We have already given away too much of the payment system to nonbanks. We don't have to play into the hand of the competition!

I am afraid some people are in a big hurry about electronic processing, and they may be killing the king without much justification. And so I think we are utilizing the perfect strategy—talking and implementing EFT services wherever they make sense but continuing to process the paper check. The most successful businessman is the man who holds onto the old just as long as it is good and grabs the new just as soon as it is better. So what's the hurry? We are making money whether the customer uses paper or electronics.

It saddens me that this speech is needed; that the check is not widely regarded as the most efficient payment mechanism in the world. It saddens me that we are prepared to replace the check with electronic transactions without caring about whether this is a profitable strategy. It saddens me that the government is making electronic banking mandatory for their payments. It saddens me that check processing people are not defending the check inside and outside their bank. It saddens me that we let promoters of electronic transactions present bad data that promotes their electronic products without refutation. It saddens me that we are not letting check processing be run as a business.

So finally, I want to end this talk as I began it, by asking forgiveness of the king, the benevolent king that has been so good to all of us. I have sinned in cursing the check, in believing it had evil ways, and in trying to kill it. It has taken me a long, long time to realize that creating an efficient payment system is no easy task. In fact, it is very difficult. We have much to do to make our future electronic banking systems more efficient than the paper checks they are supposed to replace because we have built the most efficient payment system in the world, the check. I want to pay homage to the king; long live the check.

Another company failure occurred in 2002 with the launch of GCI Europe. The concept was simple. We had a very successful business in the United States and a foothold in the UK with the UK Cheque Forum. While Europe had gotten away from writing checks and embarked on moving rapidly toward electronic payment systems, there were many opportunities that could build a consulting practice there. My son, Leo, was living in Europe and was interested in starting a consulting practice on payment systems in Europe, and he had the requisite background to do it.

Together, he and I set up a separate company called GCI Europe, but I had to deal with a number of important issues. We had to determine Leo's salary as well as how the profits and losses would be handled for the bonus pool. Since Leo was not ready to take on a major consulting assignment on his own, we expected Leo to sell the work and have the consultants at GCI complete the assignments.

Leo worked hard at trying to launch GCI Europe, but he was a one-man show with virtually no experience on how to do this on his own. I made several trips to Europe to help him, but I concluded that my contacts were undeveloped, and I would need to move to Europe for six months or more to really have a chance at making this work. I concluded that I couldn't do it as I had other obligations at home and in running GCI in the United States. In addition, my staff was not interested in helping Leo to any degree, and Leo found himself isolated from the rest of the company without many contacts himself. I felt terrible seeing Leo suffer in Europe, unable to get a good start because he didn't have the contacts, and no one else had those contacts either, including me. I realized that the culture of Europe even more so than the United States required proper relationships with bankers to gain consulting work, and none of us had them. After a year or so of agony, Leo and I both decided that we had made a mistake and closed the company down. I should add that Leo worked for several companies after that in payment systems, established the contacts he needed, and then started his own payment system consulting firm, which after several years is now doing extremely well.

Sometime in 1998, my staff approached me to discuss another new idea related to benchmarking. Our typical benchmarking ratios were produced once a year, which made this a static analysis. We had no idea whether these ratios changed over time, but we believed that not only could a bank produce these ratios on demand but also that a bank could do it dynamically during the processing of its checks.

What we proposed was the concept of a dashboard for the management of check processing. We would define the ratios that management needed because we knew the ratios that mattered from our benchmarking studies. What we needed was a company that could write software that would connect online with the check-processing systems of the bank to gather the necessary data to calculate the benchmark ratios during actual processing. We found such a company. It was a small software company owned by five partners with Kevin the most senior of them. The company was called Genisys Corporation.

Based on discussions with Genisys, our two companies agreed on a fifty-fifty ownership of a new company that would own the software and promote it to the major banks and others. We played around with a number of names for the company, and I proposed that the software be called Lumen because it shed light on how to manage a process dynamically.

Even though Lumen was a software product and Global Concepts did not have software engineers to develop the product, we felt that the concept of a dashboard played to the strength of our company for several reasons. We knew benchmarking in detail, we understood why banks did what they did, and we believed that clients would require us to consult with them for their initial installation as well as continuing consultation to make the dashboard as effective as possible.

In February 1999, after working on Lumen for six months, I wrote out the basic principles for the new company and sent them to Kevin. Shortly after I wrote the memo, I learned that Genisys had agreed to sell their firm to Carreker Antonori. Kevin was not anxious to sell his company, but he had four other partners, and a majority of the stockholders voted to sell out. There was nothing that I could do but deal with the development. The key issue was whether to sell our interest to Carreker or find another software company to replace Genisys.

I was unhappy at the prospect of working with Carreker Antonori because they were much bigger than my company and unlikely to play fair in dealing with me. I had turned down selling my company to them years earlier because I didn't want to work with them, and I didn't think we could work together on Lumen.

I had one ace up my sleeve. The joint venture that Genisys and GCI signed allowed my company the right to buy out Genisys if it was acquired. I knew that Carreker Antonori would want to own the software because they were a software company, and we weren't. Sure enough, Kevin asked me what it would take to sell our ownership to Carreker Antonori. I knew that Carreker Antonori would want to own the software, and I had a bargaining chip in the negotiations.

The bargaining chip was our legal agreement, so *for joint ventures, the legal agreement is critical*, especially when you are sharing the costs and the revenues. It is best to define the legal agreement without the lawyers being present and then have the lawyers make it legal. In this way, the professionals decide what is important and what is unimportant for them. There is only one problem with this approach. Joint ventures always begin on a positive note. So long as everything goes smoothly, there is no issue. When things go wrong or not as planned, that's when a legal agreement is needed, as in the case of Genisys being acquired.

While businessmen focus on the positive aspects of a joint venture, lawyers focus on everything that can possibly go wrong. Together they make a good team, but it is best to bring the lawyers into the negotiations after the positive aspects of the business have been worked out, and then let the lawyers deal with the many "what if" aspects of the venture that can go wrong. If the lawyers bring up all the negatives first, they can kill a deal or complicate the negotiation process, which can stop a good idea in its tracks.

After much discussion with Carreker Antonori, they made an offer to buy all of the rights and interest in Lumen Group. It was a reasonable offer given that we did not have a single sale at the time. I accepted the following offer: $284,000 in cash, no responsibility for income taxes, Lumen will not compete with our benchmarking programs, and Carreker will make its best efforts to involve us in the two outstanding proposals using Lumen.

Once we sold our ownership of Lumen, I did not believe that we would be involved in any contract regarding Lumen, and none occurred. Shortly after the sale of Lumen to Carreker Antonori, Kevin and a couple of other owners of Genisys left Carreker Antonori.

We remained in the check-benchmarking business after Lumen was sold, and we never heard of a Lumen product thereafter. It is possible that the name changed and something came of Lumen, but I was happy to be out of the software business with nearly three hundred thousand dollars. Together with our other revenue, the income produced an excellent consulting year for GCI.

I don't remember where I first met Bob Seltzer, but once I met him, he was an unforgettable man. Bob could sell anything and make you want to buy more. He was the president of Meta Software (Meta), and we immediately connected because he wanted desperately to grow the business he had in the banking world, and the software he had could enhance our consulting business.

Meta had a software package that provided modeling capability to design a simulation of the actual production process in a bank. Bob and I saw the possibility of building a computer model of a bank's check-processing operation with his company's software. This would allow us to simulate the actual check-processing workflow using actual arrival times of checks from branches and elsewhere providing an analysis of the bottlenecks in the process along with an analysis of the proper staffing needs at each function of the process hour by hour during the day and night.

Meta's staff did not have the capability to understand the intricacies of check processing to accurately build a model of the process on their software while our staff did. On the other hand, we did not have the software to build the model ourselves. Together, we were a perfect team to build a simulation model of check processing, and we knew it. We just needed to convince a bank that we had the capability and commitment to make that happen. We needed a name for the simulation model that we would build. I searched around for a name that would be simple to say and would convey what that software did, and we settled on the name *ABLE*.

Both companies had strong relationships with Bank One (now J. P. Morgan Chase), especially the senior management responsible for check processing. After some discussion with the bank, they agreed to let us model one of their check-processing sites, and in October 1999, Bob and I issued two press releases indicating the services we'd be providing to Bank One.

ABLE was a terrific product for GCI and Meta since it generated a large revenue stream for both companies. Often the project to build a simulation model of a check-processing site produced revenue of three hundred thousand dollars or more and added significantly to the bottom line of Global and Meta. Bank One was extremely generous to both companies because they had many check-processing sites, and we eventually modeled almost all of them over a period of years. This proved very valuable to the bank as they improved the efficiency of their check-processing operation far more than they paid us. As a result, these sites were among the best check-processing sites compared to other banks in our benchmarking annual study.

In mid-2000, Meta Software was having financial problems. The company was bigger than my company in terms of staff and revenue, but it wasn't pulling in enough revenue to sustain itself even though the joint venture it had with my company was doing fine. As a result, I discussed with Bob the possibility of merging both companies. Unfortunately, he was a minority shareholder in his company and reported to his board of directors. Bob asked me to put together a memo on what I might be willing to do to merge the companies. I did produce a detailed memo summarizing the essence of what I had in mind.

In the end, the Meta Software board did not want to merge with my company because they would have had to give up their control and accept a much lower evaluation for their company than they expected because of the unprofitability of Meta Software. They believed they could put in additional investment, reduce their expenses, and get Meta back into a profitable company on their own. I had no right to argue with them and gave up the one real chance I had to add a software company to my company, which would have allowed me to do what Carreker Antonori did several years earlier. It would have been a great strategy for both companies. For a merger, all the pieces have to fit, and everyone has to see the merger as a win-win. Meta's board didn't see it that way.

In 1979, the Federal Reserve Bank of Atlanta conducted a study of the number of checks written in the United States that year. The estimate of the annual checks written during that year was 32 billion checks. I had some small input to that study since I was close with the Atlanta Fed staff conducting the study. I had worked at the Atlanta Fed a few years earlier and had a close relationship with the Atlanta Fed's management. In the intervening twenty-two years, no one had a really accurate measurement of check volume, which was then the largest payment system in the United States and in the world. The banking industry had some measures of the growth rate year by year, and this was used to grow the volume, which was estimated to be as high as 68 billion checks. No one really knew, and the entire check processing industry was flying blind based on a twenty-two-year-old 1979 study.

Many people suggested to the Fed that they undertake the study again. Jerry Milano, then in charge of the California Clearing House and a long-standing friend of mine, told me that he had encouraged the Fed to undertake such a study, and he thought my company was best able to accomplish it. I was encouraged, especially when we were invited to submit a proposal to do just that. I knew that we would be up against tough competition from some of the largest consulting firms because this study would take substantial effort and could cost from five hundred thousand dollars to one million dollars or more to complete.

The Fed study was in three parts: estimate the number of checks written in 2001, survey a large random sample of individual checks to determine the various categories of payees that checks were written too, and survey all of the other payment systems to obtain an overall picture of the total US payment system. For the first part, to survey the number of checks written, it was not effective to survey the entire population of over twenty thousand financial institutions that had checking accounts because not everyone would respond to the survey, and we would then have to deal with nonrespondents. We focused on selecting a random sample of banks, savings and loans, and credit unions, and this required a stratified random sample. The key to the study was picking a truly stratified random sample and then gaining support from them all to fill out the survey accurately. The same problem existed for surveying a sample of checks. The selection of a random sample had to be done in such a way that it represented an accurate picture of all the checks paid. The discussion with the Fed in Atlanta and with some of the statisticians at the Federal Reserve Board went on for many sessions until they were satisfied that we could do the job accurately, and we won the first two parts of the project. The third part of the project, to survey credit cards, debit cards, ATM, ACH, and wire transactions was given to Dove Consulting, another small consulting firm.

For many years, I wondered why small companies could compete successfully against much larger and much stronger companies. I thought that the large companies would be able to produce a product more cheaply than small companies, would be able to pay more money to hire the best talent in the business, and would be able to provide better customer service than a small company. Under that theory, the big companies would be able to drive out the small companies, and eventually, there would be no small companies at all. Yet the majority of companies in the United States are still small companies.

The answer is that small companies survive with overwhelming expertise. Most people like working for small companies. They are friendlier, they are more productive, and they are more driven than large companies. Large companies don't make quick decisions; there is a decision-making process that often requires several levels of approval. In a small company, if the CEO wants to do it, and employees can get to the CEO quickly, the decision can be reached in a matter of minutes, and certainly within days. Large companies will take much longer. Small companies, by definition, cannot have a broad set of products and services to offer to a large market. They don't have the people to do that, so they must concentrate on one or a few services they can excel at.

That overwhelming expertise can occur in software, in marketing, in technology, in efficiency and effectiveness, in customer service, or in a variety of other factors that clients know are important. Some small companies do that by assessing the competition and then building a better mousetrap. While that is important, *the best way to gain overwhelming expertise is by working closely with clients*. Understand their needs, define their problems, study their costs, and review how they make a profit, and then creative juices will define new services. These new services will define your expertise, and when you have a proven track record with these new services, you will have achieved overwhelming expertise. It is for all these reasons that *small firms beat large firms competitively with overwhelming expertise*.

To return to the Fed payment system study, we won the major part of the assignment after a very lengthy set of deliberations with the Federal Reserve, and I considered that win to be the biggest and most important win in the firm's history. It turned out to be one of the most important assignments for the entire payment system industry as it changed the outlook on check processing for the industry.

While not the only reason for generating the very positive results for GCI in 2000, ABLE studies had a material impact on our performance for 2000, and the Federal Reserve contract looked like it would guarantee the financial performance for 2001 if we delivered as promised. Given below is the memo I wrote at the end of 2000 to my staff.

December 21, 2000
To: Global Concepts Staff
From: Allen Lipis

The financial performance of Global Concepts in 2000 has exceeded my expectations. I projected that we would reach $3.5 million revenue at the start of the year with strong performances by all our products, but we have actually reached $3.84 million in revenue. Our revenue growth over 1999 is 35%. If we eliminate the extraordinary sale of Lumen in 1999, the revenue growth for this year over last year is 52%. Either way, the firm is firing on all cylinders.

This year has produced remarkable performances and I want to take note of a few of them:

1. Forums: All four existing Forums are at peak levels with high profit margins. Renewals appear to be very strong. The new Payments Forum is off to an excellent start and has a high probability of being successful in its first year. Jenny has an excellent crew doing first class work.

2. Benchmarking: With a stable amount of revenue, the benchmarking staff has managed to produce profitable products by streamlining their approach to these assignments. The Cash Vault benchmark study has increased substantially and should continue to grow next year. The Check benchmarking study is getting high marks as they present their final results, and this will lead to

future consulting assignments, particularly in the Research and Adjustments area.

3. ABLE: Our joint venture with Meta Software continues to produce substantial revenue and profits. We doubled our growth over last year and we could double again next year. Steve, Michael, John and Todd have contributed mightily to this result and they have convinced Meta and us that ABLE is a very profitable product with strong growth opportunities. Ron, our newest employee will focus on ABLE, along with Michael and John, freeing Steve to grow the rest of our consulting practice.

4. Federal Reserve System: We have just landed the largest consulting contract in our history that will not only provide a solid revenue base for 2001, but also will continue to reinforce our reputation as the premier payment system consulting firm in the country. Dave and Tom deserve the credit for doing a first class job proposal writing in the spring for the initial assignment, and then doing the work on that assignment, which established our reputation at the Fed. Finally, the recent proposal that won this huge assignment was a masterful job by them again in persuading the Fed that we would do better than KPMG, PricewaterhouseCoopers, and others.

5. Sales and Marketing: There is a positive correlation between Karl's arrival and revenue growth. It could be that revenue went up because Karl is here or Karl is here because revenue went up. In any case, for Karl it is perfect timing. We don't seem to have problems selling lately and that is a good thing.

The bonus used to be 20% of the profits allocated proportional to actual salaries for the time period of the bonus, excluding Jenny, Michael, Steve and myself. On June 30, Jenny, Steve and Michael sold their shares back to the company, and we increased the bonus pool to 30% of the profits to compensate for the fact that Jenny, Michael and Steve were returning to the bonus pool.

In addition, 1.5% of your annual salary will be put into your 401(k) program this December for those not in the high paid category defined by the government. For this group, Global Concepts will also add an additional 1.5% to meet its legal requirement. This money is totally vested.

You may recall that in July we paid the largest bonuses in the history of the firm, both in amounts and percentages. The bonus percentage then was 30%. For this bonus period, we will top that percentage. The percentage for the last six months (July 2000 through December 2000) is 37%, making year 2000 the most profitable year in our history, and the largest bonuses every paid to employees. We used to tell new employees that bonuses would usually range from 10%-15%, but we have obviously moved the firm to a new, higher level of profitability.

The reason for our success is clear: it is all of you pulling together, and each and every one of you producing first class work. All of you made this happen! We used to think Forums were good at $200,000 in revenue and now they are pushing double that amount. We used to be happy with a $50,000-$75,000 consulting contract and now $100,000 contracts occur often, ABLE contracts exceed $200,000 and the Fed contract will reach about $675,000. We are now operating at a different level than in past years and this is a result of good strategy, a premier reputation and excellent products that provide value for the money.

The year 2001 looks even better than 2000. At this writing we can reasonably forecast $2 million in Forum and Benchmarking revenue, $1 million in ABLE revenue and more than $1 million sold in consulting. We begin 2001 with more revenue than all of 2000! It should be another very exciting year for the company.

> Thank you for a great year. When the going got tough, the tough
> got going. Now the tough can go shopping.

The 2001 Fed Study on the state of the payment system in the United States was remarkable in many ways. First, it was the first scientific study of all the consumer payment systems in the United States. There had been studies of the number of checks written or the number of credit card payments or ATM payments, but no one had completed all of them at the same time. Second, the number of checks had not been studied in detail for more than two decades, and this was a groundbreaking study for the largest payment system in the world. Third, the study had to be as accurate as possible because it had the Federal Reserve's name on it, and their reputation for accuracy could not be questioned.

The key to the Fed study on checks focused on how to achieve a representative sample, and our staff, along with the Federal Reserve staff, focused on this issue for quite some time. It was important to know the total population of financial institution to generate a representative sample to estimate the total number of checks. We also had to deal with nonresponding financial institutions. All this was spelled out in great detail and was published after the study for anyone to review.

For the sample of checks to review, it wasn't possible to get a financial institution to copy the front and back of the checks and send them to us for analysis because the banks wanted to protect the privacy of the individual checks selected. We had to prepare a detailed explanation for every participating bank, explaining how to capture the data off of the checks. We wanted sufficient data to categorize the checks into whether they were used at the point of sale or for bill payment or for other reasons. This was not obvious since a check made out to Sears, for example, could be a check used at the point of sale or to make a credit card payment. These and other issues had to be dealt with in detail.

When the results were tabulated, the number of checks paid in the United States in 2001 was estimated to be just over 42 billion checks. This was a radical result from the number the banking industry was told time and time again—68 billion. This was no small difference, but it indicated that the volume of checks paid per year was one-third less than anyone thought. Check volumes were not increasing as fast as the industry believed, and indeed, there might be evidence that the number of checks paid in the United States had peaked and was on its way down.

There were a few people that questioned the results of the study and said so in print and from conference podiums, but no one of importance questioned the study. After all, the study had the backing of the Federal Reserve, and in a short period of time, the study was considered to be definitive. Senior management in the major banks then took an entirely different view of check processing. Checks were still a major revenue stream for the banks but no longer thought to be supported with new technology, with one exception. That exception was image technology, for image technology was firmly established as the direction for check processing. In all other aspects, the major banks concluded that the volume of checks was and would decline over time, that revenue would decline, that staff would have to be cut, that some check-processing sites would be closed, and that the industry would have to ramp down the volume instead of increasing it.

In every respect, this study was the most important study that I ever did in my banking career because it had such a dramatic impact on the entire payment system business. While I thought the first study I did in 1971 that began my career in payment systems also had a great impact on the industry because it helped to launch the world of electronic banking, that study was only useful in educating the industry about the future of payment systems. The 2001 Fed study, on the other hand, had immediate implications for thousands of people working in the industry as well as billions of investment dollars that had to be spent wisely on payment systems in the immediate future.

The Federal Reserve was impacted as well because it was a major check-processing organization with check-processing sites in most of the forty plus Federal Reserve locations around the country. In addition to the reduction in check volume, the use of image technology would give depository banks the ability to transmit the image of the check through electronic exchange to the paying banks without moving paper checks. While the Federal Reserve could be the electronic exchange, and it did enter that business, other banking organizations could easily compete with the Fed when it came to electronic interchange of images. As a result, the Federal Reserve developed its own strategy to close its check processing sites since geography was not important for image exchange. The Fed eventually narrowed its check-processing sites down to four and expected to end up with one site as paper checks converted to images for exchange grew substantially. That is only one example of the impact the study had on the industry. The major banks in check processing implemented similar strategies.

To continue to monitor the US payment system, the Federal Reserve committed itself to complete similar studies every three years. As a result, my company was rehired to complete a similar study in 2004, in 2007, and in 2010. Dove Consulting continued to conduct the study of noncheck-processing payments in 2004 and 2007, but after they were sold to a Japanese company, the Federal Reserve gave the entire study to us in 2010. In 2010, the number of checks paid in the United States was down to 24 billion, a 43 percent drop in volume over nine years. However, 24 billion checks was still a sizeable number, almost five times the volume of UK checks that were handled at the peak of its check volumes.

Throughout the first decade of the twenty-first century, our Check Forum continued in place because there was still a tremendous volume to process. On the other hand, the UK volume of checks was declining so substantially that the UK Cheque Forum was no longer necessary, and the industry was pushing the UK government to eliminate the check as a payment instrument.

In the late 1990s, I had the wonderful chance to honor the check with my "Check is King" speech. I believed at that time that is was important to give that speech because checks had had such an important impact on my professional life as well as my company's. I had treated the check not just as a payment mechanism but also as a patriarch to be respected and to be honored. After all, it had given me a wonderful career, it had made me a lot of money, and it had supported the revenue for many of the major banks in the country. I gave the speech at the right time when the check was at its peak and deserved the accolade. Now it was a dying payment system, and eventually, it might disappear. I had come to love and appreciate the check-processing business. I was happy to have the chance to honor it.

I have one final thought about check volumes. On several occasions, the Financial Stationers Association asked me to speak to them about check volumes. This association, initially called the Bank Stationers Association, is composed of the companies that print the checks for the banks and others. These check printers print virtually all of the personal checks but do not print large-company checks. Nevertheless, they had a very good idea of the number of checks that were printed, but that number was somewhat different from the number of checks written, for many printed checks are never written because of closed accounts and other reasons. Still, they had their own estimate of the number of checks written and paid, and it was close to the Federal Reserve survey. However, when everyone else in the industry was thinking 68 billion checks, they knew differently, but it wasn't in their interests to question the number and suggest a much, much lower number. After all, their business was to support check processing with check printing, and they did not want to suggest that check volumes were much lower. Every time I told them the high number of checks written throughout the '70s, '80s, and '90s, they never gave me a clue that they knew differently. Sometimes, it is best to keep your mouth shut if it will hurt you to open it.

I would be remiss if I did not discuss the problems presented by a commitment I made to a telephone communication system offered by NorVergence. The story began in January 2004 when a NorVergence salesman made an appointment at our company to explain their telecommunications service. The salesman proposed a substantial savings in our telephone bill. We provided several months of our telephone bill. He analyzed them and then offered us a new service that would save $904.26 per month for a period of five years, over $54,000. Their proposal provided unlimited domestic calls, an unlimited conference calling service, and reduced international rates. Based on those savings, the paperwork was signed for the telecommunication service.

In February, a representative from NorVergence arrived with two Matrix 2003 units and mounted them on our wall in our communications room, but they were never connected to anything. The units remained on the wall for months without being connected. We had accepted delivery of the units but had no idea what was inside them, whether they worked or whether they could deliver any telecommunication service, let alone the services contracted for at the price agreed upon in the lease.

An installation by NorVergence for service was given for June 15 and then pushed back to June 30. The installation never occurred. Thereafter, NorVergence filed for bankruptcy under Chapter 11. When

I signed the lease, I did not read the fine print and relied on my financial officer to determine what details I needed to know. Neither of us knew that as part of the lease NorVergence had the right to sell the lease to another company, and it did. The lease for one of the two Matrix boxes was sold to the US Bancorp Business Equipment Finance Group, and in turn, US Bancorp assigned the lease to Lyon Financial, one of their subsidiaries. The lease on the second Matrix box was sold to Bank Branch & Trust (BB&T).

We had no idea that the leases had been sold to the banks or that we had an obligation to continue to pay on a lease for a Matrix box regardless of whether the telecommunication service worked or not, or whether the Matrix box functioned at all. We were willing to write off our three months of payments because NorVergence was in bankruptcy.

Lyon Financial sued us in November 2004 for the entire amount of the five-year, sixty monthly payments on the lease, which amounted to over fifty thousand dollars. BB&T wrote off the loss and decided not to sue.

Because of this lawsuit, if I am required to sign my name to a legal contract, I read the fine print. NorVergence was a Ponzi scheme, and I might have signed the agreement after I read the contract, but at least I would have had a chance to stop the mistake by reading the agreement. *Read the contract carefully, no matter how long it takes. When in doubt, have counsel review it.* Take nothing for granted when it comes to legal agreements.

I contacted a local Atlanta attorney to try to resolve the lease, but she made no progress whatsoever. Our cost was about two thousand dollars for the attorney's time. The lack of progress was because US Bank was determining its strategy regarding the hundreds if not thousands of leases it had scattered around the United States. In November, we were sued by Lyon Financial representing US Bank in Marshall, Minnesota for the entire remaining amount of the NorVergence lease, $50,037.98 plus interest at 8 percent per year and legal expenses. Working in Atlanta, I had to find a law firm in Minnesota to represent my company. After a couple of months of negotiations, Lyon Financial and GCI agreed on an out-of-court settlement to dismiss the lawsuit with prejudice. Instead of paying 15 percent of the outstanding amount, which was recommended by various attorneys general, I negotiated a 10 percent payment that amounted to $5,700. My attorney's cost was just under five hundred dollars, so the rest of the retainer was applied to the payment to Lyon Financial. The total cost to get out of the lawsuit was about $8,200. I didn't want to pay a penny to Lyon Financial, but the legal costs to continue the lawsuit would have exceeded the settlement cost. I put practicality over principle.

There are three other events that are worth mentioning to sum up my review of those wonderful consulting years. The first is that MasterCard hired us to write an authoritative report (white paper) about the impact that the Internet was having on the retail industry. Tom Murphy and Steve Ledford worked on this study by surveying a series of merchants regarding their views about selling over the Internet. MasterCard liked the report so much that they published it in one of the major retail magazines. The magazine decided to make it their cover story and spent considerable effort to prepare a series of multicolored exhibits to highlight the various charts that were in the report. MasterCard was doubly impressed with the result and submitted it to the advertising industry's CLIO Award, the main award for outstanding advertising. The report in the magazine made it to the finals in New York, where it won honorable mention. It showed the industry the quality of our work, and the award hangs on the wall at GCI today.

Another important event was created and implemented by Dave. He had moved to Chicago to support his wife's job at the University of Chicago, and he naturally gravitated to conducting a good deal of the research for the company since he could do that work extremely well. His idea was to conduct a series of independent research reports annually and charge for them as a group. Each year, we put together a list of payment system subjects and settled on six of them to be packaged for sale. We priced the reports so that an organization could buy three, four, or all six. Dave managed all the reports and assigned a report to an individual staff member. After a review by Dave and others, the reports were issued throughout the year. These reports became a wonderful source of new revenue for the firm and kept the firm current on a variety of payment system issues. It also led to individual consulting efforts on specific topics related to these reports.

The third and final event that we accomplished in 2003 was to win a contract with the New York Clearing House to help implement an image exchange system for them. The New York Clearing House was originally composed of only the major New York City banks, but as the law changed to allow banks to merge across state lines, it became obvious that the strategy for the New York Clearing House to remain influential in payment systems was to expand its membership to other major banks around the country, which it did. The New York Clearing House had a sizeable staff, unlike other bank clearing houses. It also had significant computer capacity to run the ACH for the Federal Reserve Bank of New York. Since Steve had worked closely with APACS in London on the development of their interbank data exchange system, he was a natural choice to work on the selection of a vendor for the check image exchange at the New York Clearing House. When the system was completed, Steve had made a major contribution to that development, and our small firm could take pride in having been a part of that significant implementation. Today, that system is the major image exchange system in the United States.

I took great pride in the accomplishments of GCI from 1989 until I sold it in 2004. The financial results over those fifteen years speak to the growth of the firm, its innovative products, and its profitability. I was in business to make a profit and to eventually sell the firm and retire. It was a terrific ride for my staff and me because not only did I do well but also my staff grew in expertise and either left my company for greener fields or stayed on continuing to be amply rewarded.

In 1989, Steve White and I took no salary but, rather, paid back our investments and loans made to the company. This reduced our taxes while giving us the income remaining after all costs were paid. I made about the same amount of money that I made at BEI, which convinced me that consulting in my own business would eventually pay off handsomely.

In 1990, we made a decent profit, about a hundred thousand dollars. That was in addition to the normal salaries that we took, which were just over a hundred thousand dollars. We paid that out as a bonus, so that the company's profit was negligible. In early 1991, Steve decided to leave, and he knew that I did not have sufficient money to pay him off. However, we were renewing the two check forums and a lot of money arrived at the year-end of 1990 and early 1991, so that the firm had lots of cash early on in 1991. That allowed me to pay Steve the $125,000 he requested to sell me his 50 percent of the company without me having to borrow any money or write a check on my own limited resources. This was a huge benefit that flowed from forums—receiving the fees up front early in the year. It allowed me to buy out Steve easily though I knew that I would struggle near the end of the year unless we had a substantial profit. As it turned out, the first half of 1991 was strong, and the rest of the year was weak and showed the lack of revenue resulting from Steve's leaving GCI. It was the only year that GCI had a substantial reduction in revenue compared to the previous year. The loss that year reflected half of the cost to buy out Steve.

The year 1992 was a real struggle. We did not increase staff and worked back up to the revenue of 1990, making just enough profit to match the cost of paying off Steve for selling his ownership of the firm. The profit was based on a reduced salary level for the staff for much of the year, and the salary reduction was eliminated in 1993. The increase in salaries in 1993 over 1992 allowed the firm to grow its revenue but again provided no profit for the firm. By the end of 1993, the firm was able to pay me a decent salary as well as the staff but had not produced a decent profit.

For the next two years, the company went over one million dollars in revenue and began to make a reasonable profit. Even though we added people to strengthen our staff, the productivity of our staff substantially grew to well over a hundred thousand dollars per person. That made the difference in generating the beginning of real profitability for my company. All of that was done while increasing salaries and bonuses, as well as offering stock to select senior staff.

In 1996 and 1997, there was an explosion of new product offerings in benchmarking, forums, and consulting, which grew revenue substantially. Even with the addition of staff, revenue grew to over one hundred fifty thousand dollars per person. Believing that our growth would continue unabated, we added four staff in 1998, but the revenue did not materialize as we had planned. Still, I maintained control of our costs so that even with the reduction in revenue per person, we still produced a substantial profit.

Nineteen ninety-nine to 2001 were the glorious years for me. In that period, we won the largest contract in the firm's history, almost a million-dollar contract with the Federal Reserve, very strong forum revenues from four to five very active forums, revenue from our joint effort with Meta Software and benchmarking programs. The growth rates were powerful with little addition to our staff, and together, these three years produced substantial profits. These years were also the high-water marks for the check because until the Fed released its study of the number of checks written in the United States, substantial investments were being made by the major banks in check processing, and our firm was one of the major firms benefitting from consulting on a variety of issues related to check processing.

The growth could not continue in 2002 because we could not replace the loss of the large Fed contract in 2001. Nevertheless, with over $3.7 million in revenue, the firm still produced a substantial profit. In 2003-2004, the company once again took off in terms of revenue growth partly because the Fed once again hired us to conduct its nationwide study of the US payment system and partly because we had acquired a substantial reputation in payment systems and continued to be asked by the major banking organizations to work with them on the implementation of the latest systems affecting the payment industry.

In thinking about our success, the most difficult and the most exciting part of the consulting business is the need for continuous creativity in offering new products and services to the marketplace. The reason is quite simple. Clients hire consultants to solve a problem, usually a problem they have not faced before. Once the problem is solved, the consultants are thanked, paid well, and asked to leave. There is no sense in continuing to pay consultants the high prices they charge if there is no problem or issue to solve. Therefore, *consulting firms require continuous creativity of new services.*

As a result, it is necessary for consultants to know what the new problems are that their clients face. Clients often identify the problems they have, and consultants are asked to help solve them. Sometimes the consultants can propose to solve a problem they know their clients have or will have shortly. We were successful because we continuously created new products and services that our clients saw the need to buy. We focused on new forums, on new benchmarking studies, on regulatory changes, on market research, and on developing and implementing new technology systems for one client or a group of them in an association. As you read through this chapter, you will see a continuous stream of new services being created for an industry generally receptive to what we had to offer.

Creativity for new services comes from staying in touch with clients. Clients know what is working and what is not, and if they trust you, they will tell you where they have problems and often allow you a chance to propose to solve them. Sometimes new technology and new legislation and regulation make it obvious to a consultant what the new problem is that a client will face, but often, the client will know long before anyone else. The answer is to *stay close to your clients*: call them often, take them out for lunch or dinner, and meet them at conferences. There is no substitute for building close relationships with them. It is the secret to staying creative and building new services.

Staying close to the market is not something that the CEO or the head of marketing should do alone. It is what everyone in the company should do, all of the staff who deal with clients. In a small company, new product ideas should be everyone's concerns, and senior management has to be open to accept ideas for new products wherever they come from. At my company, I tried to put that culture in place. Virtually all of the staff was in touch with clients, and I tried to implement new ideas generated by my staff whenever they had them if they looked promising.

The other thing I learned was that *large contracts are far more profitable than smaller ones*. It should be obvious that large contracts are more profitable than small contracts because there is more money to play with. As a small consulting firm, I was used to completing ten-thousand-dollar contracts, twenty-five-thousand-dollar contracts, and even fifty-thousand-dollar contracts. Large contracts above a hundred thousand dollars or more were out of my range in the early years of my consulting career because my clients did not think a small firm like mine could do as good a job as a large firm. It took overwhelming expertise to convince them otherwise.

Once I won a few six-figure contracts, I recognized that my staff could do the work more efficiently than I thought, and we could put more junior staff on the job with senior staff and still do an outstanding job. With small jobs, the client knew approximately what it would take to get the job done. For much larger contracts, it was more difficult for the clients to know the full extent of the work, and therefore, proposals had a cushion of money added to be sure we would make a decent profit. When we did the work efficiently, we not only made money by using junior staff on the assignment but we also had the added bonus of cushion money. It made all the difference to win one or two big contracts a year to make my business quite profitable.

In looking back on the banking industry, *one study or one event can change an industry or a company*. When we completed the first survey in twenty-two years of the number of checks written in the United States, the entire industry was totally surprised at the low number, and it changed the direction of the industry. It was clear that check volumes had peaked and were heading down. When a study by the Federal Reserve pointed out that check fraud was on the rise, the industry focused on solutions and came up with them even though there was no way to completely eliminate fraud. When the Internet could be made secure for banking at home, electronic bill payment over the Internet took off. When banks were allowed to issue both Visa and MasterCard, Citibank, who had only been a MasterCard bank, promoted their Visa card to the entire country and picked up millions of new Visa cardholders to become the largest credit card bank in the country.

These one-time big events occur more often than you think. In coming out of a recession when the stock market has been beaten up badly, it is inevitable that good company stocks will recover strongly. On many occasions, the world is not as complex as it looks. One event overshadows all others, and the direction of the industry or a company is clear from that one event. It is not always obvious, but the more you know about a subject, the more obvious the direction will be.

Finally, it is worth noting that the success I had was a direct result of the productivity of my staff. People are creative, people will perform with incentives, and people will rise to the occasion by being challenged. Charles Kettering, the legendary inventor and manager at General Motors in its early days, visited an automotive plant and saw that production was not as strong as he wanted it to be. When the day shift ended, he wrote a huge six with chalk at the entrance to the factory to indicate that six cars were produced. At the end of the night's shift, the six was crossed out, and a seven was written instead to indicate that the night shift could do one more car than the day shift. In a famous study of AT&T operators at the Hawthorne Works, no one knew why productivity was going up although the theory was that it resulted from improved lighting. It turned out that productivity went up because management showed an interest in their workers. If the lighting was improved, if the factory was cleaner, if the workers could eat on the job, and if the day was shortened by thirty minutes, all of these items increased productivity.

I saw productivity in my own staff. Under the pressure of a deadline, productivity improved. When we were very busy and supposedly understaffed, productivity improved. When bonuses depended on the profitability of the company, productivity improved. In check processing, we encouraged banks to offer bonuses for the production process of putting the dollar amount on checks. Up to 15 percent in bonus money for hitting certain milestones improved productivity. People can and will work harder than normal and often can sustain improved productivity for long periods of time with the right incentives.

With all of my success, in 2003, I was then sixty-five years old, and I had been involved in payment systems for thirty-seven years. I had made enough money to retire, and I thought seriously about retiring. I began to look seriously at selling my firm.

Chapter 16

Selling Global Concepts, Inc.

Why did I sell my company? The honest answer is that I did not want to sell my company. I loved what I was doing. Payment system consulting was a love affair of mine. I had the educational training, the passion for the business, the intellectual ability to deal with complex issues, and a wonderful staff that complemented my weaknesses. In addition, I was making serious money, more money than I ever thought I would make, and it was wonderful seeing all that money materialize. There seemed to be no real reason to sell, except for several thoughts. I was heading toward the normal age for retirement, I had no one in my family to take over the business successfully, and I wanted to do other important things with the rest of my life. The business was running at an all-time high, and if I ever thought I could get a good price for the business, it was now.

I reviewed the decision about selling my company many times over many years. In the first two years, Steve White and I were building the business. After Steve left, I had several tough years to recover our growth and shift the business into becoming the preeminent check processing consulting firm that it became. In the late 1990s, as I began to make serious profits, I started thinking about whether to sell or not, but I was still young, I wanted to grow the company a lot more, we were continuing to create new products, and the company was on top of its game, winning a lot of work. It was only after five good years of growth and profits, from 1998 through 2002, that I began to realize that I was accumulating enough money to retire comfortably, that the business would be of interest to a number of companies, and I was no longer enjoying being CEO as much as I had enjoyed it in the past. It was for these reasons that I decided to sell my company.

I thought on many occasions that someone in my family could take over the business, but nothing ever seriously materialized. Consulting is based on the skill and talent of the people who work there. We weren't selling widgets; the product was the people, and payment system expertise was not acquired easily. As a member of TEC, a group of CEOs that met monthly with a consultant to discuss our business issues, the other CEOs made it clear that it would be a mistake to bring family into the business. Their position was that if family members needed money, it was better to give them the money than to hire them into the business. They were opposed to taking family members into the business because it was a bad business practice. I thought I might be able to do it and tried on several occasions, but it never really worked. These CEOs were right, and I should have listened to them.

I dismissed considering my daughters for the business as both were married and raising families, and neither had the talent or the interest in taking on the business. My son was living in Europe, too far away from Atlanta to run the company even though he had the talent to do it. And certainly my wife wasn't interested as she was a science teacher and looked forward to retiring herself. I also had serious discussions with George, my son-in-law, who lived in Atlanta and who was somewhat interested in joining the company, but he and I realized that he would have to spend several years to become a senior consultant in payment systems while convincing a hostile staff that a family member could hold his own and then gain their support as CEO. It would be an uphill fight, and while George was a very talented consultant, he and I didn't think the fight was worth it. My family thought that it would be better to sell the company and use the proceeds from the sale of my firm to support the growth of the family's assets away from my business. That is what I did even though I would have preferred to hand the business over to one of my family. It wasn't to be.

I also considered retiring, keeping the ownership of my company, and reviewing the progress monthly. In 2001, I had appointed Steve Ledford as president of the firm to manage the day-to-day operations of the company. Steve was the obvious choice to run the company, and he was smart enough in payment systems to do it. However, I knew he didn't like the forums business as much as I did, and he preferred consulting. This was fine as a senior staff member, but I had doubts about his ability to manage products he did not personally like. I wasn't sure if he would be as focused on making the sizeable profits I was making. The company had created one new product after another, and I wasn't sure whether Steve was naturally focused on doing that, which was the fundamental reason why my company had become the success that it had become. Steve was just too risky for me to let alone without my daily involvement.

I also considered Dave as a possible CEO before I picked Steve to be president. Dave had all the credentials to do the job. He was talented, very creative, clearly a leader, but he lived in Chicago, apart from the rest of the company. I could not see how he could manage the business remotely. Had Dave remained in Atlanta, he might have been my first choice to be president, and I might have let him run the company after I retired, but that wasn't the case. I wasn't willing to risk letting a remote person run the company even if he had all the credentials. My son had similar credentials to Dave, and I couldn't see letting him run the company from Berlin, Germany, although I am sure that Dave would have been more warmly received. In the end, there was no one that I had faith in to run my company without me. The risks were too high, and the alternative of selling the company was much safer and potentially more profitable in the short term and the long term.

There was one final concern that I had about staying around as CEO. I had focused on check processing as the main consulting area in payment systems for my company. Throughout the 1990s, check processing was a huge business, the biggest payment system in the world in terms of transactions, and there was a significant need for the services that our company provided. In 2001 our own study for the Federal Reserve indicated that the number of checks written and paid had peaked, and the volume of checks would decline over time. That study changed the perception of check processing at the major banks, and it was unlikely that these banks would continue to invest in check processing to the same degree that they had in the past. The decline in check volume would probably be slow, and there would still be plenty of consulting work for a business in decline. It might take a decade or more to cut the transaction level in half, which would still be a major payment system. Still, it was worrisome, and it might be better to sell the company when the volume of checks was at or near its peak than to do it after the volume of checks had a significant drop. We were hired by the Federal Reserve to conduct the same study of the number of checks written and paid in 2004, and I suspected that we would find a significant drop. It was not a major concern about selling, but it kept nagging at me to move forward to sell the firm.

There was still another possibility that I evaluated, and that was an ESOP, an employee stock option program. The concept was based on gradually selling the company to the employees through a trust that would buy the stock of the company over time. Initially, the trust would decide how to allocate its ownership of the company to the various employees, and there were several alternative ways that it could be done, but I wouldn't care.

The value of the company would be appraised professionally, and the trust would buy, for example, one-third of the stock by borrowing money from a bank. The bank would lend the money based on the value of the company and its operating performance. As the company made a profit, one-third of the profits would go to the trust, and the trust would use that money to pay off the bank loan. Once the first bank loan was paid off, the trust would buy more of the company using the same procedure, and eventually the trust would own the entire company bought from the ongoing profits of the company. The company would then be 100 percent owned by the employees.

There was one fundamental problem with this approach. I was too late because it might take five years for the trust to acquire one-third of the ownership. Even though there were tax advantages to doing this, it might take fifteen years to get totally out of the business using an ESOP, and I didn't want to wait even five years. In conversations with my senior staff, none of them was willing to put their own money up to buy a serious percentage of the business. Selling the business to my employees was not a real possibility.

To maximize the value of my company, I knew I had to have a good story. My business was growing at between 15 and 20 percent per year in revenue and profits and that was a great story. We had conducted the largest contract in our history with the Federal Reserve in 2001, and they were so pleased that they renewed the contract for implementation in 2004. That contract guaranteed that 2004 would produce great financials for any company that might consider buying us. In addition, about 50 to 60 percent of our revenue for 2004 was recurring. The year 2004 was going to be strong in terms of revenue and profits. We had no legal issues that would raise concerns for the buyer and no short—or long-term loans.

Over the years, I had left much of the profits in the company, investing them conservatively in the stock market. I had made a mistake at my first company of taking most of the profits out during its first few years, and that left no cushion for a shortfall in revenue. Most companies fail for lack of cash, and I wasn't going to be put in that position again. By keeping the profits in the company, I avoided having to borrow money and grew the company organically. It also allowed me to sleep well, knowing that the company could sustain a downturn for a year or more. With strong revenue growth, no major liabilities, and strong retained earnings, we had a strong balance sheet.

Most important of all, we had a culture of excellence. I was willing to support the recommendations of my staff in telling our clients not what they wanted to hear but what we thought was best for them, even if it hurt. We had become the most knowledgeable consulting firm in check processing by virtue of the Check Forum meetings that we ran in the United States and the UK, through the check processing benchmarking studies that measured the cost to process checks bank by bank, and the nationwide Federal Reserve study of the number and type of checks written and paid. In anticipation of selling the company, I had selected my replacement a couple of years earlier, and I had put a handful of senior consultants in key parts of our revenue stream so that the company would have the strength it needed to continue to grow. My staff was impressive for our clients, and they would be impressive for anyone looking to buy us. I believed I had put all the right pieces together to make my company as attractive as possible.

I *established criteria for selling my company and rated offers according to them.* I offer the following to you as you go through the process of developing your own strategy to sell your business. In evaluating the buyer of your company, consider the following:

- Compatible Missions: Have a strategic fit to enhance your company's ability to help both the buyer's company and your company to grow your businesses. The better the strategic fit, the higher the price for your company.

- Growth of Both Companies: Both companies have the potential to bring more business to each other.
- Culture Compatibility: This means that the two companies had similar philosophies about business. One might have an entrepreneurial culture—that was mine—while the other might have a culture that is more intense and supports an "up or out" process for its professional staff. Common values for the culture are key, and that means compatibility on creativity, integrity, intellectual knowledge, and expertise.
- Good Price: A lot goes into the overall price for the company: the payout period, whether cash or stock, and whether the stock is public or private. I wanted an all-cash deal.
- Organizational Structure: This means that your company stays as a separate entity or is merged into the buyer's company, and it defines the role you play in the new organization. I wanted to retire.
- Fringe Benefits: The package can include salary growth, profit sharing, and other financial sweeteners.
- Known Acquirer: A big name increases the potential of the deal.

Before I committed to sell my company, I had paid for a professional assessment of it, and the appraising firm suggested that the company was worth from .8 to 1.2 times the revenue of the firm or from 5 to 7 times the profits of the company.

Feeling self-assured that a decent offer was likely for selling my company, I discussed my desire to sell my company with my family. It just so happened that the family meeting was also a board meeting since I had put my wise wife, our children, and their spouses on my board because I trusted their judgment and many of them had worked for the company. They all agreed that this was an appropriate time to sell the firm, but the decision was mine.

I held off telling the entire staff about planning for the sale of the company so that business would continue as usual. Once prospective buyers show interest, it is necessary to tell the staff what you intend to do because buyers generally want to meet with the entire staff first and then meet with senior staff individually. The buyer has two main reasons to meet with the staff: talk about their company and talk about the role that the staff will play going forward. While both are important, the least threatening strategy is to suggest to the staff that their company will remain an independent entity. It generates the least amount of concern. Understandably, the buyer wants to retain staff and minimize their concern about the deal. If the staff focuses on the buyer's company, then it inevitably raises lots of concerns about whether the staff likes what the company does, how they will fit in, and whether they will have a new boss. These issues are best left out of consideration until the acquisition is completed or for as long as possible. But I had to tell a few of the senior staff, especially the lady who handled all of the financials of the company.

With those issues settled, I focused on finding a professional advisor that had strong experience in mergers and acquisitions. While I could have tried to sell my company by myself, I thought that I did not have the expertise to do it alone and that there were professionals who had done this before and could protect me from making a bad mistake. This was going to be the biggest financial decision of my life, and I wanted the best advice I could find to get the best deal possible. I knew the value of hiring a consultant; that was my business. I had to take my own advice and hire my own consultant.

Since I had no experience with mergers and acquisitions, I had to start from scratch in picking my advisor. I asked many people for recommendations. I received a few names from my CPA firm, law firm, and family and friends. I did Web research and looked in the newspaper. In the end, I came up with six names.

I met with the six and eliminated three easily. For the remaining three, I prepared a request for proposal (RFP) similar to the RFPs that I normally received from my clients prior to hiring my firm. I had seen so many RFPs in my work that it was a normal activity for a new assignment. I followed a formal process I was quite familiar with because I believed, like my clients, that it was necessary to be formal about the process if I expected to get the best firm from among the three candidates. After the presentations, it was obvious that Roger Orloff was my first and only choice. Roger had a vast experience in selling small companies, was easy to work with, and was a brilliant strategist. He was to work with Powell Goldstein, my law firm that happened to have a masterful negotiator named Lou Spelios.

I can say unequivocally that, *when it's the biggest financial deal of your life, find the best professionals you can find.* Don't try to cut corners by doing the sale yourself or by using relatives. My family knew better than that—and that's why they were on my board. The sale of your company is too important, and there are too many legal and accounting traps to deal with. Get professional help.

I made the decision to sell my company March 2003, and it took six months to discuss what to do and select Roger. Once Roger joined my team, he and I discussed what I could do to increase the value of my company. The focus was always on increasing revenue, increasing profits, and setting in place the proper organization. These are the three key factors in setting the sales price for a firm.

The biggest issue up front was creating the business memorandum, and that fell mostly on me. Several months and eighty pages later, with me writing the original draft and Roger cleaning up the language, the document answered most of the questions that any buyer might ask.

Next, I focused on the companies that might be interested in buying Global Concepts. Key staff and I created a huge list of companies with key contacts because we were connected with most of them one way or another. Roger did his homework too; our combined list contained more than a hundred companies.

Ultimately, companies that were interested wanted to negotiate directly with me since I was the decision maker. As a result, Roger became my advisor on the key negotiations when I had to be present; other times, he took over as much as possible. Nonetheless, Roger was essential to the final price that I got as well as all the other issues that arose. He created the outline of the memorandum and took my initial writing and turned it into a finished product. He forced me to decide which companies to approach in a first wave, a second wave, and a third wave. He was at my side on all the key negotiation decisions and served as an excellent advisor on price, data presentation, staff issues, timing, and legal issues.

After we had constructed our huge list of companies and contacts, we prepared a one-page letter that Roger sent to the judiciously selected group in the first half of the first wave of companies, about fifteen of them. We agreed that we had a very specialized company that would appeal to companies in the payment system business such as banks, consulting firms, and software companies.

In picking out the companies from our huge list, we looked at companies that had synergy with us, that knew us by having worked for them as subcontractors, worked with them as consultants on a joint effort, or competed against them. In a couple of cases, we selected joint venture partners who knew us intimately. For a few companies, I eliminated them because I didn't think we wanted to be a part of that organization. I just didn't like the culture of the company. We also tried to determine if the company had the money to buy us. If a consulting firm or a competitor were interested in buying GCI, then we would be perceived as a horizontal fit, enlarging their expertise. If it were a software firm, then we would be perceived as a vertical fit, expanding their product line to tie software with consulting. In either case, I believed that we would be a good fit. With the fifteen companies for the first mailing of the first wave, Roger followed up with each of them individually.

The generic letter that we sent explained that I was the owner of Global Concepts, and I was looking to sell my company. We explained that Global Concepts was a first-rate consulting firm in the payment system business, and if they were interested in pursuing the possibility of buying Global Concepts, then we had an eighty-page memorandum that explained the company in detail. To receive the memorandum, they merely had to call or email their interest to Roger, sign a nondisclosure agreement, and the memorandum would be sent to them.

Once I decided to go public in announcing that I wanted to sell my company, it was nerve racking waiting to hear if any of our first round of potential buyers was interested in pursuing the purchase of my company. A lot of companies, of course, were not interested in pursuing GCI. The responses ranged from not being a strategic fit, to GCI losing neutrality, to not enough recurring revenue, to GCI being too small, to their company not making acquisitions, and to simply not having the money to do it. Responses like that were discouraging, but I kept telling myself that I only needed one good company to show serious interest.

I did not initially consider how our clients would react to the company that purchased us, but it became clear quickly that prospects considered this issue seriously. Maintenance of our neutrality became an important issue. If we sold the company to a bank, that could undermine our sense of independence with other banks. The same might be true if a software company owned us, but I thought less so. One company that was very serious initially called several of our clients to see their reaction, and these clients reacted quite negatively to them acquiring my company, for the buyer was mainly in the software business, and my clients believed that our neutrality would be jeopardized if they acquired us. That convinced me that the best group of interested companies would be other consulting firms involved in payment systems.

Of course, for me, the price to sell my company was important, but I thought that I would get a fair price once the buyer was interested. I knew that consulting companies do vary somewhat in how they are evaluated, and my company would hold up very well because of its strong growth rate and excellent profit margins. I also had a minimum price; I knew what an acceptable price was going into the sales process; that made me feel comfortable about selling.

Finally, the attitude my staff had toward the company wishing to acquire us grew in importance. The buyer would depend totally on the quality of my staff, and my staff would stay at the company only if they respected the buyer. As it turned out, this became a key issue.

Until I became seriously involved in selling my company, I had concluded (in a logic-driven process) that the following had to occur to complete the deal:

- Prepare a detailed memorandum to explain the company.
- Gain buyer interest.
- Have the buyer make an onsite visit to explore critical issues.
- Provide financials.
- Have the buyer meet with senior staff.
- Visit the buyer's company to meet their staff.
- Receive an offer.
- Negotiate the terms of the letter of intent.
- Allow the buyer to perform due diligence.
- Draft the contract.
- Allow lawyers for both sides to rewrite the contract to their satisfaction.
- At closing, sign the legal documents and exchange funds.
- Wait for final settlement to occur for the funds held after closing.
- Integrate the company into the buyer's company.

As the process unfolded, it became obvious who the final few companies were that should sit across the table from me in negotiations and why the simple bullets above weren't so simple.

There were four serious offers:

1. US Data Works (UDW)—a software company in payment systems
2. International Data Corporation (IDC)—a large research company that served the banking industry
3. Edgar Dunn—a consulting firm in payment systems
4. McKinsey & Company—a worldwide consulting firm across the economic spectrum

Each of them had different reasons for wanting to own my company, so it is useful to understand each of their motives and the way in which they approached the acquisition of Global Concepts.

Surprisingly, the first offer came from a company I had never heard of, US Data Works. The offer was virtually all cash and a small amount in UDW common stock. In addition, my salary would go up substantially. The surviving name of the merged companies would be Global Concepts. Coming after so many rejections from other companies, it was a stunning offer.

In my judgment, the CEO of UDW was looking for me to run the merged companies. My company was a perfect fit for UDW. We knew the business, we had an outstanding reputation, and UDW's CEO thought that I could take over the software products of UDW and integrate them into our consulting practice. From his perspective, GCI could do a great deal for UDW, and he was willing to pay handsomely to merge with GCI. In addition, since UDW was a publicly traded company on the American Stock Exchange, the value of GCI's earnings would be valuable to UDW's stock.

I quickly discovered that US Data Works was losing money. The company had a software business offering products that were competitive with banks and banking associations. US Data Works was going to have an uphill battle to grow their company, and perhaps they perceived my company as a possible savior for them. UDW didn't have the cash to match the offer they made to buy my company, but the CEO was confident that he could raise the money.

In reviewing the possibility of merging into UDW, I considered the benefits that my company could bring to the merger:

1. Global Concepts would double UDW's revenue and double their earnings per share.
2. Any restatement of UDW's financials incorporating Global Concepts' would significantly improve UDW's financial performance.
3. There was upside potential for the UDW stock, and a small increase would cover the total cost to acquire Global Concepts.
4. Global Concepts had the capability to improve UDW's existing products to remain the best of breed. We could generate add-ons to the existing products and develop new products for UDW.
5. Global Concepts had two hundred payment system clients, invaluable for UDW.

While the benefits were clear, there were major issues to deal with.

1. UDW didn't have the money to make the merger happen. The continuing lack of earnings, the short amount of cash on their balance sheet, the shortfall in revenue, and the prospect that this could continue for some time were serious concerns. I wanted a letter from a third party to assure me that UDW had the funds to consummate the transaction.
2. Global Concepts would lose its neutrality by becoming a software company. Our consulting services might be significantly affected after the acquisition.
3. After a presentation by UDW to my staff, my staff concluded that UDW's products were not likely to succeed because UDW would be up against strong competition. The staff did not believe the company had a long term future. The most important questions asked of UDW were not dealt with adequately, still leaving serious questions unresolved.

4. UDW wanted an exclusive arrangement to purchase GCI. They knew we were talking with other companies and wanted to head off any competition. I was reluctant to do this.
5. Most important of all, if we went down the road with UDW for several months trying to consummate the deal and it failed, then this might have turned off all the other merger candidates, undermining the possibility of selling the company to anyone. I wanted assurances that this merger would occur, which UDW could not deliver.

Had we worked more closely with UDW, we might have been able to solve the staff issues and my issues, but everything was done long distance, by phone or email. There was not enough detailed discussion to resolve the issues that bothered my staff and me, and in the end, merger discussions ground to a halt.

I never regretted walking away from the UDW merger. I never looked back, and I never thought much about it. I was convinced that the merger had little chance of occurring. Recently, I looked at the price of the UDW stock from early 2004 through 2010, a seven-year period. The stock peaked at about four dollars per share in early 2004, exactly when the company wanted to merge with my company. Thereafter, the stock went into a downturn, gradually declining to three dollars, then two, and then under one dollar per share. Today, the company is delisted from the American Stock Exchange, and the last share price I found was $.19. All my stock options would have been worthless. That my employees saw this in 2004 is a compliment to their wisdom.

Perhaps the merger with GCI could have changed everything for UDW. Certainly our earnings would have bolstered the merged company for several years, and it is possible that my staff and I could have changed the nature of the company and even enhanced UDW's product line. This is all speculative and a road not taken. No one will ever know.

The possible deal with UDW was unwinding late in February 2004, and a week or so later IDC, International Data Corporation, expressed strong interest in the company and wanted to come to Atlanta from Boston to discuss the acquisition of GCI. The part of the company interested in acquiring GCI was IDC Financial Insights. They were a leading independent provider of research-based advisory and consulting services to the financial services industry. They advised executives on technology investments, helped banks benchmark themselves against industry peers, and worked with clients to adopt industry best practices. Their business had many of the same elements as my company.

In April, IDC made the following initial offer:

- Significant cash at the closing.
- An additional earn out each year over five years based on the profits of GCI.
- GCI would remain an autonomous entity within Financial Insights.
- Any new payment systems related business undertaken by IDC would be the responsibility of GCI.
- I would report to the CEO of Financial Insights.
- I would be permitted to withdraw the prior earnings from GCI so long as it did not hinder the operation of GCI.

After several weeks of discussion, a second offer was made that increased the minimum payment. After I analyzed the offer, I still thought it wasn't good enough. I flew to Boston, met with IDC, and returned with the following observations:

1. While Financial Insights (FI) had a desire to be 25 percent of the four hundred-million research business, it was a long way from it and so was my company. Even combined we had a long way to go.
2. IDC's revenue per staff was smaller than we were achieving. GCI had the best financial performance that I knew of, and I could enhance IDC's profitability.
3. Neither company was one of the top two companies. To dominate the research business, it would be necessary to be one of the two top companies, so acquiring GCI would be an important strategy in making that happen.
4. We had an excellent client base critical to growing the research business.
5. We had a payment system line of business that would deepen the sale and enlarge the ways in which Financial Insights could

sell its products. Combined, it would make us a formidable competitor in the research business.

Based on our discussion, IDC promised to revise its offer, which it did. A third offer was made that:

- reduced the earnout period from five years down to three years,
- reduced the maximum value of the offer,
- increased the share of pre-tax earnings for the earn out,
- added a sizeable retention bonus, to be paid for retaining the staff at GCI.

While it was frustrating going through the various proposals that IDC made and then deciding what our counter proposal was, it was a very positive development. The reason was that other firms were interested in buying GCI, so Roger and I were trying to move all of them along to a point where I had a choice as to which one to select. IDC started in February, and the various proposals from IDC had taken us up to May. The other companies had come into the picture after IDC, so I was thankful that we could prolong the negotiations with IDC until I knew how serious the other firms were. The whole process of negotiation was complex, nerve racking, and difficult to know how much to push for a final and best offer.

While the earn out was down to three years, I wanted no earn out at all. I would have accepted a small earn out percentage, but the IDC offer had a much higher percentage than I found acceptable. As a result, we continued having discussions with IDC to sweeten the terms, and that continued to provide the time we needed to move along the other companies toward an offer from them.

At the end of June, IDC responded with its best and final offer that increased the cash at closing and offered to pay interest on the earn out. I believed that the IDC offer as it stood was a good offer from a good company, that I would be comfortable working there until I retired, and that my staff would be well taken care of financially as well as professionally. IDC and GCI were in similar businesses, and we could significantly enhance their business and they could do the same for ours. While we negotiated on price and terms, I thought that Roger

Orloff and I had done an exceptional job where I could not only live with the deal but would be happy about it as well. Still, I had revenue growth and profit objectives to meet in terms of the acquisition, and it was possible that I could be fired for lack of performance. I was determined to get a better offer if that was possible.

In April 2004, Edgar Dunn & Company became interested in buying GCI, and I met with several of their partners. Edgar Dunn was a significant bank-consulting firm focusing on plastic cards rather than check processing. After the initial discussion, Edgar Dunn decided in late May to make the following offer to buy GCI:

- A small amount in cash.
- The rest would be a note, bearing interest, paid quarterly, and paid off after four years.
- I would have an ownership of Edgar Dunn similar to the other owners.
- For three years, I would receive a small percentage of the growth in net revenues from GCI.

The offer was much less than the IDC offer, especially if you discount the loan back to its present value at a reasonable interest rate. I thought that their offer was the best they could do with the cash they had and the risk they wanted to take. I knew they wanted us, but didn't want to pay the price.

When I analyzed the offer more carefully, I concluded that the offer was unacceptable for a number of reasons. I would become a partner in a significant consulting firm, but I didn't want to sell my company to become an owner in another consulting company. I also didn't know how much the other firm was worth. I wanted cash up front and the opportunity to retire soon. Even if I grew GCI significantly, this would not produce enough earn out money to match the IDC offer. While the ownership of Edgar Dunn was interesting, it was a private company, and I had no idea what that ownership might be worth down the road. We made a series of assumptions about the growth of my products, assumed various levels of expense for each product, and worked up a spreadsheet of the potential value of Edgar Dunn over a three-year period. The bottom line was that even with an optimistic set of assumptions, the proposal amount was way below the IDC offer. I could not consider this offer seriously.

I concluded that Edgar Dunn wanted me more than I wanted them. They mentioned that the synergy of the two companies together could bolster their international business. We were only in the UK and Ireland and only in check processing. It was a big stretch to think that we could substantially help Edgar Dunn internationally.

In short, I didn't think they had the money to buy my company. If they expected that most of the cash to buy my company would come from my own profits, why would I not continue to own and run my company and keep all of the profits? The bottom line was that I told the principals of Edgar Dunn that we had a better offer than they were offering, and we did not wish to continue negotiating with them.

I now turn to McKinsey & Company. McKinsey is a world-class consulting firm, perhaps the best consulting firm in the world, a firm that consults at the highest levels in business and government, and has offices worldwide. My staff and I were very familiar with McKinsey because we had worked together on several banking assignments with them. On several occasions for payment system projects, a banking organization would first hire McKinsey to address the strategic issues and then ask McKinsey to subcontract to GCI to undertake some of the detailed analyses that might be required for the assignment. As a result, the partners at McKinsey that dealt with payment system issues knew of our capabilities.

McKinsey was on our A-list of companies to approach, and Steve Ledford, who had worked with them extensively, suggested that he approach them first. I agreed, and Steve got in touch with Jack Stephenson, the main partner at McKinsey whom Steve knew. Jack was immediately intrigued with the idea of acquiring GCI and took the leadership within McKinsey to move the idea forward. In February, McKinsey signed our standard nondisclosure agreement and, shortly afterward, received our memorandum.

In March, we provided the company with our latest financial documents. This was the end of our first quarter for 2004, and we had very impressive results. Revenues had increased 35 percent from the same period of 2003, and operating income was way up. At that point, I still considered McKinsey a long shot, for while they knew our capabilities, they rarely made an acquisition.

Still, they persisted. In April, Jack came down to Atlanta with Andy Eichfeld, another McKinsey partner, and several other staff members to meet our staff. Andy led the discussion about McKinsey's culture, and he made it abundantly clear that the most important issue for McKinsey was whether our corporate culture matched with their corporate culture. On this issue, it quickly became clear that both companies were in agreement to produce high quality work without shortcuts, to put the client first and foremost, to demand a high level of integrity by telling the client the unvarnished truth, and to focus on those client problems that could provide the greatest impact to their business. McKinsey was doing that at the CEO and board levels of companies while we were working in payment systems at a slightly lower level in the organization. The more we discussed the possible synergies, the more interesting the acquisition appeared to be for McKinsey.

The corporate culture issue was of paramount importance to McKinsey, so important that a confidential information agreement had to be signed by every member of the firm, obligating each staff member to maintain client confidences and to protect client sensitive data and information. Having to deal with McKinsey's very restrictive confidential guideline, two examples below provide real issues we had to deal with:

1. Under our benchmarking program, participants agree that their data will be shared with other study participants. The reports, charts, etc., are labeled anonymously (Site A, Site B, Site C . . .) but each participant is given a key to identify the name of the bank for each site. This is fully disclosed to participants, and agreement is a condition of participation in the study. After the acquisition by McKinsey, GCI eliminated the practice of identifying the names of the sites to avoid any legal conflict.

2. McKinsey restricted consultants from working with competing clients. This did not apply to specialists who are not involved in confidential discussions with clients at the decision-making level in the client organization. This allowed GCI consultants to play the role of information provider or third-party analyst to multiple competing clients without compromising McKinsey's policy.

This last point turned out to be a reasonable way for GCI staff to work with McKinsey and still serve competing clients. GCI staff was used to providing their expertise to a McKinsey assignment but were left out of the confidential discussions with clients at the highest levels.

At the end of April, McKinsey sent a note to me with the following points:

1. McKinsey was intrigued with the idea of acquiring GCI and wanted to move to the next stage of negotiations. The next stage would be to arrive at a sensible organizational model. A strong possibility would be to keep GCI as a reasonably stand-alone/ self-contained entity, which is what occurred.
2. McKinsey's idea for GCI was to expand the benchmarking and research capabilities beyond payments into other areas of financial services. This would give McKinsey access to proprietary research and would require ramping up the staff and building expertise on nonpayments topics.
3. GCI would also partner on McKinsey consulting assignments as deep subject matter experts. This would give clients a much better and more cost effective end product while keeping GCI distinct to avoid conflicting with the McKinsey policy against having individual consultants serve direct competitors.

For McKinsey, the senior partners had to decide whether to make an offer to buy GCI, and that was a complex process. For UDW, the CEO showed up and decided to make an offer unilaterally. For IDC, the senior man gained permission to negotiate from his CEO and made an offer. For Edgar Dunn, the small number of partners made their decision quickly and an offer was made. However, for McKinsey, the two partners wanting to proceed to acquire GCI had to ask permission from the head of the banking practice in North America. In turn, he needed approval by the worldwide group of partners that met once a quarter. Their meeting was to take place in June, and we were informed that formal negotiations would begin in earnest only after that meeting. Informal negotiations would occur before the meeting to establish a negotiating range and a deal structure. That meant that we would have to negotiate the deal with McKinsey and then wait on approval from the partners meeting. And while this negotiation was going on, I had to keep the other companies interested in buying GCI as backup. It was getting nerve racking to deal with three legitimate possibilities at the same time, but it was also wonderful. I had what Roger described as a high-class problem.

The McKinsey partners wanted to come to Atlanta to discuss the deal and then invite Steve and me to New York for a "get to know you" session with some of the financial industry partners. At these meetings, it became clear that one major argument supporting the merger was that GCI could help win a large contract for McKinsey that McKinsey would not have won without GCI. While this was speculative about the future, it was clear that the staff of GCI had contacts at virtually all of the major banks, banking associations, and vendors serving the banking industry. Our reputation could influence the decision, and McKinsey only needed one major win a year to justify buying GCI. That made it clear to me that the profitability of GCI was of secondary value to McKinsey. McKinsey would be satisfied if GCI broke even financially.

Shortly after McKinsey's partners' meeting in June, Jack told us that they had met and approved the acquisition of GCI. Jack informed us that this was a significant step for a firm as large as McKinsey. He went on to say that Andy and he were both very excited to continue our discussions over the next several weeks. I was elated.

The McKinsey staff came to GCI in early June, and the meeting went extremely well. My staff was enthusiastic about the prospect of growing our business under the McKinsey name, and McKinsey did a great job presenting their firm and handling the issues that came up. Out of that meeting, I quickly came to the conclusion that dealing with McKinsey was totally different from the other companies that I had been dealing with. The other companies focused on gaining agreement on the price to buy GCI as well as the other financial conditions related to the sale. McKinsey was more focused on legal considerations, on protecting McKinsey's reputation, and on being assured that any violations and damages that might result from GCI actions prior to the acquisition were not McKinsey problems. I was encouraged that McKinsey was thinking about these issues because it implied that an offer from them was more and more possible. As a result of all these legal concerns, my attorneys were already in discussion with McKinsey attorneys.

I then wrote to McKinsey that we needed to discuss the letter of intent (LOI) and the entire due diligence process as the lawyers were making the process difficult. I had an ideal negotiating process in my head based on dealing with lawyers in the past. The ideal as I saw it was that all business issues be defined up front, then discussed first between buyer and seller, then the attorneys would be informed about the decisions reached between buyer and seller and told to make it legal. Once an issue was resolved, the issue would no longer be on the table. And finally, we would avoid focusing on very improbable events. It never happened.

Even when the deal is big, insist on driving the process because attorneys always want to take control. When dealing with money issues, insist that your attorney play a secondary role. You must be the decision maker. Attorneys are aggressive, and they insist on taking over to focus on the worst-case scenarios, and they can create many of them. Regardless of the give and take, insist that you decide on the business issues even though the attorneys do the writing.

Lawyers focus on the worst possible cases, however improbable they might be. McKinsey's lawyers were focusing on improbable events, such as my disparaging McKinsey, which I knew would not happen. It took me a while to realize that this was just lawyer stuff, but it never went away. The McKinsey lawyers were raising new issues with my counsel, and that's not the way I wanted the process to work. Very quickly, the legal issues became confrontational instead of a partnership between the two firms. The McKinsey staff had fought hard to make the acquisition happen, and Steve and I had worked hard to get our staff enthusiastic about being a part of McKinsey and indeed to be excited about the prospect. I was worried that the lawyers could screw up the process. I did, however, make one small change in the McKinsey legal team. I forced the senior banking partner at McKinsey to remove one of his lawyers from working on the acquisition, and he agreed with me that the lawyer was being too aggressive. In the end, the lawyers had to have their say, and there was nothing much I could do about it.

As another example of the lawyers muddying up the process, McKinsey's lawyers suggested that my employees be liable in the event of a material breach. Since my employees would own shares in GCI and benefit from them, McKinsey asked if my employees could participate if any violations or damages to McKinsey occurred. My lawyer let me know that while it would be difficult to have all of my employees sign the asset purchase agreement, it would be entirely within the realm of fairness to ask those employees who were taking part of the purchase price to share the risk with me, pro rata. To that extent, my lawyers could prepare a contribution agreement between the other employees and me, whereby they would agree to share pro rata in any claim which I was required to satisfy. This would allow me to recover some of my losses in a worst-case scenario. While in principle it seemed fair, I was opposed to it because it could hold up the sale of my business, and the likelihood of an occurrence was remote. I was asking my employees to pay for a damages claim they probably did not cause and had no understanding about whatsoever. Furthermore, it would be uncomfortable for me to have to sue my employees if there was a claim they did not want to pay. This was just another legal matter that I had to be practical about because the risk was negligible, and not get caught up in an improbable situation.

Keep in mind that in June we were in serious and final negotiations with IDC. I wasn't happy with the IDC earn out, and I preferred to sell the company to McKinsey if their offer was equal to or better than the IDC offer. Informally, McKinsey had suggested that they would be willing to pay an amount similar to the IDC offer, but it wasn't formally made. Finally at the end of June, McKinsey made the following offer:

- McKinsey would buy the assets of GCI and leave me responsible for any liabilities of GCI.
- McKinsey would pay an amount virtually equal to the IDC offer and in cash.
- A small percentage of the amount would be held back to be paid at the end of twenty-four months with interest, provided there was no definitive breach in the agreement.
- McKinsey wanted an exclusive period through the end of August to prevent any other company from buying GCI. This was later extended to the end of September.
- McKinsey wanted no public announcement and no disparagement by either party of the other.

At this point, I had to tell IDC that their offer was not going to be accepted and throw all my effort into making the McKinsey offer work. I also had to get my legal team actively involved in the negotiations because I knew that we would have to define what a breach in the agreement meant, as well as many other legal issues that were sure to come up.

I was generally satisfied with the McKinsey offer, but I didn't want to wait for two years to get the money held back. I argued that I would not be the CEO after the acquisition, and I would have little control over the direction or profitability of GCI. I did not want to be at the mercy of someone else even though I thought the selection of Steve to run GCI after the acquisition was an excellent choice. I therefore proposed that the money held back to protect McKinsey be for the next eighteen months instead of two years. It was not a big leap for McKinsey, and it worked. The deal put the McKinsey offer at a similar amount to the IDC offer but with much more cash up front. With that in mind, I again approached McKinsey and told them that we had another offer of a similar amount, and I would prefer to be with McKinsey. However, I would like slightly more money to assure myself that I was selling to the highest bidder. He quickly came back with another small amount, and that closed the deal. I would receive the money held back if there was no breach of the agreement, and there never was one. Finally, all the stock appreciation rights (phantom stock) that had been issued to employees would be cleared just prior to the purchase agreement being signed. This would guarantee that all the employees were properly compensated when the deal was consummated. I thought I got the best company at a price that was fair. I was happy. I was happy that the senior staff was to receive some of the purchase price because *where the staff is the product it is good business to give them ownership in the company.*

After the deal with McKinsey was agreed upon, I then sent the following to my staff:

"I am pleased to inform you that as of yesterday Global Concepts reached a verbal agreement to be acquired by McKinsey & Company. Since this information is strictly confidential, do not tell anyone. The announcement to the industry will be an important marketing tool, and I want to work closely with McKinsey on how and when to make it. There is much left to close this deal. I will be signing a letter of intent to sell the company in the next few days, and then we proceed to the due diligence process where McKinsey checks that we do have the cash we say we have, the accounts receivable, the contracts, the membership in our various programs, and the rest of the assets of the firm. I hope we can complete the process in the next thirty to forty-five days. More details will be given to you verbally at the staff meeting."

There were a number of money issues that needed resolution for the letter of intent. After discussion with McKinsey, we agreed on the interest to be paid on the money held back for eighteen months, that in the event of a lawsuit related to work contracted with GCI before the sale to McKinsey, I would pay for the settlement of any dispute, and in the event that violations or damages exceeded the money held back, then McKinsey would have to sue me for the additional money. I was okay with this, for there was nothing that I knew that would generate a material breach, and none occurred.

I wanted the right to serve as an expert witness once I retired from McKinsey. McKinsey made it clear that so long as I worked for McKinsey I would not be able to accept expert witness work. The reason was that two McKinsey clients might be suing each other, especially among the major banks, and McKinsey did not want me to be on either side of the case.

There were some unwritten agreements that were clear: the stockholder equity in Global Concepts would belong to me since I paid taxes on the money or would have to pay taxes on it—this money was essentially the profits at Global Concepts prior to closing; Steve would assume day to day control of the running of Global Concepts after closing; my job after the closing would be to work as an advisor to Global Concepts, work with McKinsey staff to create new products and launch them, and help to sell and deliver major consulting assignments; the money given to employees for their phantom stock had to be treated as ordinary income.

With all of the key issues resolved, McKinsey and I signed the LOI and then moved on to the asset purchase agreement. This was the major legal document that spelled out everything in detail, and it took a great deal of negotiation on many, many issues before it was completed.

It was clear to me why I picked McKinsey. The partners were men of integrity. The synergy of the firms was perfect: we would enhance their research capability and increase their chance of winning payment system consulting. The price and terms were acceptable. We continued to maintain the firm as having neutrality in the marketplace. The staff had many more opportunities than any other choice. McKinsey had a first-rate reputation for excellence. And finally, I had the best chance to continue to enjoy working or retiring as I saw fit.

However, it is useful to summarize the various deals that were presented to me because they were so varied.

- In terms of pure dollars, the lowest offer was less than 50 percent of the highest offer.
- The highest offer was not selected because it did not fit the culture of GCI.
- The two best offers were extremely close in terms of dollars, though the terms differed.
- The offers fell in the range of .7-1.5 revenue, and 5-7 times EBITDA (earnings before interest, taxes, depreciation, and amortization).
- The McKinsey offer was better because it offered cash up front while the other good offer was associated with an earn out. On the other hand, the McKinsey offer had no possibility of an increase in value depending on the firm's performance, while the other offer did and could have resulted in a greater value if GCI continued to perform well.
- The McKinsey offer eliminated my role as CEO and suggested that I retire whenever I wanted to retire while other offers required me to stay on for several years as CEO.

Each of the companies interested in buying GCI had a different vision for GCI depending on its needs. In one case, the buyer's objective was survival—they wanted access to GCI's clients. In another case, the company saw GCI as synergistic to its existing business—they wanted GCI to help grow its revenue. Another company focused on extending its product line—they wanted GCI to become the biggest in the business. And finally, there was a company interested in GCI for its in-depth knowledge and research capabilities—they wanted GCI to help win large consulting contracts.

To a large degree, the LOI defines the nature of the asset purchase agreement. In my case, the acquisition was a purchase of the assets of the company, not the stock. As a result, McKinsey set up a new company named Global Concepts Holdings, Inc., GCHI, to buy GCI. After the purchase of GCI's assets, I still owned GCI, a shell of a company. I then changed the name of my company, and McKinsey then changed

GCHI back to GCI. In that way, McKinsey continued to own the name GCI without having to buy the stock of the company. It was a neat legal trick.

As we got involved in the asset purchase agreement, a variety of issues arose. We compromised on a two-year noncompete and a four-year nondisparagement agreement. Lawyers can impose major restrictions in a noncompete agreement. The initial language stated that neither Steve nor I could perform consulting services for a client of GCI or McKinsey or for a competitor of any client of GCI or McKinsey. It also prevented us from taking a job with any firm that competed with an existing client or previous client, which included virtually everyone. The language was so broad that neither Steve nor I could work if we left McKinsey. We eventually agreed that the noncompete agreement was designed to prevent me from competing in any way with McKinsey or GCI. However, I would be allowed to advise my family members on their careers, give speeches on payment systems, write a book on payment systems, speak on other issues not payment system related and perform expert witness work with consent from McKinsey, and that consent to be not unreasonably withheld. The noncompete would last for two years and begin the day I left McKinsey.

The nondisparagement clause initially proposed implied that I could not speak disparagingly about McKinsey or Global Concepts even within the firm or in court as an expert witness. I finally got a partner at McKinsey to say that internally the firm would not want to confuse disparagement with the obligation to dissent. There seemed to be a fine line between the words *dissent* and *disparage*, and I did not want to leave that to some legal interpretation.

There was also the issue of defining a material breach. Some examples helped me to understand what it meant: a client contract goes into dispute, the assets purchased were not correct, some of the intellectual property was in error, staff salaries were incorrect, or a financial statement was in error. Whether these types of breaches were material would depend on the specific situation. No breaches ever did occur, but if they did, it probably would be cheaper to resolve them through arbitration.

Regarding a breach, it depended on the definition of a single word—*knowledge*. My lawyers and I argued that knowledge applied to what we knew, and not to what we should have known. The McKinsey lawyers wanted to define knowledge as what "we should have known as a result of the ordinary and reasonable exercise of our duties with respect to the business." We ended up including the phrase "to our knowledge," and that was important. With that phrase, I would not be in breach of the agreement when I had no knowledge of it beforehand.

There was also the issue of consequential damages, not just the out-of-pocket loss in the event of a breach, but what flowed from the breach. The consequential damages that could occur as a result of a breach could be lost staff time at McKinsey, additional travel time and their costs, lost profits at McKinsey, and lost business opportunities that might be related to the breach. Consequential damages are very speculative. I couldn't go down this road. It was conceivable that McKinsey could argue that it lost many millions because of some breach we caused and wipe out everything they paid me.

I never knew about the legal concept, but I quickly concluded that *consequential damages are very dangerous for the seller. Don't do it.* A material breach can be defined in many ways, and if it occurs and it is tied to consequential damages, then it can wipe out your entire sales price. Taken to the limit, it can bankrupt you. Do not accept this legal idea, and be willing to walk away from the agreement if it is included.

I agonized over consequential damages for days because I thought it might kill my deal. I didn't know how important this was for McKinsey, but I knew that their reputation was paramount. My lawyers and my advisor told me to walk away from the deal if consequential damages were included in the agreement. In the end, I followed their advice; McKinsey caved.

The noncompete agreement for my staff had so far been vaguely discussed. This turned out to be a very important issue, and it became one of the major sticking points to complete the acquisition. McKinsey insisted that most of the staff would have to sign noncompete agreements, though less restrictive than Steve's or mine. It came up as a surprise for me because I had never required my staff to sign a noncompete agreement. I knew it would be an issue that had to be dealt with, but it was put off until the very end of the negotiations. My staff was deeply concerned about signing them even though it was a standard practice in the industry.

Noncompete agreements may be difficult to enforce, but *insist on noncompete and confidentiality agreements for key employees*. Even in states with strong right-to-work laws, you will want to implement noncompete and confidentiality agreements, and this is especially true for a small consulting firm where the people are the product or where the staff has strong expertise, and it is essential to retain them.

Finally, after a lot of discussion, upset, and threats by the staff, the noncompete agreement was structured to last for two years and included all the consulting firms in payment systems. If a staff person was fired not for cause nor for performance, then most of the salary for the remaining time of the noncompete period would be paid until a new job was found; if for performance, then a lesser amount would be paid for the remaining time of the noncompete period until a new job was found; and if for cause, then no salary would be paid.

The staff reacted quite negatively to this offer. McKinsey made it clear that they would not negotiate with my staff on the two-year restrictions related to (1) joining a recognized competitor in payment systems consulting/research and (2) forming a competing firm in payment systems consulting/research. McKinsey saw these as the essential points of the noncompete. McKinsey also made it clear that they would not allow my staff to "rip off" either McKinsey or GCI in order to sign the noncompete agreement. McKinsey was not prepared to pay any money or offer some benefit to the staff to get them to sign the noncompete, and they didn't want me to do it either.

I was unwilling to risk having the deal crumble because key staff members were unwilling to sign a noncompete agreement. I urged them to meet as a group and suggest a solution. The group did meet and asked me to meet with them afterward as a group. I was extremely nervous going into that meeting because I had no idea what they had in mind, and I knew I could not put money directly in their pocket. At the meeting, several of them spoke up about the frustration they had with McKinsey overall, leaving the issue until the very last minute when all the other issues had been settled. That said, they proposed that GCI pay two hundred thousand dollars to various charities of their choosing as a way to compensate them without putting money in their pocket. I agreed that this was a brilliant solution, but I countered with a hundred thousand dollars, telling them that two hundred thousand dollars was just too much. They responded that there were eleven in the group, and they would be satisfied with ten thousand dollars each to the charity of their choice. I agreed.

Shortly after the sale of the company, each of the eleven staff members told me their charity, and I made a check out to each of those charities and gave their check to each staff member so they could mail it to their charity and take the credit for doing so. I was not happy writing a bunch of checks that totaled $110,000, but I thought it was worth it to guarantee the sale of the company. I also made it clear that the donation was not compensation to the staff. It was a charitable donation by me. The arrangement was not tied contractually to the staff member signing the noncompete. It was a "gentleman's agreement" that tacitly recognized the value of the noncompete agreement.

As we headed toward the signing of the agreement, there were an incredible number of agreements—a total of twenty-seven—to be signed. The United States is a country founded on the rule of law, and the sale of my company proved it in spades.

There was still one final hurdle to get over, and that was the approval of the senior partners at McKinsey. In the interests of making a final pitch to them, here is an excerpt from what I wrote to them:

> Clients come ahead of the firm. Each assignment is unique and requires an open mind to find the best solution; clients receive the very best advice we can provide regardless of the consequences. Consulting engagements are based on real facts, hard data and in-depth knowledge; recommendations are based on understanding the implications of the whole picture. The staff is motivated to be the best they can be, and the staff is organized according to what a client needs.

Shortly thereafter, I received the following email from McKinsey: "Congratulations! Our Board approved the proposed purchase of GCI assets and integration plan."

The closing took place on September 23, 2004. The actual asset purchase agreement came to be a fifty-page document excluding a number of exhibits that included definitions and terms, purchase and sale of the business, representations and warranties of the seller, representations and buyers of the buyer, covenants, conditions to closing, survival, indemnification, certain remedies, termination, miscellaneous, and exhibits and schedules.

I kept ownership of GCI, but McKinsey wanted the name. In deciding what name I would pick for the shell of GCI that remained, it occurred to me that I could take the first initials of my six grandchildren and arrange them into some sort of name. My grandchildren were named Bari, Menachem, Harry, Binyomin, Sophie, and Emanuel, so I had to play with the letters *B, M, H, B, S, E*. The best I could come with was B B SHEM, and that was the name I used for my new name. It turned out that *Shem* in Hebrew means "name," and it can refer to the Name—God. It was a good choice, one that is easy for me to remember.

The most important thing that went right was that it was the right time for me to sell my company because I was sixty-five and didn't have the same enthusiasm for the business as I had in the past. It was also the right time because I wanted to do other important things in my life. I had become more involved in Judaism, in serving on nonprofit boards, and I wanted to write about my life. I needed more time to do these things along with spending more time with my family.

My good luck was that several companies had an interest in buying my company at about the same time. This allowed me to be in a stronger bargaining position with each of them. To some degree, Roger and I planned the negotiations with each company to end near the same period so I would have a real choice as to whom to sell my company. When another company matched the McKinsey's offer in total—although they would have been paid out at different periods—I used that knowledge to ask McKinsey for another small amount of money and got it. That amount can be attributed only to having two bidders at the same time bidding approximately the same price.

The selection of McKinsey was definitely the right one. McKinsey had a great name, and their culture was similar to our culture in putting clients first and being truthful in whatever they did for their clients. McKinsey was the only buyer that offered me an all-cash deal, with most of it paid up front. And McKinsey made it easy for me to work there, and to decide without any pressure when to retire. In short, McKinsey was the very best choice and a feather in my cap for selling to a company that rarely made an acquisition and was one of the finest consulting firms in the world.

In selling your company, remember that *the price is important, but the overall deal is more important*. Consider an earn out to be risky and a major negative. As negotiations drag on, if your company continues to make a profit as mine did, then insist that the profits flow to you instead of the buyer right up to the day of the closing. Finally, satisfy your staff. If they reject a company out of hand, even if you might have gotten the highest selling price to that company, walk away from the deal.

I never thought the process of selling my company would be easy, but I never thought it would take eighteen months to do it. There were multiple rewards as I've mentioned, but probably the most important was the congratulations that came in from our clients. The banks knew McKinsey very well, knew that we had worked well together, and they knew the combination of both companies would be good for them as clients and for the banking industry. I learned that in addition to gaining approval from my staff for the deal, it was just as important to gain approval from our clients.

With all of the discussion before the deal closed, the integration of GCI into McKinsey went smoothly because there was little change for the staff except for appointing Steve as CEO and making me an advisor to my company. As a result, the staff adjusted well, and I started enjoying my new job as an elder statesman. As I found out quickly, senior McKinsey staff retired at about age sixty, and I was now five years older than their retirement age. No one said much about this, but it was obvious that I could retire whenever I wanted to retire.

With my family and I now financially secure, I had to change my financial perspective from making money to investing the money wisely. That was to be the new career for me—a very high-class problem.

Chapter 17

McKinsey and Retirement

With the largest financial transaction of my life completed, I was satisfied with the result. I had gotten a decent price for my company, and I had sold it to a world-class consulting firm that made very few acquisitions. My company was only the third acquisition in McKinsey's history, and I was pleased that their management saw the value my company would bring to enhance their consulting practice.

For the first few weeks, I did whatever I could to make the transition for my staff as easy as possible. Everyone was hired, salaries continued as they existed before the acquisition, and the only financial issue was moving onto McKinsey's benefit structure. The organizational structure of GCI changed in only one major respect: Ledford was running GCI, and I was the advisor with little power. I felt the loss of control immediately, but I was content that I had sold my company, and in that process I gave away control.

We issued a press release about the acquisition, informed all of our clients by letter, phone, or email, but the strategy was to be low key about it because GCI was to continue as a separate wholly owned subsidiary doing what it did before the acquisition.

I had to find a role for myself. I thought that I could take the multiclient products that GCI had developed—forums and benchmarking—and find applications within the large number of McKinsey practices. Over the first six months, I decided that I would look at a variety of ideas and see if I could convince one or more McKinsey partners to launch these products within their specialized practice.

I quickly discovered that McKinsey partners were satisfied with their existing profitable practice, and it would take a huge marketing effort on my part to persuade any of them to spend their time and effort launching my ideas when they really didn't need to do it. I had to find someone within the practice to be my supporter, or else I would be fighting an uphill battle.

I knew that *selling a new idea can only be accomplished by selling it to top management.* This applies whether you are selling internally or externally. Every new idea requires one or more senior managers to endorse the idea. Even when lower-level staff endorses the idea, it can be quickly killed when the partner or owner has other ideas. For a small company, the owner makes the decisions. In large companies, decisions are moved up the management ladder, requiring several layers of approval before the decision to proceed is confirmed. Selling a new idea internally takes time, and sponsorship by a senior manager is critical. The higher up the sponsorship is, the easier it is to gain approval. If you have an idea and want to implement it, then sell it to a person as high up in the company as you can.

With no clear focus, I had to *establish a major role after being acquired. I had to pick one direction and focus on it.* The best way is to pick a single project and do it remarkably well. It doesn't matter what the project is if it is done well. Some people can handle multiple assignments and do a good job on all of them. However, you establish your reputation through the work you do in the business you are in, and it is better to do one thing exceptionally well than to do many things acceptably. In some cases you don't have the luxury of working on one project. In that case, you do the best you can do, but you are judged by the quality of your work and not by the amount of work you do. For management jobs, quality is more important than quantity.

Listed below in no special order are some of the ideas I came up with:

- I recommended that McKinsey launch a US study on cash as a payment mechanism. The concept went nowhere and I moved on.
- Within McKinsey there was a group that focused on the collection process in payment systems, especially credit card collections. One of the senior consultants became interested

in launching a benchmark study. The idea was a good one, and together we produced a prospectus that described the concept. Several credit card companies seemed interested, but then the consultant I was working with was assigned to a revenue generating project and the idea died. I did not have the contacts to carry on the marketing effort myself.

- I had worked on a fraud forum, but Ledford dismissed the idea once he was in charge. I liked the idea and pursued the concept with a bank lawyer that was knowledgeable about check fraud. It needed a strong marketing person to help me gain at least ten participants, but no one stepped up to work on it. The idea died.

- There was another benchmarking idea that surfaced—asking leading retail banks to provide service-to-sales performance data to evaluate product selection, call segmentation, specialization, call flows and scripting, bonus incentives, coaching, and metrics reporting. If the project was to be launched, it was without my involvement, so I moved on.

- I had the opportunity to review a major study of all types of payments in various European countries. The study was published and concluded that payments accounted for a major portion of the revenue and cost base for European banks, representing almost 25 percent of their banking revenues and 35 percent of their operating costs. Overall, however, payments were not very profitable, generating only 9 percent of bank profits. An interesting conclusion was that all the countries accepted cash payments, and they were consistently more expensive than anyone thought. I thought I might become involved in working on a study of cash, but no one seemed interested in involving me. This was a European idea.

- I had another idea. I proposed to establish a top 100 payment system panel that would answer short questionnaires on payment system issues and the panel would attend a conference from time to time with their peers. The idea was to charge a membership fee to be a part of the panel, putting together a group of knowledgeable payment system people throughout the industry. The panel would respond to a variety of payment system issues, and we would summarize their responses. I sent emails to about fifteen bankers that I knew. The responses were generally positive. The idea went nowhere.

- I proposed that McKinsey launch a one-week course for its clients called The US Payment System: From Paper to Electronic. We had access to a huge amount of GCI material, and a base of experts that could deliver a brilliant set of lectures that would be hard to match. When the idea did not seem to be going anywhere, I sat down and prepared a set of over two hundred slides on the history of the ACH, the history of credit cards, and the history of debit cards, and gave that presentation to the GCI staff. My presentation was well received, but the concept of a payment system university for the banking industry went nowhere.

After nine months of frustration in not being able to launch a single project, I decided that it was time to retire. I had learned that *after you sell your company, if you stay on then define a significant role for yourself*. Without staff and in an advisory role, you are essentially an employee without portfolio. You report to no one, and no one reports to you. You are an employee without much to do, and you have to find a new role for yourself. In that atmosphere, you either find something important to do or you retire. I tried several approaches to finding an important assignment, concluded that none of them would easily work, and gave up after nine months.

It was debilitating for me to go to the office day after day with little to do. If you run your own company, then you aren't cut out to sit around idly getting paid well and play games on your computer. You can continue this way for some time, but most ex-CEOs don't need the money, and they don't want to waste their time. I had more important things to do with the remaining time I had left in my life.

I put my thoughts down in a memo to the senior partner at McKinsey, but I decided not to send it. Some of what I wrote said,

> I am retiring because there is no compelling reason for me to stay. I don't do the GCI work—more junior staff can do it. I have had no great success launching multiclient studies with McKinsey, for it's a difficult culture to succeed in. Studies for potential clients are conducted for little or no money, designed

to sell individual consulting, rather than to turn the effort into an ongoing revenue stream.

McKinsey is not focused on GCI's financials, so there is no commitment from McKinsey to grow GCI's business. Rather, the focus is to have GCI help grow McKinsey's business, which is fine. I want to make a clean break, and not work part-time. I will offer my services as an expert witness because I like doing it, but I will not make it a permanent business.

I had spent almost a year at McKinsey with no success. I concluded that *if you cannot find a satisfying role in a year in the company, move on.* It is long enough to know the business and short enough to know where you fit. Beyond a year without a well-defined role, you will be frustrated.

Having made the decision to retire, I wrote to McKinsey and Ledford in June 2005 as follows:

It has been nine months since the acquisition of GCI by McKinsey & Company and by my reckoning the acquisition has been a success. The staff is generally happy with McKinsey, GCI has an excellent strategy for becoming a major research arm of the firm, and Steve as CEO has taken the helm with strength and leadership. By all accounts, I have found a good home for GCI, properly planned for my replacement and essentially made it easy for me to consider retiring.

After considerable thought about my future, I think it is time for me to retire. My job is no longer critical, as Steve does not need an advisor, and I have not found a new opportunity at McKinsey so compelling that it was essential for me to lead it. I must admit that it has been difficult trying to launch multi-client programs in a McKinsey culture that is structured around serving one client at a time.

Since the GCI acquisition occurred on September 23, 2004, I would propose to retire on September 30, 2005, which would be a week and a year after the acquisition. The only payment related business I envision is serving as an expert witness for payment system legal matters that may arise.

I would like to announce my intentions to the staff at GCI, and then to those I know at McKinsey. From there, I will begin to inform the people I know in the business, with the intention of making the transition as positive as possible.

I knew that I was retiring with the knowledge that the values I had established at GCI would continue at McKinsey as McKinsey had a similar culture. As we approached September, it occurred to me that bonuses would be paid in early December, so I decided to stick around for another two months. It also allowed the GCI staff to organize a retirement party well in advance so some of my family and friends could attend. The retirement dinner took place on December 1, 2005, and several people spoke glowingly about me.

At the retirement party, Steve spoke about the value I had in persistence and attributed it to my chutzpah. He said he often didn't know where the hell I was going, but he knew I would not take no for an answer. He also appreciated that I gave folks a chance to do things when they would not have had a chance in another company. The staff's gift to me was an atlas map of the world published in 1892 because they knew that I loved maps. He was right.

Jenny spoke about the passion that I had about the work that we did, and that passion made her job fun and interesting. She knew that I loved doing the work that we did, and that passion was contagious to the rest of the staff. She noted that even on my last day at work, I was working on a strategy for the company. She was kind enough to say that the industry would not be the same without me.

Jack Stevenson spoke about the unlikely possibility of acquiring GCI when Steve approached him. With approval from his boss at McKinsey, the more McKinsey looked at Global Concepts, the more interested they became until it was clear that the acquisition made sense to McKinsey because we had similar cultures. As a farewell gift, he gave me a thirty-year-old bottle of Macallan scotch and a paperweight map of the world. Macallan scotch has been the celebration drink in my household from the time my son-in-law, and I celebrated after he asked to marry my daughter Pamela. The paperweight sits on my desk, and the scotch is still half full, waiting for yet another special celebration.

Pamela related two stories from her childhood. She said,

> The first story occurred when I was in the tenth grade. I was particularly attracted to a rock and roll band and listened to their music all the time, even when I was studying. My father approached me one night and wondered why I listened to rock and roll music instead of classical music when I studied. I didn't have a particularly intelligent reply, but we decided to wager a bet. If, in one year's time, I still studied to this band's music, he would pay me twenty dollars. We wrote up a contract on a piece of notebook paper and taped it to one of his office walls. After a year, I was still listening to this band, even more than I was the year before. One evening as I was asking him a question in his office as he sat at his desk, I remembered the contract. I climbed on the desk and pulled the yellowed piece of paper off the wall and collected my twenty dollars right then and there. I remember him smiling as he handed over the twenty dollars reluctantly. I was ecstatic that I won my first bet with my father ever. I learned from this the power of keeping one's word and following through.
>
> The other story all three of us kids remember. When we were growing up, we all remember our dad saying, You go do your homework and I'll go do mine. It is a vivid memory because it happened almost every night. We would eat together as a family, clean up the kitchen, and then proceed upstairs to our respective desks and begin an evening's worth of homework. To this day, I am still impressed with my father's persistence and diligence. I always wondered what kind of homework could a grown man, a father, have? While we were slaving over geometry and Georgia civics, he used to study stock trends, write speeches by hand, and prepare his weekly SAT classes, which he taught at our high school for many years, or simply read a book. We learned from him the power of always being curious, of always wanting to learn more, and that learning is a lifetime pursuit.

Why do I share these stories with you tonight? I share them because our father is a man who has always been committed to following through and always had a passion for learning. He has transmitted that to us, his children and even his grandchildren. So, Dad, upon your retirement, our blessing to you is that you should remember your own lessons to us: make bold commitments, follow through on them and always learn every day.

Then my other daughter, Lori, my middle child, spoke about me as her father:

Dad was always present in our lives no matter how busy he was at work. He is always there for our mother and squeezed in time for all of us together and individually even when there wasn't time.

I remember the hours spent on math homework and the many short cuts dad tried teaching me. I remember him editing and proofreading my papers in high school and college. I remember being his SAT prep experiment when he was teaching the Allen Lipis SAT Prep Course, equivalent to Stanley Kaplan. Unlike my father, I don't have the gift of multiplying three numbers times three numbers in my head in twenty seconds, nor did I have a sizable vocabulary. So to catch me up to speed, I was forced into confinement for weeks until I regurgitated SAT words, like arcane, blandishment and dolorous in my sleep and pretended to know the math short cuts he taught me. He wasn't happy until I went up three hundred points on the SAT exam.

I remember all the things Dad made for us as kids. The stilts, our tree house in the backyard, the remodeling of our basement, his feeble attempt at roller skates that broke in one day, a zip line swing, jig saw puzzles made with his jig saw, and a massive igloo that would have made the Eskimos proud. His second love, second to our mom, of course, is his chain saw. When he pulls the cord and the engine roars, we all go running in the other direction.

And who could forget about the car he built, that crazy car that began as Herbie and ended as a replica of a 1929 Roadster. How and why he chose this one-year project remains a mystery, but yet another example of our dad taking on something big just because he could.

Retirement isn't the end for Allen, but the beginning of another journey that will not leave us wondering why he retired, but curious to see what challenge he chooses next.

Will you join me in a toast to this amazing husband, father, grandfather, teacher, creator, inventor, writer—the man, Dr. Allen Lipis, AKA my dad.

Jay Mehaffey spoke about how straight-laced he was when he worked at the Federal Reserve Bank of Atlanta, and that working for me put him on a different growth path in his career. He was kind to say that his father had once told him that if you can influence three people in your life, then you should consider yourself a success. He put me down as one of the three people who influenced his life.

Michael Fisher made note of the fact that both professional and personal people were at my retirement dinner. He knew that my children and grandchildren called me Zeyda, a Yiddish word for *grandfather*, and it provided a sense of quality for him. He said in many ways that he wished that I were a Zeyda to him. He said that he, too, came from the Atlanta Fed where there was always structured training, but GCI expanded his vision and gave him a different perspective. He loved the idea that I merely told him, Go make money and prosper. He too recognized that I allowed people like him to try new things and never condemned a staff member for failing. He said he was now at JPM Chase because of GCI, where they have the same type of heritage. He toasted me for the way I stood tall for the staff.

Jimmy Jarrell spoke of our long-time relationship where early in our careers he worked for me, and then I worked for him. Being the southerner that he is, he made it clear that he sometimes had to bail my ass out. Through it all, he enjoyed working with me because I never came down hard on people. I was upbeat, humorous, and often downright jolly. Since he had retired well before me and was about my same age,

Jimmy ended by saying that I finally wised up and understood that it was time to retire.

Anne Morgan Moore spoke of working in the same office with Richard Speer, who was a tough guy to deal with. She said that experience toughened her up and allowed her to start her own business with Bill Adcock. She noted that I helped sponsor a number of consulting firms in payment systems besides my own, and I was an inspiration to her. She called me one of the pioneers in electronic banking and thanked me for all that I did for so many others in the business.

George Budd also left the Atlanta Fed and noted that we grew up together in the payment systems industry. Each of us parlayed our early work into a thirty-plus-year profession, and he appreciated my intellectual honesty, especially the work we did together.

Bob Cady told how he moved from Cleveland to Atlanta to work for me and then became my partner in my first company. He noted that I could take a complex problem and provide a simple explanation of what it was. He said I could bring the problem down to a level so that others could understand it clearly. Bob said that we had a great time together, and he knew that I was a great family man.

Calvin Johnson spoke with great emotion about me, saying he could not have become the professional that he became without working with me. He called me a gentleman and a scholar.

Bill Moore spoke about our eight-year early affiliation. He said that I was the most fun guy to work with and a smart guy because I always kept searching for answers. He believed that I had creativity and was an inspiration to others.

Based on what was said by friends and family, I can identify eighteen character traits that they recognized as important elements for becoming an entrepreneur. These character traits include

1. Chutzpah (Confidence): This is the result of a process that occurs over more than a decade.
2. Profit oriented: That is not trivial, and I did not succeed at first. It was the failures that taught me about how to finally succeed, and the courage to keep trying.
3. Can hire great people: Deciding that a person was great for my company was one of the hardest things I did. Judging others is difficult to do at any time, and worse, the hiring process is often

superficial. You never really know, and I often went on instinct and the judgment of my staff in picking new staff. Our batting average turned out to be pretty good.

4. Integrity: Without that, I knew I would fail in the consulting business and perhaps in any business.
5. Open to disagree culture: I set the tone, but the staff played a major role in fostering that culture too. That culture was a high degree of integrity in what we did, the right to disagree openly with the boss, and the commitment to tell the client the unvarnished truth, even if the client did not want to hear it.
6. Bold commitments: I saw other senior people in business do this and I learned from them that some risks are worth taking.
7. Inspires others: I ran my company the best way I knew how, and it apparently inspired my staff to grow and become the best that they could be. I was merely the spark that ignited their career.
8. Pioneer: I was certainly in on the early research and development of electronic banking, but many others implemented what I could only envision.
9. Keeping one's word: I learned this from my family and from my wife. It turned out to be good for business too.
10. Trust others: I had to trust myself first and then I trusted others. This took courage, and it occurs gradually because I saw others failing at it.
11. Can fix problems: My daughter was certainly exaggerating that I could fix everything, but then she is my daughter and she has that right.
12. Passion for work: Passion comes from knowledge of the business, from believing that the business is exciting and that it will grow and prosper. More than anything it is an attitude, and it can be acquired.
13. Can define the issues: This is one of my strengths, and it came from my approach to test taking in school—reduce knowledge down to its essence.
14. Sense of humor: Business should be fun, not a chore. You spend too much time there to not enjoy it.
15. Smart: The smartest thing I did in business was to hire smart people. They made me look smart.

16. Perseverance: You learn this from your fear of failure, and that fear shows up often.
17. Learn every day: This is easy to do when you work with bright people.
18. Teacher: You get better over time, and the key is preparation and understanding the people you are teaching.

Using the eighteen character traits, you can evaluate yourself in terms of whether you have these capabilities to be your own boss. The entire evaluation will take a couple of minutes to complete. On each trait, you assess yourself as either being strong (+), moderate (0) or weak (-). I put them in rank order in terms of importance. Give yourself the points indicated below for the areas you fall in and add up the total. If you get over a hundred points, you have the characteristics to become an entrepreneur. I scored 190 points after being an entrepreneur for more than twenty-five years. At the time I was starting out as an entrepreneur, I would have given myself only 105 points, just barely enough to make the cut. Of course, you can give yourself points in between the numbers if you think that's where you belong. This is not scientific but merely my sense of what it takes to be your own boss.

Trait	Strong (+)	Moderate (0)	Weak (-)
Chutzpah (Confidence)	20	-5	-10
Profit Oriented	20	-5	-10
Can Hire Great People	20	0	-10
Integrity	15	-5	-10
Have Working Culture	15	-5	-10
Bold Commitments	15	0	-5
Inspire Others	15	0	-5
Pioneer	15	0	-5
Keep One's Word	10	-5	-15
Trust Others	10	-5	-10
Can Fix problems	10	-5	-5
Passion for Work	10	0	-10
Can Define Issues	10	0	-10
Sense of Humor	10	0	-10
Smart	10	0	-10

Perseverance	10	0	-5
Learn Every Day	5	0	-5
Teacher	5	0	-5

Days before I was to speak, I thought about what to say and concluded that I had to *be as gracious as possible to those who made significant contributions to my success.* I could not have succeeded without help from so many people. My parents were first and foremost, for they set me on a path early in my life. My relatives also had a remarkable impact on me, including my sister, who was a part of my early childhood. Then came my friends, who mostly showed me what not to do as I watched them make mistakes. After that came my teachers, all the good ones. They taught me the basic training that I needed to write, to speak, to become good at math, and to act ethically. The list is long, and each had an impact on me. Then I had to add the bosses I had in business, their bosses, and the colleagues that I worked with. Add to that all the books I read, TV, radio, the Internet, and the variety of people that I met across a lifetime. When you add them all up, there are many more than a thousand people who had some influence on me. I can only say thank you to all of them for their help, their kindness, and their desire to pass on to me what they learned from the others before them.

Whatever your success, know that you could not accomplish it alone, and you stood on all their shoulders.

When it was my turn to speak, I said the following:

> You know the most famous quotation in all of music is It ain't over 'till the fat lady sings. Well, the fat lady is singing. That was fun for me to say, but let me start at the beginning. Judy and I came to Atlanta in May 1971 from Citibank, committed for one year to work on what was then very new—electronic banking. We rented a house, our son Leo was born three weeks after we arrived, and we literally knew no one. During those early years, I worked closely with some of you here tonight, and we have been friends ever since.
>
> Back then, it was exciting to be a part of the new world of electronic funds transfer as it is today, and so Judy and I decided to stay in Atlanta and make payment systems my professional

career. I think we all knew back then that electronic banking was a very big idea, and that it would change the face of banking, and it has. Today it is a two-hundred-billion-dollar business—bigger than the airline industry—and I am proud to have had some small role in that accomplishment.

I retire with the knowledge that the sale of Global Concepts to McKinsey was the best business decision of my life. I think McKinsey is happy with the result, and I believe that the staff at Global Concepts must see that they have a very bright future ahead. I'm pretty happy too. Some people have suggested that if they were me they would have retired long ago. I didn't because I loved the work, I enjoyed the consulting and the research, and I especially enjoyed the people I worked with and the clients I served. However, it is time for me to move on. I have unfinished business to complete.

I was lying in bed a few days ago, just waking up, dreaming about what I could do after I retired—the possibilities of another hour in bed, a leisurely breakfast, and even just lying around doing nothing. I was really enjoying the dream and almost fell back to sleep when my wife, who was up for more than an hour, came into the bedroom and let me know that I had to get up, go outside to the carport, and get rid of the possum stuck in the bottom of our garbage can. My first thought was that if this is what retirement is all about, I want to go back to work. When I looked at the poor little possum at the bottom of the garbage can, I didn't know who was more scared, the animal or me. I had to turn the garbage can upside down to get the poor animal to leave, and then I had to pick up the garbage scattered all around. That brought me back to reality. I was not the boss of a successful business empire, a man with a staff to do the work, a senior executive; no, not anymore, just a husband with responsibilities. And you and I know who is in charge.

People always ask me what I intend to do. I want to finish at least two books. I have yard work that will take a year or more to complete, even with hired help. I can use the exercise, but as always, I will spend most of my time directing the work. After all, a good consultant analyzes the problem, suggests a solution, and lets others do the implementation. I've got lots of rationalizations for others to do the work: too old, too lazy, and too fat.

Judy and I expect to travel to places we have never seen, places like Alaska, Asia, Africa, Australia, and Antarctica. Notice they all start with the letter A. Of course, we will go to see our children and grandchildren.

As I look back on a successful career, I attribute it to several factors. First, to my parents and my wife who pushed and supported me to acquire a great education. Second, to all my teachers who not only taught me business skills but also gave me confidence to dream big. And finally, to my colleagues across a lifetime of work, many of them here tonight, who taught me how to write, how to speak, how to think beyond my narrow perspective, how to manage, how to lead, and yes, how to make money.

When Bob Cady and I sold our first company it was because we weren't making much money, and selling the company was the best decision. Working at BEI taught me to focus not on what I liked doing, not on what I wanted to do and not on what I was comfortable doing, but rather on what the customer wanted. I learned to focus on the customer's needs, even when it was not in an area I was an expert in, but the staff had the expertise. I learned that there is more work in day-to-day payments, like checks and credit cards, than in electronic bill payment and fashionable new payment services that might have a future a long way off. Focusing on the ordinary was more valuable to our clients than the new and fashionable because that's where the biggest problems are and where the most money can be made and saved.

There is a two-thousand-year-old famous Jewish saying, Let the honor of your student be as dear to you as your own; the honor of your colleague as the reverence for your teacher; and the reverence for your teacher as the reverence for Heaven. As the CEO of Global Concepts, and even back over thirty years ago when I was just starting out in this business, I shared in the accomplishments of each of you, but I knew that many of you were doing what I could not do. Your honor was my honor, and I cherished the prestige that each of you achieved as if it was my own, but I knew that it was your doing and not mine. As the owner of Global Concepts, I tried to listen to what the staff had to say, for I again knew that while your ideas may not have been perfect they were diamonds in the rough, only needing polishing to shine perfectly. I insisted on working as a team because we benefited from each other's wisdom, and I think I viewed you all as my teachers. Respect and honor, be it new staff, colleagues, or the boss, is the key to an ongoing fruitful relationship. I always believed that the people I worked with had a sixth sense about whether they were trusted or not and whether we worked authentically to reach the proper decision or recommendation for those we served.

In this world, we have a strong tendency to criticize others, to put ourselves up by putting others down. Because of this, I think we need to overcompensate by honoring others, perhaps more than they deserve, so that we all can aspire to greatness.

I have had the privilege to learn from each of you, and I hope I taught you something in turn. The most important lesson I learned in life is to trust others. The best way to deal with a professional staff is to trust them. I hope I did that. I also trusted my children, and I think they have returned that trust by turning out so remarkably well. And last of all, but certainly not the least, I trust my wife's instincts. When it comes to decisions, I can say this with certainty: trust your wife or your husband or your significant other.

I wish for McKinsey and Global Concepts to go from strength to strength and let it be that from this point in time you continue your long and distinguished career helping to serve others so successfully. Thank you all for sharing this important evening with me.

Once I stopped working, I realized that I had many other interests that would keep me interested in life and in helping others. I now had to worry about investing my money wisely. I asked several friends who had money what they did with it. Some provided vague answers, and I understood that this was an area they did not want to discuss openly. Others did say the obvious—the stock market, property, or find an investment advisor. I had to find my own way here, which gradually emerged.

What was abundantly clear was that instead of running a business to make a profit I had to become an investment company with me and my wife as the only employees. I established a board of directors composed of my family members. I had legitimate investment expenses for a home office, car, and travel to investment opportunities.

I decided to use two investment advisors, a private company and Morgan Stanley. I stayed with each for about two years, decided that the guys at Morgan Stanley were the better choice and moved my stock market investments over to them. When they moved to Wells Fargo Investment Advisors, I moved with them. Doug Aldridge and David Purcell there have served me well and continue to provide me with excellent investment advice.

Over time, I took an interest in options and decided to study them in detail. I developed an option strategy based on selling puts and calls that turned out to be effective. In addition, Wells Fargo provides a series of investments strategies that I participate in.

I found a couple of companies that invested in real estate, one buying pure land and the other buying office buildings. I invested in these deals, and the office park turned out to be profitable when we sold it a few years later. The land investments will require more time given the major recession that we are in.

Judy and I decided to travel a good bit, and so we took trips to Cuba, Peru and the Amazon, the Galapagos Islands, a riverboat cruise in Europe, the Antarctica, a Caribbean cruise, and St. Petersburg, Russia. I was also invited to speak in France a couple of times, and that brought us to Paris and the French Riviera. Add to that our family vacations in the Canadian Rockies, in Mexico, in Jamaica, and Berlin, in addition to visits to our children. Retirement after the sale of my business allowed my wife and me to travel to places we always wanted to see and didn't have the time or money to do before.

After retiring, I decided to teach SAT preparation again and offered my expertise to a Jewish girls' high school in Atlanta because I loved doing it, and it helped the girls. Some of the girls did remarkably well.

When Torah Day School of Atlanta, a fulltime K-8 elementary school in Atlanta, asked me to be the treasurer of their school, I took on the task, and it involved me again in education. My job became quite sizeable, looking after the budget, raising money to pay off the school's bond, and sitting on the Board of Trustees. The school took up a great deal of time, but I was thrilled to be of help, especially with the financial consulting background that I had. I recently was elected to be president of the board.

I started studying a famous area of Jewish study called Pirkei Avos, Ethics of the Fathers and fell in love with Jewish ethics. That led to helping a group of friends organize a once-a-month study on that subject with a rabbi leading the group. That led to a breakfast meeting once a week with my wife and other friends dealing with the same subject. Jewish ethics has become a passion for me, and I am committed to bringing the subject to a much wider audience.

I continued my expert witness business in payment systems and bank operations and handled several cases a year, mainly dealing with bank fraud and patents affecting check processing. These cases continue to be challenging and intellectually stimulating, but over time, I knew my expertise would atrophy.

I invested in a local craft beer company that made Red Brick beers and their best-selling beer, Laughing Skull. I joined their board.

When my wife and I found that some of the Jewish people in our community were having a difficult time putting food on their table, we organized with others a monthly program to buy food in bulk at wholesale prices and sorted the food according to the requests of the needy families. We collected money from more fortunate families, had the local rabbis assure us that a family receiving the food was needy and had a separate group deliver the food to the needy families anonymously. The program has been in place for several years now.

Retirement has been a blast. I am as busy as ever, totally committed to making a difference in this world so long as I have my health and the money to do it. Retirement has given me a chance to give back in many ways what so many people gave to me when I needed their help. I hope you can do the same.

CPSIA information can be obtained at www.ICGtesting.com
Printed in the USA
LVOW051027090413

328224LV00002B/5/P